The Book of Whole Foods: Nutrition & Cuisine

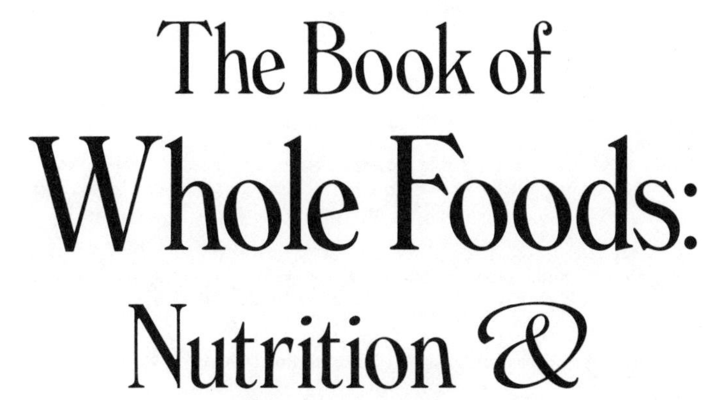

The Book of Whole Foods: Nutrition & Cuisine

Karen MacNeil

Vintage Books
A Division of Random House
New York

A Vintage Original, June 1981

Copyright © 1981 by Karen MacNeil
All rights reserved under International and Pan-American Copyright Conventions. Published in the United States by Random House, Inc., New York, and in Canada by Random House of Canada Limited, Toronto.

Grateful acknowledgment is made to the following for permission to reprint previously published material:

A&W Publishers, Inc.: Table adapted from *The Book of Waters,* by Steven Schwartz. Copyright © 1979 by Steven Schwartz and Steve Heller. Reprinted by permission of A&W Publishers, Inc.

George Braziller, Inc.: Excerpt reprinted from *Fabulous Feasts: Medieval Cookery and Ceremony,* by Madeleine Pelner Cosman, by permission of the publisher, George Braziller, Inc. Copyright © 1976 by Madeleine Pelner Cosman.

Macmillan Publishing Co., Inc.: Two tables from *The Science of Nutrition,* 2nd ed., by Marian Arlin. Reprinted with permission of Macmillan Publishing Co., Inc. Copyright © 1977 by Marian Arlin.

The New York Times: Graph entitled "Normal Prenatal Weight Gain," © 1979 by The New York Times Company. Reprinted by permission.

Nilgiri Press: "Grain Cooking Chart" reprinted by permission from *Laurel's Kitchen: A Handbook for Vegetarian Cookery and Nutrition,* by Laurel Robertson, Carol Flinders and Bronwen Godfrey. Copyright © 1976 by Nilgiri Press, Petaluma, California.

University of Texas Press: Material adapted from *Biochemical Individuality,* by Roger J. Williams. Copyright © 1966 by Roger J. Williams. Used by permission of University of Texas Press, Austin.

Year Book Medical Publishers, Inc.: Two tables reproduced from *Clinical Nutrition: A Physiologic Approach,* by Meredith H. Overton and Barbara Lukert. Reproduced with permission from Meredith H. Overton and Barbara Lukert. Copyright © 1977 by Year Book Medical Publishers, Inc., Chicago.

Library of Congress Cataloging in Publication Data
MacNeil, Karen, 1954–
The book of whole foods.
Includes index.
1. Food, Natural. 2. Cookery (Natural foods)
I. Title.
TX369.M3 641.3'02 80-5490
ISBN 0-394-74012-2 AACR2

Book design and illustrations: Charlotte Staub
Manufactured in the United States of America

To Leslie Voremberg
and Chuck Holt

Acknowledgments

For her considerable research and wisdom, I thank Carmela Vittorio. For his skill at drawing out the brillance and humanity in those around him, but especially in writers, I thank Randall Greene. And for his keenness, sensitivity, and unending creativity, I thank Alan Milberg.

Those who, in ways as infinite and varied as they are, also deserve thanks include: my father, Robert MacNeil, plus: Jamie Canton, Annemarie Colbin, Jackie Entwhistle, John Gottfried, Gordon Haight, Judy Holt, Frances MacNeil, Juan Metzgar, Richard Price, Jackie Schoner, Tung Fu Wang and, of course, my editor Gail Winston.

Contents

Part One
Food and Diet

The Tao of Food

The fundamental concept in Chinese philosophy is that of the Tao. There is no single word in English that encompasses what is meant by *Tao* in Chinese; but, to come as close as possible, it expresses the integrated and all-inclusive order of the universe.

The principles of the Tao originated in the ancient rural wisdom of people who saw themselves and every speck of life as part of and dependent on the cyclical processes of nature. Nature flowed continually—every force moving in a great sea of forces—creating an unending and unified whole. Though the Tao had reality and evidence, it had no form. It was its own essence and its own root. For the humblest mind, the Tao was simply the way of nature. For the philosophic mind, it became a profound insight that integrated life and gave it meaning.

At the beginning of this century the ancient Chinese idea of the Tao and the fundamental principles of science met when modern physicists began to unfold a vastly different picture of the universe than had ever gone before. That picture would take nearly half a century to develop. But in the end it would begin to change the way we look at modern sciences—including the science of nutrition.

For three centuries the scientific world view had been based on Newton's mechanical model of the universe. According to the model, physical phenomena took place in three-dimensional absolute space, moved in absolute time, and were characterized by material particles.

Then, in the first three decades of the twentieth century, Albert Einstein's relativity theory and research in atomic physics shattered the simple Newtonian constructs of space, time, and matter. According to the new physics the basic components of matter were not *things* at all, but *interconnections* between things. Atomic research went on to suggest that subatomic particles did not so much exist as show tendencies to exist. These tendencies were what defined the nature of matter. Moreover, there were no isolated building blocks to be discovered. Instead, nature seemed to be a web or network of forces bound together in intricate relationships that created a unified whole.

Many physicists noted the striking parallel between the new laws and ancient Eastern mystical beliefs such as the Tao. But the work that illuminated the parallel with singular clarity was Fritjof Capra's *The Tao of Physics.* In it, Capra wrote:

> A careful analysis of the process of observation in atomic physics has shown that the subatomic particles have no meaning as isolated entities, but can only be understood as interconnections between the preparation of an experiment and the subsequent measurement. Quantum theory thus reveals a basic oneness of the universe. It shows that we cannot decompose the world into independently existing smallest units. As we penetrate into matter, nature does not show us any isolated "basic building blocks," but rather appears as a complicated web of relations between the various parts of the whole.[1]

What do the fundamentals of modern physics have to do with food? Everything. By looking at nourishment from the perspective of modern physics, in which matter cannot be reduced to things and processes cannot be stripped of their contexts, we can begin to see the flaw in our post–World War II assumption that food can be taken apart and put together again like Tinkertoys.

Food and the process of nourishment are at the very core of nature. The life force of an apple becomes the life force of a human being; the human body decomposes into the very mineral compounds that gave the plant itself life. Each species is devoured as food for a next, slightly more complicated species in the huge design. Nourishment performs a constant cosmic dance, the whole ecosystem turning in grand, self-generating cycles, where even the tiniest living cells die and become life again through a constant molecular transformation that allows one biological entity to be converted into another and life itself to be carried on.

In this delicate and exceedingly complex biological agreement between the life being eaten and the life doing the eating, there is no way to measure the mystery of integration. Yet, like the early physicists looking for building blocks, nutritionists and other scientists have tended to explain the process of nourishment in terms of parts and numbers. The problem with having isolated approximately sixteen vitamins, seventeen minerals, eight essential amino acids, as well as fat, carbohydrate, and protein molecules, is that these numbers and names tell nothing about the way food *works* in living organisms —which is exactly what nourishment is about. Nourishment is the

[1]Fritjof Capra, *The Tao of Physics* (Berkeley, Calif.: Shambhala, 1975), p. 68.

principle of the Tao in action. It is an example of what physics has learned about the nature of organic matter.

Interestingly enough, it wasn't until food was taken apart and restructured into new forms of processed food that science attempted to isolate whatever it was that made food nourishing. Vitamins and minerals were in fact discovered by necessity, for science could not ignore the deficiency diseases that sprang up along with the increasingly imbalanced diets of nonwhole foods.

Once the major nutrients that prevented visible deficiency diseases were discovered, however, nourishment became a whole new ball game. Instead of avoiding disease by returning to whole foods, food technologists used the new knowledge to rearrange the composition of processed foods with even greater chemical precision. Nutritional analysis became chemical analysis, and nourishment was reduced to a mathematical formula. The danger in this wasn't immediately apparent.

When whole foods are broken down, processed into new forms, and chemically and structurally modified, a connecting link in the ecological cycle snaps. Humans begin to feed themselves "foods" that have no basis in nature. Food technologists, having successfully taken food apart, reassemble it in ever more extraordinary configurations, sometimes throwing whole parts of the original food away, manipulating other parts into previously unknown structures, and injecting thousands of completely new synthetic chemicals along the way. A sweeping change occurs in the nourishment of the whole species. For the first time a radical breakdown in the ecological cycle has taken place.[2]

This gives the question of nourishment and adaptation a new twist. Technologized forms of food are not simply the product of a rapidly evolving world in the same way that new technologized forms of transportation are. A fundamental organic process—one that changed little in fifty thousand years of *Homo sapiens'* evolution —is destroyed. There was—and is—no basis for believing that humans will simply adapt, for the very assumption that, on the basis of a knowledge of some fifty nutrients, science can put food together as well as nature can is false in the first place.[3]

[2]A thorough analysis of this is given by Ross Hume Hall, director of En-trophy Institute, Hamilton, Ontario L8P 3K2 Canada. See *En-trophy Institute for Advanced Study Review,* Vol. 1, No. 2 (January–February 1978); Vol. 1, No. 3 (March–April 1978); Vol. 1, No. 6 (September–October 1978).

[3]Numerous current health problems and the rise in diet-linked disease are thought to be potential first repercussions of the ecological shift. Anthropologists point out that it may take several generations before the genetic effects of chemically modified food become apparent.

For the first time in history people must go out of their way to eat whole, natural foods. And so food has been divided into two camps: fresh fruits, nuts, and whole-grain breads on one side; hot dogs, shakes, and sugar doughnuts on the other. But in the vast middle ground (where most of us eat) there are insidiously dangerous foods, such as commercial whole wheat high-fiber breads, which have been colored with molasses, fortified with super doses of vitamins, then packed with wood-pulp shavings for extra fiber; or nitrite-free hot dogs; or protein carob candy bars. These are the new "natural" foods. More than ever, the focus is on names and numbers, rather than on the whole context of nourishment—the Tao of food.

When cholesterol was implicated in heart disease, for example, health-conscious people began eating dramatically fewer eggs. Then fabricated eggs, low in cholesterol, were invented. They have become the second most widely used imitation food after imitation bacon. Consumers and food researchers alike focused on the safety of the various chemicals from which fabricated eggs were made. But the effect unreal eggs might have on the total scheme of nourishment was not given much attention.

As it turns out, test animals fed fabricated eggs do not die of cancer, they don't develop liver tumors, they don't become sterile. But if they're fed only fabricated eggs, they do die—unlike animals that are fed only real whole eggs. Why they die hasn't been figured out: As far as scientists can determine, fabricated eggs are made without carcinogenic chemicals and can be fortified with all of the vitamins and minerals known to be essential. As mystical as it may seem, in the final analysis, people are nourished not by vitamin A but by carrots.

Nourishment simply can't be reduced to analytical chemistry, yet in the continuing debate over specific foods, specific additives, specific methods of processing, each of us loses our grip on the fundamental issue: *Nourishment is a holistic process,* a delicate balance between every known *and unknown* component in foods. These interact with and are changed by body substances through thousands of unknown complex relationships.

Throughout the centuries human beings have survived on a diet made up *completely* of whole, natural foods.

Biochemical Individuality

The human body is an integrated organic system in a constant state of motion. At the very heart of it is the single cell, which never remains static. Inside the cell, metabolic transformations move through endless cycles until the cell itself, as part of a larger metabolic cycle, dies.

Plant cells are the first loop in a huge spiral of bio-transformations. Grain cells become chicken cells, which become human cells. Every species is tied to the one before it and after it in a complex web of biologically dependent relationships. There are no gaps, no dead ends, nothing that does not fit, nothing that does not contribute. Everything is intricately connected for one purpose: nourishment. The eaters and the eaten, then, create the overall ecological design.

In a very real sense, eating food is the way we participate in our own evolution. Through giving and taking energy from the ecosystem (breathing and eating), energy itself is sustained, passed on, and life continues. The key to evolution is differentiation; it is only by being different from one another that some of us are guaranteed to possess whatever bodily characteristics are needed to survive a constantly and sometimes radically changing environment. Organic differences are not the exception, but the rule.

If we are all different from one another, it stands to reason that each of us has different food needs. Yet because eating healthfully today almost seems to require chemophobic caution, we find ourselves walking around with mental lists of good foods and bad. We ask ourselves, with "black or white" directness, "Is this food healthful or not?" But we forget the fundamental issue: healthful *for whom?*[1]

We know that no two people (except identical twins) are genetically the same. No two people look alike, no two are alike in bodily structure, and no two have the same chemical transformations taking

[1]Certain foods, such as potato chips, are not particularly healthful for anyone. Other foods, such as fish, almost always are. But in the vast middle ground are foods that may or may not be healthful for a given individual: eggs, nuts, cheese, wheat, and honey, for example.

place in their organs, tissues, and cells. Our anatomy, biochemistry, and heredity *are* inextricably tied together, but in multiple relationships that are ours alone.

In *Biochemical Individuality* Dr. Roger Williams gives the example of healthy people who differ so much structurally that when the size and shape of their hearts are compared, some are so different that it's nearly impossible to determine if the hearts even belong to the same species![2] In his research Williams measured the individual variations among people's enzyme patterns, endocrine activity, excretion patterns, pharmacological responses, metabolism, growth patterns, pain sensitivities, effects of oxygen deprivation, blood flow, blood pressure, and even taste sensitivities. He found enormous differences—differences that, expressed mathematically, often varied ten- to twenty-fold.

The more different people are from one another, the more different their nutritional needs. In the body, nourishment is determined by the structures that receive, process, and store food.

If, for example, a person's esophagus is large, swallowing food may be quite easy. The person may be able to swallow large pieces of food; he or she may be able to eat fast and chew less. The speed of eating and chewing will determine how smoothly and efficiently that person's food is digested. The faster the meal, the slower and more difficult the digestion, because when food is bolted down, enzymes in the mouth that begin carbohydrate digestion don't have a chance to work. A double burden now falls on the stomach and intestines, which will have to complete the mouth's work plus their own. Because a person with a large esophagus can eat easily, he or she may in fact also eat a lot. This, too, will determine the way nutrients are processed by other organs down the line—the stomach, intestines, liver, and colon.

The size, position, and shape of other organs and body structures also affect the way food is used in the body. Consider the circulatory system. Blood transports food, oxygen, and the waste products of metabolism. Since nourishment is dependent on the quality and quantity of the blood that reaches the tissues with fresh supplies of oxygen and nutrients, the size and number of arteries a person has will affect the nourishment of every other part of his or her body. Oxygen, via the blood, via the arteries, is especially important for the brain. An insufficient supply causes the brain's regulating mechanisms to stop operating, which in turn causes vital processes such as breathing and the heartbeat to stop. And so there begins, with something as simple as arteries, an important chain of command.

[2]Roger J. Williams, *Biochemical Individuality* (Austin: University of Texas Press, 1956, 1969).

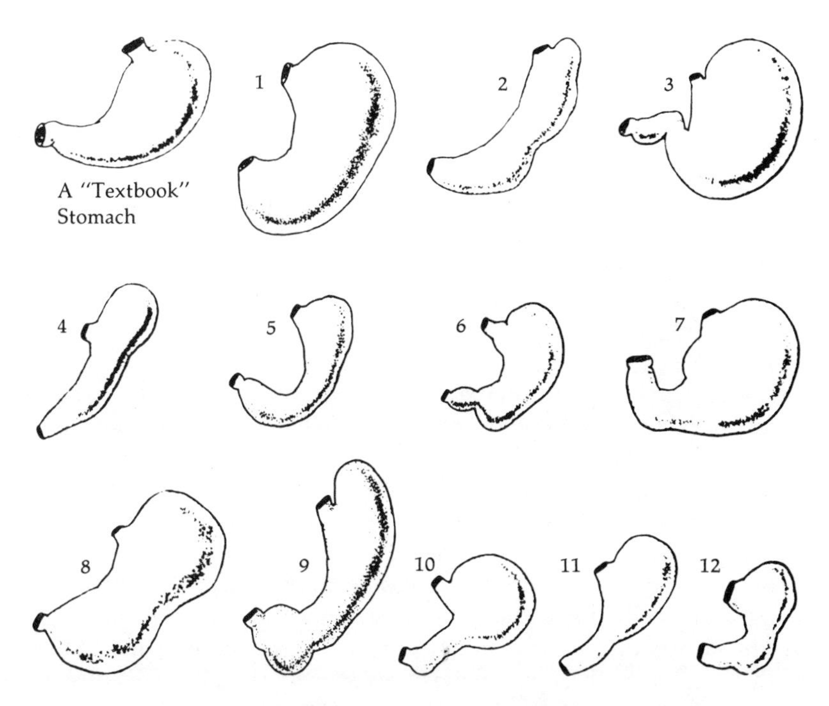

These drawings of actual specimens show how anatomically different human stomachs can be. Originally from Barry J. Anson, *Atlas of Human Anatomy* (Philadelphia: W. B. Saunders, 1951) and reprinted in Roger J. Williams, *You Are Extraordinary* (New York: Random House, 1967).

Before anyone could come to a consensus about what constitutes an optimal diet, then, he or she would need to know what the structure and chemical makeup of the average person's body is. As it turns out, there is no such thing as an average body.

Here's some of the data Williams collected based on his own and others' investigations, as well as a survey of literature in the field:

- In select groups of healthy people, the size of the esophagus varies greatly. Some individuals have an esophagus four times larger than that of others. Some human stomachs can hold six to eight times as much as others. The position of the stomach varies from one to nine inches below the breastbone. Various digestive juices flow into some people's intestines through the same duct; in others, through separate ducts; and in still others, through ducts that merge together.
- There is no set pathway for the colon; various people have colons ranging in positions that are different by more than a foot, so it's not surprising that the number of stools varies from person to

person. Among healthy babies, some pass twelve to fourteen stools in twenty-four hours, while others pass none.

- Human livers were found to vary as much as five times in size.
- Heart rates in young men were found to vary from 45 to 105 beats per minute from individual to individual. Two arteries come directly out of the aorta (the main artery of the heart) in some individuals; in others there are four. The sizes of the arteries are also dramatically different, with some arteries capable of carrying three times as much blood as others.
- Blood itself shows wide variations in makeup. For adults the normal red blood cell count varies from 4.6 to 6.2 million. The blood cell count of newborn babies varies significantly at birth and continues to show different patterns at different stages of development.
- Nerve structures are extremely different from person to person and from muscle to muscle. No two people will ever have the same handwriting because the musculature of their hands is different, the nerve pathways are different, and the speed of the nerve impulses (even between the two hands of one individual) is different.
- The position where the spinal cord ends varies in every individual by as much as three vertebrae. Nerves from the different muscles and organs enter the spinal column at different places in different people. Even the number of major nerves varies. Some people have two sympathetic nerves connecting the spinal cord with the digestive system. Other people have three. The differences in nerve patterns, nerve endings, nerve impulse speeds, and the number of nerves accounts in part for the different sensitivities people have to pain, to hot and cold, and to touch.

Anatomical individuality also determines the sensations produced by food. Food is a composite of taste, smell, texture, and temperature. Different nerve sensitivity thresholds, different nerve pathways, and different numbers of nerves all mean that each person tastes, smells, and feels food quite differently. Even the number of taste buds varies from individual to individual and changes over time. We all lose taste buds (at different rates) as we grow older, which may explain in part why children—who have the most taste buds—can be extremely sensitive to food, tending to choose bland or sweet foods, while older people, who literally have fewer buds to taste with, usually prefer highly flavored food (discounting problems of digestion).

In addition to anatomical differences, there are specific biochemical differences between people.

- The percentage of body water in healthy people has been found to range from 45.6% to 70.2%.

- Williams shows that even though, for practical purposes, blood can be grouped into four types, there are actually no specific types, but rather gradations of blood, each of which varies immunologically.
- Each person has a unique pattern of amino acids, a unique blood sugar concentration, and individual concentrations of vitamins in blood, skin, hair, and milk. Every person's saliva is different, both in the number of substances it contains and in the concentrations of those substances. In fact, before a person can taste certain substances, they must be dissolved in that person's saliva. If the substances are dissolved in water or in another's saliva, the test person cannot taste them.
- The gastric juices necessary for digestion are different in each person.

In fact, there is no body substance that does not vary from individual to individual. What is even more surprising, however, is that everyone who is judged by standard clinical tests to be healthy and normal will actually be abnormal in some specific area. For example, groups of people who have been judged normal by standard clinical tests but who have then been tested for specific complex values, such as blood lipid content, salivary amino acid secretion patterns, or the amount of calories, fat, ash, and nitrogen excreted in the feces, generally show extreme values in at least one area. Each of us would probably prove "abnormal" in some regard if a large number of diverse and repeated measures were made on us.[3]

Finally, different nutritive and non-nutritive substances affect individuals in different ways. There is always an interaction between any substance introduced into the body and some part of the body itself. In general, the more complex the organism, the more difficult it is to pinpoint what that interaction will be. With humans, it's not even always known which organs, tissues, or enzyme patterns might be involved in an interaction with another substance or exactly how various chemicals will affect any one person.

Take the simple example of alcohol. Studies have shown that one-quarter of an ounce of alcohol can have the same effect on some people that ten times that amount has on others. In one study of the effect of alcohol on a thousand people, 10.5% became intoxicated when the level of alcohol in the blood was .05%, yet 6.7% of the people were still sober after the alcohol percentage had been raised

[3]Scientists use terms like *normal person* or *average person* cautiously, if at all, since describing a person as normal or average is rather like describing a painting or book as normal or average. Humans, like paintings and books, are, by design, different—unique. The American Association of Clinical Chemists, among other scientific bodies, has questioned the acceptability of "normal values" as a clinical device (Annual Symposium, American Association of Clinical Chemists, New York, 1973).

to .40%. The authors concluded that even though some of the differences may have been due to adaptation (the people who drank more over time may have learned to handle more), most of them were due to innate differences in each person's biochemistry.

Differences in biochemistry (in addition to genetic and environmental differences) necessarily affect the way the body uses the vitamins and minerals it gets, since vitamins and minerals work cooperatively with other nutrients in the body and are always subject to varying amounts of glandular substances that can catalyze or bind them. For example, calcium absorption occurs in the upper part of the duodenum, near the stomach. The stomach itself provides an acid environment conducive to calcium absorption. However, pancreatic secretions, which are alkaline, periodically affect the stomach and intestines as they are carried through along with food during digestion. Thus anything that causes food to be passed through the stomach and intestines abruptly, such as nervous tension or diarrhea, may cause a shift in the internal acid environment of each organ—in this case a shift that keeps calcium from being optimally absorbed.

The amount of any one vitamin or mineral needed to keep some individuals healthy may also not necessarily be enough to keep others healthy. Typical genetic, biochemical, and environmental differences are enough to cause the minimum requirements for some individuals to vary twofold, if not more.[4] One of the clearest ways this has been demonstrated has been by looking at how, when, and in what manner deficiencies occur. In 1966 Williams and colleagues fed sixty-four weanling rats an exclusive diet of white bread.[5] The individual life spans of the rats ranged from 6 to 144 days. (The distribution was fairly even; no one rat either died much sooner than all others or lived much longer than all others.) The rats' individual weight gains also varied significantly—from 2 to 212 grams. Moreover, although general clinical signs of nutrient deficiency exist (see opposite), deficiency itself may be evidenced by a wide variety of pathological conditions. To give one example, chickens deprived of pantothenic acid develop a condition known as chick dermatitis—unhealthy skin and feathers. But pantothenic acid plays a generalized role in healthy cell function, and when a deficiency exists, widespread impairment in the chicken occurs. Its blood, muscles, liver, kidneys, and brain, for example, are all affected. In the literature, pantothenic acid defiency has contributed, in addition to dermatitis,

[4]George M. Briggs and Doris Howes Calloway, *Nutrition and Physical Fitness* (Philadelphia: W. B. Saunders, 1979).

[5]Roger J. Williams and R. B. Pelton, "Effects of Vitamin A Deficient and Other Deficient Diets on Experimental Animals," *Proceedings of the National Academy of Sciences, U.S.A.*, Vol. 55 (1966), p. 126.

Clinical Signs of Nutrient Deficiency, United States, 1971–72

Nutrient	*Clinical Sign*
Protein	Dyspigmented hair Abnormal texture or loss of curl of hair Visible or enlarged parotids Liver enlargement Potbelly Apathy Marked hyperirritability
Vitamin B complex: Riboflavin	Angular inflammation of eyelids Angular lesions of lips } bilateral Angular scars of lips } bilateral Cheilosis Magenta tongue Nasolabial seborrhea
Vitamin B complex other than riboflavin: Niacin	Changes in tongue surface Fissures of tongue Serrations or swelling of tongue Hyperpigmentation, hands and face Pellagrous dermatitis Scarlet beefy tongue
Thiamine	Absent knee jerks Absent ankle jerks
Vitamin D	Bossing of skull Beading of ribs Bowed legs Knock knees Epiphyseal enlargement, wrists
Vitamin A	Bitot's spots Keratomalacia Xerophthalmia Xerosis of the conjunctiva
Vitamin A and/or essential fatty acids	Follicular hyperkeratosis of upper back Follicular hyperkeratosis, arms Dry or scaling skin (xerosis) Mosaic skin
Vitamin C	Follicular keratosis Small subcutaneous hemorrhage Bleeding and swollen gums
Iodine	Enlarged thyroid gland, Group I Enlarged thyroid gland, Group II
Calcium	Positive Chvostek's sign

Reprinted from S. Abraham, F. W. Lowenstein, and D. E. O'Connell, *Preliminary Findings of the First Health and Nurition Examination Survey, United States 1971–1972, Anthropometric and Clinical Findings,* DHEW Publ. No. 75-1229, HRA (Rockville, Md.: 1975).

to keratitis, ulcerations of the gastrointestinal tract, anemia, depigmentation of tooth enamel, sterility, congenital malformations, failure to produce antibodies, fatty liver, kidney damage, heart damage, bone marrow hypoplasia, allergies, and milder effects such as headache and decreased resistance to stress.[6]

Where, then, do such biochemical differences leave us? Since nourishment is a biological agreement between the chemical structures in the body and those in nature consumed as food, doesn't it make sense that for every person, optimal nourishment would entail a slightly different equation? Yes, and groups whose purpose it is to set nutritional standards recognize it. Recommended allowances are set from 25% to 100% higher than the amounts thought to be needed by most members of a population, not counting those who've had prior dietary inadequacies, diseases, or traumatic stresses. But simply by setting such standards, groups like the National Research Council have provided us with an easily misinterpreted tool. Average nutrient intakes, as set by the NRC, are often debated for their accuracy, given existing data. Nonetheless, the real point to hang on to is that they are meaningless anyway, except as gross generalizations.[7]

An old English physician, Parry of Bath, commented that it is "more important to know what sort of patient has a disease, than what sort of disease a patient has."

It may also be more important to know what sort of person is eating than to know whether that person eats cheese or cheesecake.

[6]Roger J. Williams, *Physician's Handbook of Nutritional Science* (Springfield, Ill.: Charles C Thomas, 1975), p. 55.

[7]The U.S. recommended *daily* allowances (U.S. RDAs), printed under the nutrition information panel on food labels, were set by the Food and Drug Administration (FDA) and are based on the recommended *dietary* allowances (RDAs) established in 1943 by the Food and Nutrition Board of the National Research Council. The recommended dietary allowances are levels of intake of essential nutrients that the board has determined adequate for preventing visible dietary disease in practically all healthy people. When the dietary allowances were originally established, the board stressed that the recommended intakes were not requirements and that nutrient requirements could only be determined on an individual-by-individual basis, taking into account an individual's genetic makeup and various special needs that person may have.

The dietary allowances have been revised by the Food and Nutrition Board seven times since they were first published. It should also be noted that the dietary allowances established here are not the same as the specific nutrient intakes recommended by other countries or those recommended by the United Nations Food and Agriculture Organization/World Health Organization (FAO/WHO).

In the 1970s, public concern over the nutritional quality of food forced the government to declare some public policy concerning nutrition and to attempt to develop a nutritional standard for the food industry. The FDA took on the job. It adopted a set of nutritional standards—based on the recommended dietary allowances—that could be used for food labeling. These were called the U.S. recommended daily allowances. The FDA's daily allowances and the Food and Nutrition Board's dietary allowances are not the same values. Nonetheless, they are frequently confused with each other. The entire RDA concept has been criticized by nutritionists who assert that an "average/healthy" standard (the recommended dietary allowances) makes the complex process of nutrition misleadingly simple, and that labeling foods with similar standards that actually have a different purpose (the U.S. recommended daily allowances) generates confusion and gives the illusion that all individuals should get 100% of all nutrients from all foods.

Body Wisdom

One of the most fundamental of innate wisdoms is the wisdom to eat. Long before scientists discovered vitamins or began to chart the relationships between fats, carbohydrates, and protein, people survived quite well on the foods they found in their environments. People ate when they were hungry, chose the foods they liked best, and stopped eating when they'd had enough. Today there are still people in the world who, day to day, eat foods of the right character in the right proportion, even though they haven't a shred of modern nutritional knowledge.

The body's wisdom is highly sophisticated. Take, for example, a middle-aged man who has maintained approximately the same weight his whole adult life. In the last ten years he's gained 5 pounds because he isn't quite as active as he used to be. This means that for most of his life his intake of food matched his burning up of food with remarkably little error. During the last ten years he would have eaten about 12,000 pounds of moist food. A long-range error in balance of 1% would have made him gain or lose 120 pounds. An error of .1% would have caused him to gain or lose 12 pounds. Actually, since he only gained 5 pounds, the wisdom of his body was such that it struck a balance with an error of less than 1/20 of 1%.

How extensive is the body's wisdom and where does it come from?

The first significant study in this area, and one that has since become a classic, was conducted by Clara Davis in 1928.[1] Davis was a nutritionist who studied three eight- to ten-month-old, healthy, breast-fed infants kept in a hospital setting for six months. At mealtime the children were allowed to select any foods they wished from a large assortment of foods presented in individual glasses and dishes. The children indicated which food(s) they wanted by pointing to the food, at which point an attendant would place the food before them. Each child could choose as much of any food he or she wanted. And if, for example, the child wanted the same food over and over again,

[1]C. M. Davis, "Self Selection of Diets by Newly Weaned Infants," *American Journal of Diseases of Children,* Vol. 36 (1928), p. 651.

that food would be given until the child was satiated. Each child was allowed to keep eating for as long as he or she wanted.

The foods presented to the children were unmixed (no combinations such as soup or bread, for example), unseasoned, and unadulterated (except for slight cooking). They were as follows:

Meats (muscle): beef, lamb, chicken
Meats (organ): liver, kidneys, brains, sweetbreads
Seafood: haddock
Cereals: whole wheat, oatmeal, whole-grain barley, yellow cornmeal, rye
Bone products: bone marrow (beef and veal), bone jelly
Eggs
Milk: grade A raw
Fruits: apples, oranges, bananas, tomatoes, peaches, pineapple
Vegetables: lettuce, cabbage, spinach, cauliflower, peas, beets, carrots, turnips, potatoes
Sea salt

Though this study is often cited as evidence that children instinctively choose healthful food, the results of the study cannot support such a weighty conclusion. Davis found that the children did, indeed, choose a healthful diet and seemed to make their choices randomly (no child became fixated on any one food). However, as has often been pointed out, the likelihood of choosing a healthful diet was high, for no cookies, candy, high-fat, high-sodium, or highly processed foods were among the choices. The only thing that was conclusively demonstrated by the Davis study was that children do have definite food preferences—specific likes and dislikes, which may change abruptly at any time and seemingly without reason.

Aside from whatever small amount of insight the Davis study offered, it did serve to get the ball rolling. In the 1940s an endocrinologist named Carl Richter began to work with the idea that one of the most powerful biological urges of any organism is to behave in such a way that the body's internal environment is maintained in a healthful state (homeostasis).

Richter experimented with rats that had had their parathyroid glands surgically removed.[2] He noted that such rats died within a few days unless they were given free access to a solution of calcium lactate, in which case they ingested tremendously large quantities of the solution and kept themselves alive. Richter also noted that while the rats drank copious amounts of the calcium solution, they also automatically decreased their intake of foods high in phosphorus.

[2]C. P. Richter, "Decreased Phosphorus Appetite of Parathyroidectomized Rats," *Endocrinology*, Vol. 33 (1943).

When the rats were forced to ingest phosphorus, they all died. But given a free choice, all of them automatically selected a diet low in phosphorus.

Richter's question was, How does an animal (specifically a rat) know how to regulate its food intake in such a way that its health is maintained? Two possibilities presented themselves: Either the animal possessed a built-in recognition system for substances its body needed or the animal learned which foods made it better and which foods made it ill, coming in this manner to select foods that ultimately provided it with proper nutrients.

One of the first experiments in support of the learning hypothesis was conducted by Scott and Verney in 1947.[3] They presented nutrient-deficient rats with a vitamin-supplemented flavored food and an unflavored deficient food. After a period of time, the rats developed a distinct preference for the flavored (enriched) food. However, when the flavored food was offered without enrichment and the vitamins were switched to the unflavored food, the rats continued to eat the flavored, but now deficient, food, suggesting they'd learned a behavior that they did not automatically give up.

Later, in 1964, Rozin, Wells, and Mayer simplified the experimental design. They raised weanling rats on a thiamine-deficient diet for twenty-one days. The rats showed obvious signs of thiamine deficiency: weight loss and anorexia. At this point the researchers offered the rats a choice between a thiamine-rich and a thiamine-deficient diet. The thiamine-deficient rats strongly preferred the thiamine-rich diet, even though a control group of rats (who were not deficient in thiamine) did not.[4] Moreover, in another experiment, rats were made deficient in thiamine, then recovered from the deficiency by injection. After recovery the rats were offered the choice between thiamine-rich and thiamine-deficient diets. Rats that had once been deficient consistently chose the thiamine-rich diet.[5]

Again the question remained: If a rat injests two or more foods and, following injestion, recovers from a deficiency, how does one of the foods acquire positive properties? Furthermore, how is it that a rat associates getting better with eating? After eating, but before recovery begins, the rat does, after all, perform a wide variety of behaviors: smelling, sleeping, grooming, exploring, and so forth. Why is a single food associated with recovery?

[3]E. M. Scott and E. L. Verney, "Self Selection of Diet. VI. The Nature of Appetites for B Vitamins," *Journal of Nutrition,* Vol. 34 (1947), pp. 471–80.

[4]P. Rozin, C. Wells, and J. Mayer, "Thiamine Specific Hunger: Vitamins in Water Versus Vitamins in Food," *Journal of Comparative and Physiological Psychology,* Vol. 57 (1964), pp. 78–84.

[5]P. Rozin, "Specific Hunger for Thiamine: Recovery from Deficiency and Thiamine Preference," *Journal of Comparative and Physiological Psychology,* Vol. 59 (1965), pp. 98–101.

Several experiments in the 1960s yielded clues. To begin with, in 1966 Rodgers and Rozin studied the specific motor behavior of deficient rats.[6] They found that deficient rats show an immediate and almost complete preference for new foods. That is, something about the condition of deficiency seems to encourage experimental eating in animals. This holds true even if a new food presented to deficient rats is itself deficient, while the old food (on which the rats developed the deficiency) is later made nutrient rich. The experimenters hypothesized that new-food eating wasn't so much a "love of new food" as it was an "aversion to old food which had led to deficiency." In other words, the rats definitely knew what not to eat. And their initial preference for new foods followed that fact.

However, experimenters working in the field of food intake and body wisdom realized the simplicity of the experiments that had been performed. In a two-choice situation, it was easy to understand that a rat would develop an aversion to a food that did not support its health and would subsequently eat a new food. But what would happen in a more realistic situation in which the animal would be presented with many food choices? A classic piece of early research seemed to give some clues.

In 1933 L. J. Harris and associates found that deficient rats could *not* select the one food containing B vitamins when the rat had many choices (six to ten) but only one food contained the vitamin.[7] However, as a startling auxiliary bit of information, they found that if the rats were offered only the B-vitamin food for a few days—if, in other words, they were "educated" about the food—the deficient rats would then be able to discriminate between a series of foods and to choose the one containing the vitamin. What this and subsequent experiments indicated was clear: Before an animal can develop a strong preference for a food, it must be "educated" about the outcome (positive or negative) of the food.

Interestingly, experiments by different researchers in 1969 showed that rats were capable of learning a preference for tastes associated with recovery and would prefer these to tastes associated with deficiency or entirely new tastes.[8] However, the experimenters noted

[6]W. Rodgers and P. Rozin, "Novel Food Preferences in Thiamine-Deficient Rats," *Journal of Comparative and Physiological Psychology,* Vol. 61 (1966), pp. 1–4.

[7]L. J. Harris, J. Clay, F. Hargreaves, and A. Ward, "Appetite and Choice of Diet. The Ability of the Vitamin B Deficient Rat to Discriminate Between Diets Containing and Lacking the Vitamin," *Proceedings of the Royal Society, London,* Series B, Vol. 113 (1933), pp. 161–90.

[8]C. Campbell, "Development of Specific Preferences in Thiamine-Deficient Rats: Evidence Against Mediation by Aftertastes," Master's Thesis, University of Illinois, Chicago, 1969; D. M. Zahorik and S. F. Maier, "Appetite Conditioning with Recovery from Thiamine Deficiency as the Unconditioned Stimulus," *Psychonomic Science,* Vol. 17 (1969), pp. 309–10.

that there were drastically fewer examples of rats showing positive preferences than rats showing aversions.

As to the association between food and recovery or illness, it seems that an adaptive mechanism, termed belongingness, is at work. Taste receptors and gut receptors are both, as far as the brain is concerned, visceral sensory inputs. And neurologically, the two are intimately connected—especially in the hypothalamus, the part of the brain that regulates food intake. In a compelling experiment in 1966, Garcia and Koelling showed that there was a specific tendency for taste to be associated with gastrointestinal function, while other stimuli, such as light and sound, would more often be associated with external sensations such as electric shock.[9] The experimenters paired light, sound, and taste simultaneously with either electric shock or poisoning in animals. The shocked animals developed an avoidance of light and sound, but not taste. The poisoned animals exhibited the reverse behavior. They avoided taste, but not light or sound.

What, then, do experimenters know about body wisdom? Based on animal (principally rat) studies, which can still only be generalized to humans, they know that body wisdom is an innate adaptive mechanism. And its function is most clearly demonstrated through avoidance of foods that do *not* support health. It seems, however, that animals do have preferences for foods on which they have recovered and that these preferences are learned and not easily diminished.

Researchers also know that there is a specific and strong association between food and recovery or illness. This has even been demonstrated with humans, who will maintain an aversion to foods they ate prior to becoming nauseous, even when they are sure that something else was responsible for the sickness.

And finally, it is known that animals respond to changes in caloric density by increasing or decreasing the amount of food they take in.[10] When a rat's standard diet is nutritionally diluted, the rat will eat larger meals (though not more frequent ones) until the nutritional deficit is made up for.

What is known about body wisdom and the precise way in which body wisdom works remains two different issues. It is likely that body wisdom in humans is a highly complex set of processes—processes that may operate slightly differently today than they did a century ago, given the fact that the human diet has changed radi-

[9]J. Garcia and R. A. Koelling, "Relation of Cue to Consequence in Avoidance Learning," *Psychonomic Science,* Vol. 4 (1966), pp. 123–24.

[10]C. T. Snowdon, "Motivation, Regulation, and the Control of Meal Parameters with Oral and Intragastric Feeding," *Journal of Comparative and Physiological Psychology,* Vol. 69 (1969), pp. 91–100.

cally in the last thirty years. It is clear, however, that the anatomy of taste is a central and complex part of the problem.[11]

On the basis of preliminary evidence, it seems feasible that the chemical state of the taste buds and olfactory nerves is affected by the learned experiences an animal has with the food it takes in. What may in fact happen is that taste thresholds for various foods change depending on the outcome of eating a given food. If a food produces deficiency or sickness, that message is carried to the brain via the blood. The brain may then sensitize the receptors near the tongue to foods the body either needs or needs to avoid.

Because so much of the research on body wisdom has been conducted on animals, few conclusions about body wisdom in humans can be drawn. However, mere observation provides some interesting data. If, for example, you've ever tried to decide with several other people what all of you would like to share for dinner, you'll sometimes note a curious phenomenon. One person might say, "All day I've been in the mood for eggs. Why don't we try that new salad and omelet restaurant?" At this point you can almost see the other people envisioning what it would feel like to be eating eggs. And even though the others might like eggs in general, they might not be indifferent to eating them at that moment. One of them, for example, might really be hungry for Mexican food—lots of rice, beans, cheese, and tomato.

How does one account for such unmistakable preferences? The answer may be body wisdom. Though as we'll see in later chapters, body wisdom has its limits.

[11]According to Robert H. Cagan, biochemist, the Monell Chemical Senses Center, Philadelphia, as reported in "Behavior Clues Seen in Taste and Smell," *New York Times,* June 5, 1979, taste nerves do not actually reach the surface of the tongue, as was formerly believed to be true, nor are there four specific kinds of taste nerves, each capable of responding to one of four sensations: bitter, sweet, sour, and salt.

Creating Your Optimal Diet

To have a vigorous, healthful life, you need to consume food of a correspondingly high level of quality. For each of us there exists, in theory, an optimal diet—one that is flexible rather than fixed, dynamic rather than static, and yet so synchronized with our needs that whatever potential we possess for a strong body and long, healthful life is naturally fulfilled. But given biochemical individuality and given the multiple cycles of overlapping genetic factors that shape us as individuals, there's no *one* optimal diet that works for all. Each of us must define our own needs and create our own optimal diet. This chapter provides the framework and tools to begin the task.

To begin, why is it that virtually none of us has been taught how to develop a healthful diet in the first place? The answer lies partly in the fact that for the first time in history, developing an *unhealthful* diet is not only possible but nearly probable. Prior to World War II, food was food in the same way it had been for centuries—whole. It was ground, mashed, mixed, cooked at home, and eaten according to season. With the exception of a few foodstuffs such as bread, very little food was factory processed. And the food made in factories was processed using techniques that weren't very different from the way food was made at home. The factory simply produced food on a larger scale.

After World War II, food processing was launched into a new realm—food technology. For the first time, food processing meant *chemical* processing. In the thirty years after World War II, the percentage of calories that each of us derived from chemically fabricated and structurally modified food jumped from 10% to 70% of our total diet.[1] For the first time ever, we had to know how to read in order to know what "food" we were buying.

By the 1970s food was extraordinarily different from the food that had supported life throughout thousands of years of human evolution. But most of us were not aware of how sharply we had veered

[1]Ross Hume Hall, "Thirty Years of Laissez-Faire in Human Nourishment," *En-trophy Institute for Advanced Study Review,* Vol. 1, No. 3 (March–April 1978), p. 2.

off the track of fundamental nourishment, for in almost all cases the new technologized food was chemically molded into familiar traditional forms. As a result, few of us questioned the possible risks of foods like extruded, spun, and molecularly altered soy protein, for example, because, when you got right down to it, it was never decimated, chemicalized soybeans on the plate; it was a food that looked so much like bacon or eggs or butter or whipped cream that no one stopped to question its composition.

Only when relatively large numbers of people began dying from the same new diseases did scientists take a serious look at what we'd been eating. In 1977, for example, the National Cancer Institute put the number of cancer cases tied to diet at 60% for women and 40% for men. In the same year, the United States Senate Select Committee on Nutrition and Human Needs published the first edition of its *Dietary Goals for the United States*—point-by-point nutritional recommendations based on the most wide-ranging and exhaustive compilation of nutrition research and opinion that had ever been undertaken or assembled. The U.S. Senate Select Committee's final consensus? Six of the leading causes of death in the United States (heart disease, cancer, stroke, hypertension, diabetes, and arteriosclerosis) could be linked directly to diet.[2]

And so food was increasingly discussed in terms of risk/benefit ratios and margins of safety, and as a result, the need to consciously plan a healthful diet struck many of us with serious impact.

But there's another reason we haven't been taught how to develop a healthful diet. As scientists have mapped out certain aspects of nourishment, new information has clouded rather than clarified the nutritional principles that were thought to be true just a few years before.

The *Supplementary Views* of the *Dietary Goals* contain nearly nine hundred pages of conflicting research on cholesterol! And protein is another good example. A few years ago protein was *the* nutrient most often linked to good health. Athletes ate protein foods for energy, strength, and muscle development. Overweight people ate protein foods to lose weight without subjecting their bodies to health risks. Infants and children were fed as much protein as they'd eat, and some doctors felt that vegetarians risked not getting enough protein, especially if they ate no dairy products or eggs.

But recent research turned each of those tables. None of the research conducted on athletes substantiated the idea that cellular pro-

[2]Select Committee on Nutrition and Human Needs, United States Senate, *Dietary Goals for the United States,* 1st and 2nd eds. (Washington: 1977).

tein was destroyed by muscular activity. In fact, it was found that protein requirements were not affected by an increase in physical activity.[3]

Protein was shown to contain, gram for gram, the *same* number of calories that carbohydrates contain, and what diet-conscious people hadn't often considered was the enormous fat content of such high-protein foods as cheese and meat.

The protein in cow's milk—because it's different in structure from the protein in human milk and because there's proportionately nearly three times as much of it—was found to be dehydrating and stressful to many children's immature digestive tracts, leading in turn to diarrhea, anemia, and milk allergies.

One of the most significant theories shattered by the new research on protein was the idea that animal protein was better than vegetable protein. Although the structure of proteins in every protein food is different, vegetarians who ate no animal foods at all were shown to have adequate protein intakes, both in quality and in quantity, even when they took no special precautions to eat high-protein vegetable foods.[4]

In fact a staff report by the Federal Trade Commission in 1979 recommended regulations that would require protein supplements to carry a disclosure label stating, "A Fact You Should Know: Very few Americans need extra protein. Almost all of us get all we need from the food we eat."

And so the research goes, each small bit of latest information rendering some of the previous "latest" information invalid or inconclusive.

Not surprisingly, scientists are among those most aware of the limits of nutrition research, which is one reason why they're cautious about drawing conclusions that lead people to radically alter their diets. In fact the only nutrition information that science currently asserts *as fact* is that over the ages human beings have survived by eating whole, natural foods.

Beyond having a philosophy predicated on whole foods, then, how does one figure out what to eat to be healthy? To begin with, set aside the current black-and-white approach to food (this one's good, that one's bad) and begin developing a genuine understanding of the *context* in which nutrients work, exploring how your own nourish-

[3]C. F. Consolazio, "Nutrition and Athletic Performance," *Progress in Human Nutrition,* ed. Sheldon Margen (Westport, Conn.: Avi Publishing, 1971), pp. 118–27.

[4]U. D. Register, Ph.D., R.D., and L. M. Sonnenberg, R.D., "The Vegetarian Diet," *Journal of the American Dietetic Association,* Vol. 62 (March 1973), pp. 253–60. The report did note that supplemental vitamin B_{12} was necessary.

ment is affected by your specific biochemical needs on the one hand and your changing individual environment on the other.

The rest of this section on designing your optimal diet is given over to developing just such an understanding of individual nourishment. First, as important background, there is *Macronutrients and Micronutrients*—a full explanation of protein, fats, carbohydrates, vitamins, and minerals. Give these a quick once-over to refamiliarize yourself with the basics. Next, also for your background reference, the *Dietary Goals for the United States* are presented in condensed form. The goals are the most highly respected recommendations to date of foods that should be *avoided or limited* in the healthful diet. To round out the *Dietary Goals,* there are the guidelines in *How to Plan a Whole Foods Diet.* These spell out the most important principles associated with eating natural foods. The fourth part explores the limits of body wisdom and offers information on cravings and fatness. Part five, *The Effect Life-style Has on Nutritional Needs,* presents many of the special conditions and life-style factors that you must take into consideration when you begin to create a healthful diet for yourself. And finally, there's part six, *The Food Workbook*—individual charts for determining exactly what your current food patterns and diet are and how they compare with the recommendations set forth in the *Dietary Goals.*

A last word of support:

You're going to have to be *very committed* to wanting to eat more healthfully. Eating patterns are long-established learned behaviors, and as such, they are among the hardest behaviors to change. During World War II, Army officials complained that the biggest problem in bringing people of different ethnic backgrounds from all different regions of the United States together was *not* overcoming language, housing, or social behavior differences. It was getting all those people to be willing to eat the same food and oftentimes give up the foods they were used to.

In the beginning, finding the most healthful diet for you may seem like a small war between the adult in you and the child in you. The child in you is going to say, "I want potato chips, Cokes, hot dogs, candy bars, ice cream"—all the high-sugar, high-fat, high-salt, high-calorie processed foods that have been a part of almost every American's diet for the last twenty years.

If, however, it makes sense to you that food affects the way you feel, the way you look, how much energy you have, how calm you are, then your adult is going to have to overrule your child. You're going to have to be patient and keep refusing sugary chemicalized soft drinks, even though, in the beginning, your body won't feel any different whether you drink a soft drink or not.

What will happen in time will be astonishing. The foods that you thought you couldn't live without may actually begin to nauseate you. This happens all the time to people who stop eating sugar and drinking coffee. Refined sugar and coffee act like drugs in the body, and when you first stop ingesting them, your body may go through minor withdrawal symptoms. You'll feel uncomfortable. You may get tired a lot, have headaches. Worse than that, you may crave the foods you were used to. Psychologically, you may feel deprived—and for no good reason, it seems, since you don't seem to be feeling any better physically, even though you're not eating all the old, unhealthful food.

But slowly, slowly, the cravings go away. You begin to feel a bit better. Then much better. For the first time in years you wake up in the morning full of energy. The body feels stable. The skin, teeth, and hair may begin to look better. You feel more mentally alert.

And then the magic day comes. You haven't eaten *any* sugar for, say, six months. It's Thanksgiving. You decide to have just a small slice of that warm, oozing pecan pie topped with the smallest scoop of ice cream. One bite—and bam! A shudder ripples from the top of your spinal column to the tips of your toes. The pie tastes *so sweet*—like having a mouth full of raw white sugar. You can't chew another bite without wincing. You can happily go back to the cheese and fruit.

The taste buds and the body are always being conditioned by food. If, for example, you drink the strongest cup of coffee you can brew, then drink a small bit of milk separately, the milk will taste as sweet as cream. That's because the taste buds have been dramatically affected by the bitterness of the coffee.

The idea in modifying your diet toward more healthful food is to give your body enough time to be deprogrammed. You simply can't evaluate your body's response to coffee or meat or sugar—or anything else for that matter—if your body has gradually adapted itself to the taste and physiological effect of that food.

Food is clearly not the only determinant of health. But food, along with exercise, is one of the only health-related factors you have control over. You *can* improve your diet.

Dr. Mark Hegsted, formerly a professor of nutrition at Harvard, pointed out that the American diet of today was not planned or developed with any purpose in mind. Each of us simply took it on as a matter of happenstance. The question to be asked, Hegsted says, is *not* why should we change our diet, but why not? What are the risks associated with eating less meat, less fat, less saturated fat, less sugar, less salt, and more fresh fruits, vegetables, and whole grains?

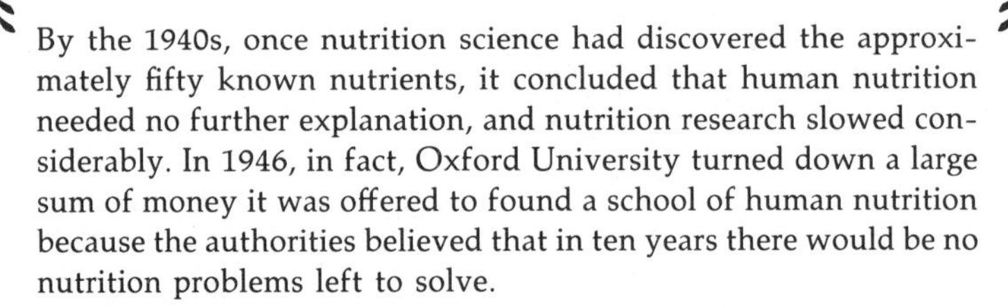

By the 1940s, once nutrition science had discovered the approximately fifty known nutrients, it concluded that human nutrition needed no further explanation, and nutrition research slowed considerably. In 1946, in fact, Oxford University turned down a large sum of money it was offered to found a school of human nutrition because the authorities believed that in ten years there would be no nutrition problems left to solve.

From: "The RDAs and Public Policy," *En-trophy Institute for Advanced Study Review,* Vol. 1, No. 1 (November–December 1977).

I. Macronutrients and Micronutrients

At the most fundamental level there is very little difference between us and the food we eat. The protein in the muscles of an Olympic athlete is made up of the same basic amino acids as the protein in a slice of cheese or the protein in a potato.

Since we are members of the animal kingdom, it's not surprising that there are biological similarities between us and animals. But the similarities also extend to plants, for plants are constructed of the same elements animals are—carbon, hydrogen, oxygen, and nitrogen—only in different combinations. These elements combine to form fats, carbohydrates, and proteins. Also, many of the structures and processes of plant and animal life are shared: cellular organization, a nucleus in every cell carrying the chromosomal blueprint for life, the ability to synthesize protein and manufacture fats and complex carbohydrates from simple substances, the presence of enzymes directing the various life processes, and the release of energy through the oxidation of nutrients.

Food nutrients are, then, to a large extent the same compounds found in our own body tissues.

Proteins, fats, and carbohydrates are macronutrients. They provide the body with energy, which is measured in calories. The amount of protein, fat, and carbohydrate you need is therefore dependent first on how much energy you need. One gram[5] of protein or one gram of carbohydrate will provide you with 4 calories, four units of energy. By contrast, one gram of fat will generate 9 calories, nine units of

[5]One gram is the basic measurable unit for computing calories, but 1 gram doesn't represent much in terms of food. Food is usually measured in 100-gram units; 100 grams = 3½ ounces.

energy.[6] So right from the start you can see that in terms of calories alone, you need only *half* as much fat as protein or carbohydrate to produce the same amount of energy (calories).

Protein

Protein is a major part of all biological systems. It occurs in all foods, whatever their origin. In the human body protein is the most plentiful substance, next to water.

Body proteins are in a dynamic state, constantly being broken down and replaced. In organs that carry out metabolism—the liver, kidneys, intestines, and pancreas—the turnover of protein is rapid. Protein in these tissues have an estimated life of 10 days.[7] In the skeletal system—the muscles, bones, and skin—protein synthesis is much slower. Here, a protein molecule lives for an estimated 158 days.

Protein is the raw material of living tissue. It must be supplied if cells (including those of the heart and brain) are to grow and continue to function. Then, as cells die, protein becomes the basis of new tissue. Like a clock that never stops running, the body carries on the synthesis, ticking out protein according to need.

The need is crucial at certain times. During growth and pregnancy, for example, protein demands are high because of the rapid growth occurring in all parts of the body. After fasting, after an infection, or after any debilitating disease, protein is again extremely important because tissues that have been damaged or have wasted away must be rebuilt.

Even when the body is not under special stress, protein is still vital. Hormones (including insulin) that regulate metabolism, spur growth, and carry out sexual development are manufactured from protein. Enzymes that keep the body in everyday working order and form the antibodies that protect against infection are formed from protein. Protein allows blood to clot and regulates the blood's acid-alkaline balance. Protein, in fact, forms the very structure of many tissues—the keratin of the skin, the collagen of the tendons, and the actin and myosin of the muscles, for example.

When protein is digested, it is broken down into amino acids. The amino acids are absorbed into the bloodstream and distributed to different tissues in a series of amino acid pools. The organs draw on

[6]One gram of alcohol (not a nutrient) generates 7 calories. It is therefore an energy source, but is toxic in excessive amounts.

[7]Gertrude E. Perlmann and James M. Manning, "Protein: Biosynthesis," *McGraw-Hill Encyclopedia of Food, Agriculture & Nutrition* (New York: McGraw-Hill, 1977), p. 532.

these pools, combining various amino acids in countless combinations to form new proteins that then become the structural and functional elements of the cells and tissues.

Of the more than two hundred known amino acids, twenty have been found in the tissues of humans. Many of these twenty amino acids are synthesized directly in the body. Eight, however, cannot be, and must be supplied directly through food. These are called the eight "essential" amino acids.

It's been a common error to confuse a food with the protein it contains and with the amino acids that make up the protein. All foods contain some protein. The amount varies from a trace in an apple to more than half the weight of a fish. *Most food proteins contain all twenty known human amino acids.* However, since the amount of protein and the relative concentration of amino acids differ in every food, some foods contain extremely small amounts of a particular amino acid.

Eggs, for example, contain the protein ovoalbumin. Ovoalbumin

Some Protein-Containing Foods

Foods	*Proteins*	*Amino Acids**
Milk	casein lactalbumin lactoglobulin	threonine tryptophan lysine leucine isoleucine
Meat (muscle)	actin myosin myoglobin	methionine valine phenylalanine histidine arginine
Egg	ovoglobulin ovoalbumin	glycine alanine cysteine cystine
Wheat	glutenin gliadin	serine tyrosine aspartic acid
Corn	zein	glutamic acid proline hydroxyproline
Gelatin	gelatin	tryptophan

* All proteins contain all twenty amino acids with very few exceptions, although the relative amount of each may vary widely. The protein in gelatin, for example, contains no tryptophan.

From: Marian Arlin, *The Science of Nutrition,* 2nd ed. (New York: Macmillan, 1977).

contains twenty amino acids, one of which is lysine. Ovoalbumin is not the only protein in eggs. Eggs also contain ovoglobulin (which also contains all twenty amino acids), and together the proteins ovoalbumin and ovoglobulin make up 13% of the whole substance of an egg.[8] Ovoalbumin and ovoglobulin also happen to be proteins that have highly concentrated amounts of amino acids.

Whole wheat flour contains two different proteins—glutenin and gliaden. Glutenin and gliaden make up 13.3% of whole wheat flour, or roughly the same percentage of protein that ovoalbumin and ovoglobulin contribute in eggs. Although wheat protein contains the same amino acids found in egg protein, the amino acids in wheat are structured differently from the amino acids in egg protein. In the end, wheat does not contribute the concentration of amino acids that eggs do, but the protein itself is in no way inferior.

The concentrations of amino acids in various proteins have been mistaken as a measure of food quality. Vegetable foods have been labeled "incomplete" protein, and animal foods have been labeled "complete" protein. Neither of these terms is used in the scientific literature, however, because the differences are *not* in quality of protein—but in the amount of protein and in the structure of the amino acids.

The problem is not that cassava, for example, is an inadequate protein for a child, but that a child would have to eat more than three pounds of cassava to get amino acids in the needed concentrations. The amount of protein in root vegetables, in fact, is extremely small, since a root's purpose is to store the starch of a plant. In parts of the world where the diet is made up principally of roots and tubers, it's almost impossible for anyone (least of all children) to eat the amount of food it would take to supply an optimal amount of usable protein.

Here is where grains and legumes show their strength over other plant foods. A cereal grain is actually a seed, which in concentrated form holds the plant's initial food, including all of its protein. As a result, grains contain the protein that the plant itself would need if the seed were planted.

Legumes become concentrated sources of protein by working in cooperation with bacteria in the soil. The roots of the legume provide food (carbohydrates) for the bacteria that grow on nodules on the plant's roots. In return, the bacteria convert nitrogen in the soil to amino acids that are absorbed along with nitrogen by the legume and

[8]The body utilizes 94% of the 13% protein in egg, 60% of the 13.3% protein in wheat, 82% of the 3.5% protein in milk, and 72% of the 3.5% protein in corn. (Sources: USDA Handbook No. 8, *Composition of Foods*; Frances Moore Lappé, *Diet for a Small Planet* [New York: Ballantine, 1971], pp. 48–49, plus corresponding tables.) See page 30 for a full explanation of net protein utilization (NPU).

stored in its seed, bean, or pea.[9] A similar process takes place with nuts. Nuts, legumes, and grains are therefore much stronger vegetable sources of protein than roots or tubers.

Since different animal and vegetable foods contribute different proteins (in differing amounts), the body receives not one, but several forms of protein substances. When you eat protein, then, there are two questions to ask. First, how much crude protein does the food contain? Fish, for example, is about 19% protein, sesame seeds are about 34% protein, and whole brown rice is about 7% protein. Second, how much of that protein is available to the body?

Depending on how the amino acids are structured, the body utilizes different amounts of the protein it's presented with. The protein in different foods has therefore been assigned different net protein utilization (NPU) values. The NPU is a measure of how much of the protein actually stays in the body and how much is excreted as nitrogen in the urine.[10]

Back to our examples, fish has an NPU value of 80, sesame seeds an NPU of 53, and whole brown rice an NPU of 70. This means that the body can use 80% of the 19% protein in fish, 53% of the 34% protein in sesame seeds, and 70% of the 7% protein in rice. There are no foods that are both extremely high in percentage of protein and extremely high in the percentage of protein the body can use.

An oddity?

Well, perhaps not. Nature has never been known to put all of her eggs into one basket. There are no multidimensional super foods. Instead, there are thousands of foods, each one making its tiny contribution, each one a speck in the nutritional cosmos. If any one of us wants to be well nourished, we have no option other than eating from a spectrum of foods (fruits, leafy vegetables, root vegetables, grains, legumes, dairy foods, meats, fish) in the widest variety a given locality allows. Because every food contributes different nutrients (and not just different proteins), a variety of foods not only assures a superior concentration and variety of amino acids but also enhances the general effectiveness of every specific food.

For example, in terms of protein, it's known that grains and legumes work well together. When the two are eaten in the same

[9]Some of the need for protein is now thought to be a need for nitrogen and various unidentified protein components as well. Amino acids, although vital, are no longer considered to be the sole determinant of a protein's nutritive value. See: Constance Kies, Hazel Metz Fox, and Eleanor R. Williams, "Effect of Nonspecific Nitrogen Supplementation on Minimum Corn Protein Requirement and First Limiting Amino Acid for Adult Men," *Journal of Nutrition,* Vol. 92 (1967), p. 377.

[10]Nitrogen and carbon are primary constituents of amino acids. When there are excess amino acids in the tissues, the nitrogen in the amino acids is converted into urea and excreted in the urine. In studies of human protein needs, researchers have used the amount of nitrogen excreted in the urine as an index of how much protein is used by the body and how much is excreted as excess. The more that is excreted, the more the person is thought to have consumed adequate protein.

meal, the body retains more protein from both. Milk protein and grain protein also enhance each other. The following model based on research cited in Frances Moore Lappé's *Diet for a Small Planet* (Ballantine, 1971) shows what the basic combinations for maximizing protein are.

↓ Milk products
↕ Grain
↕ Legumes (peas and beans)
↑ Seeds and most nuts

Each food strongly complements the food above and below it. Milk enhances grain. Grain enhances milk, peas, and beans. Peas and beans enhance grains, seeds, and most nuts.

Certainly, eating legumes and milk together (or seeds and milk or grains and seeds) will also provide the body with more effective protein than either would alone, but the relationship between legumes and milk isn't thought to be as strong as the relationship between grain and milk. Ideally , one should go for the trifecta: milk, grain, *and* legume—the classic American lunch, in other words: a glass of milk and a peanut butter (peanuts are a legume) sandwich on whole wheat bread. (Admittedly, it would be more classic—but less wonderful—on Wonder bread.)[11]

Something else to be aware of when you eat protein: With the exception of sugar and salad oils, most foods contribute a combination of nutrients. Meat, for example, which is usually thought of only in terms of the protein it provides, is also a high-fat food. While animal protein may be a plus, animal fat is definitely a minus. The animal food exception is fish, which provides a large amount of protein without much fat.

Plant foods have their own combinations of nutrients. In general, plant foods that contribute protein also contribute carbohydrates, but rarely contain fat. The exceptions are nuts and seeds, which do contribute lots of fat (although the fat is not saturated, as it is in animal food).

Protein, then, must always be considered in relation to whatever else the food it's in provides. Sources of protein containing little fat include: fish and shellfish, tofu, grains and beans eaten together, low-fat cottage cheese, ricotta and other unripened cheeses, and eggs

[11]A peanut butter sandwich on whole wheat bread accompanied by a glass of milk provides a high level of protein. As a meal, however, it's high in fat and not well rounded (low in vitamins and minerals, unless fruit or a vegetable is added).

(moderate fat but extremely high protein). Please see the following section on fat.

> The *Dietary Goals* suggest that protein make up 12% of the calories in a healthy person's diet. Currently, most American diets are in fact 12% protein. To figure out exactly what percentage of your total calories come in the form of protein, see *The Food Workbook,* page 74.

Fats

Fat has protective properties. It insulates the body against temperature changes and holds the kidneys, heart, and liver in place.

In food, fat is a concentrated source of energy, contributing more than twice as many calories (9) per gram of food as either protein or carbohydrate contribute (4). Fats also act as transporters for the fat-soluble vitamins A, D, E, and K. Since other vitamins and minerals are in turn dependent on A, D, E, and K, fats have important indirect as well as direct roles in body health.

The compounds that make up fats are called fatty acids. Different combinations of fatty acids taste different and determine whether a fat is saturated or unsaturated. Generally, saturated fats come from animals (the major exception is fish) and are hard at room temperature. Unsaturated fats come mainly from plants and are liquid at room temperature. The chapter "Edible Oils" thoroughly explains the difference between saturated and unsaturated fat and saturated- and unsaturated-fat foods. You may want to look at it now.

Most Americans eat too many high-fat foods—a practice that usually leads to slow but constant weight gain and obesity. Obesity itself often becomes a risk factor in other diseases: diabetes, high blood pressure and stroke, cardiovascular disease, arteriosclerosis, liver disease, and hernia. But even if excessive fat in the diet does not show up as disease or disability specifically, too much fat is still harmful. It causes the digestion and absorption of other foods to be very slow, for example. A sluggish metabolism, which doesn't pump nutrients as the body cells need them, undermines the whole process of nourishment.

In addition, according to research conducted by Dr. Gio Gori of the National Cancer Institute, as the amount of fat in the diet increases, there is an increase in the incidence of breast and colon cancer.[12] Saturated fat in particular seems to contribute to heart disease by increasing the amount of cholesterol in the blood.[13] Foods high in saturated fat may in fact raise blood cholesterol even *more than foods high in cholesterol do.* The section on eggs (pages 235–240) contains a thorough discussion of the fat/cholesterol debate.

A small but striking bit of research amid the volumes of current scientific reports on fat and disease comes by way of the Navy. In 1977 the Navy compared the physical health and well-being of ex-GIs who returned to America after serving in Vietnam and ex-GIs who spent more than five years in Vietnamese prison camps before returning home. The GIs who had been prisoners were more physically healthy than their American counterparts. The Navy attributed their health to the low-fat, low-cholesterol Vietnamese diet of rice, vegetables, and small amounts of fish, plus no alcohol, limited smoking, and rigorous physical exercise programs.

Fat is fat and that is that. The *Dietary Goals* suggest that fat constitute no more than 30% of the calories you eat a day, whereas 40% of the calories in the current American diet come from fat. In addition, no more than 10% of that 30% total should be saturated fat. To figure out exactly what percentage of your total calories come from fat, see *The Food Workbook,* page 74. Scan the journal to see what foods you get most of your fat from. To meet the *Dietary Goals'* 10% saturated-fat limit, only one-third of the calories you get from fat should come from animal (excluding fish) foods.

Carbohydrates

Carbohydrates are the body's most efficient, easily digested source of energy. Carbohydrates even assist in the digestion and assimilation of other foods by regulating fat and protein metabolism.

[12]Dr. Gio Gori, deputy director of the National Cancer Institute, has said, in a statement to the U.S. Senate Select Committee on Nutrition and Human Needs, July 1976, "The forms of cancer that appear to be dependent on nutrition as shown by epidemiologic studies include: stomach, liver, breast, prostrate, large intestine, small intestine, and colon. . . . I want to emphasize we are not saying there is a direct relationship between diet and cancer. We do have strong clues that dietary factors play a preponderant role in the development of these tumors. . . . As the dietary intake of fat increases, you have an almost linear increase in the incidence of breast and colon cancer."

[13]*Dietary Goals,* pp. xxxvi and 38–41.

But what comes to mind when you think of high-carbohydrate foods such as fettuccine? risotto? potato pancakes? baked beans? whole wheat raisin bread?

Do energy, balance, and strength come to mind? Do athletes come to mind? Do traditional nourishment and cultural eating habits come to mind?

More than likely *calories* come to mind. *Too many calories.* Let's begin, then, by dispelling the first myth about carbohydrates, the one that says that you gain weight when you eat them.

In 1975 Dr. Olaf Mickelsen, professor of nutrition at Michigan State University, conducted a study evaluating the effect eating bread high in cellulose (fiber) had on attempts to lose weight.[14] He took sixteen college men who were overweight by ten to forty pounds and fed them twelve slices of bread a day in addition to their meals. The men were restricted in only two food areas: They were not allowed foods high in fat or foods high in sugar. Half of the men ate bread high in cellulose and half ate regular bread. Both groups of men actually lost weight. The men who ate the high-fiber bread lost an average of 19.4 pounds in eight weeks, and the men who ate regular bread lost an average of 13.7 pounds in eight weeks.

According to Mickelsen, two things accounted for the weight loss. First, as a result of eating so much bread, the men became full before they consumed their regular number of calories. And second, those men who ate the high-fiber bread apparently eliminated more of the calories they ate.

An overview of the research on overweight people and their diets indicates that unrefined carbohydrate foods (vegetables, grains, legumes) are usually *not* responsible for weight gain. Rather, highly processed, high-sugar, high-fat carbohydrate foods (white bread, pastry, doughnuts, etc.) combined with foods containing large amounts of saturated fat (meat, butter, cream, coconut oil, etc.) form diets that almost invariably lead to obesity.

Carbohydrates come in three forms: sugars, starches, and cellulose (the nondigestible fiber found in the skins and stalks of fruits and vegetables). Sugars, sometimes called simple carbohydrates, are easy to digest and provide the body with almost instant energy. But there's a drawback. Most sugars are absorbed into the bloodstream so quickly that the pancreas releases massive amounts of insulin to deal with them. The body is flooded with the temporary energy that an onrush of insulin provides, but just as abruptly the blood sugar

[14]Olaf Mickelsen, "The Nutritional Value of Bread," *Cereal Foods World,* Vol. 20, No. 7 (July 1975).

level drops off sharply, creating a craving for sugar, plus exhaustion, and sometimes dizziness, nervousness, and headaches. The chapter "Sugars and Sweeteners" covers the specific physiological effects different sugars (natural sugars like fruit, refined sugars like white sugar, and processed sugars like honey) have on the body.

Besides sugar and fiber, the third and most important source of carbohydrate is starches, also called complex carbohydrates. Complex carbohydrates come in the form of vegetables, grains, and legumes. They break down into the same simple sugar molecule (glucose) that sugars do, except that complex carbohydrates take a much longer time to break down (they're "complex") and do not trigger a massive release of insulin. Unlike sugars, complex carbohydrates are slowly acted on by enzymes and slowly released into the bloodstream so that energy reaches the brain, nervous system, and muscle tissue in steady, even amounts.

Although most parts of the body can synthesize raw energy from fats and protein, the brain depends on glucose from specific carbohydrate sources. The source can be a simple carbohydrate (a sugary food)—but the body and brain function much better if the glucose that's provided comes in a steady stream from complex carbohydrates such as grains and legumes.

Please be aware that just as there are highly processed sugars, there are also highly processed complex carbohydrates. Even though you may technically be eating a complex carbohydrate when you eat an English muffin, you're also eating a refined, white-flour food that has little of the original wheat's worth. Gone are nearly all the original B and E vitamins, fiber, and minerals. What's left is a starch that provides calories—but nutritionally empty ones.

The *Dietary Goals* recommend that complex carbohydrates (grains, vegetables, legumes) and naturally occurring sugars (sugars indigenous to food, such as the natural sugar in milk or in an apricot) make up 48% of your diet. Currently, these two make up about 28% of most diets. In addition, the goals suggest that each of us reduce our consumption of refined sugars (cane and beet) and processed sugars (honey, molasses, corn syrup) from 18% of our diet (the average in 1974) to 10%. To figure out what percentage of calories in your diet come from carbohydrates, see *The Food Workbook,* page 74.

Vitamins

A vitamin is any natural organic substance that cannot be synthesized by—but is essential for—a living organism. Vitamins themselves are found only in the living tissues of plants and animals. When the plant or animal is eaten, the vitamins that were a part of its body become the constituents of enzymes that provide the consumer with life and energy. Vitamins are never the building blocks of body structures; instead, they're indispensable in activating nearly every body function.

There are roughly twenty known vitamins essential for human nutrition. However, a vitamin in the human body is not necessarily a vitamin in another animal's body. Vitamin C is a perfect example. Primates must get C from food sources; without it, all species of primates develop disease and die. Rats, on the other hand, manufacture vitamin C within their own body tissues.

It is thought that the need for a specific vitamin is common to all members of the same species. If, for example, the vitamin thiamine is necessary for the release of energy in any one human being (which it is), then it's necessary for the release of energy in the whole species. Individual needs for vitamins, however, do vary widely, depending on biochemical individuality, genetic makeup, and shifting environmental factors.

Two theories have been proposed explaining the evolutionary development of our dependence on vitamins. The first postulates that the enzymes necessary for the manufacture of vitamins were once available in human tissues, but that the ability to synthesize them was lost over evolutionary time. An unfortunate mutation—lucky for us there were enough vitamin-rich foods around to eat. If there hadn't been, we simply wouldn't have survived.

An alternative hypothesis suggests that as the environment grew more chemically complex, higher forms of life flourished and more effective enzyme systems naturally developed. As the human enzyme system became more and more sophisticated, humans became more and more dependent on other simple sources of the basic life components called vitamins. Many bacteria and other simple forms of life, for example, easily synthesize the vitamins we cannot.

Vitamins are described as either water soluble or fat soluble. The water-soluble vitamins (all those except A, D, E, and K) are measured in milligrams. The fat-soluble vitamins (A, D, E, and K) are measured in international units (IUs), which are a measure of the amount of a fat-soluble vitamin needed to produce a specific change in the nutri-

Vitamin	*Why It's Needed*	*Aids In*	*Food Sources*	*More Effective With*
A	Aids in general good health, protects membranes, kidneys, bladder, lungs and soft tissue, and lining of digestive tract. Builds strong bones, teeth, and rich blood, and maintains good eyesight; seems to delay senility and prolong longevity. Helps in fighting infections. Found to lower cholesterol.	Night blindness, skin blemishes, vision problems, kidney and gallstones, asthma, and acne. Signs of need include soft teeth and bones, digestive disorders, poor appetite, loss of smell, fatigue.	Fish-liver oils, dairy products, carrots, cantaloupe, peaches, squash, tomatoes, and all green and yellow fruits, vegetables.	B complex, choline, vitamin C, vitamin D, vitamin E, calcium, phosphorus, zinc
B Complex	Acts in providing the body with energy by converting carbohydrates into glucose, which produces energy. Essential for fat and protein metabolism, normal functioning of nervous system and for health of skin, hair, eyes, mouth, liver.	Constipation, burning feet, tender gums, burning and drying eyes, fatigue, poor appetite, skin disorders, cracks at corner of mouth, anemia, alcoholism, arthritis, backache, edema, infection, overweight and stress.	Brewer's yeast, liver, whole-grain cereal, blackstrap molasses.	Vitamin C, vitamin E, calcium, phosphorus
B_1 (Thiamine)	Necessary for the breakdown of carbohydrates into sugar, which produces energy. Maintains a healthy nervous system and mental attitude. Improves muscle tone.	Rapid heartbeat, digestion, nausea, fatigue, constipation, stress and emotional instability.	Brewer's yeast, wheat germ, blackstrap molasses, bran, whole brown rice, meats, soybeans, oysters.	B complex, B_2, folic acid, niacin, vitamin C, vitamin E, manganese
B_2 (Riboflavin)	Involved in the breakdown and utilization of protein, fats, and carbohydrates. Necessary for cell respiration and for the maintenance of good vision, skin, nails, and hair.	Cataracts, alcoholism, stress, diabetes, arthritis, baldness, diarrhea, cracked, sore skin, burning eyes.	Brewer's yeast, organ meats, such as liver and tongue, whole grains, mushrooms.	B complex, B_6, niacin, vitamin C

SOURCE: Puritan's Pride, Bohemia, New York. Originally adapted from *Nutrition Almanac,* Nutrition Search, Inc., 1973, 1975.

Vitamin	*Why It's Needed*	*Aids In*	*Food Sources*	*More Effective With*
B_6 (Pyridoxine)	Needed for production of antibodies and red blood cells. Helps in the breakdown and utilization of carbohydrates, fats and proteins. Helps maintain the balance of sodium and potassium, which promotes normal functioning of the nervous and musculoskeletal systems.	Acne, eczema, high cholesterol, muscular weakness, infections, thinning and loss of hair, stress, diarrhea, hemorrhoids and ulcers.	Whole-grain products, brewer's yeast, bananas, green leafy vegetables, wheat germ, pecans, meats.	B complex, B_1, B_2, pantothenic acid, vitamin C, magnesium, potassium
B_{12} (Cobalamin)	Necessary for normal metabolism of nerve tissue; helps in protein, fat and carbohydrate metabolism.	Pernicious anemia, fatigue, nervousness, irritability, depression, insomnia, lack of balance, alcoholism and overweight.	Liver, kidney, muscle meats, fish, shellfish, brewer's yeast, eggs, tempeh, kombu, *wakame.*	B complex, B_6, choline, folic acid, inositol, vitamin C, potassium
Biotin	Necessary for the body's fat production. Helps in making fatty acids and in the oxidation of fatty acids and carbohydrates.	Dermatitis, eczema, baldness, depression, and muscle pains.	Brewer's yeast, liver, kidney, unpolished rice, soy flour, soy beans, egg yolk, peanuts, mushrooms.	B complex, B_{12}, folic acid, pantothenic acid, vitamin C
Choline	Aids in utilization of fats and cholesterol in the body. Prevents fats from accumulating in the liver and aids with the movement of fats into the cells. It is necessary for the proper functioning of the liver and kidneys.	Alcoholism, eczema, hair problems, arteriosclerosis, atherosclerosis, hypertension, high cholesterol, hypoglycemia, dizziness and cirrhosis of liver.	Lecithin, egg yolk, liver, brewer's yeast and wheat germ.	Vitamin A, B complex, B_{12}, folic acid, inositol
Folic Acid	Aids in breakdown and utilization of proteins. Necessary for formation of red blood cells and formation of nucleic acid, which is needed for growth and reproduction of all body cells.	Anemia, diarrhea, stomach ulcers, menstrual disturbances, alcoholism, bruises, fatigue, stress, arteriosclerosis, atherosclerosis, and baldness.	Brewer's yeast, liver, green leafy vegetables, wheat germ.	B complex, B_{12}, biotin, pantothenic acid, vitamin C

Vitamin	*Why It's Needed*	*Aids In*	*Food Sources*	*More Effective With*
Inositol	Helps promote the body's production of lecithin, and therefore, aids in the metabolism of fats and helps reduce blood cholesterol. Aids in brain cell nutrition. Vital for hair growth and can prevent thinning hair and baldness.	Constipation, baldness, arteriosclerosis, cirrhosis of liver, high blood cholesterol and overweight.	Unprocessed whole grains, citrus fruits, brewer's yeast, and liver.	B complex, B_{12}, choline
Niacin	Aids in breakdown and utilization of proteins, fats and carbohydrates. Effective in improving circulation and reducing blood cholesterol level. Essential for proper activity of nervous system, for formation and maintenance of healthy skin, tongue, and digestive tissues.	Acne, diarrhea, atherosclerosis, high blood pressure, alcoholism, stress, headache, insomnia, arteriosclerosis, arthritis and indigestion.	Lean meats, poultry, fish, peanuts, brewer's yeast, wheat germ, desiccated liver, dried beans.	B complex, B_1, B_2, vitamin C, pantothenic acid
Iron	Needed for cellular metabolism. Acts in the release of energy from carbohydrates, fats, proteins and in utilization of other vitamins. Helps to maintain a healthy digestive tract. Stimulates adrenal glands and increases production of adrenal hormones important for healthy skin and nerves.	Alcoholism, depression, fatigue, infection, stress, baldness, hypoglycemia, headache, arthritis, nausea, digestive ailments and allergies.	Organ meats, brewer's yeast, egg yolk, whole-grain cereal, nuts.	B complex, B_6, B_{12}, biotin, folic acid, vitamin C
PABA (Para-amino-benzoic Acid)	Aids in the breakdown and utilization of proteins and in the formation of blood cells (especially red). Essential in determining skin health, hair pigmentation and health of intestines.	Burns, sunburn, vitiligo (skin depigmentation or darkening), constipation, baldness, graying hair, headache, depression, fatigue.	Liver, yeast, wheat germ and molasses.	B complex, folic acid, vitamin C

Vitamin	*Why It's Needed*	*Aids In*	*Food Sources*	*More Effective With*
P Bioflavonoids	Essential for proper absorption and use of vitamin C. Aids in keeping collagen healthy.	Common cold, arthritis, atherosclerosis, arteriosclerosis, bruising, hemophilia, hypertension, varicose veins, miscarriages, bleeding gums and eczema.	Buckwheat and fruits, such as lemons, grapes, plums, grapefruit, and cherries.	Vitamin C
D	Absorption of calcium and phosphorus in the intestines, which promotes normal growth of bones and teeth; prevents rickets, maintains good health and vitality. Protects against muscle weakness. Helps regulate the heart (thru calcium absorption). Relieves nearsightedness.	Acne, eczema, psoriasis, stress, fatigue, insomnia, backache, cystitis, high cholesterol levels, allergies, and common cold.	Egg yolk, fish, fish liver oil, milk.	Vitamin A, choline, vitamin C, calcium, phosphorus
E	Prevention and treatment of heart disease. Helps keep the heart healthy. Acts as a antithrombin (clot dissolver). Anticoagulant.	Heart disease, burns, scars, abrasions, arthritis, bursitis, some eye diseases, lowering cholesterol, menopause, circulation.	Most unrefined vegetable oils, wheat germ, soybean oil, safflower oil, all seeds, eggs, leafy vegetables, beef liver, meat, milk, nuts (raw), molasses, peanuts, legumes (soybeans, peas, beans), unrefined cereal products.	Vitamin A, B complex, B_1, inositol, vitamin C, manganese, selenium
K	Essential for normal blood clotting.	Hemorrhages, cancer, nosebleeds, can prevent cerebral palsy, menstrual cramps.	Green, leafy vegetables, carrot tops, kale, pork, fish, liver, yogurt, kefir, unrefined vegetable oils.	
C (Ascorbic Acid)	Maintains collagen, a protein necessary for formation of connective tissue. Helps in healing wounds and burns, in forming red blood cells, in preventing hemorrhaging, and in fighting bacterial infections. Promotes tooth and bone formation.	Common cold, high cholesterol, hardening of arteries, infections, arthritis, low back pain, wound healing, nasal and gum bleeding, stress, fever, liver disease, respiratory ailments and diarrhea.	Fresh fruits (especially citrus), vegetables, and green peppers.	All vitamins and minerals, calcium, magnesium

tional health of a laboratory animal. Water-soluble vitamins are not stored in the body, but are excreted through the urine when supply exceeds need. Fat-soluble vitamins, on the other hand, are stored in body fat and do not necessarily need to be consumed each day. In fact, when vitamins are obtained through supplements, there is an increased risk of fat-soluble-vitamin overdose. In general, the preferred way of obtaining vitamins and minerals is through *food,* not supplements. It's nearly impossible to determine optimal supplementation, and what often happens is that by supplementing your body with one vitamin, you create an artificially exaggerated need for others. Creating a sound nutritional balance is extraordinarily complex. It's simply more effective and easier to let foods supply the nutrients you need. If you have special needs due to illness, pregnancy, or metabolic disorders, however, it is wise to seek professional help before arbitrarily buying ten bottles of vitamin pills.

Minerals

The body needs minerals as much as it needs vitamins. Minerals are constituents of the muscles, bones, blood, and nerve cells. They act as catalysts for such biological processes as digestion, muscle response, nerve transmission, and the production of hormones and antibodies. Even vitamins are dependent on the presence of minerals in the body before they can do their own work.

Unlike vitamins, minerals are *inorganic.* Plants must extract them from the earth. Animals must extract them from plants.

Seventeen minerals are known to be essential in human nutrition, but more than twice that number can be found in animal tissues. Seven of the seventeen are considered macro-minerals. These are found in significant amounts in body tissues, but it's thought that at least 100 milligrams a day should be additionally supplied by the diet. The other known essential minerals are measured in micrograms and are considered trace minerals. There are also several nonessential —in fact, detrimental—minerals that find their way into the human body. These exist in the food supply (fish and drinking water, for example) and are carried in the environment (auto exhaust, batteries, coal burning, smelter pollution, etc.). At even low concentrations these minerals can have serious toxic effects if ingested. Lead poisoning, for example, may result if as little as 60 millionths of a gram percent lead finds its way into the system.[15]

[15]Carl C. Pfeiffer, Ph.D., M.D., *Mental and Elemental Nutrients* (New Canaan, Conn.: Keats Publishing, 1975), pp. 311–323.

Essential Minerals[1]	*Why It's Needed*	*Aids In*	*Food Sources*	*More Effective With*
Calcium (Macro-mineral)	Builds strong bones and teeth. Helps to calm nerves and aids in insomnia. Helps in normalizing blood clotting and is essential for rhythmic heart action.	Cardiovascular disorders, leg and foot cramps, fever, overweight, sunburn, insomnia, arthritis, rheumatism, menopause disturbances, premenstrual tension, menstrual cramps, aging, and tooth and gum disorders.	Milk and milk products such as yogurt and cheese. Whole grains and unrefined cereals, green vegetables, and bone meal. Chocolate, spinach, and rhubarb may bind calcium.	Vitamin A, vitamin C, vitamin D, iron, magnesium, manganese, phosphorus
Chromium (Trace Mineral)	Helps in carbohydrate utilization. Involved in metabolism of glucose (for energy) and the synthesis of fatty acids and cholesterol.	Diabetes, hyperglycemia and hypoglycemia.	Unsaturated fats (such as corn oil), meats, clams, brewer's yeast, liver and whole-grain cereal.	
Copper (Trace Mineral)	Aids in the formation of hemoglobin and red blood cells. Necessary for proper bone formation and maintenance. Necessary for production of RNA.	Anemia, edema, baldness and bedsores.	Liver, whole-grain products, almonds, green, leafy vegetables and most seafoods.	Iron, zinc
Iron (Macro-Mineral)	Necessary for production of hemoglobin; builds up blood quality and increases resistance to stress and disease.	Aging, alcoholism, pernicious anemia, pregnancy, menstruation and colitis.	Liver, lean meats, eggs, whole-grain breads and cereals, fruits, vegetables, brewer's yeast, blackstrap molasses.	B_{12}, folic acid
Magnesium (Macro-Mineral)	Necessary for metabolism of carbohydrates and amino acids. Aids in	Alcoholism, backache, overweight, diarrhea, vomiting,	Nuts, whole-grain foods, dry beans and peas, dark green	Vitamin B_6, vitamin C,

[1] Many minerals are considered nonessential. Some nonessential minerals are actually detrimental and may lead to impaired functioning and serious toxic effects. These include:

Aluminum: Found in: Some white flour, baking powder, children's aspirin, chips off aluminum cookware.
Beryllium: Neon signs, electronic devices, common household products.
Cadmium: Refined flour and rice. Sugar, coffee, tea.
Fluorine: Drinking water. (There are two types of fluorine—one added to drinking water, the other found in nature. The often excessive amount of fluorine in drinking water may inhibit enzymes and certain vitamins.)
Lead: Pervasive industrial pollutant.
Mercury: Freshwater fish (especially from Great Lakes) are the major source of this industrial pollutant.

SOURCE: Puritan's Pride, Bohemia, New York. Originally adapted from *Nutrition Almanac,* Nutrition Search, Inc., 1973, 1975.

Essential Minerals[1]	*Why It's Needed*	*Aids In*	*Food Sources*	*More Effective With*
Magnesium (Macro-Mineral)	regulating the body's acid-alkaline balance. Aids during bone growth and is needed for proper functioning of nerves and muscles.	nervousness, kidney stones, blood cholesterol levels (high), arteriosclerosis, atherosclerosis, prostate troubles, and depression.	vegetables and soy products.	vitamin D, calcium, phosphorous
Manganese (Trace Mineral)	Needed for protein, carbohydrate and fat production. Necessary for normal skeletal development. Helps maintain sex hormone production, and nourishes the nerves and brain.	Diabetes, fatigue, asthma, and allergies.	Egg yolks, sunflower seeds, wheat germ, whole-grain cereals and flour, dried peas and beans, brewer's yeast, and bone meal.	Vitamin B, vitamin E, calcium
Phosphorus (Macro-Mineral)	Essential for utilization of carbohydrates, fats, and proteins for growth, maintenance and repair of cells and for energy production. Necessary for proper skeletal growth, tooth development, kidney functioning and transference of nerve impulses.	Tooth and gum disorders, backache, pregnancy, stress, healing of bone fractures, and arthritis.	Meat, fish, poultry, eggs, whole grains, seeds, and nuts.	Vitamin D, calcium, vitamin A, iron, manganese
Selenium (Trace Mineral)	Works along with vitamin E in some metabolic processes and aids in normal body growth and fertility.	When combined with protein, kwashiorkor (a protein deficiency disease).	Bran and germs of cereals, broccoli, onions, tomatoes and tuna.	Vitamin E
Potassium (Macro-Mineral)	Necessary for normal growth to stimulate nerve impulses for muscle contraction and to maintain proper alkalinity of body fluids. Aids in keeping skin healthy. Works with sodium to regulate the body's water balance.	High blood pressure, allergies, diarrhea, alcoholism, fever, stress, acne, burns, and heart disorder (angina pectoris, congestive heart failure, and myocardial infarction).	Vegetables (especially green leafy), oranges, whole grains, sunflower seeds, potatoes (especially peels), and bananas.	Vitamin B_6
Zinc (Trace Mineral)	Aids enzymes in digestion and metabolism. Essential for general growth and development of reproductive organs and normal functioning of prostate gland.	High cholesterol levels, atherosclerosis, healing of wounds, infertility, cirrhosis of liver, alcoholism, diabetes, and retarded growth.	Brewer's yeast, bone meal, beans, nuts, seeds, wheat germ, fish and meat (especially liver).	Vitamin A, calcium, copper, phosphorus

Because minerals are inorganic, they are not destroyed by heat or long lapses of time as vitamins are. Instead, minerals present their own problem. On the one hand, many minerals are poorly absorbed by the body. Only a tenth of the iron that's consumed is actually absorbed, for example. On the other hand, the need for some minerals is extremely small. Chlorine, for example, is essential in blood and liver functions. But the amount of chlorine in drinking water is thought to destroy vitamin E and intestinal flora.[16] In addition, the Environmental Protection Agency has found that when chlorine is used to destroy bacteria (in swimming pools, for example), chlorinated hydrocarbons are formed in the process. Chlorinated hydrocarbons are carcinogenic if ingested over a long period of time.

Although minerals are listed separately in the graph, all minerals function as a team—the way they're usually found in food.

II. Dietary Goals

In the face of despair, confusion, and cynicism, it's remarkable how far public consciousness about food and nutrition has come. For decades food and health had moved along in parallel security, but then in February 1977, the United States Senate's Select Committee on Nutrition and Human Needs, chaired by Senator George McGovern, took the bull by the horns. In examining the exorbitant rise in medical care costs, the committee traced many of the major killer diseases back to the dangerously poor state of American nutrition. The committee concluded that food was the key solution; estimates, based on studies by the Department of Agriculture, suggested that improved nutrition could cut the country's projected 1980 medical bill ($230 billion) by one-third.[17]

A synopsis of the committee's *Dietary Goals* follows.[18] The goals focus primarily on protein, fats, and carbohydrates and are based on animal research, metabolic studies and clinical research on humans, and epidemiological investigations. Although the goals were revolu-

[16]*Nutrition Almanac,* Nutrition Search, Inc., director John D. Kirschmann (New York: McGraw-Hill, 1973, 1975). See also: Robert H. Harns and Edward M. Brecher, "Is the Water Safe to Drink?" *Consumer Reports,* June, July, August, 1974.

[17]Based on the testimony of Dr. George Briggs, professor of nutrition, University of California, Berkeley, 1972.

[18]*Dietary Goals for the United States,* 2nd ed., December 1977, can be obtained in full by writing the U.S. Government Printing Office, Washington, D.C. 20402. Be sure to specify Stock No. 052-070-04376-8.

tionary when they first appeared in 1977, they actually sketch only a very rough outline and are more helpful in pointing out foods to avoid than they are in choosing foods to eat.

The Dietary Goals

1. Increase the consumption of fruits, vegetables, and whole grains.
2. Decrease the consumption of refined (cane and beet) sugar and processed sugars (honey, maple syrup, molasses, etc.) and foods that contain those sugars.
3. Decrease the consumption of foods high in total fat, and as much as possible substitute polyunsaturated fats (mainly vegetable fats) for saturated fats (mainly animal fats).
4. Decrease the consumption of animal fats in general, and choose meats, poultry, and fish that will reduce saturated-fat intake. (Fish contains very little saturated fat to begin with, and poultry, eaten without the skin, is the best choice among meats.)
5. Except for young children, substitute low-fat dairy products for whole-fat products.
6. Decrease the consumption of high-cholesterol foods. (The *Dietary Goals* notes that premenopausal women, children, and the elderly may not need to be as concerned about this goal, especially if dependent on high-cholesterol foods like eggs for other positive nutritional benefits.)
7. Decrease the consumption of salt and high-salt foods.

III. How to Plan a Whole Foods Diet

Eating much less sugar, limiting high-fat (especially saturated animal fat) foods, watching out for salt—each and every point made by the *Dietary Goals* is absolutely important. But it's by means of the next step—deciding what foods to eat and how to eat them—that you begin to shape a healthful diet for yourself.

Here are some guidelines for eating whole foods:

1. *Eat a variety of foods in a variety of forms.* A stable, natural ecosystem is dependent on a diversity of plant, animal, and micro life, all of which function together for the survival of the whole environment. The human body is a micro ecosystem. We, too, function more heartily when our nourishment is derived from diverse sources. Also, no

single nutrient can function alone. Bone formation and bone strength, for example, are dependent on calcium, but whether or not the calcium we take in is actually used by the body is dependent on the presence of vitamin D, without which calcium is not absorbed in the intestines. The dependent relationships between foods are so extensive that eating from as many different sources of food as possible is the only way to make sure you're getting adequate amounts of all known and unknown nutrients.

In cultures that still eat close to the land, nearly every local edible substance is eaten. For some cultures this means hundreds of different vegetables plus as many as thirty to sixty species of animals may be eaten. In the United States, supermarkets create an illusion of diversity by presenting as many as eight thousand to ten thousand food items. Actually, most of those thousands of food products come from the same four not-very-diverse crops: wheat, corn, soybean, and sugarcane. But by shopping in a variety of markets, eating in many different restaurants, and experimenting with all local foods in their season, each of us can begin to round out our nourishment.

Also, eat a good portion of your fruits and vegetables in their natural form (raw for fruits and some vegetables; cooked but whole for vegetables that can't be eaten raw). Eating applesauce is not the same as eating an apple, even if the applesauce is made without sweeteners. An apple provides fiber that applesauce doesn't, and more nutrients since it isn't cooked.

2. *Eat all parts of foods.* Leaves (spinach), roots (carrots), stems (celery), seeds (rice, corn), fleshy fruits (apples), vegetable fruits (cucumbers), and flowers (honey, artichokes). Nutrition is improved when all parts of a plant are eaten. Essentially, this is what food combining accomplishes, since eating nuts with grain (as in a nut-butter sandwich on whole wheat bread) is really eating a dried fruit with the seeds of a grass.

Use every edible part of every vegetable and fruit. Toss carrot tops into salads. Roast squash seeds and add them to granola. Every stem, leaf, cap, or peeling you don't eat directly can be kept in the refrigerator for a few days until you've saved enough odds and ends to throw them all in a stock pot with herbs and water. (See the chapter "Cooking: Techniques for Preserving Nutrients.")

3. *Eat locally and seasonally.* Eating foods grown in your region and eating them according to their season creates a physiological equilibrium between you and your environment. If you eat a lot of leafy green salads and citrus fruits in the dead of a harsh New England winter, you may feel cold and physically vulnerable all winter because raw fruits and vegetables, although nutritious, do not provide

the condensed carbohydrates, fats, and calories that a person needs to counteract the environmental stress of cold weather. This doesn't mean that anyone should give up fruits and vegetables during the winter, simply that *cooked root vegetables* rather than leafy greens, *baked apples* rather than sliced oranges, and *lentil soup* rather than lentil sprouts are all better suited to cold weather.

Cold-weather foods take the shape of living things exposed to cold: They're dense, compact, drawn inward. (They usually grow downward, away from the cold air.) The carrot is a good example of a cold-weather food.

Warm-weather foods, by comparison, are lighter and often larger. They grow outward; they're more moist (and so provide the added benefit, when they're eaten, of replacing water lost through sweating during summer). Watermelon, for example, is a summer food.

When the kitchen was the focus of the home, people automatically ate seasonal foods and cooked in a way that was suited to the environment because foods were chosen and cooked for a reason other than eating. Soups, stews, casseroles, breads, roasts—foods that required hours of cooking—were eaten in winter because cooking them also kept the house warm. In summer, food was eaten raw or minimally cooked, not only to keep the eaters cool but also to keep the house cool.

Another factor to consider when you're tempted to eat Hawaiian pineapples for breakfast even though it's February and you live in Maine is that, with most foods, nutrients are lost over time. The "fresh" fruit a New Englander buys in winter is harvested thousands of miles away in semitropical climates, where it is picked unripe. It then spends several days in a truck en route to the airport or the docks, and even then it may spend several days or a week before it's sold in your market.

To eat fruits and vegetables at their full nutritional potential, you must focus on those that are grown in your area and eat them in their natural season. (See the chapter "Vegetables.")

4. *Buy food as frequently as possible.* Buying food frequently is very important for maximizing taste and nutrients, but it's important for another reason as well.

When you buy a food, some part of your conscious choice is operating out of bodily need. (See "Body Wisdom.") Both humans and animals can select foods that contain nutrients that the organism needs at that moment. This innate body wisdom is, in humans, often overruled by habits, susceptibility to advertising, or cultural preferences. Still, it's often apparent when your craving for a food is merely psychological and when it may, in fact, be physiological.

When you say to yourself, "What do I feel like eating?" in part, you're also asking, "What does my body feel that it needs?"

If you buy a whole week's worth of groceries on Saturday, you can't possibly know what your body may feel like or need next Thursday. This may explain in part why, in the morning, people find it difficult to know what they'll want for dinner and why it's difficult to plan a whole week's menu in advance.

If you live in a rural area and must buy large quantities of food that will last a long time, buy *very* different kinds of food and a lot of it, so that you'll always be able to have a number of choices.

If you shop for food for people besides yourself, ask them, before you shop, what they've been feeling like eating. (If they say an ice cream sundae, buy them some yogurt, raisins, nuts, and fruit instead.) And if you're a woman, don't forget about what *you* feel like eating, too. According to the *Journal of Nutrition Education,* of the women who did all their family's menu planning in 1978, only 9% based the food they bought on their own food likes, whereas 52% bought food based on their husband's food likes.[19]

(See "The Psychic Side of Food.")

5. *Eat for nutrient density.* Many foods can be considered nutritious, but the best foods from a health standpoint are those that provide maximum vitamins and minerals for a minimum of calories. The best sources of protein and carbohydrate are those that are high in either of these, but low in fat, sugar, and chemicals.

You can, for example, consume 1,200 calories worth of fish, tofu, vegetables, and whole grains—in which case, you'll be very full and extremely well nourished with hefty amounts of vitamins, minerals, proteins, and carbohydrates, while taking in no refined or processed sugar, extremely little fat, and a relatively small amount of chemical toxins, depending on the fish and the extent to which the vegetables have been sprayed.

By comparison, you could use up those 1,200 calories on a hamburger, a Coke, and a piece of cake. Now the situation is reversed: high levels of fat, sugar, lots of salt and an unknown amount of chemicals in the meat, white hamburger bun, and wedge of cake. For all of that, you've received few vitamins and minerals, almost no fiber, refined carbohydrates only, and a moderate amount of protein.

If you rarely eat high-sugar, high-salt, high-fat, or highly chemicalized foods to begin with, you still need to be conscious of nutrient density. The most commonly eaten vegetable—corn—is one of the least valuable vegetables nutritionally. Broccoli and spinach, for ex-

[19]Jill Vornauf Burt and Ann A. Hertzler, "Parental Influence on the Child's Food Preference," *Journal of Nutrition Education,* Vol. 10, No. 3 (July–September 1978).

ample, are leagues above corn in almost every nutritional dimension. The following list shows the ten vegetables in each category that contribute the most of that particular nutrient in the American food supply. The number preceding each vegetable indicates how the vegetable actually ranks compared with thirty-nine other vegetables in the amount it contains of that nutrient. For example, oranges are the second leading source of potassium for most Americans, even though oranges rank twenty-seventh as compared with other fruits and vegetables in the amount of potassium they contain. Although peas are the third highest source of iron as compared with other vegetables and fruits, peas are comparatively unpopular and so end up ninth on the list of foods that contribute most of the iron in the

*Relative Nutrient Content of Major Fruits and Vegetables and Their Place in the American Food Supply**†

Vitamin A	*Vitamin C*	*Thiamine (B_1)*
1 Carrots	7 Oranges	8 Potatoes
2 Sweet potatoes	18 Potatoes	12 Oranges
9 Tomatoes	16 Tomatoes	4 Corn
4 Cantaloupe	9 Grapefruit	19 Tomatoes
7 Peaches	8 Cabbages	1 Peas
21 Oranges	20 Corn	19 Lettuce
3 Spinach	1 Peppers	8 Watermelon
16 Corn	10 Cantaloupe	33 Apples
17 Lettuce	32 Apples	24 Bananas
14 Peppers	26 Bananas	28 Grapefruit

Potassium	*Calcium*	*Iron*
5 Potatoes	38 Potatoes	19 Potatoes
27 Oranges	32 Oranges	1 Spinach
20 Tomatoes	30 Tomatoes	24 Tomatoes
2 Watermelon	6 Cabbage	14 Corn
16 Corn	14 Lettuce	39 Oranges
8 Bananas	13 Onions	14 Bananas
30 Lettuce	3 Snap beans	24 Lettuce
38 Apples	9 Carrots	36 Apples
9 Carrots	25 Grapefruit	3 Peas
26 Peaches	8 Celery	19 Watermelon

*Fruits and vegetables are listed in rank order according to the amount of each nutrient contributed to the food supply (based on 1970 fruit and vegetable production).

†The number before the fruit or vegetable indicates the relative nutrient content, based on a comparison with thirty-nine major fruits and vegetables (equal portions).

SOURCE: Marian Arlin, *The Science of Nutrition,* 2nd ed. (New York: Macmillan, 1977).

food supply. As a general rule, the vegetables and fruits with the highest nutritive value are not the ones we most commonly eat.

6. *As much as possible, eat fresh and freshly cooked food that has undergone little or no processing, and minimize your intake of toxic substances.* Every chemical, whether it's a nutrient or not, must be broken down and made water-soluble before it can pass through the body. Those chemicals that are not water-soluble may be stored indefinitely in the body's fat tissue. Since all of our body processes are themselves chemical, our biochemistry can be easily and directly altered by other chemicals.

There are currently an estimated 70,000 manufactured chemical compounds in the environment (including the food supply), and several hundred new ones are being introduced every year. If you are an average American, you pop the equivalent of sixty aspirin-size tablets *a day* in food additives alone (110 pounds per year).[20]

Chemicals have two very dangerous characteristics: They're cumulative and synergistic. Because they're cumulative, chemicals which don't give you cancer today could very well give you cancer tomorrow. Because they're synergistic, chemicals which may have been found safe independently have the capacity to be carcinogenic when combined.

Most of us think about chemicals in the same way that scientists look at them, and the same way government agencies rule on them, and the same way that writers write about them: *one at a time.* But by focusing on the isolated dangers of nitrite or saccharin, for example, we allow ourselves to hide from the big picture—which is that we're now in a sea of chemicals, and cutting back on bacon and diet soda, although wise, is in reality a drop-in-the-bucket tactic.

Don't discriminate between chemicals that have been associated with cancer and those that have been deemed—or presumed[21]—safe (always only at certain levels). Avoid them all and eat whole, unprocessed foods whenever you can. No one really needs to eat chemicalized or fabricated foods—ever.

IV. Cravings, Fatness, and the Limits of Body Wisdom

Ideally, each of us could simply assume that the foods we like best are in fact the ones we need. But a number of other factors—habits, social pressures, television and radio advertising—have all been

[20]Ross Hume Hall, "Toxicology," *En-trophy Institute for Advanced Study Review,* Vol. 2, No. 2 (March–April 1979). See also: Jane Borchers, "Chemicals in Your Food," *Working Papers* (Commonweal Research Publication), Vol. 1, No. 10 (1978).

documented as powerful influences that cloud the basic nutritional messages that are a part of our body wisdom.

For example, food technologists who develop new foods based on computer calculations of individual taste preferences say that if you put a bowl of cereal in front of a child and ask him about the taste, he'll tell you first about the prize, then about the celebrity figure who advertises the cereal, then he'll say he likes it because it's green, then maybe he'll say it's crunchy.[22]

Body wisdom is also overruled by subtle social and cultural forces that define our food habits though we may not be aware of them. In 1973 the *American Journal of Clinical Nutrition* described the case of a man whose brain had been affected by gas poisoning so that he was unable to remember anything for more than a few seconds. As a result his eating was totally governed by his bodily needs and not by his emotions or memories. He appeared for meals only when he was hungry or thirsty. He never overate. And once he was satisfied, nothing on the table attracted him.[23]

But why do some people seem more body-wise than others? Putting social pressures and food advertising aside for a moment, when it comes to diet, what else influences body wisdom?

At the base of the two hemispheres of the brain is the hypothalamus, the area of the brain that controls feeding and satiety, body temperature, blood pressure, and sexual arousal. At the beginning of this century French pathologists conducting autopsies on obese individuals noted that the obese sometimes had lesions or tumors in or near the hypothalamus at the time of death. Later, American physiologists strengthened the connection between the hypothalamus and the regulation of food intake by conducting experiments on live laboratory animals in which surgical incisions were made in the animals' hypothalamuses. The experimenters were able to induce voracious appetites in such animals, as well as other behaviors that paralleled behavior in obese humans.[24]

In the 1970s the hypothesis that a specific mechanism in the brain controls appetite and satiation was substantiated even further. While conducting research on normal-weight and obese subjects, T. Van

[21]The GRAS list—or Generally Recognized as Safe list—is made up of more than six hundred substances that are exempt from the FDA's testing and approval requirements for additives. These six hundred GRAS chemicals have been *presumed* safe because each of them was in the food supply, without apparent harm, prior to 1958, the year the government enacted the first widespread testing requirements for additives.

[22]Patricia Wells, "Calculating America's Taste," *New York Times*, January 3, 1979.

[23]S. Lepkovsky, "Newer Concepts in the Regulation of Food Intake," *American Journal of Clinical Nutrition*, Vol. 26 (1973), p. 271.

[24]Anne Scott Beller, *Fat & Thin: A Natural History of Obesity* (New York: Farrar, Straus & Giroux, 1977), pp. 202–28. See also: Neal E. Miller, C. J. Bailey, and J.A.F. Stevenson, "Decreased 'Hunger' but Increased Food Intake Resulting from Hypothalamic Lesions," *Science*, Vol. 112 (1950).

Italie of Columbia University and Robert Campbell of the University of Rochester were able to show that normal-weight subjects automatically and unconsciously adjusted the amount of food they took in so as to maintain their normal weight. Overweight subjects, by contrast, lacked the ability to regulate their intake.[25] In other experiments Stanley Schachter of Columbia University was able to demonstrate that the internal satiation mechanism in obese individuals does not operate effectively in the presence of external cues.[26]

Under normal conditions, hunger is translated into eating through a series of neural reactions. First, stomach (hunger) contractions are relayed to the hypothalamus through the splanchnic nerve, a major nerve running from the trunk to the head. The animal or individual responds by obtaining food, putting it in the mouth, chewing, and swallowing. A multiplicity of sensations—taste, texture, temperature, and so on—are flashed back to the hypothalamus, and if the hypothalamus approves, the animal or individual goes on eating (this doesn't mean the food is necessarily beneficial). As the food is eaten, nutrients are digested and passed on to the blood. The blood sends the nutrients to the cells, including the cells of the brain. The brain then memorizes the message and may activate sensory cells lying just below the taste buds, possibly altering the taste threshold for various foods (so that, over time, the foods we need are often the ones we learn to want), and signals the cells that govern feeding to stop when enough nutrients have been taken in.

As described here, the process seems simple, but in truth, it is extremely complex neurologically. Every physical component, too, must be working soundly if the whole system is to work. Digestion must operate correctly for the nutrients—especially glucose—to be released into the blood. Receptors in the brain must accurately pick up, then transmit, the incoming messages. A variety of hormones and enzymes involved in countless metabolic reactions must be present in the required amounts at just the right times. Too little or too much of any one substance (insulin, for example), and the process easily goes awry.

For body processes to operate effectively, the body itself must be supplied with the nutrients it needs. Ironically, then, the mechanisms controlling food intake and satiety are not only susceptible to faulty neurological and physiological processes, they're also susceptible to faulty nutrition. Or to turn the idea around, the better fed your body,

[25]T. Italie and R. Campbell, "Multidisciplinary Approach to the Problem of Obesity," *Journal of the American Dietetic Association,* Vol. 61 (October 1972).

[26]S. Schachter, "Some Extraordinary Facts About Obese Humans and Rats," *American Psychologist,* Vol. 26 (1971).

the more accurately body wisdom can operate (assuming the body itself is in good working order).

The most basic example of body wisdom, for example, is our love of sweets and aversion to bitter foods. The evolutionary preference for sweet food stems from the time when sweet was synonymous with nutritious fruits and vegetables. Correspondingly, bitterness was a warning to avoid sickness-producing plants containing bitter alkaloids. Normally, when the diet of healthy humans and animals is well balanced and based on whole foods, the mechanisms that regulate intake and detect nutritious and illness-producing foods operate effectively. As an extreme example, it was shown very early in the research on food-intake mechanisms that rats can select the less toxic of two toxic diets,[27] and that animals have the ability to adjust the amount of food they take in so as to obtain an optimal supply of nutrients.

In the chapter "Body Wisdom" it was shown that aversions to food that has once caused illness are extremely strong, even when the bad-effect food and the resulting illness are separated by time and clouded by other factors or other foods. But once again, this ability may be affected by diet. For example, a natural aversion to a "bad" food may be weakened, even displaced, if the brain's intake mechanisms are not operating optimally. Rats, for example, whose brains have been injected with the thirst-provoking hormone angiotensin will drink huge amounts of water, including water so salty that they'd never touch it under other circumstances. What is important to note, however, is that the hormone seemed to alter the brain's thirst mechanism semipermanently, for the rats continued to drink the excessively salty water for days, even after the hormone injections were stopped.[28]

What, then, happens if the diet is based on chemically manipulated foods? The instinctive ability to choose foods the body needs may break down. The theory is that processed food, by chemically altering the sensitive brain/body mechanisms that monitor intake, or simply by failing to provide adequate nutrients, may have a negative effect on an individual's ability to choose food wisely. The individual may not lose the ability to control intake to the extent of becoming overweight, but preferences for certain foods, cravings, and appetite might all be skewed in an unusual direction. Why? In satisfying appetite, nutrients in the body work in teams. The nutrients in highly

[27]K. W. Franke, "The Ability of Rats to Discriminate Between Diets of Varying Degrees of Toxicity," *Science,* Vol. 83 (1936), p. 330.

[28]Alan N. Epstein, University of Pennsylvania, testimony during the National Institute of Health's Conference on Nutrition, reported by Harold M. Schmeck, "Studies on Nutrition Show Brain-Diet Link," *New York Times,* June 20, 1979.

processed food, however, are not arranged or present in the original complex ratios that the nutrients in whole food are. When processed foods are eaten solely and continually, the body, finding itself stuffed with exaggerated amounts of certain nutrients yet deficient in others, may cry out for more nutrients to balance the metabolism. It's been suggested that, as a result, highly processed food may actually have the effect of *increasing* the appetite, even when caloric needs have already been met.[29]

To give a simple, but specific, example, white flour, which is devoid of nearly all of the nutrients in whole wheat flour, is often fortified with iron. But the iron that's added to white flour is in neither the same form found in the original whole wheat flour nor the same proportion. The effect such iron has on the body's food-intake mechanisms is unknown. The subsequent nutrient needs that may develop when many fortified white-flour-food products are eaten is also unknown. But there is good cause to believe they exist.

The more deficient the diet, the greater the potential for the body's food-intake mechanisms to be thrown out of synch. Be very careful, then, in interpreting your food cravings as body wisdom. If you eat little or no processed food, it's still important to distinguish between actual bodily need and psychological desire. Is a craving for steak, for example, a psychological craving for steak or a physiological craving for protein, fat, and iron? If you ate a grain-bean-and-nut casserole that was equivalent to the steak in amount of usable protein, equivalent in fat, and equivalent in iron, would your craving be satisfied?[30]

Fifteen million Americans are thought to be obese to an extent that seriously endangers their health. Tens of millions more are overweight by sixteen to thirty-five pounds—a less acute but still serious condition.[31] Whether it's by ten pounds or one hundred pounds, being fat is nearly always unhealthful psychologically. In America, stress, guilt, and insecurity stem from the unspoken but implicit belief that fat is as much a moral and psychosomatic problem as it is a physiological one and that fat people lack the self-respect and self-control to eat normally.

But the history of human obesity indicates that fat is an extremely complex ecological issue that may not be due entirely to irrational

[29]Ross Hume Hall, "Natural Cravings Versus Policy for Obesity," *En-trophy Institute for Advanced Study Review,* Vol. 1, No. 5 (July–August 1978).

[30]It's usually apparent whether your mind wants a food or whether your stomach wants it. And even when you're feeling healthy and in good control of your nutritional needs, you'll find your mind sneaking in with the memory of a luscious chocolate-walnut crepe. Mind cravings are hard to ignore.

[31]Overweight has generally been defined as between sixteen to thirty-five pounds above ideal weight for one's age and height as set by the Build and Blood Pressure Study of 1959. Obesity has been defined as 10% to 25% above normal weight for a given height.

bouts of overeating or even chronic metabolic imbalances that upset normal body wisdom. This is not to say that overweight people don't overeat or don't eat the wrong kinds of food. Usually they do. It does mean, however, that before we can individually readjust our diets to lose weight, we have to understand some of the complex factors that make so many Americans fat in the first place.

One of the areas where biochemical individuality shows up the clearest is in gaining and losing weight. Two people living under identical conditions vary enormously in the amount and type of food they must eat to keep their deep body temperatures stable and to maintain an equilibrium between their skin temperature and the temperature of the surrounding air. Certain people also have a greater tendency to manufacture fat than others, no matter what they eat. And, for each of us, the way and rate at which food is metabolized is innately different depending on our biochemistry, immediate environment, and heredity. The truth is that some of us could lose weight on a diet that would make another person fat. But, as we'll see, many Americans have a tendency toward fatness that is unavoidably a part of their northern European ancestry.

Built into the basic adaptive equipment of all mammalian species is the ability to store food. Anthropologist Anne Scott Beller points out that territoriality in animals is based on staking out a nutritional domain as much as a defensive domain and that for almost all animals, except those living in the most food-abundant warm climates, storing food is a physical necessity.[32] The beehive, for example, is not just a nest—it's also a systematized food factory. The red fox stashes away rodents' corpses in its burrow during the winter. The European mole may store as many as a thousand earthworms in underground tunnels. Polar wolves and bears bury part of their kills in the snow. Rodents, squirrels, and hamsters are, of course, known for their capacity to store as much as two hundred pounds of cereals inside their home territories.

When humans migrated from their warm subtropical lands of origin northward to climates (like our own) characterized by extreme shifts of temperature throughout the seasons, they had to adapt their eating behaviors and learn to store food as other cold-weather species had. But human adaptation was slightly more ingenious. Rather than storing next month's body fuel as *food,* human beings stored it as *fat.* Anthropologists connect the human adaptation of storing future fuel

[32]Anne Scott Beller, in *Fat & Thin: A Natural History of Obesity,* vividly and with a great deal of intelligence traces the evolution of body types through interaction with the environment from an anthropologist's perspective. The complex reasons behind fatness are thoroughly chronicled.

as fat to the fact that our northern European ancestors were meat eaters (curiously enough, linking meat eating and fat once again).

Life in glacial Europe was one long winter. The slushy, wet months of July and August hardly constituted a growing season. Since very little vegetation was cultivated, storing food was an ecological impossibility; there simply wasn't enough food suitable for prolonged storage. The major source of food was meat, and Pleistocene humans were, necessarily, hunters who followed the herds of reindeer, bison, mammoth, and other game wherever the climate took them. In the long stretches in between successful hunts, human beings stored food as fat.

Modern humans do not have to deal with glaciers or long stretches of time between meals. Still, bio-adaptation to cold is a trait that has lived on in our gene pool, and fat has, even in modern times, contributed to human survival. (Historical records of the early colonists' ability to survive the harsh winters on extremely small rations are a good example.) In fact, our physiological response to the coming of cold weather has also lived on symbolically. The two great feasts of permissible unrestrained eating are Christmas and Thanksgiving—winter celebration feasts that have an absolute ecological logic to them.

Even the way appetite works in the body seems to indicate that we are programmed for fatness more than for leanness. Appetite is not nearly as precisely experienced as breathing, sex, or thirst, for example—even in people with the best diets. Beller points out that we all know when we've taken a breath, had an orgasm, or quenched a thirst. But knowing when we've had enough to eat isn't as simple. Since the body was originally programmed to process and store as much food as possible at any one meal, it sometimes seems as though we're receiving nonstop eat-eat-eat signals. Our only choice (painful as it sometimes feels) is to overrule these archetypal hunger signals with a mental decision to stop eating.

The problem here is that not eating when hungry seems self-defeating and feels like an undeserved punishment. Every instinct we have wants to give in to the hunger. So give in we do. Whether we gain weight in the process depends on how we give in.

Feeling satiated takes some time after the process of eating has begun because nutrients aren't absorbed immediately into the bloodstream. It can take up to six hours for proteins and fats to leave the stomach and be absorbed through the intestinal wall.

Water and minerals are the first nutrients to be absorbed, followed by sugars, then starches and proteins; fats, as pointed out, are last. In part, then, one of the easiest ways to satiate hunger quickly is to eat foods in the order of quickest digestion: water, juices, fruits, vegetables, and grains first; eggs, nuts, meats, cheese and other dairy products last. When storing a lot of fat was essential, eating high-fat, high-protein foods from the beginning to the end of the meal made sense, since maximum amounts of food could be eaten before the person felt full. But since we no longer need such heavy accumulations of fat tissue, one of the ways we can control a seemingly irrational ravenous appetite is by eating slowly and eating first those foods that give the body a full feeling, such as a hearty soup.

To be meaningful, body wisdom must be balanced with plain common sense, and food instincts must be integrated with rational eating behaviors.

V. The Effect Life-Style Has on Nutritional Need

In the simplest sense, life is the interaction between a cell and an environment. Since the nourishment that supports life is a complex process taking place in an integrated context, optimal nourishment involves much more than simply providing the body with enough protein, carbohydrates, and vitamins—in other words, assuring all of the necessary chemical interactions between food and body substances. Optimal nourishment also becomes a question of providing a psychosocial environment in which good nutrition can take place.

Food and life-style are interdependent and work synergistically. Biofeedback research, for example, has shown that the more healthy and relaxed a person becomes through biofeedback training, the more the person benefits from food (easier digestion, better assimilation of nutrients, etc.). Longitudinal studies show that among key factors responsible for continued health, a positive mental outlook and regular physical exercise are at least as important as a diet of good foods.[33] You know yourself that all of the whole wheat bread in the world doesn't make you feel any better if you're chronically overworked, underexercised, and overweight.

In determining your own best diet, then, it's important first to examine your life-style and define your needs. By factoring your individual needs into the general guidelines outlined by the *Dietary Goals* and *How to Plan a Whole Foods Diet,* you can come up with an approximate idea of what a healthful diet tailored *to you* might be like.

[33]See: Rene Dubos, *Man, Medicine, and Environment* (New York: Praeger, 1968); Dubos, *Man Adapting* (New Haven: Yale University Press, 1965); and Rick J. Carlson, *The End of Medicine* (New York: John Wiley, 1975).

Some of the biochemical conditions and life-style factors that you'll need to take into consideration in planning your diet include your age, weight, state of health, sex, the stress related to your job, how much you relax, how much you worry, the type of environment in which you live, how much alcohol you drink, what your food habits are, and the influence cultural food patterns may have on your choice of foods.

Think of your total food needs in two ways: in terms of the amount of food—or total number of calories—you need to be active and healthy; and second, in terms of the specific foods and nutrients you may need. For instance, if you are under a great deal of stress, you may want to eat more high-protein and high-vitamin-B foods. In general, special conditions that require *more calories,* like pregnancy, also require a correspondingly higher intake of nutrient-dense foods.

The two sections that follow are aimed at helping you define your needs. The first section covers individual needs determined by height, weight, sex, age, and so forth. The second explores some of the special circumstances known to affect how nutrients are used in the body.

Metabolic Needs

The human body has a demanding need for energy. At rest (and in a fasting state) the body needs energy to sustain breathing, heartbeat, cellular metabolism, glandular secretions, circulation, and body temperature. This essential minimum of energy is called the basal metabolic rate (BMR), and it differs for every individual. On top of the BMR, each person has additional specific energy needs based primarily—but not exclusively—on the amount of exercise the person gets.

Food energy is measured in calories. Since the BMR is a measure of the minimum amount of energy each individual needs, the higher the BMR, the more food energy—or calories—needed. The following factors affect the BMR:[34]

- *Body size.* The greater the body size, the higher the BMR. A large body surface or skin area means that a greater amount of body heat is lost and, as a result, more energy is needed to keep the body temperature constant. A tall, thin person has a larger body surface area than a short, stout person who weighs the same. A tall, thin person, therefore, has a higher BMR and requires more food.

[34]Marie V. Krause and Martha A. Hunscher, *Food, Nutrition, and Diet Therapy* (W. B. Saunders, 1972).

*Suggested Weights for Heights and Calories Needed to Support the Basic Metabolic Rate of Adults**

Height		Median Weight Men		Median Weight Women	
(ft)	(in)	(lb)	BMR (kcal/day)	(lb)	BMR (kcal/day)
5	0			109 ± 9	1,399
5	2			115 ± 9	1,429
5	4	133 ± 11	1,630	122 ± 10	1,487
5	6	142 ± 12	1,690	129 ± 10	1,530
5	8	151 ± 14	1,775	136 ± 10	1,572
5	10	159 ± 14	1,815	144 ± 11	1,626
6	0	167 ± 15	1,870	152 ± 12	1,666
6	2	175 ± 15	1,933		
6	4	182 ± 16	1,983		

Following is a simple formula for estimating the desirable weight of an adult:†

- For women, allow 100 pounds for the first 5 feet and 5 pounds for every additional inch.
- For men, allow 110 pounds for the first 5 feet and 5 pounds for every additional inch, and:
- Allow 10% variation above or below the calculated weight for individual differences.

*Adapted from the recommended dietary allowances of the Food and Nutrition Board, National Research Council.

†Meredith Overton and Barbara Lukert, *Clinical Nutrition: A Physiological Approach* (Chicago: Year Book Medical Publications, 1977).

- *Periods of growth.* The BMR rises during periods of rapid growth such as early childhood and during puberty. The time of most rapid growth is during infancy, when the brain and central nervous system develop rapidly. The basic energy requirements for infants are therefore greater than for any other age group. As the body grows old, the BMR declines.
- *Sex.* Women have a 5% to 10% lower BMR than men of the same height and weight. This is due in part to the male and female hormones that affect metabolism, but it is also due to the fact that muscle tissue (which men have more of) requires more oxygen and more energy to sustain it than fat tissue (which women have more of). Women, with their greater amount of fat tissue, also lose body heat less rapidly than men, which also contributes to their lower BMR. During menstruation, a woman's BMR increases.
- *Pregnancy and lactation.* During pregnancy and lactation, women have a greater BMR because the uterus and placenta develop more muscle tissue; the fetus itself is developing muscle tissue and growing

rapidly; and the woman's respiration rate and heartbeat have increased to meet the fetus's needs in addition to her own. Milk production also takes a lot of energy (about a thousand extra calories a day, since an ounce of breast milk has about 30 calories, and a lactating woman produces about 30 ounces a day).
- *Cold climates.* As the environment gets colder, the BMR rises to compensate and keep the body temperature constant.
- *Disease.* Disease increases the BMR, since the body's immune system is activated to combat the disease and the disease itself consumes body energy. Fever, for example, raises the BMR 7% for every 1-degree rise in temperature.

On the average, a full-grown adult needs 1,300 to 1,800 calories a day to sustain his or her basic metabolism. To calculate more closely the number of calories your body uses for its basic metabolism, multiply your weight in kilograms (to get your weight in kilograms, divide your weight in pounds by 2.2) by 24 calories (one for every hour of the day). This will represent the minimum number of calories you need each day to keep the essential functions of your body operating smoothly. For people who are tall, male, ill, pregnant or lactating, growing rapidly, or living in a cold environment, basic calorie needs will be somewhat greater. For infants, the BMR will be significantly greater. During the first six months of life, an infant's *total* energy requirement (BMR plus all other energy needs) is 50 to 55 calories for every pound of body weight. Between six months and one year, the infant's total energy requirement is reduced slightly to 40 to 45 calories for every pound of body weight.

Special Situations

Infection and illness, drugs, vitamin supplements, environmental pollutants, food additives, emotional stress, pregnancy, aging, exercise, athletics—these are some of the special situations known to affect nutrients *and* nutritional needs. As the body ages, for example, the metabolism of all nutrients is affected (slowed down) by aging organs. At the same time, aging creates special nutritional needs, such as the extra calcium older bones need to combat brittleness.

The special situations explored here are not the only ones that exist, but they are the ones we're most likely to encounter on a frequent basis. Please remember, however, that every individual's response to any special situation varies, and the nutritional measures you may need to take are not necessarily appropriate for someone else.

Infection and Illness

Every disease involves nutrition. Either the disease itself was prompted by faulty nutrition (not enough and/or not the right balance of nutrients), or the disease will affect the way the body uses the nutrients it receives.[35] Diseases of the gastrointestinal tract, diabetes, hypertension, heart failure, atherosclerosis, renal disease, and surgery require specific nutritional attention since a number of nutrients may be altered or blocked by the disease or the nutrient itself may be harmful—refined carbohydrate, for example, to the diabetic.

But even seasonal infections and less serious illnesses may affect the way nutrients are used in the body. When a cell is injured by an invading bacteria or virus, or when a nutritional deficiency leaves a mass of damaged, weak cells, the protein chains in the cells begin to break down and unfold. If the injury is prolonged or becomes severe, the broken protein chains may collapse and shrink into a mass of coagulated protoplasm. Broken protein chains are unable to carry nutrients into the epithelial cells (the covering tissue cells) that line the villi (the absorbing surface) of the intestines. In this way, even a series of colds or stomach viruses could prevent protein, fats, vitamins, and minerals from being properly absorbed by the intestines.[36]

When a cell is injured only slightly, the normal reserve compounds in the cell can resynthesize protein and other necessary components quickly, and the cell's functioning returns to normal. In fact, some protein in cells is always being broken down, and some protein is always being synthesized to take its place. During a prolonged or serious disease, however, protein chains may be irreversibly damaged, and the cell may lose its ability to synthesize new ones. Extra protein is, at this point, clearly needed. It's important to realize that cell injury and protein destruction can be significant even when the visible signs of illness are few—when a person has a sore throat or has just been immunized against smallpox, for example.

Together, infection and poor nutrition form a Möbius strip—one affecting the other, which in turn reaffects the first, with both growing progressively worse as a result. Nevin Scrimshaw, professor of nutrition and food science at MIT, has documented this cycle in children who are malnourished (but not necessarily underfed). Poor nutrition weakens the body's immune system, so that the child is ripe for infection. The infection, in turn, interferes with the absorption of nutrients and, in addition, large numbers of nutrients are lost through

[35]N. Jolliffe, *Clinical Nutrition,* 2nd ed. (New York: Harper, 1962). See also: the entire vol. 30 of the *American Journal of Clinical Nutrition* (August 1977).

[36]Krause and Hunscher, *Food, Nutrition, and Diet Therapy.*

diarrhea, the urine, sweat, and so on. Sickness also diminishes the child's appetite and, in general, reduces a sick person's ability to discriminate good, nutritious food. The food that a sick child is given will generally be watery, low in protein, and low in vitamins, rather than more nourishing solid food. As a result, the infection keeps the child poorly nourished, and the poor nourishment means that the child recovers slowly and remains vulnerable to infection because the body is still weak.[37]

Scrimshaw notes that in order to return to a state of health after an infection, both children and adults generally need additional calories and protein. Wound healing in general has been shown to be more rapid when protein in the diet is increased.[38]

Also, it may be possible for infecting microorganisms to actually compete with the body for a nutrient, increasing the individual's overall need. It takes, for example, much more vitamin C and vitamin A to saturate the tissues of a person with tuberculosis than those of a healthy person.[39]

Drugs

Drugs may deplete the body's store of specific vitamins, alter the microbial balance in the intestines, or upset metabolism. Oral contraceptives, for example, seem to alter the metabolism of lipids, carbohydrates, protein, vitamins, and minerals.[40] Although not all studies are in agreement, oral contraceptives have specifically been linked to decreases of carotene (a component of vitamin A), vitamins E, C, B_{12}, and B_6, plus decreases in calcium, magnesium, and phosphorus.[41]

One of the most well-documented relationships between drugs and nourishment is the effect that antibiotics have on the bacteria that normally line the intestines. Four to five hundred varieties of bacteria (some harmful, some helpful) live in the intestines.[42] There are three pounds of bacteria in the colon alone.

These bacteria, along with mucus and other microorganisms such as yeasts, fungi, and viruses, serve as a protective border between the

[37]Testimony of Nevin Scrimshaw, Conference of the Boston Children's Hospital Medical Center and the Department of Nutrition and Food Science, MIT, 1977.

[38]Nevin S. Scrimshaw, "Effect of Infection on Nutrient Requirements," *American Journal of Clinical Nutrition,* Vol. 30 (1977), pp. 1536–44; M. Golden, J. C. Waterlow, and D. Picou, "The Relationship Between Dietary Intake, Weight Change, Nitrogen Balance, and Protein Turnover in Man," *American Journal of Clinical Nutrition,* Vol. 30 (1977), p. 1345.

[39]Roger J. Williams, *Biochemical Individuality* (Austin: University of Texas Press, 1956), p. 158.

[40]Janet C. King, "Nutrition During Oral Contraceptive Use," *Contemporary Nutrition,* Vol. 17, No. 3 (March 1977).

[41]"Serum Levels of Phosphorus, Magnesium, and Calcium in Women Utilizing Combination Oral or Long-Acting Injectable Progestational Contraceptives," *Fertility and Sterility,* Vol. 23 (1972).

[42]In *Diet and Nutrition* (Honesdale, Pa.: Himalayan International Institute Press, 1978), Rudolph Ballantine indicates that where more natural and consistent diets are consumed, fewer species of bacteria tend to predominate and that these tend to be stable.

How Drugs Interfere with Nutrients

Drug	*Interference*
Alcohol	Folic acid, vitamin B_{12}, fat ↑ Excretion of magnesium
Analgesics	
Colchicine	Damage to intestinal wall → nonspecific ↓ in absorption ↓ Absorption of vitamin B_{12}, carotene, fat, lactose, D-xylose, electrolytes and cholesterol
Anorexiants	Appetite suppression → growth retardation
Antacids	Alkaline destruction of thiamine → thiamine deficiency; fatty acids
Anticonvulsants	
Barbiturates	Inhibition of absorptive enzymes or ↑ metabolism and turnover → deficiency in body folate and vitamin D ↓ Vitamin B_{12} and D-xylose absorption
Hydantoins	Inhibition of absorptive enzymes ↑ Metabolism and turnover Deficiency in body folate and vitamin D ↑ Urinary excretion of ascorbic acid
Antidepressants	
Tricyclic antidepressants	Stimulation of appetite → weight gain
Antimetabolites	Anti-vitamin action on folic acid
Methotrexate	Damage to intestinal wall → nonspecific ↓ in absorption Inhibition of enzyme system ↓ Vitamin B_{12}, folic acid and D-xylose absorption
Antimicrobials	Appetite suppression and diarrhea → ↓ nutrient absorption
Chloramphenicol	↓ Protein synthesis Altered hemoglobin synthesis → failure of incorporation of Fe into RBC
Isoniazid	Complexation of vitamin B_6 → ↑ excretion of vitamin B_6
Neomycin	See under Hypocholesterolemics
Para-aminosalicylic acid	Inhibition of absorptive enzymes → ↓ vitamin B_{12} absorption, folic acid, iron and cholesterol
Penicillin	Aftertaste with food → suppression of appetite Inhibition of glutathione

↑ Increases ↓ Decreases → Leads To

From: Meredith Overton and Barbara Lekert, *Clinical Nutrition: A Physiological Approach* (Year Book Medical Publications, 1977).

Drug	Interference
Sulfonamides	↓ Synthesis of folic acid, B vitamins and vitamin K
Tetracyclines	Binding of bone calcium ↑ Serum nonprotein N and urinary amino acids and urea
Autonomics	
Anticholinergics	↓ Peristalsis → ↓ nutrient absorption
Ganglionic blockers	Same as above
Cathartics	Malabsorption of protein, calcium, vitamin D and potassium
Bisacodyl	↓ Intestinal uptake of glucose
Colocynth	↑ Loss of calcium, potassium; steatorrhea
Jalap	Same as above
Mannitol	Damage to intestinal wall → ↓ absorption of glucose, water and sodium
Oxyphenisatin	↓ Intestinal uptake of glucose
Phenolphthalein	Same as above
Podophyllum	↑ Loss of calcium, potassium; steatorrhea
Chelating agents	Chelation of metals → ↓ absorption of metals
Penicillamine	Complexation of vitamin B_6 → ↑ excretion of vitamin B_6 ↓ Taste acuity and aftertaste → suppression of appetite
Corticosteroids	↓ Glucose tolerance ↓ Muscle protein ↑ Liver fat ↑ Retention of sodium ↓ Calcium and iron absorption
Diuretics (except spironolactone and triamterene)	↑ Excretion of potassium ↓ Excretion of potassium ↓ Excretion of potassium
Hypocholesterolemics	
Cholestyramine resin	↓ Absorption of potassium, fat-soluble vitamins; binds inorganic and hemoglobin Fe in vitro
Clofibrate	↓ Absorption of vitamin B_{12}, D-xylose, carotene, MCT, iron, sugar and electrolytes ↓ Taste acuity and aftertaste → suppression of appetite
Neomycin	Inactivation of bile acids → ↓ absorption of vitamin B_{12}, lactose, D-xylose, carotene, MCT, iron, sugar, potassium, sodium, calcium and nitrogen Damage to intestinal wall Steatorrhea

↑ Increases ↓ Decreases → Leads To

Drug	Interference
Laxatives	
Mineral oil	↓ Absorption of carotene and vitamins A, D, E and K
Oral contraceptives	Inhibition of absorptive enzymes Selective malabsorption or enzyme induction → deficiency in body folate ↑ Turnover of vitamin B_6 → deficiency in vitamin B_6 ↑ Blood lipids (especially TG) ↑ Intestinal absorption of iron
Potassium chloride	↓ Absorption of vitamin B_{12}
Sedative-hypnotics	
Glutethimide	↑ Metabolism and turnover of vitamin D → deficiency in vitamin D Multivitamin deficiency
Surfactants (stool softeners)	Alteration of fat dispersion and permeability of mucosal cell membrane → alteration of nutrient absorption
Tranquilizers	
Phenothiazines	Stimulation of appetite → weight gain
Chlorpromazine	Hypercholesterolemia

↑ Increases ↓ Decreases → Leads To

nutrients taken in from the external environment and the digestive organs themselves. They also help synthesize vitamin B_{12} and various amino acids. In the colon, bacteria complete the digestion of fiber and other food products, and here, as well, important B vitamins may be synthesized. Without the bacteria needed for these jobs, some nutrients may pass through the whole system and never be absorbed.

Since antibiotics are, by nature, toxic to bacteria, a large percentage of the bacteria in the body (both beneficial and harmful) are destroyed when antibiotics are taken. Some antibiotics are more destructive to intestinal microbes than others, however. Penicillin, for example, seems to affect the intestinal bacteria very little. Other "broad spectrum" antibiotics, such as tetracycline, are less selective about the bacteria they kill. Taking them has been compared to fixing a fine watch by banging it with a sledgehammer. Although the watch might be jolted back into operation, chances are greater that the damage will outweigh the benefit.

Vitamin Supplements, Environmental Pollutants, and Food Additives

At the cellular level, all of our biochemical and physiological processes are chemical and can therefore be easily altered by foreign chemicals. For example, an excessive intake of a specific vitamin or combination of vitamins may affect the biophysical balance enough to alter the way other nutrients are absorbed. This can be positive (one nutrient, for example, may increase the synthesis of other important nutrients) or negative (too much of any one nutrient may throw the body's metabolism off balance). The use of vitamin supplements may skew the outcome of biomedical laboratory tests. Also, because bacteria may compete with their host for certain vitamins, large doses of vitamins over long periods of time could promote excessive bacterial growth, with the result that more and more nutrients would be depleted from the host in order to feed the bacteria.[43]

However, the effect of vitamin supplements may be minor compared with the potential hazards of the estimated ten thousand chemical food additives that may now be in the food supply.[44] Furthermore, these chemicals are compounded by chemical contaminants in air and drinking water, bringing the total number of manufactured chemical compounds up to an estimated seventy thousand, with hundreds of new ones being introduced every year.[45] In 1919 Butter Yellow was banned because it was found to produce liver cancer. In the 1960s Orange Nos. 1 and 2 and Red No. 1 were removed from the market for causing internal organ damage. Yellow Nos. 3 and 4 were banned for causing heart damage in animals. In 1973 Violet No. 1—the certified color used by the Department of Agriculture for inspecting meat—was banned eleven years after it was first shown to cause cancer and skin lesions.[46]

Currently, seven synthetic dyes can be used in any food, although three of them—Red Nos. 2 and 4 and Orange B—are limited to one product, since each of these colors has produced either organ damage or disease in laboratory animals. Red No. 2, for example, used to dye oranges, has been shown to be a weak carcinogen; and Red No. 4, used in maraschino cherries, has been found to damage the adrenal cortex and bladders of dogs.[47] (Maraschino cherry producers have convinced the FDA to allow them to continue using Red No. 4 on the grounds that no one eats more than a few maraschino cherries at a time.)

Substances that are not nutrients are, by definition, not required

[43]Ballantine, *Diet and Nutrition.*

[44]Ross Hume Hall, "What Kind of Food Protection System Have We?" *En-trophy Institute for Advanced Study Review,* Vol. 2, No. 1 (January–February 1979). Note: The amount of food additives consumed by the average American has nearly doubled *since 1970.* According to *The Ecologist* (February 1978), the average person among us now eats nine pounds of pure additives a year. When salt and sugar are included, the figure jumps to 140 pounds of additives per person per year. One type of additive, certified food dyes, are among the most dangerous, yet least necessary, of artificial substances added to food. Each year four million pounds of certified dye are added to food products solely to improve their looks.

[45]Michael H. Brown, "Love Canal USA," *New York Times Magazine,* January 21, 1979, p. 23.

[46]Borchers, "Chemicals in Your Food."

[47]Ibid.

by the body. But once they are ingested, unnecessary chemicals, just like nutrients, must be broken down and made water soluble before the body can excrete them. This takes place in the liver, where everything from the nutrients in an apple to the toxic compounds in the insecticide it's been sprayed with are sorted out for use or as waste.

If the liver is overloaded with chemicals (likely) and debilitated due to lack of nutrients (also likely), the rate at which it can metabolize toxic substances may be substantially lowered. The longer toxic material resides in the body, the worse the effects on health. Liver cells themselves may begin to break down, and when that occurs, the bloodstream can be flooded with undetoxified chemicals, unprocessed sugars, and denatured proteins.

The fact that toxic chemicals must be metabolized along with nutrients presents an even more complicated Catch-22 situation. During the metabolism of toxic compounds, the compounds themselves can be broken down into more reactive substances. These substances have the ability to bind to other molecules in the cell, including nutrients. When these chemicals bind to DNA, the final result may be cancer, birth defects, or mutations.[48]

Emotion and Stress

Hundreds of thousands of years ago the human nervous system evolved the highly sensitive stress mechanism that allows us to respond immediately to any threat to survival. That mechanism, called the flight-or-fight response, automatically triggers feelings of fear or anger and readies the muscles for instant flight. Adrenaline shoots through the body, constricting blood vessels, raising the blood pressure and heart rate, and causing other hormonal and chemical changes that heighten physical strength and dexterity. For our ancestors, this automatic response to stress was crucial. The fact that it paralyzed digestion was beside the point.

Today we react to stress in the exact same physiological way, even though the stress we're exposed to is more likely to be psychological than physical. Hating your job, for instance, elicits the same heart-pumping, muscle-constricting tension that was used to fight polar bears. Digestion is deadlocked and nutrients drained from the tissues either way. Muscle tension can also block oxygen flow, since under stress many people develop chronic shallow breathing. Without sufficient amounts of oxygen, the body cannot even begin to oxidize (burn up) the food that's been eaten.

Our automatic response to stress would not be a problem if it

[48]For a more complete explanation of toxicity, see T. Colin Campbell, "How Toxic Is Toxic: A Commentary," Conference on Food Safety Policy, Cornell University, March 13, 1979.

weren't for the fact that we face stress *all the time.* The environment is full of anticipated stress and actual threats to survival—from heavy traffic to sickness. Digestion is interrupted incessantly. Constant muscle tension, overworked glands, constricted blood vessels, and a stressed heart sending emergency levels of blood and oxygen away from the stomach to the brain and muscles are the body's norm.

If you are under a lot of emotional pressure or are in a demanding environment, make sure you are giving your body enough nutrients to make up for those that may not be absorbed. This doesn't mean that you need to overeat (a well-documented response to stress); it simply means that you should make sure that everything you eat is packed with nutrients. Good wholesome meals are essential. Sugar, coffee, and alcohol may create more physiological stress and should be limited. Special consideration should be given to adolescents, who not only go through considerable emotional anxiety but who also need to eat high-quality, nutrient-dense foods because they are growing so rapidly.[49]

Pregnancy and Prenatal Nutrition

An infant *is* what its mother eats. Studies of primitive tribes show that during pregnancy a woman is often given the best and most favored foods so that she might give birth to a warrior.

When a pregnant woman eats poorly or doesn't eat enough, glucose and amino acids do not reach the fetus in the quantities needed. Birth defects, brain damage, and growth retardation may result.[50] Although the extent of damage may vary, it's always permanent. Stillborn and premature infants are also more frequently born to women with poor diets than to women whose nutrient intakes during their pregnancy are high.[51]

But as important as good nutrition during pregnancy is, the mother's *lifetime* dietary habits are also important.[52] In some cases, a woman's diet throughout her life has been found to have more significant consequences than her diet during pregnancy alone.

Both the fetus and the mother will sacrifice the nutrients each needs for its own body if the diet of the other is inadequate. The mother's tissues will be seriously depleted of some nutrients to provide for the fetus, and the fetus will sometimes sacrifice its own normal growth in order to share nutrients with the mother. Pregnant

[49]Krause and Hunscher, *Food, Nutrition, and Diet Therapy.*

[50]L. F. James. "Diet-Related Birth Defects," *Nutrition Today,* Vol. 9 (1974), pp. 4–11.

[51]B. S. Burke, V. A. Beal, S. B. Kirkwood, and H. C. Stuart, "The Influence of Nutrition During Pregnancy upon the Condition of the Infant at Birth," *Journal of Nutrition,* Vol. 25 (1943), p. 569.

[52]D. Baird, "Variations in Fertility Associated with Changes in Health Status," *Journal of Chronic Disease,* Vol. 18 (1965).

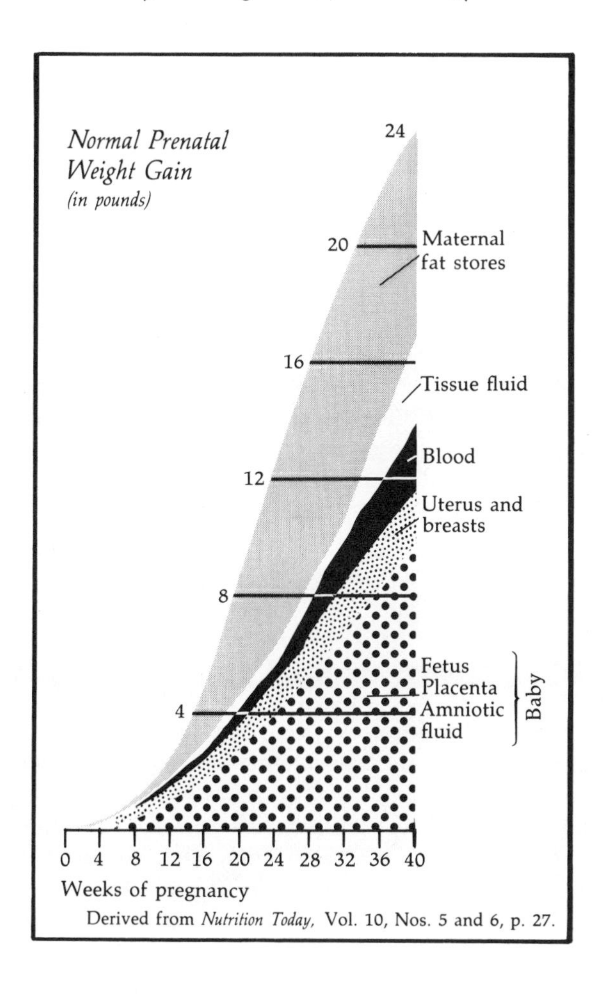

Derived from *Nutrition Today,* Vol. 10, Nos. 5 and 6, p. 27.

women, then, need to be especially conscious of the extra nutritional demands placed on their bodies.

A woman develops 50,000 calories' worth of new tissue when she's pregnant. In addition, she needs about 30,000 more calories to support the extra strain on her heart and uterus. So, *in toto,* she'll need approximately 80,000 calories' worth of energy to support her own and the fetus's body throughout pregnancy. Based on the recommendations of the United Nations Food and Agriculture Organization/World Health Organization (FAO/WHO) Joint Committee on Pregnancy, 80,000 calories needed for nine months of pregnancy works out to an extra 150 calories per day during the first trimester and 350 extra calories a day for the second and third trimesters. An extra 150 to 350 calories of food per day isn't really much in terms of food (one ounce of Swiss cheese, for example, has about 300 calories), but it is *highly* essential.

In addition to extra food, a pregnant woman needs to eat foods that are nutrient dense; in other words, she should seek to obtain the maximum number of nutrients possible from the calories she takes in. One of the nutrients needed most is iron. Because the blood volume in her body increases roughly 20%, the pregnant woman's concentrations of hemoglobin—and therefore iron—are reduced. At the same time, in the womb, the baby is drawing on whatever iron the mother does have, storing extra amounts in its own liver. This stored iron will be the infant's only source during the time after birth when it will be fed only milk. During the second half of pregnancy the mother transfers 200 to 300 milligrams of iron to the fetus and placenta, or about 6 milligrams daily. She gets this iron by eating a nutrient-dense diet that will provide about 6 milligrams of iron for every 1,000 calories. The healthiest American women may have some iron stored in their bodies as a reserve; yet, of all minerals, iron is the one American women are most likely to be deficient in prior to and during pregnancy, and with the birth of the child, the woman will lose even more. So iron-rich foods such as sea vegetables, blackstrap molasses, lima beans, soybeans, oysters, parsley, and other leafy greens are needed to counteract potential anemia in both mother and child. These foods should be supplemented with foods rich in vitamin B, which helps to metabolize iron.

Pregnancy may also cause amino acids to be excreted in the urine, lowering the amount of available protein, when the mother actually needs additional protein to build new maternal tissue to carry the fetus and to provide protein for the rapid growth of the fetus itself. Studies conducted at the Harvard School of Medicine show that the weight, length, and health of a baby at birth are directly related to the number of grams of protein the mother consumed daily during her pregnancy. Women who consume a high level of protein during pregnancy have also been shown to have less anemia and fewer miscarriages and premature babies. The Harvard study suggested a minimum of 75 grams of protein daily for a pregnant woman. *Our Bodies, Ourselves* by the Boston Women's Health Collective suggests 80 to 100 grams of protein per day. (This is roughly twice the recommended daily allowance of protein for a nonpregnant adult woman.) Protein of both animal origin (eggs, cheese, milk, fish) and plant origin (whole-grain cereals and breads, peas, beans, lentils, nuts) should be included in the diet, since in combination these foods will provide protein at a maximum level.

Nutritionists also suggest that pregnant women concentrate on a diet rich in B vitamins and calcium. B vitamins are not stored by the body and are needed for metabolism and growth during pregnancy; in addition, B vitamins are known to help relieve fatigue, insomnia, nervous tension, digestive upsets, and are effective in regulating fluid retention. Brewer's yeast and wheat germ are two of the most concentrated sources of B. (See also the section on vitamins, pages 36–41.) Calcium is needed so that the baby's bones and teeth will form properly, and calcium, working with the B vitamins, may help to relieve the leg, back, and joint pains of pregnancy. Calcium (found in milk, cheese, yogurt, broccoli, spinach, kale, some fish, and bone meal) is more readily absorbed by diets high in vitamin D.

Lactation may place even more demands on the nutrients in the mother's body than pregnancy. More protein, calories, calcium, iron, and vitamin A are necessary if the mother is to produce a sufficient quantity and quality of breast milk. To breast-feed a five- to six-month-old baby, a lactating woman needs an estimated 800 extra calories a day.

An excellent practical guide to good nutrition during pregnancy is a sixteen-page booklet, "As You Eat, So Your Baby Grows," by Nikki Goldbeck.

It can be obtained for $1.25 including postage by writing to Ceres Press, Old Witch Tree Road, Woodstock, N.Y. 12498. Physicians and midwives can obtain bulk orders.

Aging

In some primitive tribes the aged were always well fed because they provided wisdom for the next generation.

As people grow older, their body processes slow down, their organs deteriorate, and the nutrients they take into their bodies are utilized less efficiently. In addition, body structure changes. Bone mass shrinks, muscles lose their tone, and at the same time, the proportion of fat tissue in the body increases. Because fat tissue requires less energy than lean tissue (muscles and bones) to support it and because older people tend to be less active in general, an older person's need for calories (energy) is reduced considerably. On the average, each of us needs 5% to 10% fewer calories for each decade after we're twenty years old.

However, at the same time that older people need fewer calories, they may actually need more nutrients to help their bodies cope with aging. Older people, then, must structure their diets carefully with whole, nutrient-dense foods that provide a maximum of nutrients for a minimum of calories. Foods such as lean meats, fish, dried beans and peas, whole-grain breads and cereals, leafy green vegetables, and dairy products are best. Vegetables and whole grains, with the addition of fruits, will also provide fiber and help with slow or difficult digestion. Fiber-rich foods, even if consumed with a bit of difficulty because of teeth problems, are a much healthier way of combating digestive disorders than laxatives or mineral oils, which may actually cause the body to lose the fat-soluble vitamins A, D, E, and K.

Perhaps the most obvious nutritional need among older people, however, is the need for calcium. Calcium, along with vitamin D, helps to counteract the brittleness of aging bones and helps keep aging teeth in good condition. Calcium-rich foods include milk, cheese, yogurt, sardines, salmon, kale, spinach, and broccoli.

Finally, older people need to be especially cautious of foods that lead to diseases often encountered with age, such as diabetes, high blood pressure, heart attack, stroke, and cancer. This means that foods high in fat, sodium, sugar, and chemical additives (such as bakery products, desserts, luncheon and other fatty meats, canned vegetables and soups, processed cheeses, etc.) should be limited as much as possible.

Exercise and Athletics

Those of us who have studied food would sometimes like to give whole, nourishing food sole credit for keeping people healthy. But the truth is that food stands at the doorstep of health. Regular physical exercise is the key that unlocks the door.

Nutrients are made available by good blood circulation. Without exercise, blood circulation lags, and cells throughout the body aren't fed properly no matter what is eaten. Exercise also improves muscle tone and stimulates the digestive organs so that food is actively digested, metabolized, absorbed, and eliminated.

The brain, as the major survival organ, depends on the allied actions of eating and expending muscular energy to provide a constant supply of glucose and oxygen. Food, of course, supplies the glucose, and exercise infuses the bloodstream with oxygen. It's thought, in fact, that sedentary people tend to gain weight faster than active people for two reasons. First, they simply don't burn up as many calories through muscular activity. Second, because glucose and oxygen are essential to the brain and are carried to it together in the bloodstream, the brain may not easily distinguish between the two. As oxygen becomes less available to the brain of a sedentary person, he or she feels more and more in the mood to eat. The food hunger may, in reality, be an oxygen hunger that a brisk walk or a few minutes of jumping jacks would totally satisfy.

Just as too little exercise may affect the amount of food a person eats, a lot of exercise also has an effect. The rule of thumb is: The more you exercise, the more energy you need and the more food you should eat. Exactly how many calories more you should consume during periods of high activity depends on your body build, your age, and how strenuous the activity is. Olympic athletes have daily intakes that range between 4,000 and 6,000 calories, for example.

Studies of nutrition and athletes in the *Journal of Sports Medicine* (1969) and *Physician and Sports Medicine* (1977) suggest that an ideal average athletic diet would be 15% protein, 30% fat, and 55% carbohydrate. This is 3% more protein and 3% less carbohydrate than the *Dietary Goals* suggests for an optimal individual diet. The percentage of ideal fat is the same.

The most persistent myth regarding athletic nutrition is that athletes need copious amounts of extra protein.[53] Protein is not the primary fuel source for muscular energy. Carbohydrates are. Protein stores, in fact, have been shown to be relatively unaffected by strenuous exercise (though athletes may require an optimal level of protein utilization), while carbohydrates are readily burned as fuel. When carbohydrate stores are exhausted, the body turns to fat as its major source of energy.

For example, in studies reported in *Progress in Human Nutrition* (Avi Publishing, 1971) comparing the performance of athletes skiing, bicycling, and running, high-carbohydrate diets provided significantly more oxygen and endurance than high-protein diets. In one study, skiers were given manual work assignments after eating either a high-carbohydrate diet, a high-protein diet, or a normal diet. The high-carbohydrate skiers were able to work for 167 minutes straight, whereas the high-protein skiers averaged only 57 minutes and the skiers who ate a normal diet worked for 114 minutes.

Although the evidence suggests that protein is not the primary *immediate* fuel source for muscular energy, it's true that the stronger the body is in general, the better it holds up under athletic stress. Since protein is essential for the synthesis of enzymes, the rebuilding of tissue, the metabolism of nutrients, and healthy cell function in general, people who do exercise strenuously need to make sure that, on a day-to-day basis, their diets include an ample amount of protein. Mature athletes are thought to require 1 gram of protein per day for every kilogram (2.2 pounds) of body weight (Food and Nutrition Board, National Research Council). Growing athletes or athletes under extraordinary stress may need as much as 2 grams of protein for every kilogram of body weight.

[53]Robert C. Serfass, "Nutrition for the Athlete," *Journal of the American Pharmaceutical Association* (1978).

Athletes need to be careful about *when* they eat protein, however. It is thought that consuming excessive amounts of protein directly before strenuous exercise may actually be detrimental for an athlete, since protein metabolism requires large amounts of water to flush nitrogen by-products out of the system through the urine.[54] Athletes already run the risk of losing several pints of bodily fluid through sweat, so that anything that draws fluid reserves even further away is certainly not beneficial.

Water, in fact, is clearly the most important nutritional need for people who exercise strenuously. Water loss increases the body's temperature and pulse, puts strain on the circulatory system, leads to chronic exhaustion and, if severe enough, can lead to death. In a temperate environment an average of three pints of water a day is normally lost through perspiration, urine, and stools. Athletes lose considerably more, and at such a fast rate that no matter how much water an athlete drinks, more water is lost than can be resupplied to the tissues. It is especially important, therefore, for athletes to drink frequent small quantities of water on a daily basis, as well as during exercise.

VI. The Food Workbook

The following food journal is an expanded version of the impromptu food records I first kept several years ago when I wanted to know exactly what my diet was comprised of. I've kept a food journal for a week or two several times since then, and I'm always intrigued by the changes in diet I seem to make almost unconsciously. Changes in season, changes in age, changes in stress, environment, health—they're all reflected in food. But not until you sit down with paper and pencil will you ever really know how you are by what you eat.

Three worksheets follow. Worksheet 1 is a day-by-day food record. Worksheet 2 is a weekly total. Worksheet 3 is designed to help you figure out (easy math here) what percentage of your daily calories are eaten in the form of protein, what percentage in fat, and what percentage in carbohydrate.

Worksheet 1 is designed to help you record the amount of carbohydrates, fats, and proteins that you consume each day. It would be best to keep a record for two weeks, but one week will be useful too.

[54]C. F. Consolazio, "Nutrition and Athletic Performance," *Progress in Human Nutrition,* ed. Sheldon Margen (Westport, Conn.: Avi Publishing, 1971).

Make one copy of Worksheet 1 for each day that you will be keeping a record of your diet. Make sure you insert the date on the worksheet.

How do you find out how many carbohydrates, how much fat, and how much protein a given food contains? Several books about cooking, food, dieting, or health contain abbreviated tables of food composition. The tables of food composition are the official government values for all foods, raw, processed, and prepared. The values given include not only carbohydrates, fats, and proteins, but also calorie values and the major vitamins and minerals. I have included here a list of popular books which contain the tables. However, it's best to obtain the complete tables by writing the United States Government Printing Office, Washington, D.C. 20402. Address the letter to the Superintendent of Documents, and request either: Bernice K. Watt and Annabel L. Merrill, *The Composition of Foods,* Agriculture Handbook No. 8 (Stock No. 001-000-00768-8), or Catherine F. Adams, *The Nutritive Value of Foods in Common Units,* Agriculture Handbook No. 456 (Stock No. 001-000-03184-8). *The Composition of Foods* will give you nutrient values for "an edible portion"—roughly 100 grams of any food. *The Nutritive Value of Foods,* which many people find easier to use, lists nutrient values in common units: 1 tablespoon of butter, 1 medium-sized apple, 1 cup of rice, for example. Each book will give values for virtually every food available here. There is a small fee for each handbook.

The following books have good, but not complete, tables of food composition. You may also want to check any food books you already have in your home library.

- Nikki and David Goldbeck, *The Dieter's Companion,* Signet Books.
- Nutrition Search, Inc., *Nutrition Almanac,* McGraw-Hill.
- Laurel Robertson, Carol Flinders, and Bronwen Godfrey, *Laurel's Kitchen,* Nilgiri Press.

At the end of each day add each column to obtain a total for each nutrient and for the calories consumed for the whole day.

These daily totals will then be recorded under the appropriate day on Worksheet 2. *Worksheet 2* will help you maintain a weekly record. At the end of seven days add up the number of grams of carbohydrates, fats, and protein and the number of calories consumed during the week. Divide each of these weekly totals by seven to obtain an average of the nutrients and calories consumed each day.

Note: If you keep records for more than one week, do not take a total at the end of each seven-day period. Take a total for each nutrient and for calories for the entire period of time that you will be keeping a record. Then divide each total by the number of days for which you have kept records.

Worksheet 1
Date ________

Food Group	*Item*	*Quantity*	*Carbohydrate (g)*	*Fat (g)*	*Protein (g)*	*Calories*
Breads, Cereals, Grains, Pasta, Grain Products						
Dairy Products, Eggs, Butter, Margarine						
Meat, Fish, Poultry, Seafood						
Vegetables						
Fruit						
Beverages: Juices, Soda, Beer, Wine, Liquor						

Food Group	*Item*	*Quantity*	*Carbohydrate (g)*	*Fat (g)*	*Protein (g)*	*Calories*
Nuts, Seeds, Oils						
Sweets, Sugars						
Miscellaneous						
		Total	*	†	‡	§

*Insert this figure on line A of the appropriate day on Worksheet 2.
†Insert this figure on line B of the appropriate day on Worksheet 2.
‡Insert this figure on line C of the appropriate day on Worksheet 2.
§Insert this figure on line D of the appropriate day on Worksheet 2.

Tally

Water (Glasses)	*Coffee (Cups)*	*Tea (Cups)*

Worksheet 2

	DAY								
	1	2	3	4	5	6	7	Total	Total Divided by 7
A. Carbohydrates (g.)									AA
B. Fats (g.)									BB
C. Protein (g.)									CC
D. Number of Calories									

Worksheet 3

Average daily amount of carbohydrates (AA)	____	× 4 =	____	E
Average daily amount of fats (BB)	____	× 9 =	____	F
Average daily amount of protein (CC)	____	× 4 =	____	G
		Total (DD)	____	

Carbohydrates (E) ÷ Total (DD) =	____ × 100 =	____
Fats (F) ÷ Total (DD) =	____ × 100 =	____
Protein (G) ÷ Total (DD) =	____ × 100 =	____

The last figures on the right indicate the approximate percentages of calories that you consume from carbohydrates, fats, and protein.

What percentage of your diet is fat, protein, and carbohydrate?

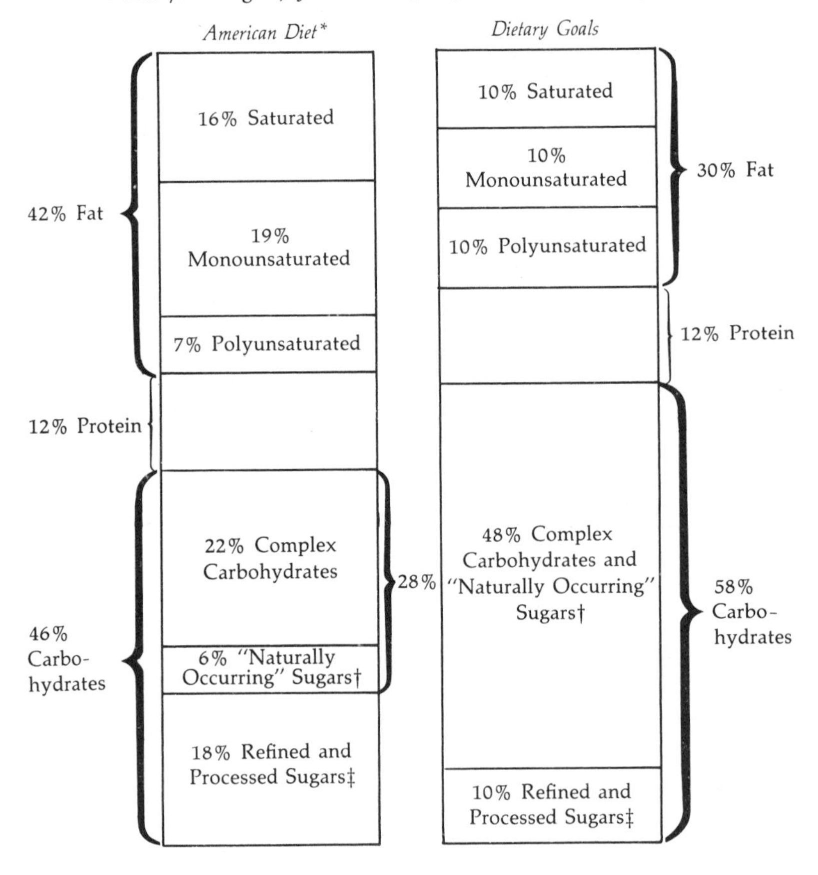

*SOURCE: *Dietary Goals.*
†Sugar indigenous to food, such as the sugar in fruit, milk, and vegetables.
‡All cane and beet sugar and sweeteners (refined sugar). Plus honey, maple syrup, molasses, corn syrup, and so on (processed sugar).

For example, if you intend to keep a record for ten days, make two copies of Worksheet 2, record the figures for the ten days, and obtain a ten-day total for each of the nutrients and calories. Divide these totals by ten to obtain the average amount of nutrients and calories consumed each day.

The average daily amounts of carbohydrates, fats, and proteins derived in Worksheet 2 can be used in *Worksheet 3* to determine the percentage of calories that each nutrient contributes to your diet.

Part Two
Food and Spirit

The Psychic Side of Food

There it is, an honest loaf of bread—a crusty brute resting squarely on the counter, still proud, still hot from the oven. Rugged but vulnerable. In the end, an almost primal strength will be ripped from its soft belly and devoured.

Food is powerfully and intimately connected to our deepest feelings; it was the basis of one of our first sensual experiences, and through it we developed bonds of love to our parents and formed our first feelings about the world.

Ask yourself why, in the final analysis, you're here reading a book about food. Your first answer might logically be that you want to provide yourself with information. But chances are, your emotions are also operating. Food and all of the symbolic meanings attached to it are too inherently a part of our psychological makeup for any one of us to have a take-it-or-leave-it attitude.

This chapter explores the other side of food—the emotional side. It may help you to understand why you make some of the food choices you do. It also provides the next step in creating an individually tailored healthful diet—that is, discovering how to heighten the pleasure you get from the food you eat. If there's a lesson to be learned from the first food experiences we had as infants, it's that eating should be sensually nourishing as well as physiologically nourishing.

Food's Psychological Impact

For the baby and for the child, food has profound psychological importance. Children who do not develop a relationship to food do not develop a relationship to the world and the people around them. It is only by seeing, chewing, and tasting real food in a real context that the child comes to understand that noodles, for example, are made from flour that began as a grain planted in a field. Psychologists say that by making the connection between food, life, and growth, a child begins to get a grasp of his or her place in the world.[1]

How and what children are fed, therefore, is extremely important. If they are fed TV dinners; premade, cardboard-wrapped hamburgers; and liquids out of metal cans, they will come to think of their own nourishment and bodies mechanistically. Food robbed of any character or value and always presented preformed will seem as though it has appeared by magic. The child will never make a true emotional connection between living things—plants and animals—and his or her own body.

By contrast, children—and later, adults—who deal with food directly, focus their attention on it while eating, and chew each mouthful well, are people who face the world cleanly and squarely, sink their teeth into each new situation, and deal with life events from beginning to end.

The reaction to food in prisons and mental institutions shows how emotionally charged and psychologically telling food is, even for adults. In a detention center in Maryland, for example, inmates had been fed premade aluminum-foil-wrapped TV-dinner-type meals for years. In 1976 the *Washington Post* reported that the inmates regularly expressed their anger about the dehumanizing food by smashing their food trays against the wall.[2] Then the food was changed. An inmate was allowed to cook whole, fresh food that tasted like real food. For the first time the inmates could see that the coleslaw had, that morning, been a live cabbage. No more trays were thrown against the wall.

The well-known child psychiatrist Bruno Bettelheim believes that sharing food is very important in developing relationships. He points out that in mental institutions, when the whole staff begins eating the same food the patients eat and begins eating *with* the patients in the same room and at the same tables, the patients become markedly better behaved.[3]

Sharing food has always been one of the strongest statements of feeling. The examples range from lovers who order one milk shake with two straws to the great food co-ops of the late sixties and early seventies. When the co-op movement began, its success was at-

[1]For an analysis of the development of a taste for food, and the use of the teeth as they relate to the ability to understand the world and get a grip on life, see F. S. Perls, *Ego, Hunger and Aggression* (New York: Vintage Books, 1969), p. 115.

[2]Marian Burros, "Feeding the Inmates," *Washington Post,* May 6, 1976.

[3]Bruno Bettelheim, "Food to Nurture the Mind," *School Review,* Vol. 83 (May 1975).

tributed to the outrageous food prices that forced consumers to buy collectively. But, in fact, few people saved a significant amount of money after dues and volunteer-work time were figured in. More probably, food co-ops were successful because, in the most basic way, they brought together individuals who shared an identity, a political vision, and—at the bottom line—the same food.

Food doesn't come to us of its own free will. We must spend a good deal of time and effort thinking about what we want to eat, taking ourselves to just the right stores, buying the food, bringing it home, storing it, cooking it, eating it, and even then digesting it.[4] All of the feelings associated with each of these activities affects how we feel about the food itself. It's important, for example, to shop in food stores that you like and feel comfortable in. You can't love the food if you don't like where it came from and resent the time you spent getting it.

No one food is inherently more exciting than any other. A plate of vegetables may be chop suey to one person, culinary gestalt to another. The pleasure you get from a food depends first on the emotional and physical associations you have with that food.

On a snowy winter morning the simplest slice of homemade bread can be as luscious and satisfying as a dinner of more complex foods —especially if you've made the bread yourself from an old family recipe and are sharing it with your own children or a husband or wife whose favorite breakfast is your homemade bread toasted and brushed with honey. As you eat the warm bread and watch the snow fall outside, you might be flooded with memories of your own childhood—and all of the feelings attached to those memories. In this way foods gather emotional associations that are passed on from generation to generation, and some foods, naturally, become strong cultural pleasures.

Some part of food enjoyment also comes from the ability to spontaneously match what you eat to the mood you're in and your immediate physical surroundings. Do peanuts ever taste better than when you're at a ballgame, cracking them open one by one and popping them into your mouth like popcorn?

[4]The average American spends 44.1 minutes a day (average) preparing meals. These meals are made up of a high proportion of processed convenience foods intended to save time and trouble. Europeans, who rarely use convenience foods, spend exactly 1.4 minutes more a day (average) preparing meals from whole, largely unprocessed foods. To a major extent, convenience foods are an American myth. In addition, our national average for food shopping time is one hour once a week. In a U.S. Department of Labor study comparing working women with families and non-working women with families, no significant differences were found in shopping time or shopping behavior, even though the working wives, in theory, had less time to spend (*National Food Review,* April 1978).

The Sensuality of Food

Imagine a crunchy, juicy Granny Smith apple that's just been picked. One bite and your teeth go wild—they just want to keep digging in. Biting into a mealy warehouse apple that's nine months old and tastes like rumpled cotton sheets just isn't as satisfying as a crisp, tart Granny Smith.

The major characteristic that heightens or detracts from the pleasure certain foods give is texture. Texture gives food what is called "mouthfeel." Foods that have a distinct texture are inherently satisfying. When a food has no distinct texture, or mouthfeel, nerve endings on the tongue are not excited, and no electrical impulses vibrate a message to the brain.

Watch a child select favorite foods. Children have taste buds not only on the tongue, as adults do, but also on the insides of the cheeks and on the roof of the mouth. With all those taste buds to excite, children invariably choose high-texture foods over low-texture foods—raw fruits and vegetables, for example, over cooked fruits and vegetables (which, if they're not cooked right, share the same mushy, indefinite texture).

Foods without definite texture are never as pleasurable as foods with texture—be it soft, springy, crisp, and so on. Commercial white bread that, crushed into a ball, feels like a wad of wet Kleenex does not—cannot—taste as good as a full-textured, chewy whole-grain bread fresh from the oven. And because it cannot taste as good, it cannot be as emotionally satisfying as bread should be.

There are two reasons a commercial white bread can't taste as good as a natural whole-grain bread. First, the more food is processed, the more its original structure is broken down and the more nutrients are lost. When you rob a food of its components, you destroy its original taste. As Henry Miller wrote in his essay "The Staff of Life," people in America used to eat well, but now the best food is eaten by machines. Second, when a food is processed, the additional flavors factored in create a final product that is an imbalanced hodgepodge of artificial and natural flavors thrown together at random (or at least with goals other than superior taste in mind). The food's final flavor (really mixture of flavors) lacks the dominance or strength that one pure flavor has. A vegetable soup, for example, has less dominant flavor characteristics than any of its ingredients do when they stand alone (especially uncooked). You can't taste *the* flavor of the soup in the same way that you can taste *the* flavor of a pea.

There is an analogy in music. A human voice, it is thought, is superior to a flute, and both are superior to a stringed instrument,

Most people are as aware of a food's texture as they are of its flavor, although women and people in higher economic brackets tend to be the most texture conscious.

In 1963 and 1970 two separate studies were done measuring the words people use to describe the textures of food. One study was done in Japan; the other in the United States. The ten most frequently used words to describe textural properties are listed below. Interestingly, seven of the ten top words are used by both countries, even though Japanese culture and food habits are different from those of Americans. Even more interesting, however, was the finding that the Japanese used a total of 406 descriptions of texture when presented with various foods, while the Americans used only 78 words.

Undoubtedly, that says something about language differences. But could it also be that American food has become so homogeneous that no more than seventy-eight texture words are warranted? Or that in some very basic sense, food here has less worth —and is therefore allotted a substantially smaller share of the working vocabulary?

Most Frequently Used Texture Words

(in descending order of frequency)

United States	*Japan*
crisp	hard
dry	soft
juicy	juicy
soft	chewy
creamy	greasy
crunchy	viscous
chewy	slippery
smooth	creamy
stringy	crisp
hard	crunchy
78 words total	406 words total

From: *Fabricated Foods,* ed. George E. Inglett, Ph.D. (P.O. Box 831, Westport, Conn.: Avi Publishing, 1975), p. 131.

because the closer you can come to the pure essence—be it sound or taste—the more intense and satisfying your experience of it will be.

In many cultures the emotional and psychological aspects of food are brought to the surface through food rituals and ceremonies. Children are taught how to treat and savor even the simplest of foods. In the mountains of China, tea for a very special person is made with rainwater and tea leaves that have been handpicked. We're more likely to spend a lifetime gulping down mugs of lukewarm, bag-made tea with never a second thought. In fact, there is no clear American ceremony for heightening the pleasure of food. Learning how to savor is not usually a part of our cultural upbringing.

Too bad, for the mouth is extremely sense oriented. In fact, it has more sense organs per square inch than either the legs or the trunk of the body. Yet despite the mouth's capacity for stimulation, it is more taken for granted than many other body parts. While our breakfast eggs are doing a French can-can on the nerve receptors of the tongue, our attention is focused on chewing up the morning newspaper. We may not even remember what we ate. So, of course, we've missed the pleasure of eating it.

As we've seen, for an infant, food is the first sensual experience. For an adult, it's the only one that can be depended on. It is important, therefore, to teach yourself food appreciation. Food sensuality —like music appreciation, like good sex—is an art of living that can be learned. The following exercises will help.

Exercise 1: Feeling Your Food

Close your eyes and take a few minutes to relax, concentrating on your breath. With your eyes closed, imagine the inside of your mouth. Think about what the different parts of your mouth can do with food. You can swirl food with your tongue. Mash it against the roof of your mouth. Grind it with your back teeth. Squeeze it against your cheeks. Mince it between your front teeth.

The Chinese are extremely dexterous with their mouths. Many of them can split a watermelon seed between their teeth, extract the meat, and carry on a conversation all at once. The most dexterous can tie one or two knots in a cherry stem with the tongue and teeth or plop a snail, shell and all, into the mouth, then suck the meat from the shell in one quick movement.

Choose a simple thin-skinned food, put it in your mouth, and see if you can peel the skin from the flesh. Grapes or lima beans are good for this. Or try separating the thin membrance enclosing an orange section from the flesh itself. And now is the time to learn how to split open sunflower seeds in your mouth so that you no longer have to pay twice the amount for shelled seeds!

This is learning how to use your body to eat. It gives you a finer understanding of food, since you feel as well as see how food is built.

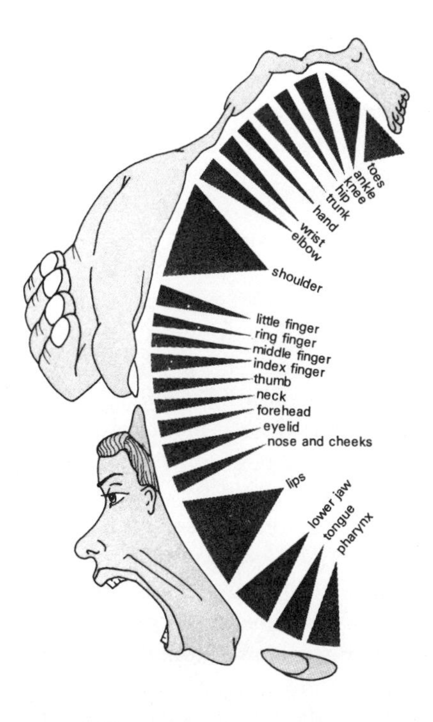

Different parts of the body are not equally represented in the brain, nor are they represented in proportion to their size. Penfield's "Homunculus," above, shows how some body parts dominate brain space on the surface of the cerebral cortex. As far as the brain is concerned, the two most important parts of the body and the two that command the most brain space are the mouth and hands. (From: Jonathan Miller, *The Body in Question* [New York: Random House, 1978].)

Exercise 2: Using Your Fingers

Another way of getting an expanded feel for food is by eating it with different utensils: wooden chopsticks for salads, porcelain spoons for rice. Eating spaghetti with your fingers is a surefire way of learning exactly how perfectly cooked spaghetti should feel.

Forks are a relatively recent eating tool, in fact. Throughout most of history, people had a more direct relationship with food because they touched and held everything they put into their mouths. Finger eating was an art. Certain fingers were used for certain foods, and some fingers were always extended out so that they'd be clean for the next course. (Extending the pinky while drinking tea with tiny sandwiches is a habit left over from this custom.)

Exercise 3: Letting Tension Drain from Your Body

Most people do not allow eating to be a sensual experience. They sit down at the table, tense on the one hand, distracted on the other. Even if they're hungry, they may not really enjoy the food they've begun to eat. We've all plowed happily but ferociously through meals that we can't even remember the next morning.

When rats expect food, they demonstrate exaggerated body tension by running excitedly in an activity wheel. Humans, too, become physiologically excited when they anticipate food. Whether we're conscious of it or not, right before we eat, all kinds of signals are flashing in the body. The mouth is secreting extra saliva, the stomach muscles are being pumped with blood, the glands are getting ready to burst open with a flood of digestive juices, the intestines are contracting, bracing themselves for the heavy load.

On top of natural biophysical tension is built the day's pressures, frustrations, worries, ambitions, joys—all of them bottled up, clenching the muscles and wiring up the stomach. When you're tense, eating cannot be a sensual experience.

A few years ago I began something that singlehandedly tripled my enjoyment of food. I began to stop, close my eyes, and take three very slow deep breaths before I ate. With each breath, I exhaled the tension of the day. And even on days when I felt totally relaxed, I stopped to breathe anyway. I found that even when I thought I was relaxed, I wasn't, because breathing, eyes closed, relaxed me even more.

These few moments of releasing tension made a big difference in my whole body. My digestion improved, I felt calmer and more physically aware of myself, and taking just those few moments allowed me to be a bit reflective. I found myself happy and thankful that I was about to eat. I found myself really maximizing the simple pleasure of food.

Here's how to relax before eating:

1. After the food is in front of you and you've been able to look at it and catch the aroma, sit up very straight in your chair with hands and feet uncrossed. Close your eyes. Take a deep breath and slowly let it travel from the top of your head down and out your spinal column, letting the tension drain from your muscles. Keep your mind as blank as possible. This is almost impossible to do if you don't close your eyes.

2. Take a second breath, pushing out your intestines and stomach as you inhale as fully as possible. Again, let the breath run down and out your spine. Stop for a moment and imagine your stomach and

intestines. See if you can trace the route that the food you're about to eat will take. Imagine what that food will feel like inside you.

This is a crucial step in developing a relationship with your body through food. The more often you imagine what a food will feel like before you eat it, the more you'll become aware of body messages and preferences and the more you'll be able to choose foods that your body needs. This is simply a magnified version of what people normally do when they run through their head an imaginary list of foods, trying to figure out exactly what they'd like to eat for dinner.

The stomach is capable of making its opinions known. We all, for example, have made decisions based on a gut feeling. Logically, if anything in the world should be based on a gut feeling, it's deciding what food to eat.

I experimented further with this idea. Each day, during those few moments of breathing, I would ask my stomach how it felt about the food it was about to have dumped into it. Sometimes the message was "I vote for the fish, but stay away from that coleslaw" or "I'd rather have bananas down here instead of an apple, and could you throw in some cheese?"

I experimented both with following the messages and with intentionally choosing those foods that my body seemed to say no to, and I found that I consistently felt markedly better when I ate in harmony with my gut feelings.

Please note that the issue here is not between wholesome food and junk food. I wasn't asking my stomach how it felt about Coke and a sugar doughnut for breakfast. Rather, given the choice of a number of good foods, which foods were the ones that my body specifically wanted and needed?

Not surprisingly, this process took mere seconds; the body knew instantaneously what it needed. But remember to follow through. After you've eaten something, close your eyes again, concentrate on your intestines, and ask yourself how you feel. Foods feel very different from one another once they're inside you. Could you, for example, list your favorite foods, then describe how they make you feel?

3. One last breath for the road. During this last breath, I usually think about the person (or people) I'm about to eat with and, just for the moment, feel the pleasure of being with them.

I did this for a year at home before I also started doing it in restaurants. I would explain to whoever I was having a meal with that I wanted to take a couple of breaths. The reactions were surprising. Those friends who, in the beginning, teased me the most are now invariably the ones who quietly breathe along, too.

Taking a moment before plowing into the food is especially important in a restaurant. For there, you have no relationship to the food you're about to eat. For example, you didn't spot the big red body of the strawberry you're about to eat at the greengrocer, and you couldn't feel its plump ripeness when it was washed. You didn't have the chance to smell its sweetness. You weren't the one to snip off its green cap, then slice it into a bowl. You simply have no relationship to it. You haven't yet touched it—or even seen it for more than a few seconds. Stopping for a second to concentrate on the food in a restaurant establishes that tiny but important link that makes eating a strawberry different from eating cardboard.

Exercise 4: Welcome to the Kitchen

To develop your sensitivity to food, you must wash it, chop it, blend it, sauté it—work with it until you know every bit about that piece of food and feel comfortable with it. It's hard to develop this kind of sensitivity in a sterile kitchen, so keep your blenders, juicers, woks, omelet pans, baskets, scoopers, mashers, pasta makers, popcorn poppers, grain mills, yogurt makers, and so forth out where you can see them, out where they can tempt you. A kitchen where the utensils and gadgets, pots and pans, and foods are all out in the open rather than tucked away in cabinets is the perfect kitchen to work in because just looking around will give you food ideas.

Suppose you're stir-frying some peppers and eggplant in a wok. If you look up and there on the open shelves are jars of dried mushrooms, almonds, raisins, lentils, coconut, caraway seeds, plus the grain mill, garlic press, nut cracker, and so on, then your mind begins to click out the possibilities. How would a few caraway seeds taste sprinkled in here? Suppose I threw in a pinch of curry and some coconut and raisins?

Walk around your kitchen. Experiment touching different foods. You've got two cucumbers? Poke them. If one's hard, the other spongy, can you imagine what the difference will be in taste? Take out the olive oil. Take out the safflower oil. Smell them and feel them. How do the smells compare? Which is more slippery to the touch? Which one would coat a salad better?

Start tasting different foods together—even ones that are not usually put together—to get an idea of the possibilities. How does sesame butter taste on a banana? What about a sesame dressing on a fruit salad? What about a sesame-fruit dressing on pancakes?

How do the flavors of food affect one another? If you've lightly steamed carrots, divide them into three batches and sprinkle a different herb over each. Try minced parsley, tarragon, and dill. Which of the three herbs best brings out the flavor of the carrots? Experiment with balancing different flavors and textures off one another. Why do cheese and bread, pie and ice cream, nuts and raisins go together? What would taste good over brown rice, and what foods would brown rice taste good over?

The more associations you have with a food, the more hunches you'll get in the kitchen for good dishes. Food will become more exciting to work with and eat, and you'll become a better cook.

Exercise 5: Potatoes for Breakfast, Pancakes for Dinner

Why is it that certain foods have been given time slots? The Dannon yogurt people say that when yogurt was first introduced in America, the most difficult thing yogurt manufacturers had to overcome was not the American dislike of tangy dairy foods. Instead, it was the fact that no one knew where yogurt fit in the American meal concept. When did you eat it? Was it a breakfast food? Was it a dessert? Could you eat it as an appetizer?

The first time they eat last night's leftover dinner for breakfast, most people discover that foods needn't be confined to specific meals. In the wintertime especially, thick, hot soups or casseroles are wonderful for breakfast.

By experimenting, you may find that you love certain foods at very unconventional times. I've spent weeks with a large, mostly non-English-speaking Chinese family. What do the Chinese eat for breakfast? Chinese food, of course. Every morning there was fish, rice, vegetables, noodles. But never bread, eggs, juice, or cheese.

Exercise 6: Food's Power to Bind People Emotionally

Because of the power food has to influence mood as well as metabolism, food has important metaphysical properties. People who share the same food share the same wavelength in a sense. For whatever life force was contained in the food they shared has been passed on in duplicate, becoming nurturing energy in each of them.

Such a process is basic in nature. A chromosome, for example, splits so that both the old and the new life share certain traits carried by the same genetic code. In the case of food, every aspect of a food's power to influence body and mind is received by each of the people who share that food.

It's important, then, to go about sharing food consciously with people close to you. When two people share the same apple, that apple's life force becomes a part of both of them and draws them emotionally together. If you and a friend each have an apple, try cutting them both in half and sharing. It's a markedly different experience than simply eating separate apples in each other's company.

Recommended books on the meaning, power, and psychic side of food include the following:

Hsiang Ju Lin and Tsuifeng Lin. *Chinese Gastronomy,* New York: Hastings House Publishers, 1969.
Don Gerrard. *One Bowl.* New York: Random House/Bookworks, 1973.
Mike Samuels, M.D., and Hal Bennett. *The Well Body Book.* New York: Random House/Bookworks, 1973.
Fritz Perls. *Ego, Hunger and Aggression.* New York: Vintage Books, 1969.
Michio Kushi. *The Book of Macrobiotics.* Tokyo: Japan Publications, 1977.

Cooking: Techniques for Preserving Nutrients

The muffins are baking. The cabinets are pulled open, banged shut. Soups simmer. Hanging herbs are crushed, ground. The room is warm.

One by one, people wind up in the kitchen. It's not just the rich smells and the happy sounds. It's the alchemy, the fascination of watching squat little squash, bulbous tomatoes, a block of cheese, a sack of wild rice, plus fresh greens and herbs all being chopped, mixed, fluffed, crushed, and stuffed into a delicious dish.

The way you handle food, the way you slice it, the way you cook it, is a symbol of the attitude you have about the food itself. Whatever the attitude—warmth, neglect, joy—it will be reflected in the final dish. Have you ever eaten a terrible meal prepared by someone who loves to cook? Probably not. People who love to cook impart their own energy and vitality to the dishes they create. Even when passionate cooks make mistakes, the mistakes usually taste good. But if the cook couldn't care less, the dish will always taste like it.

It isn't necessary to be an exceptional cook to prepare good food. No one has to know how to make a perfect soufflé, but knowing how to make good homemade pancakes for breakfast in bed—that's the sort of stuff it takes: a certain feel for what goes with what, a boundless energy and a sensitive hand, the kind of enthusiasm it takes to make fresh blueberry pancakes over a campfire on a summer morning high in the mountains.

You can tell a lot about people and their self-esteem by the way they prepare food. Joyless, oblivious cooking—throwing frozen breaded veal cutlets in the oven night after night—is a symbol of people who simply doesn't respect themselves enough to feed themselves better food.

Technically, cooking is anything you do to a food. So even a simple salad of fresh greens and raw vegetables can be "cooked" haphazardly or it can be prepared with such exquisite attention to detail that it seems as though you're eating a food garden. You can imagine which one tastes better.

The importance of cooking—both method and technique—is based in Chinese tradition and has spread to other cuisines. To this day, a Chinese chef will rate another's dishes not so much by the taste of the ingredients (which is expected to be exemplary) but rather by the purity of the cooking technique. Good cooking is considered to be the achievement of perfect balance between size, texture, and color—as much as the balancing of flavor. Asparagus to be combined with mushrooms, for example, must be cut and cooked differently than asparagus to be combined with tofu.

In many ways the real key to health-giving food is right here in this chapter: learning how to cook whole, natural foods in a way that preserves nutrients and enhances flavor, learning how to cook with integrity and instinct.

The Freshness of Food

From the minute food is harvested, it begins to lose nutrients. Foods that have a high water content, such as leafy green vegetables and meat, lose nutrients and visibly deteriorate the fastest. Foods with a low water content, such as dry seeds or beans, can be stored for years with minimal nutrient losses. To get the most nutrients from the food you eat, buy the freshest foods you can and cook them as quickly and as briefly as possible.

Nutrients are destroyed not only by time but by heat. The longer food is held at a warm temperature, the more nutrients it loses. It's important to realize that the percentage of lost nutrients is *great.* Overcooking can easily destroy virtually every vitamin in a food, most of the minerals, and a good share of the protein.[1]

This is why beginning with *fresh* food is important. Frozen and canned foods are *cooked even before you cook them.* Both are blanched in order to inactivate enzymes in the food that in time would cause the food to produce gas, soften, wilt, and discolor. Canned foods are even subject to a second heating when the container is hermetically sealed.

There's simply no way of knowing exactly how many nutrients have been lost in canned or frozen food, except to realize that the potential for losing most of them is definitely there. Be aware that when food manufacturers say, for example, that 20% of the vitamin C in peas is lost during freezing, that 20% refers to the freezing process only. It doesn't take into consideration how much vitamin C was lost when the peas were blanched nor how much is lost during storage time or later when you actually cook the peas.

Some vitamins seem to be so vulnerable to the effects of harvest-

[1]Endel Karmas, "Nutritional Aspects of Food Processing Methods," *Nutritional Evaluation of Food Processing,* ed. Robert S. Harris and Endel Karmas (Westport, Conn.: Avi Publishing, 1975).

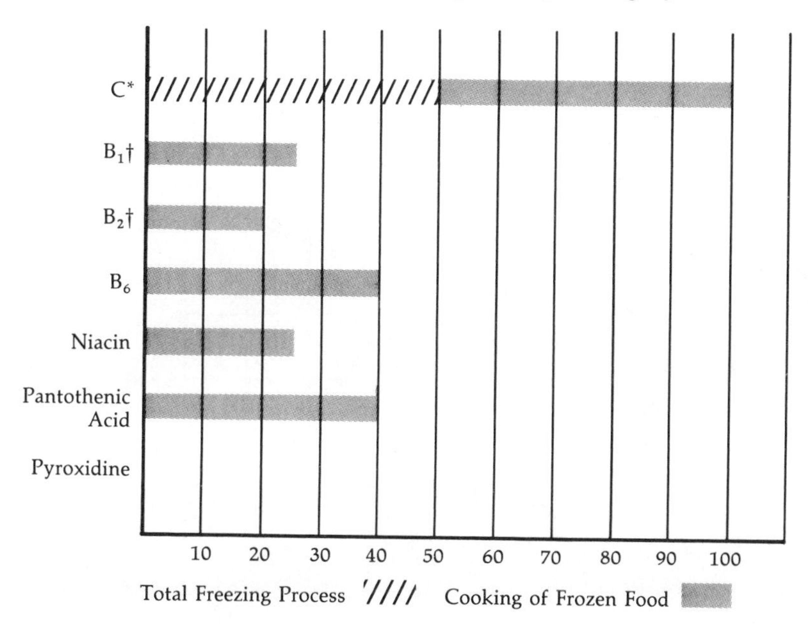

*Before food is frozen, 10% to 44% of the vitamin C may be lost through blanching.

†Loss of vitamins B_1 and B_2 during frozen storage are unknown, but thought to be moderate. Cooking losses are as shown.

Adapted from: Robert S. Harris and Endel Karmas, eds., *Nutritional Evaluation of Food Processing* (P.O. Box 831, Westport, Conn.: Avi Publishing 1975), p. 281.

ing, handling, blanching, freezing or canning, storage time, possibly thawing, and finally cooking that 90% to 100% of several vitamins may be lost. In 1971 the *American Journal of Clinical Nutrition* published a report that concluded that we cannot expect to obtain the RDA for several vitamins if we eat canned food.[2]

If you cannot always buy fresh food, frozen food is somewhat better than canned. Fruits, for example, lose two to three times more niacin and vitamins B_1, B_2, and C when they're canned than when they're frozen.

Cooking Techniques and Their Effect on Nutrients

Since heat, water, light, and time are the prime destroyers of nutrients, choose cooking methods that minimize all four.

Steaming is one of the best ways to cook and preserve nutrients,

[2]H. A. Schroeder, "Losses of Vitamins and Trace Minerals Resulting from Processing and Preserving Food," *American Journal of Clinical Nutrition*, Vol. 24 (1971), pp. 562–73.

*Comparative Losses of Vitamins in Fruits Under Various Methods of Preparation**

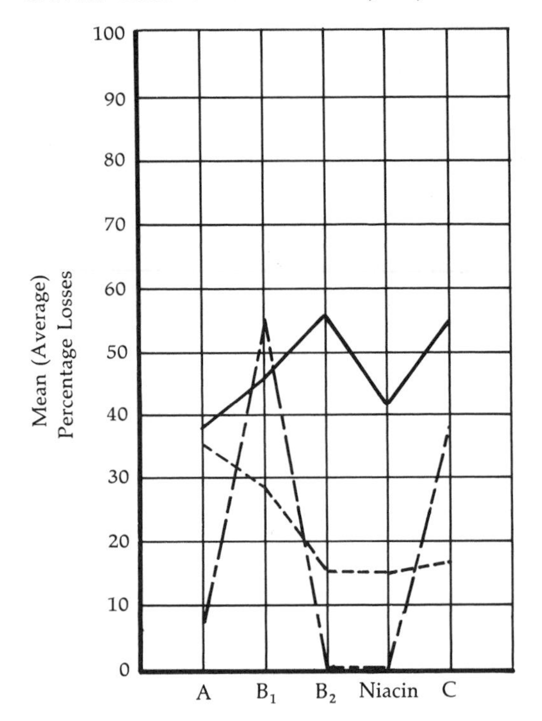

*Losses are given as averages. The range of losses were: 0% to 78% for vitamin A, 0% to 90% for B_1, 0% to 83% for B_2, 0% to 60% for niacin, and 0% to 86% for C.

Adapted from: Robert S. Harris and Endel Karmas, eds., *Nutritional Evaluation of Food Processing* (P.O. Box 831, Westport, Conn.: Avi Publishing, 1975), p. 269.

since the food comes into direct contact with only a small amount of water and that water condenses and coats the food in the end. Steam also displaces oxygen in the cooking pot, and since proper steaming requires that the pot be covered, the food is exposed to a minimum of light. In addition, steaming is fast, and food being steamed does not reach as high a temperature as boiled or baked food.

To steam, simply boil one-half to one inch of water in a generous-size pot and insert a steamer so that the bottom of the steamer is just about at water level (collapsible, stainless-steel steamers cost about three dollars). Put the foods to be steamed in the steamer and cover the pot. If more than one food is being steamed at a time, put the food requiring the most cooking in first so that it receives the most steam, then layer the other foods on top. Turn the heat down to moderate to prevent the water from boiling away and burning the bottom of the pot.

Stir-frying is another way to preserve nutrients. Stir-frying is even quicker than steaming, and the small amount of oil that is used coats the food and protects it from exposure to air. Stir-frying does not require water, so nutrients are not lost through water leaching. Water can be used, though, the advantage being that a bit of water means using less oil, thereby cutting down on fat and calories. You must, in any case, use some liquid; otherwise the food being stir-fried will scorch. I prefer to use a homemade vegetable stock, which adds flavor and nutrients. Whatever liquid is used will create a slight steaming effect, so that the food will cook even faster.

Stir-frying also happens to be one of the most interesting and easiest ways to cook, since many foods can be cooked at once and an infinite number of combinations of foods can be cooked together depending on what foods you have on hand.

To stir-fry, thoroughly heat a wok (preferable) or heavy skillet with a tablespoon or more of an unrefined vegetable oil. (You'll have to experiment here; the correct amount of oil depends on the amount and nature of the food you want to cook.) Cut and slice the food into bite-size pieces. Cut the food requiring the longest cooking a bit smaller or add it to the wok a few minutes before you add the other ingredients. The oil in the wok should be very hot before you add any of the food—you'll know that the oil is the right temperature if a chopped onion dropped into it applauds. You'll need to stir the contents continuously in order to coat each piece of food with oil and prevent scorching. Stir-frying only takes from two to eight minutes, however. Remove the food when the vegetables are still crisp. By using stock, water, a bit of wine, or a seasoning like shoyu or tamari (naturally fermented soy sauces) plus herbs and perhaps some finely minced garlic or shallots, you can make a good sauce in the wok after you remove the food.

Sautéing is about as effective as stir-frying when it comes to preserving nutrients. This is because the two techniques don't differ appreciably: Sautéing is French; stir-frying is Chinese. In sautéing, a skillet rather than a wok is used, the food is shaken rather than flipped with a utensil, butter is used more often than vegetable oil, and sometimes the food is not cut before cooking. A whole fish, for example, is often sautéed (in generous amounts of fat), but it's not stir-fried unless it's sliced first.

Braising is not an ideal method of cooking when it comes to preserving nutrients, but it is better than boiling, which is the worst method, since virtually all of the nutrients (not to mention the flavor) is leached out of food when it's boiled. Braising is also better than baking, which robs food of massive amounts of nutrients because of the high heat and long cooking time required.

To braise, preheat a pan with a bit of unrefined vegetable oil and briefly sauté the food. Next, add a good amount of liquid. As the food cooks in it, the liquid will imbue the food with flavors, so choose an interesting liquid, one that will add nutrients and form a good base for a sauce. Juices, tomato puree, cider, stock, or wine added to water are all much more delicious and nutritious braising liquids than water alone. Squash braised in apple juice is luscious.

Deep frying has small benefits and large drawbacks. Because deep frying is quick and because batters protect the nutrients in food from air, deep frying tends to preserve nutrients rather well. The obvious drawback, however, is the excessive fat and calories that deep frying adds.

On Tools

Food should taste like food, not like wet metal. After years of using stainless steel pots, spoons, colanders, and so forth, I've found that certain foods taste better when the utensils used are made from more natural materials.

The most natural, good-tasting, and versatile utensil in the world is your hand. French chefs, in fact, use their fingers to taste sauces, since the taste of a metal spoon spoils the delicate flavor of a sauce.

To the Chinese and Japanese, who are accustomed to the feel and natural taste of chopsticks, Western food almost always tastes of the metal it's eaten with. The argument can be made, however, that chopsticks, wooden spoons, and wooden spatulas taste woody and give food a woody flavor. Actually, only brand-new wooden utensils and cheap pine utensils taste woody. Cheap pine spoons and spatulas are porous, which means that they pick up and hold strong flavors. In addition, pine splinters and cracks easily.

The solution is not to give up wood, but to buy hardwood rather than pine utensils. Hardwoods (beech, cherry, and maple) are more closely grained, making them more effective, longer-lasting utensils, as well as more beautiful ones.

New wooden utensils simply need to be washed a few times for their woody flavor to disappear. Don't soak wooden utensils, however, or put them in a dishwasher, because they'll soften and crack.

To remove the woody taste of new chopsticks, a Japanese or Chinese person will stir the tea a few times with them. If the tea is hot enough, this will also sterilize chopsticks that are obviously being used again and again.

Wooden baskets, colanders, and steamers are the traditional counterparts of natural food, even though they aren't necessarily any more effective than their metal counterparts. Wooden spoons and spatulas, however, *are* more effective and practical than metal, since wood is a poor heat conductor and, as a result, you can stir for hours without scorching your fingers. Because wood doesn't hold heat, you can also use wooden utensils over very high heat one moment and in a chilled mixture minutes later without the temperature of one affecting the other.

Actually the oldest and most natural form of cookware is pottery. There is no non-nomadic culture that does not make some sort of clayware.

Pottery is the umbrella term for any utensil or cooking object made of molded wet clay. At one end of the spectrum is earthenware, which is simply pottery fired to a temperature of 1,100°F so that the clay no longer dissolves when it interacts with water. Earthenware, however, does remain somewhat porous. At the other end is porcelain (china), a translucent (glazed) pottery that has been heated to 2,000°F so that the particles of clay fuse together into a glasslike mass that is not porous.

Pottery is great for cooking (especially casseroles) because, although it takes a long time to heat up, pottery retains heat, disbursing it slowly and evenly for a very long time. When foods are cooked slowly in clay pots, their flavors are brought out strongly. The best clay pots are glazed inside (to prevent porosity) but unglazed outside for maximum heat absorption.

Other materials from which cookware—especially stove-top cookware—is made include heavy aluminum, stainless steel, porcelain enamel,[3] glass, cast iron, copper, and specially treated aluminum.

Copper, heavy aluminum, and cast iron are all good conductors of heat. Heat, in fact, is distributed entirely throughout these metals, so that the food receives heat from all sides and cooks evenly. By comparison, stainless steel and glass conduct heat poorly. When you use a stainless steel or glass pot, the heat from the burner alone is cooking the food, causing some to stick to the bottom while what is on top

[3]Porcelain enamel is a glasslike finish bonded to the outside of cast iron and aluminum and to both the outside and inside of stainless steel. The best-quality porcelain utensils have several coats. Do not buy acrylic enamel or Polyamide utensils. These look like porcelain enamel, but the coating is cheaper, thinner, and more apt to chip, scratch, and stain.

Comparison of Seven Major Categories of Stove-Top Cookware

	Heavy Aluminum	*Stainless Steel*	*Porcelain (iron coated with enamel)*	*Glass*	*Cast Iron*	*Copper*	*Specially Treated Aluminum*
Average Price of a Two-Quart Pan	$10–$15	$25–$35	$25–$35	$12–$20	$15 (hard to find iron saucepans)	$55–$65	$39.50 (2½ quart)
Durability	GOOD: can become pitted or discolored when in contact with acidic foods.	EXCELLENT	POOR-GOOD: can chip and crack with insufficient layers.	POOR	EXCELLENT	GOOD: drawbacks are the need for retinning ($15–$25 for a 2-quart saucepan) and constant polishing.	EXCELLENT
Heat Distribution	EXCELLENT	POOR	GOOD: depends upon the metal base.	POOR	EXCELLENT	EXCELLENT and very fast.	EXCELLENT
Discoloration	YES	NO	YES: use mild solution of bleach and water to clean.	NO	YES	YES	NO
How to Clean	Always cool before washing. For stains boil a solution of 2 tablespoons lemon juice per quart of water for 10 minutes.	Use detergent; dry immediately.	Soap and water. Do not scour.	Use a plastic pad and nonabrasive cleaners.	Always dry immediately to avoid rusting.	Use commercial cleaner for the copper. Do not remove surface tarnish from the inner lining.	Place pan in warm, soapy water after using. If food hardens onto surface, use plastic pad and abrasive cleanser.

	Heavy Aluminum	*Stainless Steel*	*Porcelain (iron coated with enamel)*	*Glass*	*Cast Iron*	*Copper*	*Specially Treated Aluminum*
Dishwasher	NO: can become dull or stained.	YES	YES	YES	NO	NO	NO
Effect on Food Flavor	Metallic taste to foods with high acid content.	NONE	NONE	NONE	YES: however, considered to be a good source of iron.	YES: actually poisonous if not lined with another metal or kept absolutely clean.	NO
Recommended Use	High-heat cooking: omelets, sautéing, etc.	Low-heat cooking. Liquid cooking (soups).	SEE LABEL	Microwave only. Not recommended for stove-top cooking.	Long, slow cooking because of excellent heat retention.	EXCELLENT for everything. Especially good for sauces because of sensitivity to temperature changes.	Best for high-heat cooking.
Comments	The lighter gauges are easily dented. Use the heavy aluminum only.	Very poor conductor of heat if has no other alloys. A better choice is a stainless steel pot with a copper or aluminum bottom.	Heats slowly but retains heat well. Throw out pan if the enamel finish chips.	Glass is a poor conductor which causes food to stick.	Needs to be seasoned. An overall good choice.	Hard to maintain but the best choice if price is not a factor. The price can be more competitive if pots made with copper from Chile.	These new aluminum pans are a good choice. The finish cannot be scraped off, there is no effect on food flavor, and the pan will not discolor.

Reprinted from *The Cook's Magazine* (Pennington Publishing, 1698 Post Road East, Westport, Conn.), charter issue.

remains undercooked. For this reason, the best stainless steel pots have a layer or layers of copper, aluminum, or carbon steel sandwiched between the stainless steel exterior.

The chart on pages 102 and 103 can help you choose stove-top cookware suited to your needs. Please be aware that traces of aluminum from aluminum cooking utensils have been reported to cause ulcerations, headaches, constipation, heartburn, dyspepsia, and flatulence. I recommend using the new specially treated aluminum only. By comparison, the traces of iron that cast-iron cooking utensils give off are actually good for you.

Recommended Natural Foods Cookbooks

The books listed here are the best I've found for learning the *techniques* of natural foods cookery. Ironic as it is, most cookbooks are not geared to healthful foods. Their recipes call for lots of butter, salt, and sugar, plus a heavy emphasis on oil, animal fats, cream, egg yolks, and white flour. Those natural foods cookbooks that eliminate such ingredients are sometimes just as difficult to deal with themselves. They're unimaginative, esoteric, and rarely do they make you *want* to cook, but worst of all, they fail to teach you the important rules of natural foods cookery: what to expect when you cook with honey rather than white sugar, what to expect when you substitute unrefined vegetable oil for butter, how to make a delicate sauce, and so on. This book and the ones listed below should help.

Armand Aulicino. *The New French Cooking: Minceur Cuisine Extraordinaire.* New York: Grosset & Dunlap, 1976. Strong on technique. Classical international recipes reworked with healthful ingredients.

Marion Gorman and Felipe P. deAlba. *The Dione Lucas Book of Natural French Cooking.* New York: E. P. Dutton, 1977. The authors' philosophy is that you can be a gourmet *and* be healthy and that the art of eating includes both the sensuous *and* the nutritious aspects of food. Excellent recipes.

Laurel Robertson, Carol Flinders, and Bronwen Godfrey. *Laurel's Kitchen.* Petaluma, Calif.: Nilgiri Press, 1976. A vegetarian cookbook/handbook that radiates warmth and the authors' commitment to health-giving food. Wholesome "home-style" recipes.

William Shurtleff and Akiko Aoyagi. *The Book of Tofu,* 1975. *The Book of Miso,* 1976. Brookline, Mass.: Autumn Press. The best texts for cooking these and other natural and macrobiotic foods. Historical and nutritional information is excellent.

Annemarie Colbin. *The Book of Whole Meals.* Brookline, Mass.: Autumn Press, 1979. Emphasis on grains, legumes, and vegetables. One of the few cookbooks that present recipes in entire meal sets with directions on when to begin what so that the whole meal is ready at the same time.

Part Three
Natural Food

Natural and Organic Food: Guidelines for Intelligent Buying

No single food, except mother's milk for a short period of time, can sustain life and assure health. We all know that a number of whole foods—that is, foods that spontaneously grow in nature and can be consumed in their natural state—are necessary for optimal health and a vigorous body and mind.

Yet even among whole, natural foods there are not true "health foods"—no foods that are unconditionally physically tolerable and beneficial for everyone. Let's agree, then, to put the term *health food* aside and consider the two terms that *are* important in gauging the healthfulness of food: *natural* and *organic.*[1]

The Definition of Natural Foods

Natural foods are those foods that grow spontaneously in nature whether or not they are tended by man. There are three stages in the biochemical cycle of natural foods. At the first stage, water, carbon dioxide, and organic nutrients in the soil combine in the presence of energy from the sun to produce plants. At the second stage, plants

[1]The terms *health food* and *health food store* have taken on slightly different meanings as more and more food-conscious people become progressively better educated about what healthful food is and what it's not. Many committed whole-foods people now feel that a health food store is itself no guarantee of healthful food and that one can, in fact, eat quite healthfully by shopping selectively in a supermarket. At the same time people have begun to distinguish between health food stores and natural food stores. The first can be loosely defined as a store that concentrates on *packaged* food *products* such as granola cereals and soy margarine, food *supplements* such as brewer's yeast and high-protein powders, and a full array of *vitamins* and *minerals.* Natural food stores, by comparison, concentrate on *food*—grains, beans, sprouts, cheese, loose herbs, breads, and a variety of organic and nonorganic fresh vegetables and fruits. Food supplements, vitamins, and minerals are given much less emphasis, if present at all. If the store you shop in for healthful food does not contain a wide variety of whole foods that have undergone little or no processing, begin to shop in a store that does, or rely on the mail-order list of natural food companies at the end of this chapter.

provide nourishment for herbivorous animals. And at the third stage these animals produce edible substances that are the natural products of the animal's life cycle. We eat food from the first stage (grains, vegetables, fruits, nuts), the second stage (meats and fish), and the third stage (eggs, honey, raw milk, etc.).[2]

But, as it is popularly used, the term *natural food* also refers to foods that have been prepared from first-, second-, and third-stage foods without the use or addition of additives, preservatives, artificial colors and flavors, or manufactured chemicals of any sort after harvest or slaughter. So, for example, whole-grain flours and some yogurts are legitimately considered natural foods.

In the past few years, however, the definition of *natural* has been stretched to the limit. You the consumer are faced with potatoes on the one hand and potato chips on the other, both described as natural.

The best recourse here may be to ignore descriptive terms like *natural* altogether. Decide for yourself what foods can legitimately be considered natural and what foods that *may not grow in nature*—nut butters, for example, are still acceptable under the *natural* umbrella. Here are some points to consider:

1. Foods that do grow naturally can still be significantly affected by chemicals. Apples, for example, can be grown with or without the heavy use of manufactured chemical fertilizers, pesticides, and runoff herbicides, then waxed with a food-grade paraffin—canauba wax —or a wax made from resin. Meat animals can either be raised under "organic" conditions (without growth-promoting hormones and antibiotics, without chemicalized feed, in a natural environment) or sprayed with pesticides, drugged, fed chemical-formula feeds, and raised in man-made, biologically manipulated environments. In both cases the meat is meat and could still be considered "natural."

2. Foods such as dried fruit, nut butters, and juice that are made from foods that grow spontaneously in the environment can be more or less natural depending on the extent to which they are processed. Peanut butter that is simply ground roasted peanuts packed in a jar is different from peanut butter that has added salt, added sugar, and hydrogenated fat or vegetable oil. The *most natural* processed foods are those that have simply been given a new form through the application of time, heat, or pressure, or the addition of other foods. I call these ecologically processed foods. They are foods that—like a preservative-free loaf of whole-grain bread—you could make in your own kitchen. A commercial white bread would not be included.

[2]In terms of being nourished by natural food, the goal is to eat as close to the earth as possible, so that most of your food comes from the first stage—plants—with second- and third-stage animal foods eaten to supplement it.

Neither would concentrated orange juice, a protein-carob candy bar, or a slice of American processed cheese. These foods fall into the realm of chemical processing—several steps beyond ecological processing. When chemical processing is taken to the limit, totally new artificial but edible substances such as whipped dairy toppings and burgers made from texturized, extruded, and spun soy protein are formed.

The Definition of Organic Food

Organic foods have been defined as those foods derived from soils rich in natural minerals and living organisms that promote soil fertility. These foods are raised without the use of toxic pesticides and herbicides and without chemical fertilizers. In addition, as the organic food is grown, *positive* steps are taken to *improve* the quality of the soil and environment (natural insect control, nitrogen-fixing crop rotations, the encouragement of various species of wildlife, etc.).

But even organic foods can be more or less organic depending on the level of pollutants in the air, water, and neighboring soil and depending on how long it's been since chemicals were last used on the organic plot. Although no legal standards for organically grown food exist, farmers have independently set up organic certification programs that generally require a given plot of land to be free from chemical exposure for at least three years before the foods grown on it are certified organic.

As a consumer, some of the things you need to know about food marketed as organic follow:

1. Organic food is not raised on land that is totally free from man-applied treatments. Organic farmers use "organic" soil conditioners, for example. Yet such soil conditioners are proving to be extremely frustrating for highly conscious farmers because roughly half of the thousand commonly used organic soil conditioners are considered to be uncertifiable as truly organic. These soil conditioners may contain "natural" fish emulsions that are chemically fortified, for example, or a variety of manufactured synthetic chemicals such as ammonium sulfate and synthetic urea. The most conscientious organic producers are currently attempting to explain their preferences to fertilizer manufacturers and are occasionally having soils and fertilizers tested in laboratories at an enormous cost.

2. It is important to discriminate between organic food and organically grown food. Food that is organically grown, for example, may

be later stored in bins that have been fumigated with parathion and cyanide gas, or the organically grown food may be processed using chemical substances, or the organically grown food may be packaged in synthetic materials that have been chemically treated (chemicals are known to "migrate" from packaging to food)—dozens of possibilities exist. As a consumer, you'll have to rely on the buyer at your natural food store, and that person, in turn, will have to rely on the integrity of the company that purchases, packages, and/or processes the organic food after it has left the farm.

3. The United States Department of Agriculture (USDA) makes available reports that have found no "proved, substantiated basis" for claiming that organic foods have a greater nutrient content than chemically grown food. However, in 1978 a group of American farmers, agricultural extension agents, and state secretaries of agriculture toured organic farms in Switzerland and Germany. The U.S. investigators concluded that Europe's organic farms (thousands more exist there than in the United States) were so impressive in terms of plant health, yield, disease resistance, environmental conservation, and cost control that it would be a "mistake for those of us in the U.S. to miss the boat on basic research in biological farming."[3] According to the investigators, the preliminary results in Germany and Sweden do, in fact, suggest that some organically grown crops have higher quality protein and more nutrients than chemically grown crops.

In the United States, although little research on the nutrient quality of organically grown crops has been conducted in the last fifteen years, several studies from the 1950s suggest that the mineral quality of the soil influences the mineral balance of the foods grown in that soil.[4]

4. Even though the United States has far fewer organic farms than Europe, there are more of these here than most people realize. The reason? Money. In the last dozen years, the chemical bills on some farms increased by 800%. Not only must a farmer spray five times more pesticides this year than he did in the late 1960s to control the same number of insects, but in addition, the cost of petroleum-based fertilizers has skyrocketed. There are now more than 250 large commercial organic farms in the Corn Belt and a large number of organic citrus growers. These farmers still sell to conventional wholesalers, who mix the organic produce with chemically grown foods and sell both to supermarkets.[5]

[3]Daniel Zwerdling, "Curbing the Chemical Fix: Organic Farming—The Secret Is It Works," *The Progressive* (December 1978).
[4]Mark Schwartz, *Nutritional and Environmental Aspects of Organically Grown Food* (Emmaus, Pa.: Rodale Press).
[5]Daniel Zwerdling, "Rebirth of Organic Farming," *Nutrition Action* (August 1978).

5. The term *organic* is usually used to describe fruits, vegetables, and grains. When it is applied to meat, it refers to meats that come from animals raised on land that is managed organically. Such animals are not sprayed with, injected with, or fed feed containing pesticides, herbicides, growth hormones, or antibiotics. In addition, the animals are not raised in environmentally controlled factories, but are allowed to get adequate physical exercise in the natural environment. Animal products such as eggs are sometimes called organic if they come from animals raised in an organic manner.

Guidelines for Buying Natural and Organic Foods

Anyone who is serious about eating natural and organic foods needs to be as consumer conscious as possible. That involves understanding food costs and food quality in supermarkets and comparing these to food costs and food quality in natural and health food stores. It also requires the ability to interpret food labels—especially the labels on foods that fall into the big, poorly defined category of natural food. Following are some guidelines that you may find helpful.

Food Costs

As natural food stores become more plentiful, larger, and more efficient, the price gap narrows between foods sold in them and the foods sold in supermarkets. In 1979 *The New York Times* armed a writer with a thirty-four-item shopping list in order to compare food prices in each.[6] The supermarket total was $3.73 lower than the natural/health food store total, but the *Times* concluded that if you consider quality of food in addition to price, the best bet is to shop around.

For example, the supermarkets surveyed offered the best prices on similar-quality maple syrups, unsulfured molasses, crackers, and natural cereals. But for many brand-name natural products such as Häagen-Dazs ice cream, Celestial Seasonings herb tea, and Perrier water, the supermarket price and the natural/health food store price were much the same.

Natural food stores, however, offered better prices on grains and legumes, and sometimes *organically grown grains were actually cheaper in a*

[6]Patricia Wells, "Supermarkets Versus Health Shops: Prices Compared," *New York Times,* June 6, 1979.

natural food store than chemically grown grains were in supermarkets. Because of the great turnover in dried fruits and nuts, these, too, were cheaper in natural food stores.

When it comes to dairy foods and natural food products such as eggs and honey, be careful about comparing prices. The raw-milk butter sold in a natural food store is not the same as a butter made from pasteurized milk and sold in a supermarket. You must weigh the differences in quality, then decide whether or not those differences are worth the extra cost. But before you decide, read the specific chapter in this book given over to the food you're considering, and remember, you're not comparing stereos—you're comparing substances that end up *inside* your body. For some foods, such as eggs from free-ranging, naturally fed hens or whole-grain breads, the extra cost is, I feel, justified.

When it comes to organic fruits and vegetables and organically raised meat, the decision may be difficult, since these foods can cost twice as much as their chemical counterparts. If you can't afford to buy all of your food from organic sources, decide what foods make up the largest part of your diet and buy those foods in an organic state.

Since natural food stores usually don't receive produce deliveries as frequently as supermarkets, find out which days produce is delivered to your natural food store and shop on those days so that you'll always buy food at its nutritional peak. Remember that it's difficult for a produce buyer to obtain organic fruits and vegetables every week. Sometimes the buyer must settle for nonorganic produce. If your natural food store does not post signs indicating which fruits and vegetables can be *certified* as organic (the store should be able to produce affidavits), ask to speak with the produce buyer before you buy.

Natural food stores and mail-order natural food companies are not the only sources of certified organic foods. Many natural food co-ops have contracted directly with organic farmers in their state, and sometimes organic farmers are willing to sell directly to consumers. Your state's department of agriculture will probably have a list of organic farmers in your state that they'll send to you on request. The local natural or health food store can probably put you in touch with food co-ops.

Of course, the most dependable, satisfying, and least expensive way of obtaining organic fruits and vegetables is to grow your own. Not only will you then be assured of pesticide-, herbicide-, and chemical-fertilizer-free foods, but you'll also be treating yourself to dramatically better tasting, more nutritious fruits and vegetables.

And the satisfaction that comes with growing your own food in an ecologically positive way counts for a lot, too. There's a section on seeds on pages 206 to 210 that lists excellent sources of old-fashioned, untreated seeds, and some of the best beginning manuals on organic farming can be acquired inexpensively by writing to Rodale Press, Inc., Book Division, Emmaus, Pennsylvania 18049.

Special Labeling Notes

In 1978 nearly five hundred people across the country testified in person and five thousand others submitted written testimonies at five food-labeling hearings held jointly by the FDA, USDA, and FTC. From consumers to nutrition professionals, the overriding message was: Food labels are inadequate, confusing, and often deceptive.

The government agencies agreed, and so our food-labeling laws are in the first stages of an overhaul that's expected to take years.

Whatever new labeling laws are put into effect will, it is hoped, help the consumer make more educated food choices. But there are well-entrenched aspects of food labeling and related issues that are not likely to change, and I'd like to present some of them here.

First, all food labels must contain the following:

- Name of the product
- Net contents or net weight (the total weight including the water or liquid the food is packed in)
- Name and address of the food's manufacturer, packer, or distributor

Many foods, by law, must contain a list of ingredients, but there are approximately 350 foods that fall into the categories of milk, cheese, ice cream, frozen desserts, bread, flour, macaroni, cocoa, food dressings, canned fruit, and canned vegetables that do not have to list ingredients on the label. Instead, these foods have a "standard of identity," a recipelike formula established by the FDA that describes the specific ingredients in that standardized food. The standard of identity for mayonnaise, for example, requires that the manufacturer use eggs in making the mayonnaise, but it also allows any number of other ingredients (thickening agents, emulsifiers, artificial colors, etc.) to be used. None of these ingredients has to be listed on the mayonnaise label. The only way you can find out exactly what the basic ingredients are is by looking up the food's standard of identity in the Code of Federal Regulations.

For people who want to eat foods that are as chemical-free as possible, the standards of identity present a major problem. To what extent, for example, can we even rely on labels for natural-food-store mayonnaise, ice cream, and yogurt if the manufacturers are not *required* to list ingredients but instead choose voluntarily to print an ingredient list? By printing such a list, the manufacturer allows the consumer to believe that the ingredient list is required. In fact, because the food in question has a standard of identity, the manufacturer can selectively list some ingredients and *not list* others. A natural ice cream, for example, could have an ingredient panel listing milk, cream, and honey. That ice cream could actually contain other ingredients (emulsifiers, flavorings) allowed in the ice cream standard of identity, but the consumer would not know.

Foods that do not have a standard of identity must list ingredients. The major ingredient (by weight) must be listed first, followed by the other ingredients in descending order. But even a complete ingredient list can be deceptive. A candy bar, cookie, or snack food bought in a natural or health food store may have an ingredient list that isolates the sugars, listing them separately as honey, corn sweeteners, carob, and malt. These are dispersed among the other ingredients, so that even if you read the label, chances are you'll fail to realize how much total sugar the product contains.

There's an even more serious problem when it comes to the labels on natural food products. By carefully stringing together words such as *natural* and *pure,* which have no legal definitions, and adding short "no" phrases ("no added sugar," "no artificial ingredients," "no cholesterol") a natural food label can make a food seem wholesome without really telling you much at all about the food or the way it was made.

Most natural food manufacturers *are* committed to producing wholesome, nutritious food, and as your respect for and trust in specific natural food companies grow based on those companies' philosophy and manufacturing integrity, you can, to some extent, assume that most of the companies' products will have a similar level of quality. But sometimes natural food companies are restricted by inherent characteristics in a food, technology, or excessive cost. A manufacturer that mills stone-ground whole wheat and rye flour, for example, may produce a buckwheat flour that is not stone ground. (See the chapter "Grains and Legumes" for a full explanation.)

Therefore, consumers must read every label carefully—and cautiously. Natural food labels that indicate what a food *does not contain* still don't tell you what the food does contain—or, equally important, how and to what extent the food was processed.

Food labels may never give completely specific consumer information. As a result, learning about specific food companies is a good idea, as is reading every label with a critical eye and, most importantly, becoming more knowledgeable and confident about food.

The purpose behind the food chapters that follow is to provide you with exactly the sort of specific information you need to make educated food choices and to eat well. This book, in fact, grew out of my own frustration and lack of information. Dozens and dozens of times, it seemed, I'd ask the manager of a natural food store what the difference was between one food and the next or between a natural-food-store product and a similar product in the supermarket. The reply was usually, "This one is better for you." But "better" didn't answer my questions.

I hope the food chapters that follow answer some of yours.

Sources of Organic and Natural Foods

The food companies listed on page 116 can supply you with a mail-order list of the natural and organic foods they produce or distribute, or they can help you locate a natural-food store or market in your area that carries their products. On request, each of the companies will include certifications of their organic products.

Natural foods ordered through the mail may be marginally more expensive than store-bought natural foods because of mailing costs. However, you can actually save money buying directly from the natural foods company if the order you place is large enough. Through a school, church, or social organization you may find several other families or groups of people who'd be willing to share in one large order, which would save everyone money.

About the Recipes

As much as possible, I've tried to make the recipes in this book simple, flexible, and nourishing—but also imaginative and, of course, delicious.

To maximize the healthfulness and flavor of each dish, use the freshest ingredients you can obtain. If the recipe calls for an herb, for example, use fresh herbs if you can. Always use the freshest fruits, vegetables, fish, and meats. Please refer to the buying guide for natural and organic produce before buying foods labeled either (see page 111).

	Herbs	*Grains and Flours*	*Beans*	*Cereals and Mixes*	*Pancakes, Cookies, Muffins*	*Oils*	*Nuts and Seeds*	*Cheese*	*Meat*	*Other Products**
Arrowhead Mills P.O. Box 866 Hereford, TX 79045		•	•	•	•	•	•			honey, jams, peanut butter, fruit butter
Chico-San P.O. Box 1004 Chico, CA 95926		•								rice syrup, rice cakes, tamari
Diamond K Enterprises Rt. 1, Box 30 St. Charles, MN 55972		•		•	•	•	•			birdseed
Erewhon Inc. 3 East Street Cambridge, MA 02141		•	•	•	•	•	•	•		many: carob, tamari, pasta, utensils, etc.
Manna Milling 827 NW 49 Street Seattle, WA 98107		•		•	•					
Nichols Garden Nursery 1190 North Pacific Albany, OR 97321	•	•	•	•	•	•				many: planting seeds, flour, corn, garlic
Shiloh Farms, Inc. Box 97, Sulphur Springs, AR 72768 Eastern Office: White Oak Road Martindale, PA 17549	•	•	•	•	•	•	•	•	•	many: specialties: organic meat, fish, pizza, apple butter
Walnut Acres Penns Creek, PA 17862		•	•	•	•	•	•	•		dried fruit, pasta, honey

* The best sources for some foods are local sources. For top-quality honey, write your state department of agriculture for a list of local apiaries. For unpasteurized juices and fresh and dried fruits and vegetables, request a list of local orchards and farmers' markets. For raw cow and goat's milk and cheese, request a list of certified dairies.

Follow the recommendations throughout the book when choosing each ingredient. When the recipe calls for eggs, for example, use eggs from free-ranging hens if possible. When the recipe calls for honey, use honey that has been heated and filtered as little as possible. Use cornmeal that is undegerminated and flour that is stone-ground.

Whenever oil is called for, please use an unrefined oil, as explained in the chapter on edible oils. Also, when dairy products are called for, use low-fat versions. When butter is called for, you can, if you prefer, substitute an unrefined vegetable oil in some of the recipes. This will change the flavor, however. In all cases I've tried to keep the amount of butter required to a minimum. Always use sweet (unsalted) butter.

Some of the recipes call for large cakes of tofu (Japanese tofu). The smaller, firmer Chinese-style cakes may also be used. When the recipe calls for well-drained tofu, please make sure as much moisture as possible has been removed. See page 160 for instructions on draining tofu.

Other recipes call for yogurt to be drained of its whey (the watery liquid). To do this, line a sieve with cheesecloth and allow the yogurt to drain for several hours or overnight in the refrigerator. A paper coffee filter can also be used, as can a yogurt cheese maker—a simple cheesecloth stand used for draining yogurt. The one I'm familiar with is marketed by Dannon. Note that the whey contains a good portion of nutrients and should be saved for another use: stocks, soups, blender drinks, etc.

Many of the recipes call for vegetable stock, which is preferred over water because it adds both nutrients and flavor. Vegetable stocks are easy to make from vegetable trimmings (see page 166), and it's a good idea to have a jar of stock in the refrigerator for easy use at all times. If a recipe calls for vegetable stock and you do not have any on hand, a quick substitute can be made with Morga vegetable bouillon cubes or Marmite (brewer's yeast extract with dried vegetables).

Finally, I've chosen not to include numbers of servings for each of the recipes. The number of people one dish will serve depends, of course, on many factors: who's doing the eating, how hungry they are, and also when the dish is being served. A vegetable casserole, for example, serves more people as a side dish than as a main dish.

Both from a cooking and an eating standpoint, I'd prefer to let you judge how many people a certain recipe will serve. By simply reading through each recipe first, I think you'll have a clear idea of the amount of food you'll be working with. You can then adjust the recipe up or down based on your own needs.

Grains and Legumes

Grains and beans are a Southerner's shibboleth: hot and crumbly spoonbread, grits, bowls of buttered black-eyed peas. In New England they're an American tradition: baked-for-hours baked beans, oatmeal, raisiny Boston brown bread. When the West was a boom town, grains and beans were life itself. As the frontier grew tame, the chili grew hellish.

The culinary partnership between grains and legumes (beans, peas, lentils) is pervasive. Virtually every national cuisine combines the two in a special regional dish: pasta, polenta,[1] and white beans (Italy), cassoulet and French bread (France), tortillas and red beans (Mexico and South America), millet or rice and tofu, miso, shoyu (China and Japan), lentils, split peas, and rice (India). Grain and legume dishes aren't coincidental. The two foods are plentiful and taste good together for a reason: Combined, they have extraordinary nutritional clout.

Both contain large amounts of protein compared with other plant foods. Grains are seeds; they contain, therefore, the concentrated protein and other nutrients that allow the seed to burst into life. Legumes are plants that have a special capacity to convert nitrogen in the soil to amino acids—the substances from which proteins are made. Those proteins are then stored in the plant's seed, bean, or pea. And when grains and legumes are eaten together, the protein of each is better utilized by the body. (Please see the chapter "Protein.")

Grains and beans share other nutritional assets. Because they're plants, both are low in fat. The exception is peanuts, a legume relatively high in unsaturated fat much like the nuts with which it's usually grouped.

Also, like all plants, grains and legumes are low on the food chain —in other words, their nourishment comes directly from the earth. As a result, even though grains and legumes may be sprayed with

[1]Polenta is a thick cornmeal porridge that is sometimes eaten soft and very hot, usually dripping in a rich homemade sauce, and sometimes eaten after it's cooled and hardened, whereupon it's cut into squares, spread with fresh butter and sprinkled with freshly grated Parmesan. Hardened polenta is also sometimes sliced and arranged in layers with slices of sautéed mushroom, chicken liver, and veal. The whole dish is well sauced, then baked.

chemicals, they don't accumulate and concentrate chemical residues in their tissues as animals do by eating plants. Meat, fish, and poultry contain about thirteen times more pesticide residues than plants or plant products.

The Grains

Wheat

Wheat has been harvested somewhere on the earth every month of the year for the last eight thousand years.[2]

Almost all of that wheat (*trillions* of bushels each year) has been, and continues to be, made into bread. Wheat seeds have a protein/starch structure that allows them to be worked and worked until a sticky tension develops between the wheat cells. The tension—a kind of elasticity and resistance, pushing and pulling at the same time—is the mark of gluten, a protein substance formed from the two specific proteins gluten and gliadin. Bread results when gluten is attacked by yeast cells and the carbon dioxide bubbles that are given off stretch and swell the wheat's starchy core into large, upstanding loaves.

The earliest wheat farmers, however, did not bake their wheat into bread. Leavened bread—bread that has risen with the help of yeast—was not made until roughly 3,000 B.C., when the Egyptians began milling flour by grinding kernels of wheat between stones. Before that, grain was pounded by hand in mortars, but the meal that formed was simply not cohesive enough to hold the carbon dioxide bubbles that puff wheat dough into bread.[3]

Strangely enough, by the time stone-grinding was developed, fermenting wheat with yeast was already a common practice. Hand-pounded wheat meal was mixed with wine or simply set in the sun where wild yeasts would ferment it naturally. The result would be a soured porridge that could be added to coarse dough, shaped into a flat oval, and baked into a sort of sourdough pancake. By allowing half-baked sourdough pancakes to ferment further and using the

[2]More than 2 billion bushels of it are harvested in the United States each year from almost every state in the union. Most of that wheat, however, has its seed in the soil of a grain triangle that sweeps across northern Ohio, along the Great Lakes and the Canadian border to Washington, then works its way down until both sides, stretching south, meet at a point somewhere in Texas.

Here, too, more corn is harvested than in all the rest of the world combined (excluding the U.S.S.R.). Nearly all of the world's soybeans grow here, as well as a good half of the world oat crop.

[3]The term *leavened* is used to describe *all* breads that have been raised by yeast, including what are called "unyeasted" breads (breads left to rise by natural yeast in the air). Unleavened bread contains no yeast and therefore hasn't risen. Crackers and matzo are examples.

yeast liquid that resulted, the Egyptians made their own version of beer.

Wheat is separated into two broad categories: winter wheat and spring wheat. Winter wheat is planted in warm and temperate climates during the fall, grows a bit before the cool weather, lies dormant, then grows rapidly throughout the spring and is harvested in summer.

Spring wheat is the opposite. Planted in northern climates as soon as the ground is warm enough to work, spring wheat grows throughout the summer and is harvested in the fall. The further north wheat is planted, the higher its protein content. In this country, wheat raised in Montana may have as much as 4% more protein than wheat raised in Colorado.

The many varieties of winter and spring wheat are grouped into five classes. When you buy whole wheat kernels in a natural food store—or in bulk from a feed store—you have the option of choosing among them.

Hard Red Spring Wheat. The flour that is ground from hard red spring wheat is topnotch bread flour—high in protein. The kernels are short, thick, and hard.

Hard Red Winter Wheat. More than half the U.S. wheat crop is hard red winter wheat, for it is hard red winter wheat that is planted throughout the Midwest. The kernels are longer and narrower than hard red spring wheat kernels. The flour is used for bread and general baking. The protein content varies widely depending on the soil.

Soft Red Winter Wheat. Soft red winter wheat is grown in the eastern United States and is high in starch and lower in protein than the hard wheats. Soft red wheat is ground into pastry flour for cakes, crackers, snack foods, and commercial pastries. Because it is low in gluten, it is not good for bread baking.

White Wheat. White wheat is used for commercial bakery products other than bread. It's low in protein and low in gluten and an all-around poor choice.

Durum Wheat. Durum is an extremely hard wheat grown in the northern United States for pasta and all macaroni products. Some pasta is made from semolina, a ground durum that is coarser than durum flour.

Wheat Berries

Before wheat was used to bake bread, it was eaten as porridge. The grains were toasted, mixed with water, and boiled into a gruel. Toasted wheat has a delicate nuttiness, and even the original porridge makers must have mixed berries and nuts with their wheat to give it a sweeter flavor. Whole wheat berries can still be eaten this way. Soak the berries overnight, cook them for two to three hours to a chewy softness, then add milk or cream, nuts and raisins, fruit, honey, or a drop of maple syrup. Today most of the wheat not eaten as bread is eaten not as whole-wheat-berry porridge, however, but as cracked wheat, bulgur, couscous, or pasta.

Cracked Wheat

Cracked wheat is simply wheat berries that have been broken up into smaller pieces so that they'll cook faster. You can do this yourself by grinding wheat berries to a coarse texture in a flour mill or grinding them carefully in a blender (straining the cracked wheat from the bit of flour that will result). Cracked wheat will require different cooking times depending on the size of the pieces, but 20 to 30 minutes on the average.

Bulgur

Bulgur, the staple grain of Eastern Europe and used throughout the Mideast, is cracked wheat that has been cooked before it's cracked. Bulgur can be used interchangeably with cracked wheat; it is, however, a bit nuttier in flavor and cooks in a shorter period of time since it has been precooked.

Bulgur can be bought in any natural food store, but you can also make it at home. Homemade versions can be given slightly different flavors by varying cooking times and by adding different herbs, seasonings, or sweeteners (apple juice or raisins) to the wheat berries as they cook.

To make bulgur:

Gently boil whole wheat berries in twice their volume of water or stock for 45 minutes to 1 hour. If you're going to use the bulgur in main-dish casseroles, to stuff peppers, squashes, eggplant, chicken, or turkey, or to eat it along with roasted meat, you may want to tie a few bay leaves, sprigs of parsley and thyme, and chopped celery, carrots, and onion in cheesecloth, then drop the whole bag into the cooking pot to simmer along with the wheat.

When the wheat is soft but firm, drain it well and spread it on a baking sheet. Place it in a 225° F oven, stir the berries occasionally, and cook them until completely dry—45 minutes to 1¼ hours. Turn the oven up to 400° and toast the berries lightly for 5 minutes. This will give them an extra nuttiness. Be careful, they scorch easily.

Wheat Taboos

In rural Turkey, wheat is considered to be God's blessing. Ears of it are hung over doorways to protect the home and assure fertility, health, and general good fortune. An ear of wheat is the emblem of Turkey's new left, reformist political party.

Its significance is so great, in fact, that wheat is almost personified. Offenses against it are divinely punished. Bread is never allowed to touch the floor or ground, and to step on it is the worst transgression. Turkish children are taught to kiss fallen bread and to touch it to their forehead as an apology to God.

It is forbidden to urinate, defecate, or have intercourse in a wheat field, or to perform any of those three acts with wheat or bread on one's person. Bread, it is taught, should never be left uneaten at a meal, and when it is eaten, it is kept carefully above the waist and away from the lower, or profane, half of the body. Often, in fact, bread is placed on a small pedestal so that it is raised even higher than other foods.

Never is it thrown away, for to waste bread would be to defy God.

To an American, Turkish wheat taboos may seem severe. But anthropologists say that wheat, as the most powerful symbol, serves a key purpose in Turkish life. Wheat is a reminder of one's relationship to God. It gives a person an expanded perspective so that what is fundamental, what is valuable, and what is proper is not lost sight of.

Adapted from *The Anthropologists' Cookbook,* ed. Jessica Kuper (New York: Universe Books, 1977), pp. 61–68.

Let the wheat cool, crack it coarsely in a blender, and you now have bulgur. Store the bulgur in clean, dry containers and cook it as you need it. Homemade bulgur will cook up in 15 minutes.

Couscous

The best couscous is made when whole wheat or millet flour is made into a dough that is then worked into tiny pellets of grain, or couscous. When these bits of grain are steamed, they become incredibly light and fluffy. In North Africa the grain couscous is seasoned with saffron and mixed with lamb and vegetables to make a dish also called couscous. Traditionally the dish is made in a couscoussiere—a double boiler of sorts, where the lamb is braised in the lower half of the pot and the couscous grains steamed above.

The couscous available in the United States—especially the packaged couscous found in supermarkets—is made from semolina wheat, a type of durum wheat used in pasta. This produces a good couscous, although you can make a more nutritious one yourself by grinding whole millet in a grain mill until each piece has been cracked into three or more smaller pieces.

A couscoussiere is not essential for cooking couscous. You can fashion your own steamer by placing cheesecloth in a colander or strainer and fitting this inside a pot over boiling water or stock or, if you're making a traditional couscous, over a simmering stew of lamb and vegetables. Couscous steamed this way will require at least 30 minutes cooking time.

Couscous can be cooked more simply, however, by sautéing some minced onion (or leeks, peppers, or scallions) in an unrefined oil (I use sesame for this). Then, in the same sautéing pan, make a strong broth by adding Madeira, sherry, or tamari and stock. Season the broth with herbs or spices, bring it to a gentle boil, and immediately add

Couscous with Mushrooms and Cinnamon

- 1 T. safflower oil
- 1 T. butter
- ½ lb. mushrooms, sliced
- 1 clove garlic, minced
- 3 t. dried tarragon
- 2 t. dried oregano
- 1½ c. vegetable stock
- ¼ c. tamari
- 1 t. curry powder
- 2 t. ground cinnamon
- ½ c. raisins (optional)
- ½ c. chopped parsley
- 1 c. uncooked couscous

1. Combine the safflower oil and the butter in a large, heavy skillet. Sauté the mushrooms and garlic over moderately high heat for 2 to 3 minutes, or until they begin to brown. Sprinkle with the tarragon and oregano.

2. Add the vegetable stock or water, tamari, curry powder, and cinnamon to the mushrooms. Bring to a boil. Add the raisins and cook for 1 minute.

3. Quickly stir in the parsley. Stir in the couscous. Cover the skillet with a tight-fitting lid and remove from the heat. Allow the couscous to rest off the heat until all of the liquid is absorbed (about 10 minutes). Do not stir during this time.

4. If the couscous seems dry, sprinkle lightly with water, toss, and heat briefly before serving in a warm bowl. If it's sufficiently moist, simply toss, heat momentarily, and serve with something moist—pureed vegetables or creamed eggs, for example.

the couscous. (In Morocco, couscous is often made with raisins. If you like raisins, now is the time to add them too, since the hot broth will plump and warm them.) Cover the pan, take it off the heat, and allow the couscous to sit undisturbed while it absorbs the broth—about 15 minutes. Cooked this way, the couscous in effect steams itself. One cup of dry couscous absorbs 2 cups of boiling broth. After the broth is absorbed, the couscous will be lumped together. If it seems dry, you can sprinkle it with a bit more hot broth and allow it to rest again. Finally, oil your fingers lightly and gently toss the couscous until the grains have separated. Mix with fresh herbs and something interesting: nuts, fruits, or sautéed mushrooms, peas, zucchini, or peppers are just a few possibilities. Couscous—since it's the lightest grain—can also be sprinkled cold over salads.

Cooking Pasta and Noodles

*Here is the technique for cooking Italian pasta, Chinese noodles, Japanese wheat noodles (*udon *and* hiyamugi*), and the traditional Japanese buckwheat noodle* —soba.

- One pound of pasta or noodles requires a minimum of a gallon of water. When too little water is used, the noodles clump together and cook slowly and unevenly.
- The water must be boiling rapidly before the noodles are added to it. A bit of sea salt, added to the water, will bring out the noodles' flavor.
- Drop the noodles into the rapidly boiling water, without breaking them. As they soften, they'll naturally slip beneath the water.
- Keep the water boiling and stir the noodles occasionally. Test them for doneness by pulling a strand out and biting into it. The noodle should be firm.
- The instant the noodles are done, drain them in a colander, transfer them to a warm bowl, and toss with a sauce. If noodles aren't covered with sauce, they become gummy.
- Few foods are as versatile as pasta when it comes to a sauce. Besides tomato sauce, which can be spiced tens of different ways, you can make a delicious vegetable sauce. The Italians, for example, puree cooked carrots and combine them with parsley, butter, and freshly grated Parmesan. *Pesto,* another traditional Italian sauce, combines fresh basil, olive oil, garlic, pignolia nuts, and Parmesan cheese. Oriental sauces are also excellent. One of the simplest is achieved by blending in a blender a cake of tofu with ¼ to ⅓ cup sesame oil, ⅓ cup tahini, the juice of half a lemon, 2 cloves garlic, and—if you like a more piquant sauce—a dash of tamari.

Spaghettini Primavera in Lemon–Cream Sauce

1½	lemons
¼	lb. mushrooms, thinly sliced
1	T. butter
1	c. broccoli flowerets, separated into small pieces
1	c. shelled fresh peas
3	T. chopped fresh basil leaves
1	lb. uncooked whole wheat or spinach spaghettini (very thin spaghetti)
1¼	c. light cream
¼	c. kirsch
1	t. freshly grated nutmeg
	pine nuts (optional)

1. With a very sharp knife or citrus zester, remove the lemons' zest (outer yellow skin), being careful to avoid the white pith, which is very bitter. Mince the zest as finely as possible.

2. Briefly sauté the mushrooms in the butter, just enough to take away their rawness. Remove to a warm bowl.

3. Separate the broccoli flowerets into small pieces. Steam them, then the peas, just until crisp tender. This will take about 3 to 4 minutes for the broccoli, 1½ to 2 minutes for the peas. (Both can also be dropped briefly into boiling water, then removed with a slotted spoon when just tender.) Sprinkle the broccoli and peas with the basil, then add to the warm bowl with the mushrooms.

4. Cook the pasta in boiling salted water until tender, approximately 8 to 10 minutes.

5. As the pasta cooks, combine the cream and lemon zest in a large skillet. Cook, stirring, over medium-low heat for 5 minutes. Add the kirsch. Stir in the juice of half a lemon. Grate the fresh nutmeg into the sauce.

6. Drain the spaghettini. Quickly add the vegetables to the sauce. Stir lightly. Add the spaghettini. Toss lightly, keeping a low flame if necessary. Remove to a warmed serving platter and serve with a bowl of pine nuts for sprinkling on top.

Pasta

If I could eat wheat in only one form other than bread, it would be pasta. Not brittle, pale white straws of dried spaghetti cooked into a tasteless mass, but broad sashes of fresh green lasagna, long strands of nutty whole wheat fettuccine, and gnocchi made with spinach, potatoes, egg yolk, Parmesan cheese, and whole-grain wheat or millet crushed to a cereal-like texture.

There are many varieties of pasta: noodles—flat or round, thin or fat; tubular rounds of macaroni, such as ziti and rigatoni; long spaghetti types, such as linguine. Fresh, these pastas have an unmistakable luscious, delicate flavor, but unless you live near an old-fashioned Italian market or make it yourself, fresh pasta is hard to find.

Of the dried forms of pasta, an overwhelming majority is made from semolina—coarsely ground durum wheat. In natural food stores, however, you'll find whole-grain pasta, increasingly in many shapes and sizes.

Whole-grain pastas (and whole-grain Japanese and Chinese noodles), like whole-grain breads, are more nutritious than pastas made from refined flour and have a heartier, slightly nutty flavor. You may need to cook them half a minute longer. But all noodles should be cooked *al dente*—firm to the bite. If you can mash a noodle against the roof of your mouth easily, it's too soggy to be worth eating.

Rice

Of the 200 million pounds of rice harvested in the world each year, only 1% is harvested in America, though, ironically, we're the world's third largest exporter. While other countries eat every bit of rice they produce, we hardly touch ours at all.

Rice is the bread of Asia—eaten every day, usually with every meal. But it holds a different place in Eastern ideology than bread does in the West. For many Americans bread is a second-class food, a filler—something to drop an egg on, melt cheese over, pick up sliced meat with. By itself bread lacks identity.

Rice, on the other hand, is an esteemed food in precisely those countries that consume the most of it. It is the core of a meal; vegetables, seafood, and bits of meat are balanced around it. Westerners often think this is because people in Asian countries can afford no better. But that explanation is a projection of our own bread-as-filler philosophy. In Japan the poorest farmers sell their rice for money and eat millet or wheat instead. In China the poor eat a lower quality rice mixed with potatolike tubers. Throughout Asia good-quality rice is considered an extremely valuable food—one that has a flavor so pure that it cannot be fabricated. Among the wealthy, the philosophers, and the gourmets of the East, rice has been (and continues to be) exalted for its utter simplicity and its nourishing, calming effects on the stomach and body. In Japan the standard meal for the highest samurais was miso soup and a bowl of rice. The best Japanese *sushi* chefs are said to know exactly how many grains of rice will balance perfectly the flavor of different fishes, and they make their *sushi* accordingly.

Rice is thought to have a series of flavors, beginning with a mild

Brown Risotto

- 1 T. safflower oil
- 1 T. butter
- 1 medium-size onion, finely chopped
- ½ lb. mushrooms, sliced
- 1 c. uncooked long-grain brown rice
- ½ c. dry white wine
- 1¼ c. vegetable, fish, or chicken stock
- ½ c. water
- ½ c. almonds, thinly sliced
- ¼ c. minced parsley
- herbal salt to taste
- ½ c. freshly grated Parmesan cheese (optional)

1. In a large, heavy skillet, heat the safflower oil and butter. When hot, add the onion and sauté until transparent. Add the mushrooms and toss over high heat for 2 to 3 minutes, or until the mushrooms just begin to brown.

2. Add the rice to the mushrooms and onion. Turn the heat down to moderate and stir the grains continuously so that they don't burn. Roast this way for about 3 minutes, or until the grains themselves begin to take on a tinge of deeper brown.

3. Splash in the wine. Stir. Add the stock and water, stir again, then cover the skillet. Allow the mixture to just come to a boil.

4. Stir in the almonds and parsley. Cover the skillet and turn the heat down as far as possible. Allow the rice to cook undisturbed for 1 hour. Do not stir during this time, or the rice will be gummy. Five minutes before the rice is done, sprinkle lightly with salt and grate in the Parmesan. Stir briefly over high heat for a few minutes. Fold the risotto into a warmed covered bowl and serve.

textural chewiness, progressing to a delicate, sweet juiciness, and ending with a slightly nutty aftertaste. As the grain is eaten, more and more of the flavor is unlocked. Japanese and Chinese chefs are meticulous when cooking it, in fact. An ounce too much or too little of water can make rice tasteless, they say. On the other hand, different tastes are achieved by varying the amount of water and type of rice. The Chinese, for example, often eat *congee* (usually for breakfast) in place of fluffy cooked rice. *Congee* is short-grain rice made into a grainy gruel, the rice and water so interlocked as to form almost a pudding. Too much water here and the grains simply rest in a puddle of water. Too little water and the *congee* is pasty.

Each different variety of rice available in America has its own flavor and cooking characteristics and is therefore well suited to some dishes and poorly suited to others.

Rice Bread

⅔	c. uncooked brown rice	4	c. water
⅓	c. uncooked sweet brown rice	5	c. whole wheat flour
		1	t. herbal salt

1. Put both kinds of rice into a heavy saucepan and cover with water. Bring to a boil, cover, turn the heat very low, and allow the rice to cook for 45 minutes.
2. Place the saucepan full of cooked wet rice in a warm place. Allow it to stand, uncovered, for 24 to 30 hours, or until sour.
3. Mix together the whole wheat flour and salt. Add to the soured rice mixture. The dough will be soft and sticky, but knead it as best you can until the rice and flour are evenly mixed throughout. Add more flour if the dough is too moist. Allow the dough to rest and dry out for 30 minutes.
4. Separate the dough into two masses. Oil 2 small loaf pans and fill them to two-thirds capacity with dough. Cover the pans with a cotton towel. Place them in a warm, moist environment until the dough has risen above the top of the loaf pan (this may take several hours).
5. Preheat oven to 400°F.
6. Bake in the preheated oven for 15 minutes; then at 350° for 1 to 1¼ hours.

Makes 2 loaves.

Short- and Medium-Grain Rice. These short, plump grains cling together after cooking and are tender and moist. Some people find them sticky, but it is precisely short-grain rice's cohesiveness that makes it best for croquettes, puddings, and rice balls.

Long-Grain Rice. Long-grain rice is preferable with seafood or meat or in curries, stuffings, and salads, since it is lighter and fluffier than short or medium grain.

Wild Rice. Wild rice isn't really a variety of rice, but a rare aquatic grass. Wild rice has not been successfully commercially cultivated, so the wild rice that's available is literally harvested in the wild (in this country, near the Great Lakes).

Depending on the extent to which it's processed, rice can be one of the following:

Brown Rice. The whole, unpolished grain with only the hull and a small bit of the bran removed. Brown rice is nutritionally superior to white rice: more protein, carbohydrate, fiber, calcium, iron, thiamine, and niacin; much more phosphorus and potassium; and 100% more vitamin E. Brown rice requires a bit more water and slightly longer cooking. It's chewier and has a nutty flavor. Wild rice, like brown rice, is whole and unpolished.

White Rice (sometimes called polished). White rice that has had the hull and bran milled from it until only a white kernel remains. Because most of the vitamins, minerals, and some of the protein are concentrated in the bran layers that have been removed, white rice is not as nutritious as brown rice and is sometimes sold enriched. Only a fraction of the original nutrients (.7 mg iron, .09 mg thiamine, and .6 mg niacin per 100 g) is added back, however.

Parboiled Rice (sometimes called converted). Rice that has been steamed and pressurized before being milled into white rice. This process drives some of the nutrients into the rice kernel so that after it's milled, parboiled rice contains more of the original nutrients than regular white rice does. If you must buy white rice, parboiled is preferable.

Precooked Rice. White rice that has been partially cooked after milling, then dehydrated so that it will cook faster.

Rice is often heavily treated with pesticides and herbicides because it is a delicate crop, highly susceptible to disease, infestation, and weeds such as the aquatic sedge—the nemesis of American rice farmers. One of the major organic rice farms in America, for example, reported as many as five hundred sedges to every ten rice plants the first few years they tried growing without herbicides. To combat the sedge, most nonorganic rice farmers use a highly potent weed killer. Organic rice, then, should be a priority even if you don't buy other organic grains.

Only in the last few years have small organic farmers—through ground preparation, flash-flooding, and special hoeing—been able to lick the problems of growing rice without chemicals. The production of organic brown rice is still small, therefore, and the cost high. In natural food stores the brown rice usually sold in bins is not organic unless a label specifically states that it is.

Oats

Compared with other grains, oats are fat little nuggets. The edible inside, called an oat groat, rests between two inedible outer husks that must be removed before the groat can be milled. To remove these husks, the oat is steamed, dried in a kiln, then rubbed between a horizontal pair of milling stones until the dry, brittle husk pops loose.

The best way to cook whole oat groats is the way they're cooked in Scotland—slowly, in an iron kettle, all night long. By breakfast time the oats are reduced to a thick, creamy porridge—an extraordinary breakfast early on a winter morning when the house itself is aching with cold and the sun seems to shatter like glass in the freezing air.

But, of course, most oats are not cooked whole, nor are they cooked all night.

Oatmeal Cookies

1¾ c. rolled oats
1 c. whole wheat flour or ½ c. whole wheat flour, ½ c. rye or corn flour, plus ¼ c. wheat or rye berries cracked in a blender
1½ t. baking powder
½ t. herbal salt
6 T. butter, softened
2 T. date sugar, finely ground
2 T. honey
1 egg, well beaten
1½ t. vanilla extract
2 T. apple juice
½ c. or more raw cashews, chopped*
½ c. raisins
⅓ c. chopped dried apples

1. Preheat oven to 350°F.
2. Mix together the oats, flour (or flour-berries mixture), baking powder, and salt. Set aside.
3. In a large bowl, cream together the butter and date sugar until it is blended as much as possible (it will remain slightly grainy).
4. To the butter add the honey, egg, vanilla, and apple juice. Mix well.
5. Slowly stir the dry ingredients into the liquid ingredients. Adjust as necessary by adding a bit more apple juice if the batter seems dry.
6. Fold in the cashews and then the raisins and dried apples.
7. Drop by the spoonful onto a greased cookie sheet and bake in the preheated oven for approximately 15 minutes. Cookies should be lightly browned when done.

Makes 1 to 2 dozen, depending on size.

*Cashews are suggested because their flavor goes very well with oats, but almonds or walnuts could be substituted.

Steel-Cut Scotch Oats. Steel-cut rolled oats, sometimes called Scotch oats, are made from groats cut into tiny pieces. When the pieces are rolled, the oat flakes that result are much thinner than whole groats, cook in half the time (about 1 hour), and are just as tasty and nutritious as whole groats.

In Scotland today, 1 cup of steel-cut rolled oats is cooked with about 3 cups of water and a pinch of salt for just a few minutes, until the oats are softened. The oats are then put in the refrigerator overnight, to be brought out the next morning and cooked in a double boiler for 30 minutes, then eaten with cream and sugar.

Instant Oats. The quick-cooking or "instant" oats you find here in supermarkets are the result of more modern processing. These oats are cut, then steamed before they're rolled into extremely thin flakes. They do cook quickly but seem to have a raw taste. Quaker oats in the red cylinder are the quick-cooking variety. Instant *oatmeal* is not the same as instant *oats,* however. Instant oatmeal is invariably packaged with sugar.

Rolled, Table-Cut Oats. The oats sold by natural food stores are usually rolled, table-cut oats. These are virtually the same as Quaker's quick-cooking oats, but perhaps a bit thicker, which makes them chewier in a bowl of oatmeal and in homemade granola.

Oats are always better tasting if you toast them first. To do this, simply spread them on a baking sheet and slip them into a 400°F oven for 5 to 10 minutes. Turn them often with a spatula so that they toast evenly.

Oats can be made into more dishes than anyone would ever think possible. A good old-fashioned bowl of oatmeal, though, is oats in their glory. Breakfast is the perfect time for eating them because, relative to other grains, oats are high in unsaturated fat (so they're filling and warming) and one of the higher protein grains.

Barley

Like wheat and rice, barley begins as a dull brown grain encased in a protective hull. A barley hull, however, is several nutrient-rich layers thick and is tightly fused to the grain's starchy core below. Scraping these layers off is no easy process, but when the milling is finally complete, what's left is a small white "pearl" of barley, a polished bead of almost vitaminless starch.

Pearl barley is the barley most often sold for eating in the United States and the only form of barley found in supermarkets. Natural brown barley is difficult to find even in natural food stores. When you do find it, the barley will already be partially hulled, but it won't be milled down to a naked white pebble. Natural brown barley is sweeter, nuttier, chewier, and more nutritious than pearled. In vegetable casseroles it's delicate and superb.

The best variety of barley for eating purposes is actually a hull-less barley grown in the Orient and only occasionally available here. Hull-less barley does have a thin hull, but one that can be easily removed without significantly damaging the nutrient-rich layers below. Hull-less barley is almost never grown here because most of our barley is not eaten; it's drunk as six packs of beer, and hull-less barley is simply not as well suited to making beer as hard-hulled barley is.

Buckwheat

In the Ukraine and Eastern Europe, it's called kasha, and you have only to whisper "kasha varnishkas" to be welcomed in a warm embrace.

Buckwheat requires a developed taste, for the groats are big, chewy, dry, and have a very strong flavor all their own. If you've never tried them, *don't* cook up a pot and eat them alone (alone, their flavor has been described as "chopped doormat"). Break yourself in gradually. Find a good Russian, Hungarian, or Jewish cookbook and make one of the traditional buckwheat dishes. Make sure it has a sauce.

In China, where buckwheat has been a staple for centuries, the groats are ground into buckwheat flour, which is mixed with other flours and made into a delicious bread. In my house every ounce of buckwheat flour seems to find its way into a stack of no-beating-around-the-bush pancakes that wrestle with the maple syrup for the heavyweight taste title.

Millet

Millet is a light, tasty grain that can be used in most dishes and meals that call for rice (and may be preferable to rice in stuffings and casseroles, since it's lighter).

Millet was, in fact, the staple grain in China before rice and is still eaten today, especially in northern China, where it's made into cakes, cookies, breads, and puddings.

The millet you find in natural food stores is hulled, but hulling is unavoidable, since the tough millet hull is inedible.

Storing Grains

No matter how thoroughly a grain is cleaned, nor how careful the farmer, distributor, and store owner, a sack of grain or seed may contain one or two dormant insect eggs. If it does, that loose, old-fashioned bag of rolled oats you buy may be draped with a webby cocoon in no time, that box of grain or pack of seeds hung with molds, which grow when free-floating spores in the air settle down on moist, warm kernels.

Neither insects nor mold will be a problem, however, if you store grains and seeds in tightly closed clean, dry *jars* and keep the jars in a relatively cool, dry dark place. In the summertime, or in hot, humid climates, you may want to refrigerate them.

When buying grains and seeds from open bins or bulk gunny sacks in natural food stores, make sure the storekeeper has taken some care, too. The temperature in the store should be cool, the air dry, and although open fifty-pound sacks of millet and rice look homey, covered bins are better.

Cooking Grains

A heavy pot with a close-fitting lid is all you need to cook any grain perfectly well. You may want to use a pressure cooker for whole grains (brown rice, whole barley, millet), but cracked grains such as bulgur or cracked wheat will clog the vent, so they must be cooked in a regular pot. One of the best ways to cook any grain is in a double boiler, since the grain will cook more slowly and evenly and never scorch, and the final texture will be uniformly smooth.

Here is the most basic method for cooking grains:

1. Rinse the grain in cold water and drain.
2. Bring water, stock, or milk to a boil.
3. Pour in grain, then add a bit of sea salt.
4. Let liquid come to a second boil. Stir the grain once and turn the heat down as far as possible.
5. Let the grain cook, covered (or mostly covered), until all the water is absorbed. If you stir the grain often, fiddle with the heat, cover and uncover the pot to "see how it's doing," the grain will probably become gummy.

Whole grains by nature are more chewy and sticky than refined grains. You learn to love this (and chew with more gusto), but in the beginning you may want to lessen the stickiness by mixing dry grain with a beaten egg (1 egg to every cup of grain), then cooking the mixture in the pot over low heat until the grain is dry again and the

Grain Cooking Chart

*1 Cup Dry Grain**	*Water†*	*Approximate Cooking Time‡*	*Yield*
Barley (brown)	3 cups	1¼ hours	3 cups
Buckwheat (kasha)	2 cups	15 minutes	2½ cups
Bulgur	2 cups	25 minutes	2½ cups
Cornmeal (polenta)§	3½ to 4 cups	30 minutes	3 cups
Couscous (quick method)‖	2 cups	10 to 15 minutes	3 cups
Cracked wheat and rye	2 cups	30 minutes	2⅓ cups
Millet	3 cups	45 minutes	3 cups
Oats (rolled)	1½ to 2 cups	1 hour or more	2 cups
Rice (brown)	2 to 2½ cups	1 hour	3 cups
Whole wheat berries	3 to 3½ cups	2 hours	2⅔ cups
Wild rice	3½ cups	1 hour or more	3½ cups

* Grains can be toasted for 10 to 15 minutes in a dry frying pan before cooking to bring out their nuttiness. Use a low flame. Stir often. Adding a beaten egg to the grain during this time will reduce the grain's stickiness later. Stir until egg is absorbed.

† Use cold water or stock and add a bit of sea salt. The amount of liquid should be increased if you like grain softer and moister or are cooking it as a porridge.

‡ In a covered pot. Pressure cookers take less time.

§ Polenta scorches easily and is best cooked slowly, uncovered, in the top of a double boiler.

‖ See page 122.

kernels separate. Make sure all the egg is absorbed before adding the water and proceeding as usual.

Although natural grains cooked in water and eaten alone with a dab of dairy or nut butter are fine, they're not nearly as good-tasting as grains can be made to be. The nuttiness of grains is always improved if you first toast them (in a dry pan, over a low flame, for 10 to 15 minutes), then sauté them in a bit of unrefined oil with onions, leeks, red or green sweet pepper, mushrooms or sesame seeds, and lots of any fresh herb (and *garlic*). As a cooking liquid, use something more flavorful than water (or in place of half the water): wine, stock, juice, etc. Roasted nuts or seeds, sautéed vegetables, and a final sprinkling of fresh herbs can all be added after the grain is cooked, just before it's served.

Whole-Grain Flours

Excellent whole-grain flours are so available, adaptable, and challenging that you may never want to bake the same bread twice. When, for example, I'm standing in my kitchen surrounded by jars filled with grain, I can't help speculating. What would a little chestnut flour do to the flavor of corn muffins, I wonder; and, inevitably, chestnut-corn muffins are born.

Every grain yields a whole-grain flour with a character all its own.

Some flours are better in pies, others in breads, still others produce delicate crepes and pastries. Mixed together in unlimited numbers of combinations, whole-grain flours can make a muffin, cake or even a waffle drier, lighter, crisper, softer, chewier—whatever texture or taste you'd like.

The taste and nutritiousness of a whole-grain flour is affected by the way it's ground. Flour may be ground in high-speed roller mills, steel-plate mills, or hammer mills. The first two processes grind flour quickly by tearing grain between rotating cylinders; hammer mills pound grain into flour with hammers that whorl around an axis. In both cases, the heat that is generated destroys vitamins and enzymes and oxidizes the natural oils in the grain, turning them rancid. Lumps of rancid oil collect in blotches throughout the flour, making it taste bitter and bake unevenly.

Many millers who produce whole-grain flours use hammer, steel-plate, and roller mills. The best mills, however, are made from natural stones, and the best flour is unquestionably *stone-ground.* In a stone mill, grains are dropped between two natural stones that slowly—and without heat—crush the grains without tearing the germ. The oils remain inside the germ, evenly distributed throughout the flour.

Sadly, there are few traditional millstones left. Most of them were cut in Europe and imported before the 1920s, and only one firm in the United States still makes them today. Not surprisingly, smaller milling companies are usually very proud of their traditional mills. The people at Manna Milling in Seattle, Washington, for example, named their stone mill Alice after the person who built it in the early 1900s.

If a flour is stone-ground, the label will definitely say so. But there seem to be no general rules of thumb governing stone-ground flour. Some companies stone-grind their whole wheat flour but not their whole wheat pastry flour. Other companies stone-grind their pastry flour but not their rye. Most companies use several milling techniques. You'll have to read each label of every brand to be assured of stone-grinding.

Actually, the best method of grinding flour—the one that makes for the tastiest and most nutritious breads of all—is grinding your own flour at home. The process is easy and quick. The whole grains themselves are very inexpensive. The only drawback is the grain mill—it's expensive. On the other hand, whole-grain breads themselves are becoming more expensive all the time. So if you eat a lot of good bread and enjoy baking, a grain mill may be worth the investment.

One of the best grain mills on the market, the Magic Mill II, is described on page 146.

Before reviewing each of the whole-grain flours, their uses, flavor, and characteristics, it's important to understand why whole-grain flours are desirable in the first place.

A whole wheat berry contains almost all of the forty-odd known nutrients (lacking six: vitamins A, D, B_{12}, and C; sodium; and chlorine). But if that wheat berry is ground, sifted, and bleached until it becomes white flour, every nutrient in it (including the proteins) will be ravaged, and some will be lost forever.

A wheat berry has three parts: a germ, an endosperm, and the bran. The germ is the innermost part—the part that grows into a new plant if the wheat berry is planted. The germ contains most of the wheat's thiamine, a good share of the pyridoxine and riboflavin, and almost all the vitamin E. The germ is surrounded by the endosperm, which makes up 83% of the kernel. The endosperm, or starchy part, contains 70% to 75% of the wheat's protein. Finally, the endosperm is covered with several protective layers called the bran. The bran contains almost all of the wheat's B vitamins plus large percentages of other vitamins and minerals and 19% of the wheat's protein.

When wheat is ground into flour, the nutrient-rich bran and germ may be allowed to remain—in which case the result is whole wheat flour. If they're removed, the result is a white flour that commercial bakers love and laboratory animals shun—ironically, for the same reason: It's nutritionally sterile. Lacking the natural oils and nutrients present in the germ, white flour does not go rancid.

In the 1930s, surveys of the health of Americans showed marked deficiencies in B vitamins and iron. As a result, plain white flour, under the FDA's authority, was enriched with niacin, riboflavin, thiamine, and iron.

Percentage of Nutrients Lost When Whole Wheat Is Milled into White Flour

Nutrient	*% Loss*	*Nutrient*	*% Loss*
Thiamine (Vitamin B_1)	77.1	Sodium	78.3
Riboflavin (Vitamin B_2)	80.0	Chromium	40.0
Niacin	80.8	Manganese	85.8
Vitamin B_6	71.8	Iron	75.6
Pantothenic acid	50.0	Cobalt	88.5
Alpha-tocopherol (Vitamin E)	86.3	Copper	67.9
Calcium	60.0	Zinc	77.7
Phosphorous	70.9	Selenium	15.9
Magnesium	84.7	Molybdenum	48.0
Potassium	77.0		

Reprinted from Henry A. Schroeder, "Losses of Vitamins and Trace Minerals Resulting from Processing and Preservation of Foods," *American Journal of Clinical Nutrition,* Vol. 24 (1971).

Triticale

A field of wheat left to fend for itself soon becomes a field of wheat and rye, for rye thrives in and among wheat plants. Throughout most of history, in fact, the wheat harvest was really a wheat-rye harvest, and the breads and cakes made from the wheat were as much—if not more—rye.

Such breads also contained something else. In the field, wheat and rye not only coexist, but they produce spontaneous crosses, or hybrids, which by nature fail to produce seeds. These hybrids were harvested and made into flour along with the wheat and rye. In time, a hybrid flour of wheat, rye, and wheat-rye came to be considered superior pastry flour, especially by French bakers.

From the early 1800s on, farmers and scientists watched wheat-rye hybrids closely. They sought a wheat-rye cross capable of producing seed, for the plants that could be bred from such seeds might be expected to have rye's sturdiness and high lysine content plus wheat's overall high protein and high gluten content. After years of research and plant breeding, such a hybrid was developed. It's called triticale (from wheat, *Triticum*; and rye, *Secale*).

Triticale flour is an excellent bread flour that can be used alone to produce a loaf that is more tasty than wheat but not as strong-tasting as rye. The flour has a good gluten content (the factor that makes bread light and gives it a smooth, fine texture), but triticale dough must be kneaded more gently than wheat flour dough for the gluten to develop. Letting triticale bread rise only once is preferable, since the delicate cell walls in triticale flour may collapse under too much pressure from the carbon dioxide given off by yeasts.

The enriching of white flour does not make it the nutritional equivalent of whole wheat flour. Only four of whole wheat's original nutrients are added back and these not in the original proportions. In 1970 the American Bakers' Association and the Millers' National Federation officially petitioned the FDA to permit bakers to triple the amount of iron added to white bread. Bakers, of course, could use triple iron as a selling point.

The FDA deliberated the case for seven years, finally deciding that too much iron (as many hematologists had testified) could be dangerous. The FDA commissioner, Donald Kennedy, ruled that tripling iron in white bread would be like conducting a full-fledged experiment on the U.S. population.

Though enrichment always sounds positive, the underlying reality is that if a food has to be enriched, it's inferior to begin with. But the

Whole-Grain Flours

Flour and Type	*Characteristics and Flavor*	*Combine With*	*Best Uses*	*Home Grinding*	*Notes*
Barley	Soft, starchy; earthy, sweet taste	Always combine with wheat or another strong flour.	Cakes Pies Cookies	Easy; use unhulled barley if possible.	Gives a coffee-cake texture to foods. Commercial barley flour is ground from pearl barley.
Buckwheat: Light Dark	 Strong Stronger	Always combine with wheat or rye flour.	Pancakes Waffles Breads Cakes Dumplings	Easy; use buckwheat groats.	Dark buckwheat flour is ground from unhulled groats, bits of which remain in the flour and give a strong flavor.
Chestnut	Delicate texture, nutty flavor	Always combine with whole wheat or whole wheat pastry flour.	Sauces Crepes Biscuits Pastry	Ground from shelled chestnuts.	Used to add flavor rather than body.
Corn: Degerminated Undegerminated	 Limp white powder; little flavor Contains germ and nutrients; good body, corn flavor	Rye flour to add flavor and density.	Breads Muffins Tempura	Use flour corn kernels only. Becomes cornmeal, then corn flour.	Sweet corn (the corn-on-the-cob eating variety) cannot be ground into corn flour. Flour corn kernels can. They are available from Nichols Garden Nursery (see page 207).
Millet	Light, delicate texture and flavor.	Always combine with whole wheat flour.	Flatbreads Dumplings Croquettes Sauces Cookies Cakes	Easy; use whole millet.	A very versatile flour that can be used to lighten baked goods.
Oat	Chewy texture; oat flavor	Always combine with whole wheat flour.	Cookies Cakes Breads Muffins	Oat groats do not grind to a powdery flour. Put through a mill, they emerge as soft flakes good for baking.	

Flour and Type	Characteristics and Flavor	Combine With	Best Uses	Home Grinding	Notes
Rice:		Combining is not necessary but produces interesting results.	Bread Crepes Sauces Tempura	Easy; use brown rice.	Makes a delicious bread that's softer, sweeter, and more moist than other breads (like rice pudding in bread form).
White	Very light texture and flavor				
Brown	Light texture; nutty flavor				
Rye:		In bread, combine with wheat flour to make it less dense. Combine with other flours for added flavor.	Breads Fruit breads Waffles Pancakes Crepes	Easy; use rye berries; becomes more like cracked rye than rye flour.	Has a low gluten content, which means breads made from it are dense and heavy.
Light	Bran sifted out; light texture and flavor				
Dark	Heartier texture; better rye flour				
Soy	Adds enormous amount of protein; bitter flavor	Always combine with whole wheat flour to avoid bitterness; ratio soy to wheat, 1:8.	Add small amounts to anything.	Possible. Better to buy defatted soy flour, which is 50% to 52% protein (regular is 35% to 40% protein).	To avoid even a remote possibility of bitterness, add ground cooked soybeans or ground cooked soy grits rather than soy flour to other flours.
Triticale	Good firm body; wheat-rye flavor	Flours other than wheat.	Breads Dumplings Muffins Crepes	Whole grain difficult to find.	Requires gentle kneading, which is why it should not be combined with wheat, which requires vigorous kneading. (Can be combined if wheat is kneaded separately first.)
Whole Wheat:		Any other flour for lightness and varied flavor.		Easy; use whole hard spring or winter wheat.	Whole wheat flour can be used in place of white flour in almost any recipe. The result will be a heavier, more full-textured, full-flavored product. If lightness is essential, use whole wheat pastry flour. Whole wheat pastry flour is not good for breads, however, since it contains less gluten.
Regular	Ground from hard wheat; excellent, versatile body; wheat/nutty flavor		Breads Dumplings Muffins Cakes		
Pastry	Ground from soft wheat; lighter flavor		Cakes Pies Cookies Pastry Crepes		

purpose of enriching white flour was not to make it as nutritious as whole wheat flour anyway. When enrichment was originally authorized, it was simply decided that flour (in the form of bread) was the easiest and least expensive way to get nutrients to large numbers of people. Nutritious bread was not the goal. Bread itself was simply a vehicle for whatever vitamins and minerals were drastically absent in the American diet.

Besides enriched and not enriched, white flour is also sold bleached and unbleached. Unbleached white flour is usually not enriched. Flour is bleached and matured to make it whiter and fluffier. The chemicals involved—chlorine dioxide, nitrogen dioxide, and benzoyl (nitrogen trichloride, once used, was banned after it produced hysteria in dogs)—are among thirty-odd chemicals added to flour and dough to improve the workability of the dough or the look and feel of the loaf (not to improve the nutritional quality of the bread itself).

All whole-grain flours, like whole wheat flour, contain the grain's natural oils and nutrients. This makes them (a) stronger tasting; (b) nutritionally superior to refined flours; and (c) susceptible to spoiling. Always store whole-grain flours in the refrigerator or in a cool, dry place. Ideally, buy a small sack of fresh flour each time you bake.

Baking Whole-Grain Bread

Each whole-grain flour responds differently to water, temperature, humidity, and altitude. Freshly ground flour has a different texture and absorption rate than older flour. To make good bread, you'll need

The Politics of Bread

If any one food ties us to the earth, it's bread. Fields of grain rooted deep in the soil have always been a metaphor for nature and the bond nourishment creates. And because bread is so pervasive a life symbol, it is also the most political of foods.

The first raised breads were made in Egypt sometime between 2,000 and 1,300 B.C. Flat breads were already common fare at that time; in fact, according to archeological records, an Egyptian peasant's diet was composed almost entirely of flat bread, beer (made from fermented bread), and onions.

By the twelfth century B.C., however, rich Egyptians, nobles, and priests distinguished themselves from the poor by eating raised breads and cakes baked in as many as forty different varieties. Some were baked with honey, some with milk or eggs; all were shaped

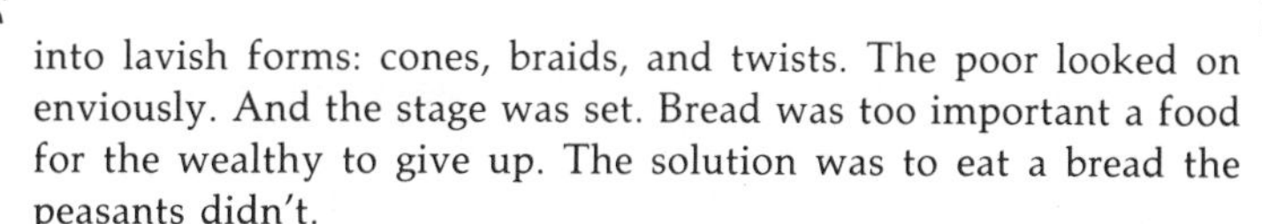

into lavish forms: cones, braids, and twists. The poor looked on enviously. And the stage was set. Bread was too important a food for the wealthy to give up. The solution was to eat a bread the peasants didn't.

When the flour that was used in raised breads became plentiful and inexpensive enough for the poor to purchase, the wealthy found themselves needing a new bread to set them apart. The answer was white bread.

The history of white bread indicates that there was no reason, other than a political one, for flour to be milled until it was white. White bread was less tasty and more expensive than whole-grain bread. White flour took inordinately more time to produce. But because white bread was neither common, easily affordable, nor the same color as whole-grain bread, it became a convenient wedge that once again could separate rich and poor. By eating white bread, a Roman citizen silently but conclusively elevated himself over those around him.

And the symbol stuck. White bread became associated with those in power; dark bread with the common man. By the thirteenth century, in the most lavish and extravagant Arabian courts, white bread, along with roast kid and wine, was considered a supreme mark of self-indulgence. A few hundred years later Paris bakeries would be kept under constant pressure filling the long lists of orders for white bread that came regularly from the households of French monarchs.

In America, if there is one political symbol that represents the new humanistic left, it is, wonderfully and simply enough, whole wheat bread. The *Wall Street Journal,* in a September 1978 front-page story, documented the whole-wheat-and-politics phenomenon. According to the *Journal*'s report, hand-shaped loaves of hearty whole-grain bread baked in small ethnic bakeries haven't changed in years, but the people who eat them are different. Rye, pumpernickel, corn, and whole wheat bread used to be eaten by immigrants. After the American Revolution, in fact, Germans, Russians, Poles, and Scandinavians in the growing industrial cities of the East shared communal bread ovens where they'd bring dough that they'd let rise overnight.

But now the market for whole-grain bread is suburban and urban American—wealthy, well-educated people who are willing to pay considerably more money for a loaf of good bread. To keep up with the new demand, in fact, bakers baked 68% more whole-grain breads between 1972 and 1977. During the same time, the demand for white bread slowed and production dropped 4.4%.

to adjust your technique every time. Begin with a good recipe, but add more or less flour, more or less water, as the situation demands. There's no way to explain how much; in time, you'll simply know from the feel of the dough whether or not it's right.

Beating the dough well, then kneading it vigorously is essential in order to develop the flour's gluten. Gluten is formed from proteins in the starch of the flour. When fully developed, gluten gives the dough an elasticity that allows it to rise and make bread light and uniform in texture.

Whole wheat flour requires a lot of kneading for the gluten to develop—more kneading than white flour needs. In fact, no other flour has as much gluten as whole wheat. So no matter how much you knead rye flour, for example, it will never develop the elasticity, nor rise as much, as whole wheat flour will. This is why all whole-grain breads, from rye to oatmeal, usually have whole wheat flour as their base. Without it, the bread would be dense, heavy, compacted.

Sourdough Whole Wheat Bread with Roasted Soy

Sourdough Starter

1 pkg. dry yeast
2 c. warm water
2 c. whole wheat flour

Bread

¼ c. blackstrap molasses
butter or vegetable oil
1 c. lukewarm water
1 pkg. dry yeast or ¼ oz. fresh yeast
½ c. uncooked soybeans
3 c. or more whole wheat flour
1 T. herbal salt

1. The starter will require from 1 to 3 days fermentation before it can be used.* Combine the yeast and water, stirring until blended. Add the flour and stir again. Cover the bowl with plastic wrap and let it stand in a warm, but not hot, place until the mixture begins to ferment. Allow to ferment for at least a day. Stir the mixture down once or twice.

2. To make the bread, put the molasses into a bowl. Stir in ¼ cup of the water. Stir in the yeast until it dissolves. Set aside.

3. Put the soybeans into a heavy skillet. Stirring and shaking the pan almost continuously, roast them for 20 minutes, or until lightly browned. Allow to cool, then grind them to a meal in a blender. They will give the bread an extraordinary nuttiness.

*You may want to begin a continuous starter by increasing the starter recipe by half. The extra half will keep indefinitely in the refrigerator. Add additional flour to this 3 days before making bread again to bring the starter level up to the required amount.

4. In a large bowl, combine the flour, salt, roasted ground soybeans, and sourdough starter. Add the yeast mixture and beat vigorously, gradually adding more water (you may actually need less than all the remaining water).

5. As a sticky mass of dough begins to form, knead it with your hands. Turn the dough out onto a floured surface and knead well for 15 minutes.

6. Gather the dough into a ball, rub it lightly with butter or vegetable oil, place it in a bowl, cover the bowl with a cotton cloth, and allow to stand until doubled in volume (1½ to 3 hours).

7. Pull the dough out of the bowl and work it on a floured surface until it has collapsed. Gather it into a ball, place again in a covered bowl, and let rise a second time until doubled in volume.

8. Preheat oven to 400°F.

9. Grease a baking sheet lightly and sprinkle it with cornmeal. Pull the dough out of the bowl. Work it briefly and divide it in half. Form 2 balls, then 2 ovals, and finally 2 French-style loaves. Place these on the baking sheet and cover again. Let the loaves rise a third time until doubled in volume.

10. Make a gash down the center of each loaf and smaller, leaflike gashes alongside it. Bake in the preheated oven for 30 to 40 minutes.

The first crucial step in baking whole-grain breads is to mix the whole wheat batter vigorously before adding other flours or cracked grains. This will give the wheat flour's gluten a chance to develop before it is weighted down by other grains.

When kneading, don't be afraid to really let loose on the dough. (Playing music with a strong beat helps.)

The correct kneading technique involves pushing the rounded ball of dough away with the heel of your hand, turning it a quarter turn while folding it over toward you, then pushing it away again. To get enough force behind your kneading, knead on a table about hip level. If your tables at home are too high for this, try kneading on a board or in a bowl on the floor, with a pillow under your knees. The dough is sufficiently kneaded when it feels roly-poly, fat, pliable, and alive in your hands.

Whole-grain bread can be made even more hearty by adding slightly cooked cracked wheat or rye or finely chopped nuts or seeds to the batter.

Soak cracked grains for an hour first; otherwise the bread will taste gritty rather than chewy. Allow the soaked grain to dry a bit before adding it to the batter.

You can also toast the grain lightly in a 250°F oven (stirring occasionally) after you've soaked it. Toasting grains, nuts, and seeds will give the bread a nuttier flavor.

Yeast

Where do they come from? Out of the air, to be exact, for yeasts are simply single-cell plants that float everywhere in the environment. There are many species, only one of which is used for baking.

A yeast cell in a warm, steamy environment will put out buds that break away from the parent cell, in turn producing more buds. Warm yeast cells fed a small amount of natural sugar will reproduce a whole generation every five hours. Kept cold and dry, yeasts remain alive but dormant.

Fresh Yeast. The fresher yeast is, the better. Fresh, or compressed, yeast is sold in natural food stores and small bakeries in small gray-white blocks that feel like a cross between clay and putty. Do not buy fresh yeast if the block has been partially crumbled, since the yeast will have begun to dry out and won't work well in the dough.

Fresh yeast should be stored in the coldest part of the refrigerator in a small dish with a tight-fitting cover. (Poke one hole in the container so that moisture doesn't condense inside, soaking the yeast.) Kept this way, fresh yeast will last 3 to 4 weeks. Fresh yeast can also be frozen. Wrap it well. To bring it back to life, soak it in warm water for 15 minutes.

Dry Yeast. Dry (active) yeast is twice as strong as fresh yeast. It, too, is alive, but the drying makes it dormant. To get dry yeast started, put a small amount of tepid water in a bowl, add a tiny amount of honey or molasses, then sprinkle the yeast over the top. Give the mixture one stir and let it sit in a warm, moist place for 15 minutes, or until the yeast has frothed.

Packages of dry yeast almost always suggest more yeast than is needed to make dough rise. With too much yeast, bread rises quickly and goes stale quickly as well. The longer dough ferments and the more it relies on natural yeasts in the air to rise (in addition to the yeast you've supplied), the better the bread tastes, the better the crust formed on it will be, and the longer it will keep moist and fresh.

Experiment with letting your bread rise overnight. You can also let it rise three times for incredible lightness and flavor. Rub the ball of dough lightly with oil so that a crust doesn't harden during all those hours. A bread that's been allowed to ferment very slowly and thoroughly is like a wine that's been allowed to do the same. Both turn out better if they aren't rushed.

Virginia Batter Bread

2	c. undegerminated cornmeal	⅓	c. or less safflower oil
½	t. herbal salt	2	eggs, lightly beaten
¼	t. baking soda	1½	to 2 c. buttermilk
		1	T. honey

1. Preheat oven to 450°F.
2. In a large mixing bowl, combine the cornmeal, salt, and baking soda.
3. Place the safflower oil in an 8-inch heavy cast-iron skillet, set it in the preheated oven, and let it heat.*
4. Lightly mix the eggs into the dry ingredients, then stir in just enough buttermilk to make a batter about the consistency of pancake batter.
5. Remove the skillet from the oven and swirl the oil around until the bottom and sides of the skillet are well greased. Pour the rest of the hot oil into a small bowl along with the honey. Mix well and pour into the batter. Stir quickly, just enough to mix.
6. Pour the batter back into the hot skillet and bake in the preheated oven until firm and lightly browned, about 25 minutes. Cut into wedges and serve directly from the skillet with a bit of molasses, maple syrup, fruit butter, or nut butter.

*Traditionally, lard was used in place of vegetable oil.

As for developing an excellent crust, the ovens in Europe are injected with steam. To create the same effect, I bought two iron wedges in a hardware store, heated them to a feverish pitch on top of my stove, then put them in two loaf pans set on the floor of the oven. Immediately after I slipped two loaves of whole wheat sourdough onto the top oven rack, I poured boiling water over the red hot iron wedges and closed the oven door quickly. The oven steamed and hissed, the sourdough baked, and in the end the bread's crust was so crackling, the loaf could have passed as Parisian.

Grain Mills

The best-tasting breads, muffins, cereals, cakes, and cookies are made with freshly ground flour. In fact, in terms of taste, using freshly ground flour rather than store-bought flour is like using garden-fresh herbs rather than packaged dried ones—the flavor is dramatically better. And so is the nutritional quality, since the flour has not lost vitamins and enzymes through oxidation.

There are two types of grain mills: hand mills, which must be bolted to a counter and operated by hand; and electric mills, which are faster, more versatile, and tend to grind more uniformly.

In most electric mills, grain is ground between Carborundum stones driven by a powerful motor. Carborundum stones are man-made from aluminum oxide that has been bonded under heat and pressure with flint and feldspar. After several years of use, Carborundum stones begin to wear down and minute particules of aluminum oxide are ground into the flour. Aluminum oxide is considered an inert material that has no effect on the body as it passes through. The R. & R. Mill Company, 45 West First North, Smithfield, Utah 84335, publishes a free catalog of the best electric mills on the market (catalog includes many old-fashioned kitchen utensils and cast-iron cookware).

The grain mill I use and consider to be one of the best electric mills currently available is the Magic Mill II. Rather than grinding grain between Carborundum stones, the Magic Mill micro-atomizes grain by exploding it into minute particles. Micronization has been used in the pharmaceutical industry extensively. In the late 1970s the concept was applied to mills and appears to have no negative effects as a method of grinding grain. In fact, because stones are not used, particles of stone do not chip off into the flour.

The Magic Mill can be used for grinding or cracking all grains—from corn to soybeans. It is quick (almost a pound of flour per minute), easy to use, light, self-cleaning, compact, and grinds uni-

Trenchers

Throughout the Middle Ages in England, individual plates were only rarely used. Instead, huge squares of bread were sliced, hollowed out, then heaped with whatever foods on the common serving platters the person fancied.

Bread plates of this sort were called "trenchers." Often they were colored and spiced: green trenchers with parsley, yellow with saffron, pink with sandalwood.

At the end of the meal, the plate was eaten or saved for breakfast, where it would become "sops"—bread pieces dunked in almond milk, wine, meat drippings, or fruit juice. If one was feeling generous, one could also give his trencher to the less fortunate who milled about outside the door.

From: Madeleine Pelner Cosman, *Fabulous Feasts: Medieval Cookery and Ceremony* (New York: George Braziller, 1976).

Wine and Natural Food

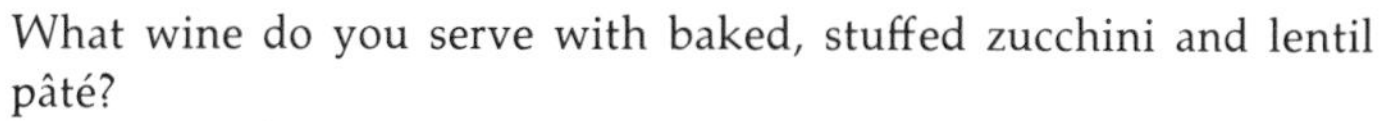

What wine do you serve with baked, stuffed zucchini and lentil pâté?

In *The Book of Natural French Cooking,* Dione Lucas points out that even no-meat, no-fish dinners deserve a good wine. The Europeans, for example, eat much less meat than we do, yet with pasta, eggs, vegetable dishes, whole-grain casseroles, and even cheese, nuts, fruit, and dessert, there's always a bottle of wine on the table.

Wine contains calcium, phosphorus, magnesium, sodium, potassium, iron and other minerals, as well as B vitamins. It is a good source of carbohydrates. You do need to be aware that excessive amounts of alcohol destroy nutrients in the body. Still, a glass or two of wine with some crusty whole wheat bread and a bit of raw-milk cheese is nothing less than delicious and nutritious.

It's true that the grapes used to make wine are sprayed and that the cheaper jug wines may have been treated with chemicals during fermentation. Many of the best wines, however, are still made naturally, the way they have been for centuries, and are clarified with natural materials from the earth.

I find that white wines go best with natural food, both because a light white wine will complement a light vegetable dish and because a light white wine will balance out a heavier grain dish, soup, or a casserole. Also, white wines tend to have a lower alcohol content than red wines—especially white German wines, which can be as little as 8% alcohol. I enjoy red wines more in winter and then usually drink them with pasta.

formly. Like the Carborundum stone mills, the Magic Mill costs in the neighborhood of $200, and like all mills, it's loud. It is available directly from Magic Mill, 235 West 200 South, Salt Lake City, Utah 84101.

The Legumes

If there was a discouraging word to be heard anywhere down home on the range, it was *beans.* And *peas* wasn't far behind. Yet for the last ten thousand years, peas and beans have been, along with grains, the major sources of sustenance throughout the world.[4]

[4]For centuries, farmers had resigned themselves to the fact that grain crops planted year after year gradually wore out the soil. But then, first by coincidence and later by intention, bean and pea crops were rotated with grains in the same field. The result was more and better bean crops plus more and better grains. The tradition of grain and bean dishes—a tradition rooted in virtually every civilization throughout history—was indelibly stamped.

*Relative Nutritional Values of Dried Beans and Peas (Legumes) and Fresh Beans and Peas (Vegetables)**

(100 grams)

	Protein Grams		Iron Milligrams		Calories
				Lima Beans	
Soybeans	20		6		240
		Lima Beans		Soybeans	
				Split Peas	
	18				
					220
		Soybeans	5	Kidney Beans	
Split Peas					
		Great Northern Beans		Great Northern Beans	
Lentils	16				
				Lentils	
Lima Beans					
Kidney Beans					
		Kidney Beans			
					200
Great Northern Beans	14				
		Lentils	4		
Black-eyed Peas					
				Black-eyed Peas	
	12				
		Split Peas			
		Black-eyed Peas			180
		Garden Peas	3		
	10				
Garden Peas					
	8				160
			2		
	6				
					140
	4		1		
		Snap Beans			
				Garden Peas	
Snap Beans	2			Snap Beans (30)	120

*Garden peas and snap beans are vegetables. All other beans and peas listed are dried and are legumes.

Adapted from: *Nutritive Value of American Foods,* Agricultural Handbook No. 456, USDA, November 1975.

According to archeological records, the dependability of peas and beans led to their becoming the backbone of nourishment. Food had been hunted or gathered in preagricultural society; but as populations grew, planting became a necessity. Approximately eight square miles were required to feed one hunter. On the same amount of land, a crop that would feed six thousand could be planted. And so the diet shifted from bison to beans.

Beans, peas, lentils, kudzu, peanuts,[5] and alfalfa[6] make up the family of legumes. Legumes all grow in a similar way: a single row of seeds is encapsulated in a pod that hangs down from the stems of the mother plant. Yet despite this similarity, legumes are strikingly different in character.

Peas and beans, for example, can be divided into two camps: those suitable for drying and those (like the garden pea or snap bean) that are cooked and eaten fresh. Among the twenty five or so varieties of dried beans, the differences are dramatic. Garbanzo beans (also called chick-peas) taste nothing like adzuki beans, and neither one tastes or looks like a great northern bean (used for baked beans). When you begin to compare the taste and texture of dried split peas, kidney beans, green lentils, and Spanish peanuts, the individuality of legumes is even more obvious. So, in cooking, you'll need to experiment a lot.

Cooking Legumes

Beans, peas, and lentils should first be washed by dumping them into a deep pot and covering them with cold water. Broken pieces and cracked or damaged legumes will float to the top. Discard them. Next, drain the water.

It can take several hours to cook a dried bean, which is why beans and peas are soaked overnight before they're cooked. Soaking softens the legume, begins to break down the starch in it, and shortens the cooking time by about ½ hour. Even after an overnight soaking, though, most beans still require more cooking than grains. Soybeans and red beans, the longest cooking legumes, take considerably longer to cook than whole wheat berries, barley, or rice, the longest cooking grains.

All dried beans and whole peas should be soaked in a pot placed in the refrigerator to prevent fermentation. A faster method than the overnight soak is to boil them for about 5 minutes, then soak them for at least 1 hour before cooking. Split peas and lentils can be cooked

[5]Peanuts, although technically legumes, are discussed under "Nuts and Seeds."
[6]Alfalfa seeds, also legumes, are discussed on pages 179 through 181.

Lentil Pâté en Croute

This pâté is wrapped in brioche dough. The result is a hearty vegetable pâté filling inside a fine-textured, buttery brioche loaf. Before beginning the brioche, note: A good brioche is light and fine textured. To achieve those characteristics, make sure you use either fresh yeast or very fresh packaged yeast. And make sure you use enough of it. Too much yeast will not harm the dough, but too little will. Yeast is also very sensitive to temperature. Make sure all the ingredients are at room temperature. Adding just one cold egg can slow down the yeast action, and hence the preparation time, significantly. Liquids should be lukewarm, not hot. Also note that because brioche dough is buttery, it requires a slower, cooler rising than other breads. A moist 70°F environment is perfect. An earthenware mixing bowl will maintain a stable temperature better than glass or metal.

Brioche Dough

- 1 oz. fresh yeast or 2 pkg. dry
- 1 t. honey
- ¼ c. lukewarm water
- 3½ c. whole wheat flour
- ¼ lb. (1 stick) butter, softened
- 1 t. vanilla extract
- 3 t. very finely minced lemon rind
- ½ t. herbal salt
- ½ c. lukewarm milk
- 3 whole eggs and
- 3 egg yolks, beaten

Pâté

- 1½ c. dried lentils (preferably ¾ red and ¾ green)
- ½ c. dried yellow split peas
- 1 t. herbal salt
- 1 bay leaf
- 4 generous slices of stale whole wheat sourdough bread
- safflower oil for brushing
- 3 cloves garlic, finely minced
- 2 T. butter
- 1 medium-size onion, chopped
- 3 stalks celery, finely chopped
- ¼ t. ground cumin
- ¼ t. dried thyme
- ½ t. Hungarian paprika
- ½ t. cayenne pepper
- 1 T. whole wheat flour
- 1 T. miso (preferably hatcho)
- ½ c. vegetable stock
- ⅓ c. dry red wine
- 2 T. Cognac
- 1 T. tamari
- 2 eggs
- ½ c. finely chopped parsley
- ½ c. or more almonds, coarsely chopped

1. *Making the brioche dough.* Crumble the yeast into a large measuring cup. Stir in the honey, then gently stir in the lukewarm water. (If dry yeast is used, sprinkle the yeast over the water, then gently stir in the honey.) Set aside. Place the flour in a large bowl and, with your hand, make a well in the center. Pour the yeast mixture into

the well. With the back of a spoon, push just enough surrounding flour into the yeast mixture to give it a pancake-batter consistency. Do not mix in too much flour. The yeast must be allowed to work on this "sponge" before all the dough is worked in. Cover the sponge with a 1-inch layer of flour taken from the sides of the bowl. Cover the bowl with plastic wrap drawn tightly. Set aside for the sponge to take hold, roughly 10 minutes, or until little cracks appear in the flour over the sponge.

2. In a separate large bowl, cream the butter by hand with a large wooden spoon. Add the vanilla and the lemon rind. Mix well. Now add just the sponge, not the remaining flour, to the butter mixture and mix together well. Add the salt to the flour left in the bowl and begin adding this to the sponge-butter mixture. Work the flour in slowly, alternating with the lukewarm milk, the eggs and egg yolks. (The eggs should each be beaten separately, then added one at a time.) Keep blending until the dough is stiff. Add extra flour if needed.

3. Lift the dough out of the bowl and place it on a floured surface. Coat your hands with flour and slap/knead the dough by throwing it from one hand to the other, back and forth, with loud slaps. Keep the dough moving. Coat the surface and your hands with additional flour as needed. Continue to slap the dough for 5 minutes. Try to maintain a round ball of dough. When the slapping/kneading is done, the dough should feel heavy, homogeneous, and silky rather than sticky and lumpy.

4. Put the dough back into a bowl, cover tightly with plastic wrap, and allow to rise until doubled in volume (1½ hours). Do not let the dough overrise. Then punch it down, slap it into a ball once again, and allow it to rise a second time for 1 hour. The dough should be doubled in size again. Punch it down once more and with a floured rolling pin, roll it into a rectangle about 12 by 15 inches. The dough at this point is ready to be filled.

5. *Making the pâté.* The pâté is best made while the brioche dough is rising. While it is rising the first time, fill a heavy pot with cold water. Add the lentils and split peas. Throw away any bits of legume that float to the top, then drain the water. Cover the lentils and peas with cold water once again. Add the salt and bay leaf. Place, covered, over medium heat until the water is about to boil. Turn the heat down and simmer, partially covered, for 1 hour.

6. *Making garlic sourdough bread crumbs.* Trim the crusts from the sourdough bread. Tap the bread slices lightly on both sides with safflower oil, using your fingertips or a pastry brush. Now sprinkle both sides with fresh garlic. Toast lightly on both sides under your oven broiler. When cool, dice into small squares with a sharp knife. Set aside.

7. When the lentils are done, drain them well in a large wire-mesh sieve or in a cheesecloth. Reserve a small portion of the liquid and

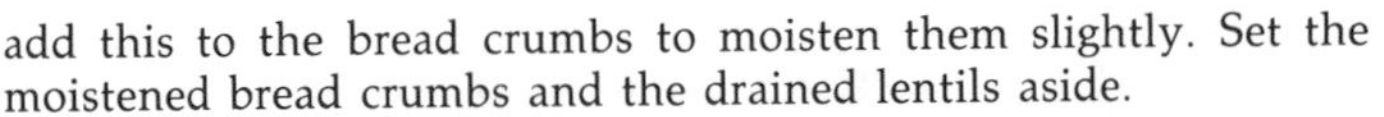

add this to the bread crumbs to moisten them slightly. Set the moistened bread crumbs and the drained lentils aside.

8. Meanwhile, heat the butter in a large skillet. Add the onion and celery and sauté until the onion is transparent. Add the garlic, cumin, thyme, paprika, and cayenne. Add the flour and stir rapidly over low heat for 1 to 2 minutes. Dissolve the miso in the vegetable stock and add this to the onion-celery mixture. Then add the wine, Cognac, and tamari. Cook for several minutes until the liquid is thickened. Remove from the heat.

9. To this mixture add 1 egg, lightly beaten; the parsley; and the almonds. Stir in the moistened bread crumbs. Stir in the lentils and peas.

10. Preheat oven to 400°F.

11. Generously oil or butter a large, heavy loaf pan. Pile the pâté mixture down the center of the brioche rectangle. Leave several inches at the ends to fold the dough closed and leave several inches on each side to wrap the dough over the pâté. Fold the two long sides up and over the pâté, overlapping them and pinching the dough together gently. Be careful not to pierce the dough. Now fold the ends up, as though wrapping a package. Pinch the seams closed as much as possible (wetting your fingers with water will help). And now the tricky part. Place the loaf pan on its side next to the dough-wrapped pâté. Lift the pâté loaf up and ease it onto the inside wall of the loaf pan. Lift the other side of the pâté loaf up and in one quick, steady movement, roll the pâté loaf over and into the loaf pan so that the seamed edge is on the bottom. Allow the loaf to rest for 5 minutes. Beat the remaining egg well and brush the top of the loaf with it. Bake in the preheated oven for 20 minutes, then turn the temperature down to 350° and bake for 35 to 40 minutes more. Allow the pâté en croute to cool before removing it from the loaf pan. Serve either warm or cold.

without soaking, although soaking them for 30 minutes helps them hold their shape after they're cooked.

The heavier and deeper the pot, the better it is for cooking beans and peas. Cover the legumes completely with cold water, allow them to come to a boil slowly, then simmer until tender, adding more boiling water as it becomes necessary. A well-cooked bean can be easily squashed against the roof of the mouth using only the tongue. If the bean doesn't give way, keep cooking.

During cooking, cover the pot only partially. Beans will boil over in a tightly covered pot. As the beans become tender, add a pinch of sea salt.

Crock pots are especially good for cooking beans and peas, since heat is distributed evenly and slowly. The slower beans and peas are cooked, the sweeter and more concentrated their flavor. Legumes that are cooked unevenly or too quickly burst open and become watery, mushy, and tasteless. Legumes can be pressure-cooked, but I have found that the foam created from the dissipating starch often clogs the vent, and what is gained in quick cooking seems to me to be lost in flavor.

Legumes must be cooked thoroughly, otherwise they'll be difficult to digest. Beans and peas contain two starches: stachyose and raffinose. In the intestine special bacteria work on the iron-clad bonds that link the elements in these starch chains together. As the bacteria work, carbon dioxide and hydrogen are given off, creating gas. When legumes are well soaked and well cooked, however, the starches in the legume are broken down during cooking, making the legume more digestible. But even when well cooked, some legumes are

Split-Pea Balls

- 1½ c. rolled oats
- ½ c. almonds, finely chopped
- ½ c. wheat germ
- ½ c. shredded unsweetened coconut
- 1½ t. herbal salt
- ½ c. dried green split peas
- ½ c. dried yellow split peas
- 1 bay leaf
- 2 c. vegetable stock
- ½ c. ricotta or cottage cheese
- ½ c. dates, pitted and chopped
- 1 t. basil
- 1 t. oregano
- corn oil for frying

1. Preheat oven to 400°F.

2. Mix the oats, almonds, wheat germ, coconut, and ½ teaspoon of the salt together. Spread evenly on a cookie sheet and roast in the preheated oven for 20 to 30 minutes, stirring often, until nicely toasted. Set aside to cool.

3. Mix the split peas together and cook them with the bay leaf in the vegetable stock until tender (about 1 hour). Drain.

4. In a medium-sized bowl, combine the cheese, dates, remaining 1 teaspoon salt, basil, and oregano. Mix well. Fold in the peas.

5. Roll the pea-cheese mixture into small balls. Roll each of these in the roasted oat mixture until evenly coated.

6. Heat about ¼ inch of oil in a large skillet until very hot. Gently add the pea balls and fry until brown, turning with a slotted spoon as necessary so that all sides cook evenly. Drain well on paper towels and serve as an appetizer, side dish, or snack.

harder to digest than others. Soybeans, kidney beans, and broad beans are the toughest, and you may want to go easy on these in the beginning until your body adapts. Beans do become more easy to digest as time goes on, because more of the specific intestinal bacteria that break down starch are encouraged to grow, the more beans you eat.

Beans and peas are more easily digested and they taste better if seasonings and herbs are added to them while they cook. You can either drain the seasoned legumes and eat them alone, bake them with other vegetables (and seasonings) in a casserole, or turn the bean pot into a stew by seasoning the bean stock. Tomato paste, chopped onion, garlic, and a bit of wine plus some crushed herbs and a rela-

Beans *

One Cup Dried Beans	*Water*	*To Cook*†	*Yield*
Adzuki Beans: These dark red beans are imported from Japan. They are small, extremely tasty, and easy to digest. You can cook them right in the same pot with rice or barley and season the whole pot with sesame seeds for an incredibly high-protein dish.	3 cups	soak + 45 minutes to 1 hour cooking	2 cups
Black Beans (also called black turtle soup beans): Famous in thick Cuban, Mediterranean, and Oriental dishes. Use in soups or casseroles, or season well and ladle over rice.	4 cups	soak + 1½ hours cooking	2 cups
Black-Eyed Peas (also called cow peas and black-eyed beans): The American equivalent of the adzuki bean, they're small and white with one black spot and can be added to soups, but are traditionally eaten alone.	3 cups	soak + 1 hour cooking	2 cups
Dried Peas: (yellow, green, and split). Green peas have a more dominant taste than yellow. Split peas are special whole dried green or yellow peas that have been cracked in half and had their skins removed. Any of the three can be used for a thick pea soup. Pureed, they can be added to casseroles or mixed with a grain as a stuffing.	2½–3 cups	whole peas: soak split peas: no soak + 1 hour cooking	2¼ cups

* When you cook beans, cook a lot of them. Leftover beans keep well in the refrigerator for days and can be mixed with grains and vegetables for new casseroles, mashed with rice and made into stuffings or croquettes, or pureed, mixed with olive oil, a bit of lemon juice, chopped peppers or pimento, onions, scallions or leeks, and herbs for a vegetable dip.

† Legumes can be soaked overnight or for at least 3 hours before cooking. To shorten soaking time, boil legumes in soaking water for 5 minutes, then soak for 1 hour.

One Cup Dried Beans	*Water*	*To Cook†*	*Yield*
Garbanzo Beans (also called chick-peas): These are mashed with sesame oil into the Middle Eastern favorite, hummus. Cold garbanzos are great in salads. Hot, they're excellent in soups and stews.	4 cups	soak + 3 hours cooking	2 cups
Great Northern Beans: These beans are often boiled, then baked. They're large and are better in casseroles and stews than in salads.	3½ cups	soak + 2 hours cooking	2 cups
Kidney Beans: These large, kidney-shaped red beans made chili famous. Kidney beans are one of the tastiest varieties of bean and can be added to anything.	3 cups	soak + 2 hours cooking	2 cups
Lentils: Disc-shaped, lentils are the easiest of all legumes to cook. They're about the size of a pea. Green are the most common, but red are tasty in a different, equally good way. Lentils should be combined with vegetables in a casserole or stew or combined with rice or barley as a stuffing rather than eaten alone.	3 cups	no soak + ¾ hour cooking	2¼ cups
Lima Beans: Limas come either large or small and are excellent in casseroles or alone with butter and herbs. They have a bean-pea flavor.	2 cups	soak + 1½ hours cooking	1¼ cups
Mung Beans: Mungs are the smallest beans, army-green in color and usually eaten sprouted rather than cooked. (See pages 179–181.) However, they're delicious and beautiful mixed in and allowed to cook with rice or barley.	3 cups	soak 1 to 2 hours + cook ½ hour, add grain and continue cooking	2 cups
Navy Beans: These include many different white beans—all are small and firm and good in casseroles. Navy beans are also used to make home-baked beans.	3 cups	soak + 1½ hours cooking	2 cups
Pinto Beans: These speckled beige beans are somewhat smaller than kidney beans, but they're also great in salads and for chili.	3 cups	soak + 2½ hours cooking	2 cups
Red Beans and Pink Beans: Reds taste stronger than pinks. Both are used in Mexican dishes—refried beans, for example. They can also be used in salads and for chili.	3 cups	soak + 3 hours cooking	2 cups
Soybeans: Soybeans are one of the most nutritious foods in the world. They can be made into casseroles or loaves, but because they're the toughest bean of all to digest, soybeans are more often eaten in another form: tofu, tempeh, miso.	4 cups	soak + 3½ hours or more cooking	2 cups

tively hardy vegetable (carrots, parsnips, beets, peppers, potatoes, leeks) all mixed into the bean pot and slowly simmered until the vegetables are cooked (but slightly crisp) will make an excellent stew.

Cooked beans or peas (or combinations of these) can be cooled and dressed with a sharp herb vinaigrette for an excellent salad. Adding apple juice or tomato juice instead of water to the beans as they cook changes the whole flavor. And finally, plain bean and pea dishes can be dressed up by tossing some cumin, coriander, oregano, curry, garlic, dill, bay leaf, sage, or basil right into the cooking pot and later, when the beans or peas are done, sprinkling them with just a few fresh herbs and some grated sharp Cheddar cheese and maybe a bit of finely minced onion.

Tofu

Just as we take wheat and from it make flour and from the flour make bread, the Chinese and Japanese take soybeans and from them make soybean curd and from the curd make tofu.[7]

Baked Tofu in Mushroom Sauce

- 2 large (Japanese) cakes of tofu, well drained
- 3 heaping T. miso (preferably hatcho)
- 1 t. honey
- ¾ c. vegetable stock
- ½ lb. mushrooms
- 3 T. safflower oil
- 2 cloves garlic, minced
- 1 t. ground cumin
- ⅓ c. tahini
- ½ cup whole-grain bread crumbs for topping (optional)
- sprigs of parsley, mint, or carrot greens (optional)

1. Drain the tofu by wrapping each cake in a cotton towel and placing a weight on top of each so that water is pressed out. Allow the tofu to drain in this way for a least 30 minutes.

2. Spoon the miso and honey into a medium-size bowl. Heat the vegetable stock gently, then pour over the miso and honey. Stir until both are well dissolved in the liquid; set aside.

3. Preheat oven to 350°F.

4. Remove the stems from the mushroom caps (Reserve the stems for a future stock pot.) Slice large caps into 2 or 3 pieces. Leave small caps whole.

[7]Tofu, however, is not the Eastern equivalent of bread. It is, in fact, much more esteemed there than bread is here. There are twice as many tofu shops in Japan as bakeries in the United States, even though the U.S. population is double that of Japan.

5. Sauté the mushrooms in the safflower oil just until they lose their rubberiness, 3 to 5 minutes. Sprinkle the garlic and cumin over the mushrooms.

6. Turn the heat down as low as possible and slowly pour the tahini over the mushrooms. Stir, gently but constantly, for 2 to 3 minutes. Do not let the tahini burn.

7. Pour the miso-honey liquid over the mushrooms and tahini. Allow this to cook for 1 brief minute, then remove the pan from the heat, give the mixture a few stirs, and set aside.

8. Carefully slice the drained tofu, lengthwise, into ½-inch slabs. Gently place these in an oiled casserole dish. Cover and place in the preheated oven for 15 minutes. During this time, baste the tofu twice with the mushroom sauce.

9. After 15 minutes, pour the remaining mushroom sauce over the tofu in the casserole dish. Replace cover and allow to bake for another 15 minutes.

10. Before serving, sprinkle with bread crumbs and sprigs of green. Serve as a side dish. As a main dish, figure 1 cake of tofu per person and adjust recipe accordingly.

Tofu was first made by the Chinese about 164 B.C. when soybeans (then considered one of the five sacred grains) were roasted, mashed into a puree, and allowed to curdle by the addition of seawater. Later the original tofu makers would discover that by straining the fibrous material out of the puree and mixing it with mineral-rich sea water, small, more compact curds could be formed. When these curds were then pressed into cakes, squares of Chinese tofu were born.

In this country tofu comes in two forms: the small, dense Chinese soybean cakes and the larger, pillowy Japanese cakes. In the Orient, however, there are dozens of varieties of tofu—all of which taste distinctly different to the Japanese and Chinese, just as various cheeses taste different to Americans and Europeans.

Here Chinese and Japanese tofu also taste different. And tofu that is bought packaged in supermarkets or natural food stores tastes different from tofu bought loose, floating in tubs of water in Oriental produce markets. Tofu on the East Coast also tastes different from tofu in the West. The differences in taste are based on slightly different production techniques, differences in the taste and chemical composition of local water, and differences in the solidifying agent that's used to form curds from the soybean milk.

Tofu is sometimes called soybean curd or soy cheese. Neither name really fits, since tofu is not bean curd per se—it is made from bean

The Tofu Master

In Japan and China tofu making has been one of the highest of culinary crafts. Traditional shops carry a lineage name dated from an original master whose skill was considered consummate. As in the French countryside where, in the early morning, entire small towns are filled with the heady aroma of baking bread, China and Japan are dotted with local tofu shops, where craftspeople have been at work from perhaps 3 A.M. making the day's supply of fresh tofu—and using perhaps seventy pounds of soybeans a day.

curd. Also, unlike cheese, tofu is neither fermented, aged, nor ripened.

Instead, tofu is pressed into existence through a time-consuming series of precise steps. First, soybeans are cooked until curds are formed. The specific curdling agent may be nigari, a mineral-rich liquid extracted from seawater, or calcium sulfate, which is ground from natural gypsum. Both give tofu its large amount of calcium. After the boiling and the curdling agent have done their work, the heavy curds are separated from the milky-white liquid whey. The curds are next pressed in cloth-lined settling boxes fitted with weights. The result is a big, slippery, glistening rectangle of tofu with a texture like milk Jell-O.

Tofu has the highest ratio of protein to calories of any known plant food—with the exception of soybean and mung bean sprouts, which ounce for ounce are slightly higher in protein and lower in calories.

Compared with meat and dairy foods, tofu's nutritional assets are dramatic. For example, one cake (approximately 5 ounces) of tofu has 86 calories, 9.4 grams of protein, and 5 grams of fat, whereas 1 ounce of Cheddar cheese has 1⅓ times the calories (113) plus almost twice the fat (9 grams) and *less* protein (7 grams). And although a whole cake of tofu is a normal amount for anyone to eat at one sitting, almost no one stops at 1 ounce of cheese.

Let's compare one cake (5 ounces) of tofu with one hamburger patty (3 ounces).[8] One cake of tofu has 86 calories; the hamburger patty has more than two and a half times the calories (235). The tofu has 9.4 grams of protein, the hamburger about twice as much (19 grams). But look at the fat comparison. While the cake of tofu has 5 grams of fat, the hamburger patty has 16 grams—more than three times the fat.

[8]Although the number of ounces is not the same, the two are compared, since one hamburger patty and one cake of tofu constitute an average portion for one person at one meal.

Blueberry Flan

- ¼ c. raisins
- ½ c. apple juice plus additional juice as necessary
- 1 t. vanilla extract
- 2 large (Japanese) cakes tofu, drained
- 1 c. fresh blueberries or raspberries
- 2 T. tahini
- 1 T. maple syrup
- ⅓ c. chopped almonds

1. Preheat oven to 325°F.
2. Place the raisins, apple juice, and vanilla in a small saucepan and heat over a low flame until the raisins are plump.
3. Cut the tofu into large cubes and place in a blender. Add all the other ingredients, including the apple juice and raisins, and blend until smooth. If the mixture seems too thick, add more apple juice.
4. Pour into 4 small baking cups. Place these in a large shallow pan. To the pan add hot water to a depth of ½ inch. Bake in the preheated oven for 30 minutes. Remove the cups from the water bath. Cool to room temperature. Chill.

In addition to being low in fat and calories while relatively high in protein, tofu is high in calcium, iron, phosphorus, and vitamins B and E. With an overall nutrient composition like this, it's understandable that for most of eastern Asia, tofu holds the place that meat and dairy hold in Europe and America. But now the ironic twist: In *The Book of Tofu* William Shurtleff and Akiko Aoyagi point out that despite the 49 billion acres of soybeans grown here, most Westerners have never eaten tofu, and they add that this is like imagining that in the largest wheat-producing country, no one had ever tasted bread. But our unfamiliarity with tofu is changing. Currently, tofu consumption by non-Orientals in the United States doubles every six months.[9]

Tofu can be made at home, and like homemade anything, a cake of homemade tofu will have a finer, fresher flavor than a store-bought version.[10] But because making tofu is time-consuming work,

[9]Although traditional Eastern soy foods like tofu are only beginning to be recognized here, Americans have eaten lots of soy for years without realizing it. Soybeans are sneaked into the diet through texturized, concentrated, and isolated soy products, which can be found in virtually every processed food: coffee whiteners, whipped toppings, imitation eggs, luncheon meats, baby foods, frozen desserts, and so on. The healthfulness of soy protein isolates and fibers is questionable. Their processing involves immersion in alkaline and acid baths, mechanical extrusion and stretching, then treatment with artificial colors and flavors.

[10]*The Book of Tofu* by William Shurtleff and Akiko Aoyagi (Brookline, Mass.: Autumn Press, 1975) gives step-by-step instructions for making tofu at home and includes over five hundred tofu recipes.

most people buy it prepackaged in supermarkets or natural food stores or unpackaged (floating in tubs of water) from greengrocers.

Always buy the freshest tofu you can find and select the whitest, firmest cake. Don't buy the tofu if the ends have been allowed to dry out, crack, or turn brown (this happens if it's kept out of water for a long period of time). Packaged tofu occasionally tastes slightly bitter—the result of age, packaging materials, or the chemical preservatives added to some packaged varieties.

No matter what kind of tofu you buy, it should be kept in a bowl of water in the refrigerator. Change the water daily. If you've bought prepacked tofu, drain the water out of the container as soon as possible and add fresh water. Kept in fresh water, tofu will last more than a week.

Tofu can be eaten as is, but only an extremely fresh cake from a master craftsperson has the silky-sweet flavor revered in China and Japan. In America tofu is better when it's flavored and/or cooked—and here the possibilities are endless.

I use more Japanese tofu than Chinese, although in certain dishes —such as scrambled eggs with scrambled tofu (cooked in butter and seasoned with fresh herbs and a sprinkling of shoyu)—Chinese tofu, because of its firmer texture, works best. The two are virtually interchangeable, however.

All tofu (especially the larger, fluffier, and more watery Japanese variety) must be drained before cooking, seasoning, and eating or the water will dissipate whatever seasonings you use and the tofu will taste wet and pulpy.

To drain tofu, wrap it in a cotton towel or paper towels and place it in a container in the refrigerator for at least an hour—and as long as overnight. The longer you allow it to drain, the firmer it will be and the more concentrated the taste.

For faster draining, place a weight on top of the tofu so that the water is pressed out of it. Anything will do as a weight, although the pressure that's exerted should be uniform. You can wrap two cakes of tofu in separate towels, place one on top of the other, and place a small wooden cutting board on top of both. In fifteen minutes, both towels will be saturated with water. A well-pressed cake of tofu can be picked up with two fingers and suspended vertically without the cake crumbling.

The grand-luxe method of draining and pressing involves steaming the tofu first, then allowing it to drain under weights. Tofu that is steamed first and then drained tastes surprisingly different from drained but uncooked tofu. The steam firms the tofu's texture, and later, after the tofu has been drained, the flavor is more concentrated and the texture is chewy.

Steamed tofu will hold up better under any sort of further cooking, such as sautéing or deep frying (for tempura). The longer you steam it, the firmer it becomes. An average time is 15 to 20 minutes of steaming, followed by 15 minutes of pressed draining. Now you're ready: Crumble the tofu and sauté it in sesame oil with garlic, shallots, finely minced onion, or scallions. Top casseroles with this as though it were cheese. Scramble eggs with it. Season it with oregano or basil and layer it into lasagna. Or cube the tofu and sauté it in sesame oil with garlic, herbs, and a bit of shoyu or wine. This can be served on top of watercress as a great appetizer or allowed to cool and added to salads. Cubed, the steamed tofu can also be added to all stir-fried dishes, where it will pick up the flavor of the vegetables and other seasonings.

Chestnut Soup

3 T. butter or 2 T. safflower oil
1 c. finely chopped carrots
½ c. finely chopped celery
1 onion, finely chopped
2 T. whole wheat pastry flour
6 c. vegetable or chicken stock
¼ c. tamari
2 c. peeled shelled chestnuts
½ c. sour cream
herbal salt to taste
chopped fresh tarragon, for garnishing
toasted whole wheat croutons (homemade from whole wheat bread), for garnishing

1. In a large saucepan, heat the butter or safflower oil until hot. Add the carrots, celery, and onion, cover, and sweat the vegetables until they're tender, about 15 minutes.

2. Sprinkle the flour over the vegetables. Slowly stir in the stock, then the tamari. Add the chestnuts, cover, and cook over low heat for 30 to 40 minutes or until the chestnuts are tender.

3. Pour into a blender and puree until smooth. Return to the saucepan.

4. Over very low heat, fold in the sour cream, then add the salt. Cook, stirring continuously, for several minutes until thoroughly heated. Serve in warm bowls, topped with fresh tarragon and croutons.

Vegetables

In 1970 the *Journal of Food Science* published a study that surveyed the food preferences of fifty thousand college students to see if there was a relationship between the vegetables people liked and the vegetables that were the most nutritious.[1]

You can guess what the study found. The vegetables *least* liked were cooked cabbage (coleslaw was liked), cauliflower, brussels sprouts, broccoli, turnips, and kale.[2] These were also among the most nutritious foods. Ounce for ounce, kale ranked higher than any other vegetable based on its cumulative content of the fifteen major nutrients; turnips ranked fourth; brussels sprouts were seventh; cauliflower was fourteenth; and cabbage was twenty-third.

As you can see from the table that follows, leafy greens in general are the most nutritious vegetables. Interestingly, if you measured all vegetables on a dry-weight basis, rather than weighing them water intact, you'd find that the nutritional contribution of leafy greens would skyrocket. The water removed, a portion of kale or collards that weighs the same as a dry portion of carrots or peppers is much more nutrient dense.

Vegetables, along with fruits, make up an enormously important part of a healthful, whole-foods diet. In this book each has been given a separate chapter. But in discussing their nutritiousness and how to preserve it, some general rules apply to both and are presented here.

First, vegetables and fruits share a special value. Both provide concentrated amounts of vitamins and minerals, but, at the same time, few calories and almost no fat. Although not particularly high in protein themselves, vegetables and fruits have a definite impact on dietary protein, since the vitamins and minerals they contain are critical to the body's ability to utilize amino acids and synthesize new protein.

[1]M. A. Einstein and I. Hornstein, "Food Preferences of College Students and Nutritional Implications," *Journal of Food Science,* Vol. 35 (1970), p. 429.

[2]Surveys by the Army in 1962 and 1967 and by the USDA in 1965–66 confirm these vegetables as among the least liked foods, with the USDA survey showing that only 10% to 20% of all individuals contacted ate dark green and leafy green vegetables.

Because vegetables and fruits are living things, they are extremely sensitive and vulnerable to nutritional destruction.[3] If you soak them, scrape them, chop them to bits, or leave them on a kitchen counter for hours; if you peel them, boil them, or eat them as leftovers days later, you simply won't get the nutrients you should from them. So treat vegetables and fruits gingerly by applying the rules that follow.

How to Preserve Fresh Vegetable and Fruit Nutrients

1. If there is a lot of dirt on a vegetable or fruit or if the vegetable is leafy and green (which usually means it's been heavily sprayed with pesticides if it's not organic), wash it quickly in running cold

Relative Nutritional Value of Fruits and Vegetables Surveyed for Their Cumulative Averages of Fifteen Nutrients

Food	*Rank for Relative Nutritional Value*	*Percentage Water*
Kale*	1	83
Collard greens*	2	85
Lima beans	3	68
Turnip greens*	4	90
Peas	5	78
Mustard greens*	6	89
Brussels sprouts*	7	85
Spinach	8	91
Broccoli*	9	89
Sweet corn	10	73
Watercress*	11	93
Sweet potato	12	71
Asparagus	13	92
Cauliflower*	14	91
Snap bean	15	91
Other Major Fruits and Vegetables		
Potato	17	80
Tomato	27	94
Orange	29	86
Apple	41	84
Watermelon	42	93

* If expressed on a dry-weight basis, the ranking could be improved in favor of these vegetables because of their high water content.

From: D.K. Salunkhe, ed., *Storage, Processing, and Nutritional Quality of Fruits and Vegetables* (Logan, Utah: CRC Press, 1974).

[3]Even after they're picked, plants continue to respire, metabolizing compounds with the help of carbon dioxide and giving off oxygen, water vapor, and heat.

Carrots Glazed with Filbert–Orange Sauce

- 6 or more tender carrots
- 2 T. butter
- ½ c. filberts, finely chopped
- 1 T. tahini
- rind of ½ orange, finely grated
- ½ t. grated mace or nutmeg
- 1 t. lemon verbena leaves, crushed
- ¼ c. orange juice (preferably fresh)
- 3 T. water
- 1 T. orange liqueur or Cognac (optional)

1. Choose tender, unbruised, medium-size carrots and scrub them well with a vegetable brush under cold running water. Do not use very large "horse" carrots; those are best for juicing. Slice the carrots on the diagonal, ½ inch thick. Steam them until just tender. While they steam, prepare the sauce.
2. In a skillet, melt the butter over low heat, then add the filberts. Toast the nuts in the butter for about 5 minutes, stirring, until they're nicely browned.
3. Remove the skillet from the heat and add the tahini, orange rind, mace or nutmeg, and lemon verbena.
4. Pour in the orange juice, water, and liqueur or Cognac, and return the skillet to the heat for a few moments, stirring, until the ingredients are well blended. Pour over the steaming-hot carrots and serve.

water, then pat it dry. If the vegetable or fruit is not dirty, wait until just before you eat or cook it to wash it.

2. To prevent rapid wilting, store fruits and vegetables in plastic bags or airtight containers in the vegetable crisper compartment of your refrigerator. In most refrigerators, the crisper is colder and more humid than the rest of the refrigerator, since air circulating in the rest of the refrigerator does not infiltrate the crisper tray. A cold, humid environment is perfect for highly perishable foods.

3. Store fruits and vegetables apart from one another. Many fruits, such as apples and pears, give off a natural ripening gas that affects the color and flavor of vegetables. Strong-flavored vegetables can also affect the flavor of delicate fruits.

4. Do not peel or trim vegetables or fruits until just before you cook them. In fact, try not to peel them at all, and use trimmings whenever you can (see "Trimmings Stock," page 166).

5. The outer leaves of cabbage, lettuce, and similar dark or leafy green vegetables receive the most sunlight while the vegetable is growing. Because these outer leaves are the most active site of photosynthesis, they're also where the highest concentration of nutrients

is found. Don't throw these outer leaves away. Eat them, make a good stock to use in cooking, or blend them into salad dressings. There are more vitamins, minerals, and proteins in the peel and just under the skin of apples, potatoes, citrus fruits, and many other vegetables than in the fleshy center. When possible, peel a vegetable *after* cooking it so that fewer nutrients are leached out into the cooking water.

6. Air and light activate natural enzymes in fruits and vegetables. These enzymes destroy vitamins. Thus the more pieces you cut a vegetable or fruit into and the longer you allow these pieces to be exposed to light and air, the more nutrients are lost.

For example, cucumbers lose 22% of their vitamin C when they're sliced. If sliced cucumbers are left for one hour, the loss jumps to 35%. If they're left for three hours, 49%. As much as 80% of the vitamin C may be lost when potatoes are mashed, and mincing cabbage causes it to lose six times the vitamin C than if the leaves are simply left whole.[4]

When you prepare a meal, cut fruits and vegetables last—immediately before you cook them. If the fruit or vegetable is to be cooked but served cold, cut or slice it *after* you cook it.

Remember to buy the freshest vegetables possible, for those will be the most nutritious. Growing your own vegetables is clearly the best option, though, in terms of nutrition and taste (see "Growing Your Own Fruits and Vegetables," page 204).

7. Buy fruits and vegetables that are exactly the size you need for one meal and use the whole food. Rather than buying one large cucumber and storing half of it, cut open, in the refrigerator for the following evening's meal, buy several small cucumbers and use a whole one each time you make a salad. Also avoid buying plastic-wrapped *halves* of large cantaloupes, melons, squashes, and cabbages. Produce markets cut large vegetables and fruits in half because wrapped halves of a huge melon sell more quickly than a whole large melon does alone. Nonetheless, halved fruits and vegetables have lost considerable nutrients because of exposure to oxygen and light.

Basic Vegetable Cooking

One of my most vivid memories is of a Swiss chard that a friend and I picked from his California backyard garden when the chard's dark red and green leaves were fourteen inches long. In a huge wok

[4]Robert S. Harris and Endel Karmas, *Nutritional Evaluation of Food Processing* (Westport, Conn.: Avi Publishing, 1975), p. 477.

we sautéed a bit of finely minced garlic and some garden-fresh scallions in sesame oil. Then we threw in the chard, tossed it a bit, covered the wok, turned the heat off, and waited. Three minutes later the chard had steamed itself and was lightly sesame-garlic flavored. We ate the chard on the spot, as though it were a hot salad. What was incredible was that, as we ate, the vegetable leaves seemed to spring around in our mouths, and the flavor was so delicious and intense we were both stupefied.

The best way to cook just-picked vegetables is the simplest way. Simple maximizes taste. To cream garden-fresh spinach, for example, is to cream the vitality, flavor, and texture right out of it. Vegetables that have not come straight from the field are better in more elaborate dishes. Early cooking manuals conspicuously lack vegetable recipes. This isn't because people didn't eat vegetables, but rather because

Trimmings Stock

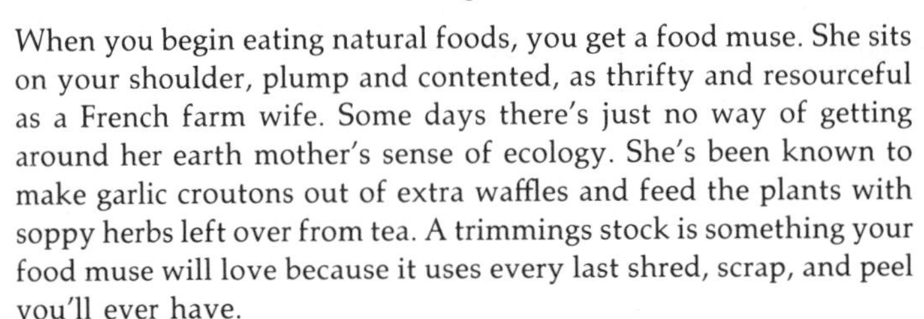

When you begin eating natural foods, you get a food muse. She sits on your shoulder, plump and contented, as thrifty and resourceful as a French farm wife. Some days there's just no way of getting around her earth mother's sense of ecology. She's been known to make garlic croutons out of extra waffles and feed the plants with soppy herbs left over from tea. A trimmings stock is something your food muse will love because it uses every last shred, scrap, and peel you'll ever have.

The purpose here is to make a soup—or, technically, a stock—that can be used instead of water in cooking. A good stock adds not only nutrients but flavor to the dishes you make. Breads taste just fine made with stock. You can use stock when sautéing and thereby cut down on the amount of oil you need. You can even drink it—half and half with tomato juice, for example—as a way of filling up with nutrients minus calories.

The easiest way to make a good stock is to do it while you're making dinner. Simply load a big heavy pot with all of the vegetable scraps you have on hand, cover the scraps with water, throw in a pinch of salt (salt draws the nutrients out of food), add bay leaves, onions, peppercorns, rosemary, ginger, or whatever herbs and seasonings strike your fancy, cover the pot, and let the stock simmer away for 1 to 2 hours. You must bring the stock just to a boil before simmering it, and a stir or two throughout the simmering is necessary.

Everything can go into the stockpot. The seeds and core from peppers, the ends of mushrooms, the tough stalks of broccoli, the

core of cauliflower, the outer leaves of lettuce, spinach, or cabbage —even the skins from onions, which will give the stock a wonderful auburn color and a slight French-onion-soup flavor. To get a full array of such good stuff, it's usually necessary to save the scraps and peelings from several meals. These will keep in a plastic bag in the refrigerator for several days until you're ready to make your stock.

When the stock has finished cooking, simply leave it on the stove to cool and a few hours later strain it into a clean glass jar. A good stock will keep in the refrigerator for one to two weeks.

A final note: If you are a meat eater, you can make an excellent stock by simmering meat bones along with your vegetable scraps. Never bouillon cubes, however. They contain salt, sugar, hydrogenated (saturated) oil, artificial flavors, modified cornstarch, and chemical additives.

Adelle Davis suggests adding a tablespoon of vinegar with the meat bones, since the vinegar will draw the calcium out of the bones.

After you chill a meat-based stock, a thick sheet of animal fat forms on the surface. Carefully lift it off and throw it away. This, however, won't remove all of the fat—nor the small amount of pesticides, insecticides, and hormones that are necessarily a part of animal foods and may be present.

Dione Lucas, in *The Book of Natural French Cooking,* suggests a very good substitution for meat stocks: Add a tablespoon of tamari to your vegetable stock while it's cooking. This will give the stock a more dominant flavor—as the addition of meat bones would have. Because tamari is naturally salty, do not add salt to the stock in the beginning.

cooking vegetables perfectly doesn't require a recipe. Just a good sense of timing and imagination when it comes to seasoning. Keep this in mind, though: Any pot will continue to cook a vegetable even after the heat's been turned off; vegetables are so delicate that even if they're removed from the cooking pot, they'll continue to cook themselves. So take a vegetable off the heat before you think it's done. By the time it's on the plate, it will be.

Following are some cooking and precooking notes for certain vegetables.

Artichokes. Cook whole. Cut the stem off close to the leaves. With a scissors, trim the pointed ends off the bottom row of leaves. Stand artichokes in a small amount of water and steam until a leaf pulled gently comes off easily. This will take anywhere from 20 to 45 min-

String Bean–Sesame Casserole

1	lb. green beans, cut into 2-in. pieces	1	T. dried oregano
			herbal salt
2	T. safflower oil	1	c. cottage cheese
1	small onion, diced	2	T. whole wheat flour
1	green pepper, chopped	2	T. raw wheat germ
1	leek chopped		juice of ½ lemon
1	clove garlic, minced	1	T. tahini
3	T. sesame seeds	1	T. sesame oil

1. Steam the green beans lightly (about 5-7 minutes). They should remain fairly crisp. Run under cold water for a minute to set color and set aside.

2. Preheat oven to 350°F.

3. Heat the safflower oil in a skillet. Add the onion and sauté for 1 minute. Add the green pepper and white part of the leek. Sauté for another minute. Add the remaining green part of the leek plus the garlic, sesame seeds, oregano, and salt, and sauté for 3 to 5 minutes.

4. In a large, ovenproof baking dish, combine the cottage cheese, whole wheat flour, and wheat germ. Add the leek-pepper-onion mixture and mix well. Fold in the green beans.

5. In a small bowl, whisk together the lemon juice, tahini, and sesame oil. Pour over string beans. Mix gently to blend. Pat down and bake, covered, in the preheated oven for 30 minutes.

utes, depending on the size and variety of the artichoke. Drain for a moment upside down on paper toweling.

Asparagus. Scrape any nubs or tough, stringy skin from the stalks. With your hands, snap the bottom end off at the point where it gives way easily. Steam gently or tie in bunches of 6 to 10 and cook upright in boiling water. The stalks should still be slightly crisp when you remove them from the water.

Cabbage. Both green and red cabbage can be washed and sliced raw into salads or quartered, cored, steamed, and seasoned.

Carrots. Use tender spring carrots or baby carrots for cooking, large carrots for juicing. Slice and steam. Or cook according to the French method—*à l'étuvée*—by placing them, sliced, in a heavy saucepan with a bit of vegetable oil and salt. Stir the vegetables, cover, and cook over a low flame. Stir again and cover. Keep up this process. The purpose here is to make the carrots sweat, so that they cook themselves in the

Baked Eggplant with Rosemary

Eggplant has a high moisture content and is naturally bitter, so it's necessary to remove some of the water before baking, otherwise the eggplant will turn mushy and tasteless and remain bitter.

- 1 good-size eggplant or several smaller ones
- 2 T. or more salt
- olive oil for brushing
- 3 heaping T. miso
- ⅓ c. red wine
- 2 cloves garlic, minced
- 2 T. minced fresh ginger
- 3 T. rosemary
- 1 T. honey
- ⅓ c. undegerminated cornmeal
- vegetable stock

1. Cut the eggplant into rounds ¾ inch thick. Sprinkle both sides of each slice liberally with salt. Stack the slices in a bowl and set aside for 45 minutes to 1 hour. At that point the eggplant will be coated with small beads of watery "perspiration." Rinse each slice well in cold water to remove the perspiration and all traces of salt. Pat the eggplant dry.

2. Preheat oven to 350°F.

3. Brush each slice of eggplant with olive oil. Place in a covered casserole dish and begin baking in the preheated oven.

4. In a small bowl, dissolve the miso in the wine. Mix in the garlic, ginger, rosemary, honey, and cornmeal. Mix in enough vegetable stock to make a loose paste.

5. Pour three-quarters of the rosemary-miso sauce over the eggplant and continue to bake. The eggplant should bake for a total of 45 minutes.

6. Just before serving, pour the remaining sauce over the eggplant and return to the oven for 1 minute more.

water vapor they're giving up. The method can be applied to turnips, green peas, and snap beans.

Cauliflower. Remove the leaves and use them in salad. Cut the head into small bouquets, remove most of the stem, and steam.

Celery. Clean stalks in cold water, trim if necessary, and eat raw or steam lightly. Celery root should be peeled, quartered, and lightly steamed.

Corn. Remove the green leaves from the cob, leaving the white leaves around the ears. Place ears in milk-water liquid (2 parts milk to 5 parts water). Do not add salt. Cook until tender (about 8 minutes) and then remove leaves.

Cucumbers. Always peel before eating and discard peels, for cucumbers are coated with a paraffinlike wax. Eggplants should be rid of

Eggplant. Eggplants should be rid of excess water by placing halves or cut slices in a bowl, sprinkling salt over them, then tossing the mixture and allowing the eggplant to sit. After 15 minutes, the eggplant will be covered with beads of water. Rinse the eggplant well in cold water and proceed to cook. This process also serves to reduce an eggplant's bitterness.

Endive. Wash endive well but do not allow it to stand in water, for it will become bitter. Steam gently, allow to cool, and slice into a salad. To cook, place in a saucepan with a touch of vegetable oil, sea salt, the juice of 1 lemon, and 2 tablespoons water. Cook, covered, over moderate heat.

Leeks. Wash thoroughly, for they always contain lots of sand. Green tops are best as seasoning or in salads. White parts can be tied together, blanched, and eaten as a vegetable.

Mushrooms. Wipe mushrooms clean with a damp cloth or paper toweling. Rub with a lemon to keep from turning brown. Trim very bottom of stems.

Onions. Peel onions and slice quickly to prevent loss of juice. To use onions raw or retain maximum juice, do not chop. Instead, cut in half, place flat side down, and slice as thinly as possible lengthwise.

Peas. Keep peas in the pod until ready to cook. Shell, then steam lightly. Or tie in cheesecloth, and drop cheesecloth and pods into boiling water and cook for a few moments only. Discard pods (they've added nutrients to the cooking water), eat peas, save water for stock.

Potatoes. Potatoes may be prepared in innumerable ways. However, certain potatoes are best suited to certain methods of cooking (see accompanying box).

Snap Beans. Cook beans as nearly equal in size as possible together. Steam briefly or steam and sauté.

Snow Peas. These are eaten as is, pod and all. Simply snip off each end and pull the membrane string away before steaming for 3 to 5 minutes.

Spinach. Wash spinach in several changes of cold water. Remove stems. Place spinach with the water clinging to its leaves and a bit

Cooking with Potatoes

The four basic types of potatoes—round white, round red, long white, and russet—come in several varieties. New potatoes are simply young, small potatoes with thin, papery skins. Several of the varieties listed below can be eaten as new potatoes. Their whiteness and firm texture make them good for potato salad. All potatoes should be cooked and eaten with their jackets on.

Type	*Appearance*	*Texture*	*Uses*	*Some Varieties*
Round White	Creamy buff-colored skin, almost shiny.	Very firm	Steaming Roasting Frying (home fries) Mashing	Katahdin Superiors
Round Red	Reddish skin that may be netted.	Firm	Steaming Roasting	Red Pontiac
Long White	Light tan, with smooth, shiny skin. Cylindrical shape with slightly flattened ends.	Extremely firm	Steaming Roasting Frying (home fries)	White Rose
Russet	Russet skin with a heavy netting. Long, cylindrical, with flattened ends.	Floury, mealy	Baking Frying (home fries) Potato pancakes Dumplings	Russet Burbanks

of sea salt in a saucepan. Cover and cook for only a few minutes, until the spinach is wilted. Four pounds of uncooked spinach reduce to 1 pound of cooked.

Tomatoes. Tomatoes can be washed, sliced, and eaten raw. To skin a tomato (as you must do before making a tomato sauce, for example) drop the whole tomato into rapidly boiling water for 30 seconds. Remove and allow to cool. The skin will now slip off easily.

Turnips. Turnips can be prepared and used like carrots. The large, waxed variety need peeling, however.

Herbed Potato Salad in White Wine

- 10 small new potatoes
- flowerets from 1 bunch (3 to 4 stalks) broccoli
- ½ c. white wine
- 2 pimientos
- 1 bunch fresh dill, finely minced
- 1 bunch Italian (flat) parsley, finely minced
- 1 t. herbal salt

Dressing

- 1 clove garlic, minced
- 1 T. Dijon mustard
- ½ t. paprika
- ¼ c. safflower oil
- ¼ c. olive oil

Garnish

- 2 ripe tomatoes, cut into wedges

1. Place the potatoes whole and unpeeled in a steamer. Cook until they are barely fork-tender. Rinse immediately under cold water to stop them from cooking and to set the color of the skins. Set aside.
2. Steam the broccoli flowerets until tender, just a few minutes, then rinse them under cold water to stop the cooking and set the color. Set aside.
3. Slice each potato into quarters, but do not peel. Place them in a large bowl and sprinkle them with the wine. Allow to rest.
4. Dice the pimientos into small squares. Chop the broccoli into very small pieces. Combine the pimientos, broccoli, dill, parsley, and salt. Add this mixture to the potatoes.
5. Place the garlic in a separate bowl. Use the handle of a wooden spoon to mash the garlic into a paste. Add the mustard and paprika and mix well. Whisk in the oils.
6. Stir three-quarters of the dressing into the potato salad. Mix well, making sure that all of the potatoes are coated lightly. Refrigerate until completely chilled.
7. Put the tomato wedges into a separate bowl and pour the remaining small bit of dressing over them. Refrigerate. Arrange tomatoes around the edge of the potato salad just before serving.

Season	What to Look For	Storage and Comments
Artichokes March, April, May	Compact, heavy, plump globes with large, tightly clinging flashy-leaf scales. Size has nothing to do with flavor.	Refrigerate promptly in the crisper section of the refrigerator. Use as soon as possible for maximum calcium and phosphorus.
Asparagus March into June	Green stalks with compact, closed tips. Avoid angular or flat stalks with large portions of white, which may be woody. Don't buy stalks that are soaking in water.	Refrigeration helps retain folic acid and vitamin C, but use as soon as possible.
Avocados all year	Bright and fresh appearing, not wilted or bruised. Should have good color, from green to purple-black, and feel heavy for their size. Irregular marks do not affect quality.	If hard, keep at room temperature until soft, then store in refrigerator. After slicing or mashing, add lemon juice to prevent pulp from discoloring.
Beans, Green all year; peak: May through August	Green, without scars, discoloration, or strings. When broken, they should snap, which is why they're sometimes called snap beans.	Store whole; if you plan to slice or french them, do it just before cooking. When refrigerated, they retain vitamin C and folic acid.
Beans, Lima mostly May into October	Pods are bright and dark green; shelled beans are plump with tender skins of green or greenish white.	Refrigerate. Very perishable, so use as soon as possible.
Beets all year; peak: June through October	Small or medium-size roots; large ones may be woody. Avoid flabby, rough, or shriveled beets.	Refrigerate. Tender green tops of early beets are high in nutrients. Tops should be used as soon as possible, roots within a week.
Broccoli all year; peak: October through May	Firm, compact, closed bud clusters of dark, sage, or purplish green. Stems should not be too thick. Enlarged or open buds and yellow or wilted leaves indicate old age.	Refrigerate. Use as soon as possible. Rich in vitamins A and C. Cook quickly in a small amount of water to retain vitamins and minerals.
Brussels Sprouts September through February	Bright green, firm, tight-fitting outer leaves. Avoid yellow, soft, or loose leaves. Small holes and ragged edges may indicate worms.	When refrigerated, they retain their nutrients for weeks, but for best eating, use them fresh.

Reprinted with permission from *Changing Times* magazine. © 1977 Kiplinger Washington Editors, Inc., July 1977.

Season	What to Look For	Storage and Comments
Cabbage all year	Three varieties: green, red and Savoy, which has crinkly leaves. Green and red should have firm, tight leaves of good color and be heavy for their size. Reject those with white, yellow or soft leaves and worm injury.	Refrigerate in plastic bag or film and use within a week or two. Fresh, all types are good for slaw and as a substitute for lettuce. When cooking, use a small quantity of water to retain vitamin C.
Carrots all year	Well formed with smooth skins and good orange color. Avoid wilted, flabby, rough or cracked carrots and those with green "sunburned" areas at the top.	These keep well when refrigerated; use as needed. High in vitamin A.
Cauliflower all year; peak: September through January	White to creamy white, compact flower clusters with green leaves. Open clusters indicate overmaturity; a speckled surface is a sign of insect injury, mold, or decay.	Retains vitamin C and other nutrients for several days when stored in hydrator.
Celery all year	Stalks should have a solid feel and fresh-looking leaflets. Soft branches indicate possible pithiness. Don't buy ones with wilted stalks, brown or black discoloration in central branches.	Store in hydrator and use as desired, preferably within a couple of weeks.
Corn all year; peak: April through September	Fresh, green husks and plump, tender kernels. Reject straw-colored husks and corn silks with decay or worm injury.	Should be refrigerated after it's harvested. Use as soon as possible. Yellow corn has more vitamin A than white.
Cucumbers all year; peak: May through August	Good green color, firm, well shaped. Avoid yellow, wilted and overly large ones; they are likely to be overripe and have hard seeds. Withered or shriveled ends indicate toughness and bitter flavor.	Keep cool and humid. Use within a few days.
Eggplant all year; peak: August and September	Firm and heavy with smooth, purple-black skin that is free of scars and cuts. Wilted, shriveled, or soft eggplants are usually bitter.	Keep cool and humid. Use within a few days.
Greens all year	Young, tender greens are best quality. Avoid greens with yellowing leaves, coarse stems, or dirt.	These include collards, turnip tops, mustard greens, Swiss chard, beet greens, spinach, and others. Keep cold and moist. Use as soon as possible.

Season	What to Look For	Storage and Comments
Leeks peak: spring; September through November	Fresh green tops with necks blanched two or three inches from the root. Wilted or damaged tops are signs of aging and tough, fibrous roots.	Refrigerate and use within a week. Wash thoroughly to remove any sand or dirt.
Lettuce all year	The solid head type, iceberg, should be fairly firm to firm with crisp, medium-green outer leaves. Butterhead, romaine, Bibb and leaf should have good color without wilted leaves, insects or dirt.	Put in plastic bag before refrigerating or store in hydrator. Discard any damaged outer leaves. Use within a few days. The greener the leaves, the more vitamins A and C and other nutrients.
Mushrooms all year; peak: November through April	Clean, closed caps around the stem; pink or light tan gills and undersides. Avoid brown or black gills, a sign of old age.	Caps are more tender than stems. Refrigerate and use as soon as possible, or sauté lightly in fat and freeze.
Okra mostly May through October	Tender green pods that will bend with pressure. Don't buy dull, dry, or shriveled pods because they will lack flavor or be unpalatable.	Deteriorates rapidly. Refrigerate and use as soon as possible.
Onions, Dry all year	Hard, firm, dry, with papery skin and small necks. Moisture at the neck indicates decay. Avoid those with thick, hollow centers in the neck or with fresh sprouts.	Leave at room temperature or refrigerate, but make sure they stay dry. They retain ascorbic acid if stored under 55°F.
Onions, Green all year; peak: May through August	Should have fresh green tops and be well blanched two or three inches from the root end. Wilted or decayed tops indicate tough fibers.	These are ordinary onions that are harvested young. Keep cold and moist and use as soon as possible.
Parsnips peak: October through April	Smooth and clean; small to medium. Avoid roots that are large, badly wilted, or flabby; they will be tough when cooked.	Refrigerate and use as needed.
Peppers, Sweet all year; peak: May through October	Red or medium to dark green glossy skin with firm sides. Avoid soft or dull-looking peppers or those with cuts or soft, watery spots, which indicate decay.	Green peppers are high in vitamin C and red peppers in vitamins A and C. Refrigerate and use within a few days.
Potatoes all year	Smooth, clean, fairly well shaped, uncut, unbruised, and without sprouts. Should not show any green.	Do not refrigerate; store at room temperature in a dark spot away from heat and cold. An important source of vitamin C.

Season	What to Look For	Storage and Comments
Squash all year	Soft-skinned types, such as crookneck, straightneck, and zucchini, should look glossy. Hard-shelled, such as Hubbard, acorn, and butternut, should have firm rinds and be heavy for their size.	Refrigerate soft-skinned varieties and use within a few days. Store hard-rind ones at room temperature or, if possible, at around 55°F.
Sweet Potatoes all year; peak: October through April	Uniformly colored skins of good copper or light tan. Avoid those with wormholes, cuts, or decay.	Do not refrigerate except after cooking; refrigeration causes internal discoloration and decomposition. Excellent source of vitamin A, good source of vitamin C.
Tomatoes all year	Well formed, free from blemishes, and slightly soft. Immature green tomatoes will eventually turn red but will not have the flavor quality of vine-ripened tomatoes.	Keep at room temperature until ripe, then refrigerate, but don't let them get near freezing temperature. Tomatoes lose vitamin C rapidly when overripe.

Squash-Nut Puree

- 3 lb. butternut squash, peeled, seeded, and cut into large cubes
- 1 T. safflower oil
- 1 T. butter
- 1 large onion, sliced into moons
- 2 eggs, lightly beaten
- 1 t. freshly grated nutmeg
- ¼ t. ground cinnamon
- herbal salt
- ¾ c. chopped pecans or walnuts

1. Steam the squash until tender. Place it in a food processor, blender, or a food mill, and puree until smooth, adding a bit of the steaming liquid if necessary. Set aside.

2. In a skillet, heat together the safflower oil and butter. Add the onion and cook until nicely browned.

3. Combine the squash puree, eggs, nutmeg, cinnamon, and salt. Mix well.

4. Preheat oven to 350°F.

5. Line the bottom of an ovenproof baking dish with the sautéed onion. Turn the squash puree into the dish on top of the onion. Sprinkle the nuts over the puree, patting them down into it so that they're not simply resting on top. Dot with a bit of butter if you like. Cover securely with aluminum foil and bake in the preheated oven for 20 to 30 minutes.

Sweet Potatoes with Ginger and Apples

- 3 lb. sweet potatoes
- 3 T. butter
- 1 large tart apple such as a Granny Smith
- 1 c. apple juice or cider
- 1 t. honey
- 1 T. grated fresh ginger
- herbal salt to taste
- cayenne pepper to taste

1. Scrub the sweet potatoes well with a vegetable brush until the skins are clean. Cut each potato into ½-inch round slices. Use 1 tablespoon of the butter to grease a casserole dish, then arrange the sweet potato slices inside it.

2. Preheat oven to 350°F.

3. Peel and core the apple and cut it into moons ¾ inch thick. Place these slices in a saucepan with the remaining 2 tablespoons butter and the apple juice. Bring this to a simmer and continue cooking for 3 to 4 minutes, or just until the apples lose their crispness. Stir in the honey. Remove from the heat and set aside.

4. Sprinkle the grated ginger evenly over the sweet potatoes. Then dust them lightly with a touch of salt and cayenne. Pour the apples carefully over the sweet potatoes, trying not to wash the ginger to the bottom of the dish.

5. Cover the dish tightly with aluminum foil and place it in the preheated oven for 40 minutes. Baste several times.

6. Turn the heat up to 400°, remove the foil, and allow the sweet potatoes to cook for 10 minutes or so more, basting again, until most of the juice has evaporated.

Sea Vegetables, Sprouts, and Salads

There are three areas of vegetable cookery that deserve special attention here: sea vegetables, because so few people know what to do with them; sprouts, because they're so varied, versatile, and easy to grow; and salads, because they're one of the best opportunities to be flamboyantly creative with food. In addition, sea vegetables, sprouts, and salads all have one very important characteristic in common: They're loaded with vitamins and minerals while exceptionally low in calories.

Sea Vegetables

Americans often call sea vegetables seaweeds—a misleading term, even when one puts the negative connotations of the term *weed* aside. Millions of years ago these vegetables came into existence (only plankton and moss preceded them) in the nutrient-rich environment of the ocean. In essence, they are nutritious, wild, aquatic plants—sea vegetables, really.

Sea vegetables reproduce by spores, gametes, and fragmentation. They do not possess separate tissues that carry out specific functions (leaves, roots, stems) as land plants do. The reason for this is simple. Land plants gather nutrients from the soil and interact with sunlight and air to carry on photosynthesis. Sea vegetables interact with their immediate environment, the seawater, by absorbing minerals and other nutrients from the ocean.

Experiment and use your imagination with sea vegetables. Wrap fish fillets in their leaves, then poach in broth. Sauté red laver with garlic and fold it into an omelet. Add *wakame* to split pea soup or fish chowder. Sea vegetables are excellent stir-fried with land vegetables or added to salads—dulse, for example, combines well with leafy greens, carrots, and avocado. Flavor your rice with sautéed scallions, mushrooms, and *nori.* Add *hijiki* to a cheese sauce.

Using sea vegetables is so simple that the only way to begin is by plunging in. Listed below—by their common names—are some sea vegetables and general guidelines for best use. Beside each sea vegetable, in parentheses, you'll find the nutrients that sea vegetable is likely to contain, although nutrients do vary among varieties, and where and when the sea vegetable was harvested will also affect its nutrient composition.

What the guide doesn't indicate is the nutrient richness of sea vegetables. *Nori,* for example, is not just protein—it's *35%* protein (higher than soybeans or steak). *Hijiki* not only contains calcium—3½ ounces of *hijiki* (dry) contains more calcium than ½ cup of milk. Of course, sea vegetables don't top the charts every time, but in general, they're extremely strong sources of minerals and oftentimes better than average sources of other nutrients.

You can obtain sea vegetables in Oriental shops or by mail from the sources listed here. The sea vegetables are usually sun-dried and require a brief soaking in a small amount of water. Mail-order items should contain directions for rehydrating.

Erewhon Trading Company
342 Newbury Street
Boston, Mass. 02115

Erewhon
8001 Beverly Boulevard
Los Angeles, Calif. 90048

Japan Food Corporation
P.O. Box 6096
Long Island City, N.Y. 11106

Nichols Garden Nursery
1190 North Pacific Highway
Albany, Ore. 97321

Uses for Sea Vegetables

As Natural Gelatin

Irish moss (pr, io, A)
wing kelp (B_6, K)
tengusa (io)
grapestone (C)
agar-agar/kanten (pr, io)

With Eggs

laver (pr, C)
nori (pr, A)
chi choy (pr)
kim (pr)

With Yogurt

dulse (f, pr, io, ph, A)
giant kelp (A, B, D, E)

In Soup

arame (sweet taste) (car, f, pr, A, B_1, B_2)
ma-kombu (car, pr, io, cal, ph)
bladder wrack (sweet taste) (pr, io, mag, ph, A)
dulse (f, pr, io, ph, A)
naga-kombu (f, pr, io, ph)
wakame (pr, ir, mag, cal)
Irish moss (pr, io, A)
matsumo (f, pr, cal)
mitsuishi-kombu (pr, io)
sea tangle (io, ir)
wing kelp (B_6, K)
rishiri-kombu (car, C)
nori (pr, A)
laver (pr, C)
sea lettuce (p, ir)
sugar wrack (cal, pr, io)

In Salad

dulse (f, pr, io, ph, A)
green *nori* (car, po, mag, cal, ph)
wakame (pr, ir, mag, cal)
sea lettuce (pr, ir)
hijiki (car, pr)
wing kelp (B_6, K)
chonggak (ir)

In Desserts

Irish moss (pr, io, A)

With Seafood

dulse (f, pr, io, ph, A)
naga-kombu (f, pr, io, ph)
wakame (pr, ir, mag, cal)
matsumo (f, pr, cal)
hijiki (car, pr)
mitsuishi-kombu (pr, io)
laver (pr, C)
nori (pr, A)

Steamed or Stir-fried with Other Vegetables

ma-kombu (car, pr, io, po, cal, ph)
dulse (f, pr, io, ph, A)
naga-kombu (f, pr, io, ph)
wakame (pr, ir, mag, cal)
Irish moss (pr, io, A)
hijiki (car, pr)
mitsuishi-komu (pr, io)
laver (pr, C)
nori (pr, A)

Key:

car = carbohydrate	io = iodine	cal = calcium
f = fat	ir = iron	ph = phosphorous
pr = protein	mag = magnesium	capital letters = specific vitamin

An excellent book on sea vegetables that gives instructions for foraging and includes numerous recipes is *The Sea Vegetable Book* by Judith Cooper Madlener, Clarkson N. Potter, New York, 1977.

Sprouts

Sprouts are delicious, nutritious, versatile in cooking, and easy to grow. Almost all seeds and beans can be sprouted, yielding baskets of sprouts for just a few cents. Elaborate equipment isn't needed—just seeds, water, a warm place for the sprouts to grow, and a large container. Always use food-grade or sprouting seeds. Planting seeds sold for gardens are chemically treated with toxic chemicals to inhibit mold and fungus growth. Natural food stores, food cooperatives, and, increasingly, supermarkets stock varieties of sprouting seeds. Of course, dried beans and lentils from any food store work quite well.

The most popular sprouts come from alfalfa seeds, wheat berries, soy and mung beans, and lentils. The chart on page 181 details quantities and sprouting times. To begin sprouting, use a large-mouth jar, such as a mayonnaise or Mason jar, a piece of cheesecloth or fine netting, and a mason jar ring or a rubber band. Place at least 2 tablespoons of seeds, beans, or seeds and beans in the jar. Cover the jar with the cloth and secure it with the rubber band or ring. Run warm water into the jar, rinsing the seeds, then drain the water. Now cover the seeds with warm water. Use about four times as much water as seeds. Let the seeds soak overnight.

Next morning pour off the water and rinse the seeds again. Save soaking and rinsing water for cooking or for watering plants. The water from soybeans, however, is toxic, and should be discarded. Invert the jar and place it in a bowl in a warm spot *out of* direct sunlight. If your kitchen is sunny and you can't find a darkened cabinet, cover the jar with a towel folded twice. Be sure that the jar can drain, or the seeds and sprouts will rot. Rinse the seeds two times a day in tepid water. Remove any fuzzy or moldy seeds if they occur. In 4 to 6 days, the jar will be full of sprouts. Alfalfa sprouts are the most nutritious and tasty when they develop their first leaves. Put them in direct sunlight at this point to green them and fully develop the chlorophyll. Finally, rinse sprouts and store them in an uncovered container (sprouts are alive and need ventilation) in the refrigerator. They will keep for about 5 days. Freshen them up every day or two by rinsing in cool water.

After growing for 2 to 3 days, alfalfa, lentil, mung bean, radish, and sunflower sprouts will burst through their seed hulls. The other varieties of sprouts have no hulls. Hulls are not harmful, but some people rinse them off in the belief that hulls may cause sprouts to mold. I've never rinsed hulls away and never had problems with mold, even when I've kept sprouts a week or more. Since rinsing the hulls away is easier said than done, I'm content to leave them.

Several companies sell equipment to make sprouting unconscionably easier, and perhaps to lend it a new-age status that cheesecloth banded to an old mayonnaise jar doesn't seem to have. Mason jars (first patented in 1858) with stainless steel mesh inserts are economical, genuinely practical, and usually available in natural food stores.

You can sauté mung or soy sprouts for just a second or two, but most sprouts are best uncooked in fruit and vegetable salads, liquefied in blender drinks or fruit juice (try blending with pineapple or tomato juice), sprinkled on top of soups or casseroles, or (in the best California tradition) layered on top of whole wheat nut-butter sandwiches. Wheat sprouts can be ground and used raw along with chopped nuts in desserts.

Sprout Chart

Seed Variety	*Dry Seed Measure*	*Yield*	*Soak Time*	*Rinse Hulls Away*	*Growing Time**	*Harvest Length*	*Sprouting Tips*	*Nutritional Highlights*
Alfalfa	1½–2 tbsp.	1 quart	4–6 hours	3rd or 4th day	4–6 days	1–2 inches	Place in indirect sunlight 1–2 days before harvest to develop chlorophyll	Tops list in content of minerals, protein, vitamins A, B complex, C, D, E, K
Black-Eyed Peas	1 cup	1 quart	8–12 hours	No hulls	3–4 days	¼–¾ inch	Allow ample room for expansion during soak time	Protein, minerals, vitamins A and C
Cabbage	¼ cup	1 quart	8–12 hours	3rd or 4th day	4–6 days	¾–1½ inches	Allow time to develop chlorophyll	Rich in minerals, vitamins A and C
Corn	1 cup	1 quart	12–16 hours	No hulls	3–8 days	½–1 inch	Experiment with all varieties; sweet corn is delicious	Niacin, folic acid, vitamin A
Garbanzos	¾ cup	1 quart	12–16 hours	No hulls	3–5 days	½–1 inch	Combine with wheat for nutritious mixture	Complete protein, numerous minerals
Lentils	¾ cup	1 quart	3–12 hours	3rd or 4th day for seed skins	3–4 days	¼–½ inch	Tasty and crispy if grown longer, but less nutritious	Complete protein, B vitamins
Mung Beans	½ cup	1 quart	8–12 hours	3rd or 4th day	3–5 days	½–2 inches	Grown in dark, at warmer temperature	Protein, vitamins A, C, calcium, phosphorus, iron
Peanuts	1½ cups	1 quart	12–16 hours	No hulls	3–4 days	¼ inch	Use raw, shelled nuts	Excellent protein, niacin, minerals
Radishes	¼ cup	1 quart	8–12 hours	3rd or 4th day	3–5 days	½–1½ inches	Develop chlorophyll, snappy flavor	Potassium, other minerals
Soybeans	1 cup	1 quart	12–16 hours	No hulls	3–5 days	½–1 inch	Best sprouted alone, do not use soak water	Complete protein, vitamins A, B complex, C, E
Sunflower seeds	2 cups	1 quart	8–12 hours	3rd day for seed skins	2–3 days	Under ½ inch	Sprout will get bitter if allowed to develop green leaves	Minerals, proteins, unsaturated fatty acids, vitamins D and E
Wheat	¾–1⅓ cups	1 quart	8–12 hours	No hulls	2–3 days or 4–7 days	¼–1 inch	Length grown depends upon intended use	Good protein, vitamins B complex, C, E, complete nutrition

*Growing time may vary due to temperature and water conditions.

Courtesy of "The Sprout People." Bima Industries, Inc. Copyright 1977.

The Art of Salad Making

A saucerlike bowl of anemic iceberg lettuce topped with one watery slice of gray-green gassed-red tomato is not a salad. It has no movement, creates no image, lacks even the smallest shred of self-expression.

True salad making takes a bit of creativity. Waltz around your kitchen. Poke into cupboards, throw open drawers, peer into those hinterlands at the back of the refrigerator. The more you let yourself get carried away, the better the salad will turn out to be. Do you have half a zucchini? Slice it in! Whole wheat crusts? A bit of garlic and olive oil and they're croutons. Chop the carrot tops with the watercress. Grate in some fresh Parmesan cheese.

- A decent salad has different textures so that your teeth must nibble, chew, grind, and bite in various interesting ways. Chewing spinach-mushrooms, spinach-mushrooms, spinach-mushrooms just isn't as much fun as chewing spinach, mushrooms, asparagus, tofu, beets, walnuts, sprouts.
- A somewhat opposite principle holds true for fruit salads. Each fruit has its own distinct and dominant personality that is quickly lost when too many fruits are mixed together. An amorphous chop suey of fruits has no striking taste or texture.

  Three fruits with the same characteristics make a good fruit salad. Bananas, pears, and grapes (all sweet, all soft), for example. Or oranges, grapefruit, and pineapples (all acidy, all watery, similar fibrous texture). Or nectarines, plums, and cherries (all fleshy, all watery, all sweet yet acidic at the same time).
- Every vegetable brings something different to a salad. This isn't the case, though, if you mix several different-textured but similar-tasting lettuces in one salad. A soft, delicate Bibb or Boston is simply upstaged by a stronger, crisper romaine. However, if you put that soft Bibb lettuce next to a crisp, fresh water chestnut instead of another type of lettuce, the Bibb's softness is brought out and enhanced by the crisp contrast of the water chestnut.
- If you contrast colors in a vegetable salad, you'll find you've almost automatically assured yourself of different textures and different tastes. Consider: white cauliflower, sprouts, and mushrooms. Lemon-green endive, army-green asparagus, and forest-green spinach. Purple cabbage, scarlet peppers, crimson beets. Brown seeds, nuts, croutons, grains. Yellow parsnips. Orange carrots. Plus rounds of multicolored skins on white flesh: zucchini, radishes, eggplant.
- The fresher the vegetables, the better the salad looks and tastes. Wash all vegetables and fruits well in cold water, using a natural-

bristle scrub brush. Leafy greens are heavily sprayed with pesticides. They, along with leeks and mushrooms, are also usually gritty with soil. Dry vegetables well by patting them with paper towels or dumping them into a cotton pillowcase and whirling it around and around (outdoors) until all the water is removed by centrifugal force. Wet vegetables will not hold a dressing.

- To maximize nutrients, never peel vegetables unless the outside

Turkey Salad

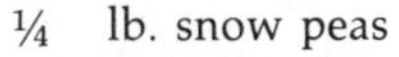

- ¼ lb. snow peas
- ½ c. diced peeled water chestnuts (preferably fresh)
- ½ c. fresh lemon juice
- 3 pimiento halves, cut into julienne strips
- 3 c. cubed cooked turkey
- ½ c. cashews, chopped
- ½ c. chopped celery
- ½ c. thinly sliced scallions
- 2 T. sesame seeds
- ¼ c. olive oil
- ¼ c. walnut, avocado, or safflower oil
- ⅛ c. vinegar
- 1 t. Dijon mustard
- ½ t. tamari
- few drops of honey
- bed of Boston or another soft, leafy lettuce
- ½ lb. Vermont aged Cheddar cheese, cut into julienne strips
- sprouts
- sprigs of fresh mint (optional)
- cherry tomatoes (optional)

1. Blanch the snow peas, then drop them into a bowl of ice water to set the color. Set aside.
2. Set the water chestnuts aside until ready to use in a bowl of cold water and ¼ cup of the lemon juice to keep them from discoloring.
3. Mix together the pimientos and the turkey, water chestnuts, cashews, celery, and scallions.
4. In a small skillet, sauté the sesame seeds in the olive oil until the seeds are nicely browned. Add the walnut, avocado, or safflower oil. Blend and set aside to cool.
5. In a separate bowl, combine the vinegar, remaining lemon juice, mustard, and tamari. In a steady stream, slowly whisk the oil in. Whisk in the honey.
6. Toss the turkey mixture with the dressing. Mound it in the center of a bed of soft lettuce. Alternating snow peas and strips of Cheddar, create a pattern like the spokes of a bicycle wheel around the turkey mound. Strew the top with sprouts, and garnish, if desired, with sprigs of fresh mint and cherry tomatoes.

skin is so bruised it's extremely unappealing (in which case, throw the whole vegetable in the stock pot). Fruits should be peeled: their slightly bitter skin can ruin the taste of a soft, sweet fruit salad and destroy the blend of fleshy textures. Most people are willing to sacrifice the nutrients in fruit peelings for a markedly better-tasting fruit salad. Fruits should always be pitted, hulled, and seeded as well.

- Greens should be torn rather than cut. Torn greens look more natural and feel better in the mouth since their naturally round, furled shapes are intact. For other vegetables, vary your cutting technique. This will intensify the different tastes in the salad. If you are using three carrots, for example, shred one, chop one into cubes, and slice the last into very thin rounds. You'll find that the three carrots taste almost like different vegetables. Shape does affect taste.

  All vegetables should be cut and trimmed so that they're easy to eat. Once it's served, you shouldn't have to cut a salad for every forkful or trim away the stems of greens such as spinach and watercress.

- Some vegetables taste better when they're lightly cooked and allowed to cool before they're added to a salad. Mushrooms sautéed

Three Beans

¾	c. navy (white) beans
½	c. adzuki beans
¾	c. garbanzo beans (chick-peas)
2	bay leaves
1	large or several small shallots, finely chopped
1	t. safflower oil
	herbal salt
1	good-size green frying pepper
1	whole pimiento
¼	c. minced parsley
2	T. safflower oil blended with 1 T. olive oil
⅓	c. sesame seeds

Garnish

if served cold: ripe tomato wedges
if served hot: sharp Cheddar cheese, grated

1. Place the navy and adzuki beans together in a pot full of cold water. Soak overnight. Similarly, place the garbanzo beans in a pot full of cold water and soak overnight.

2. Drain the garbanzo beans, add fresh water and 1 bay leaf, and begin cooking over medium heat, stirring occasionally and adding more water as necessary.

3. After the garbanzos have cooked for 1 hour, drain the navy and adzuki beans and add them to the pot with the garbanzos. Add the remaining bay leaf and more water so that the beans are well covered. Cook for an additional hour.
4. Sauté the shallot in 1 teaspoon safflower oil until wilted. Sprinkle liberally with salt.
5. Slice the pepper and pimiento into fine julienne strips, then slice again crosswise, so that the strips are no more than ¾ inch long. In a large bowl, combine the pepper, pimiento, shallots, parsley, and safflower and olive oils.
6. Roast the sesame seeds in a 350°F oven for 20 minutes, shaking occasionally. Allow to cool, then grind until smooth in a blender.
7. Add the cooked beans to the pepper-shallot mixture, mixing well, so that the beans are lightly but evenly coated with oil and vegetables. Stir in the roasted ground sesame seeds.
8. Chill in the refrigerator and serve as a cold salad, garnished with tomato wedges. Or spoon into a casserole dish, top with about ½ cup Cheddar cheese, cover, and cook in a preheated 300°F oven until the cheese has melted nicely.

just briefly in herbs and a tiny bit of butter or flavored with tamari always taste more interesting than raw mushrooms. I often steam slightly or sauté very lightly broccoli, cauliflower, and asparagus and let them cool before adding them to salads. Cooked vegetables have a different taste and texture, so a few cooked but cold vegetables in an otherwise raw vegetable salad greatly heighten the overall taste of the salad. But cook vegetables for a cold salad *very, very* briefly. If you sauté a vegetable, allow it to drain completely on a paper towel so that the cooking oil or liquid doesn't fight with the dressing.

- An extremely good dressing and a few fresh herbs can totally make an otherwise middling salad. For vegetable salads, mix heavy oils with lively tastes (French walnut, olive, sesame) with lighter oils (sunflower, safflower) so that the fresh flavor of the vegetables isn't masked by the more dominant flavor of oil.

The most common mistake in mixing up a salad dressing is using too much vinegar. Most vinegar available today is not fermented naturally from fruit but is percolated in recirculating vinegar generators using beachwood shavings, corncobs, or coke. Later it is filtered and pasteurized. Vinegar, therefore, is almost devoid of nutrients.

A good alternative is to use fresh lemon juice in place of vinegar for salad dressings. Lemon juice contains significant amounts of vitamin C and potassium and can be squeezed by hand and strained in mere seconds.

Salad dressings have a more piquant taste when they're made fresh. Begin the dressing right in the salad bowl by rubbing a wooden bowl with cut garlic (discard it afterward). Toss some dried herbs into the bowl (these will be softened by the oil); fresh herbs can be tossed directly in with the greens. Now mix in a bit of mustard, a bit of lemon juice, and maybe a well-beaten egg yolk. Finally, whisk in the oils.

Let the dressing stand a bit so that the flavors merge before you add the vegetables. Adding the heaviest vegetables first and the greens last will keep the greens springy.

Fruit salads can also be dressed: fresh whipped cream, yogurt, honey, freshly squeezed pear or apricot juice, or a bit of peach or pineapple kefir.

- Think about nutrients and don't be confined by typical vegetables. As it happens, the most nutritious vegetables usually do taste good and have wonderful textures. Romaine lettuce has six times more vitamin A and three times more vitamin C than iceberg lettuce (which not only is low in nutrients, but has a texture that dressing won't adhere to). Using mustard greens, dandelion greens, or kale instead of or in addition to spinach, romaine, and leaf lettuce will always boost the nutrient content of a salad and intensify flavor. Some other ways to heighten a salad's nutritional level and taste impact include:

  1. Sprinkle finely chopped parsley over the salad as a whole. Ounce for ounce, parsley is one of the greens richest in vitamins A and C and iron and adds a zing of flavor.
  2. Chop and add the *tops* of root vegetables to a salad. The tops of turnips and beets are actually more nutritious than the roots, and the flavor of both is extremely good.
  3. Add cooked cold chick-peas, lima beans, or adzuki beans to a tossed green salad to add protein. Cold bean salads themselves are highly nutritious.
  4. Add lightly roasted seeds or nuts (unsalted) for increased protein or a small amount of a cooked (but cold) grain. I often sprinkle tossed salads with a small amount of herbed couscous that's been allowed to cool.
  5. Add sprouts of any sort. Sprouts add considerable vitamins and minerals for very few calories. They add a special texture to salads. (See "Sprouts," pages 179–181, for guidelines on growing many varieties yourself.)

- And finally, use a generous bowl. If you have to toss your salad gently to keep the vegetables in the bowl, the bowl isn't big enough. Plants are expressive; they don't sit in a bowl like soup. Give vegetables room to fan out as they do naturally. You may also want to use a wooden bowl. Wooden bowls are traditional, since they were once plants themselves.

Salad: Infinite Possibilities

	Greens	
Arugula	Dandelion leaves	Radish tops
Beet tops	Endive	Sorrel
Carrot tops	Escarole	Spinach
Chicory	Kale	Swiss chard
Chinese cabbage	Lettuces: Bibb, Boston, leaf, romaine	Watercress
Cress		
	Raw Vegetables	
Avocado	Fennel	Scallions
Cabbage: green, red, Savoy	Jicama	Sprouts: bean and seed
Carrots	Leeks	Sweet peppers
Cauliflower flowerets	Onions: Bermuda, red, yellow	Tomatoes
Celery	Radishes	Water chestnuts
Cucumber		Zucchini
	Crisp-Cooked Vegetables (often lightly seasoned, always chilled)	
Asparagus	Broccoli flowerets	Mushrooms
Beans: yellow, green	Celery root	Potatoes: red jackets
Beets		
	Herbs	
Basil	Dill	Oregano
Borage	Fennel leaf	Parsley
Chervil	Garlic	Savory
Chives	Horseradish	Tarragon
Coriander	Mustard leaves	Thyme
	Legumes	
Garbanzo beans (chick-peas)	Lima beans	Pinto beans
Lentils	Navy beans	Red beans (kidney beans)
	Others	
Anchovies	Croutons*	Sardines
Artichoke hearts	Hard-boiled eggs	Seeds
Capers	Olives	Tofu
Cheese: fresh grated Parmesan; cubed or julienned Cheddar, Swiss, Jack	Herring fillets	
	Nuts	
	Roasted peppers	

*Whole wheat bread lightly sautéed in garlic, then toasted crisp.

Farmer's Markets

He dropped the snap beans, crisp as melon rind, and the pinkish-yellow fuzzy, ripe peaches into a small brown paper sack. And we both smiled to ourselves.

He was a farmer from a small agricultural town seventy-five miles upstate. On those peaches he'd just made 25% more than if he'd sold them to a wholesaler; on the snap beans, 20% more.

I lived in the middle of New York City. I'd just saved 20 cents a pound on the peaches, 15 cents a pound on the beans. In addition, I'd saved myself a dismal trip to the supermarket produce section, where (in most northern East Coast supermarkets) lifeless, mushy brown fruits and vegetables—fruits and vegetables nowhere near the quality of those I had in hand now—are heaped.

We were both in a parking lot full of people pinching, squeezing, and otherwise scrutinizing the pounds and pounds of fresh local produce that was being sold from the backs of farm trucks, which formed a wagon train around the entire lot.

Ironically, the people who grow food and the people who buy most of the food that's grown are the two groups with the least power in the American food marketplace. Direct marketing of food from farmer to consumer, still the most common method of food distribution in the world, has not been commonplace in the United States since the 1930s, despite the Old World tradition of farmers' markets that Europeans brought with them when America was settled.

But just like Lennon and McCartney said it would, things are getting better. In the late 1950s roadside stands made a comeback. Then roadside-stand families came up with a more feasible idea yet—PYO or Pick-Your-Own marketing operations. A variation on the PYO theme is Rent-a-Tree, where an urban family can select and rent a fruit tree with the help of the farmer in the spring. The farmer cares for the tree, but when the fruit is ripe, the renter comes and harvests, and keeps, the crop. In Pennsylvania there are small slaughterhouses where consumers can buy an entire meat animal raised by farmers who utilize a minimum of chemicals and drugs.

But there's no place like California when it comes to farm-fresh food. Since 1977 California has had a Farm Hot Line, a toll-free telephone number that fifteen thousand consumers used in 1977 to reach more than four hundred farmers. As a result of all those calls, California abounded with farmer-to-consumer markets, although surprisingly, New York still has the largest number of direct-marketing operations—1,200 in 1977.*

*Source: *National Food Review,* April 1978.

In 1978 the USDA made $1 million available to states for direct-marketing food projects. Farmers were more than willing to participate. Consumers happily envisioned vine-ripe red tomatoes. But the crucial link was a direct-marketing organizer. Oftentimes farm families simply got together and organized direct-marketing operations themselves. But in the South a group of students got together at Vanderbilt University in 1975 and formed the Agricultural Marketing Project, which has now organized food fairs in over thirty cities in Tennessee, Alabama, and Mississippi. According to the AMP, farmer-to-consumer food fairs are easy to establish, need no special equipment, and take about five to eight weeks to organize.

The AMP publishes three guides to help new groups start food fairs. The guides are available on request from the address below. In addition, your state agricultural extension service can provide you with a list of greenmarkets, "pick-your-own" farms, and rent-a-tree operations.

The Food Fair Organizer's Manual, The FARM Management Manual, and a videotape called *Organizing Food Fairs* are available from the Agricultural Marketing Project, 2606 Westwood Drive, Nashville, Tennessee 37204.

Fruits

Fruits have a slightly different nutritional role than vegetables. In general, they're not as mineral-rich as vegetables, but they're an excellent source of fiber for digestion and natural sugar (fructose) for energy. Cantaloupes and watermelon are among the most nutritious and least caloric fruits. Oranges, grapefruits, honeydew melons, strawberries, and tomatoes are all high in vitamin C. And apples, grapes, and plums are some of the best sources of fiber.

To maximize a fruit's nutritional impact and to get the full benefit of its fiber, buy fresh fruits only when they're in season (see accompanying chart), refrigerate them just as soon as they're ripe, then eat them as soon as possible. Fruits, like vegetables, are living things and very susceptible to physical and nutritional destruction if they're not handled and stored properly. The preceding chapter, "Vegetables," contains seven rules for preserving the nutrients in both.

Most fruits hit a peak of ripeness, then break down overnight. Organic fruits and vegetables are picked riper than their supermarket counterparts, making them more vulnerable to bumps and bruises. Also, please note that brokers for organic fruits and vegetables are often able to deliver only once or twice a week. The first step in getting a fresh, ripe organic fruit, then, is finding out when fruit is delivered to your natural food store. Greengrocers and supermarkets have specific fruit schedules as well, so ask for their delivery days and whether some shipments come from more local sources than others.

How to Pick a Ripe One

It isn't easy to pick a ripe fruit, and you take a big chance when you buy a hard one, place it on your sunny kitchen windowsill, then wait for it to reach that perfect state of fruity ripeness, because some fruits never will. They'll turn soft, yes. In fact, they'll go from being very hard to very soft very quickly. What this means, however, is that the fruit was picked much too early, before any of the natural sugars had a chance to develop. Such fruit will never ripen and never have a sweet flavor. Instead, by the time it's soft enough to eat, it will have already begun to turn bad.

The two best measures of ripeness are a fruit's smell and feel. Ripe fruits smell lightly fruity, clean, and airy—like a wild orchard in bloom. Fruits that have a dank, heavy, sweet smell are rotting from the inside out. A ripe fruit will also give a bit when you press it gently with the flat part of your thumb. No need to grip it in a half nelson. Just a bit of thumb pressure and you'll know exactly where the fruit is at.

Here are some specifics to watch for:

Apples. An apple should be firm and crisp. If it has a watery, soft give to it, chances are it will be mealy.

Apricots. Avoid a blond apricot. Pass by those with a green cast, too. Apricots should be fat and golden.

Bananas. Buy them bright, unblemished yellow. Eat them when they're covered with brown polka dots. Once they're ripe, you can put bananas in the refrigerator. Here, the skin will turn solid brown, but the banana itself will keep for another 3 to 5 days in excellent eating condition.

Berries. Avoid stained containers, a sign that the berries have begun to turn. Unlike many other fruits, berries should be firm. Blueberries should be a dull blue, and the silvery sheen they sometimes have is a protective coating—it doesn't mean the berries are old.

Cantaloupes. The more pronounced the lacy netting on a cantaloupe, the better. The more even, dull, creamy yellow the color, the more ripe. The blossom end of a cantaloupe (not the concave stem end) will be slightly soft if the cantaloupe is ripe.

Coconuts. A ripe coconut feels heavy for its size. The eyes on the flattened bottom should be clear and dry.

Grapefruits. Citrus fruits are among the hardest fruits to judge. Thorny scratches and brown spots are meaningless. What you're looking for here is a thin-skinned fruit that feels heavy for its size. Thicker skinned grapefruits or grapefruits that have a slightly pointed end are more pulpy and have less juice.

Grapes. Grapes will never improve in color, flavor, or amount of sugar once they've left the vine, so choosing a ripe bunch is essential. Darker grapes should not be tinged with green (underripe). Look at the point where the grape attaches to the stem. If this area looks strong and fresh, the grapes probably will be too.

Honeydews. Here again, a tender blossom end is a sign of ripeness. But the easiest way to tell a ripe honeydew is by rubbing your hand over the melon's skin. The skin should feel sticky—a sign that the sugar has moved outward and the melon is at its peak.

Kiwis. Kiwis look like furry brown eggs. They should feel like ripe pears.

Kumquats. The test of a ripe kumquat continues to puzzle fruitarians. Firm is better than soft, and bright orange is better than pale.

Lemons. A lemon is ripe for only a fleeting amount of time. Thin-skinned, heavy ones are the most juicy. Mustard-yellow lemons are too ripe. Greenish lemons are too acidy.

Limes. Limes are actually ripe when they're lemon yellow, not when they're lime green. A lime should be heavy for its size.

Poppyseed–Apple Cream Pie

Filling

- 1 c. fresh apple juice or cider
- 2 T. flaked agar-agar or 1½ T. *kanten**
- 2 T. lemon juice
- ¾ c. plain yogurt
- ¼ c. vanilla-flavored yogurt
- 4 egg yolks, well beaten
- 1 c. chopped apple†
- ¼ t. grated lemon rind
- ¼ t. grated orange rind
- ¼ c. honey
- 2 t. vanilla extract
- ½ t. grated nutmeg (preferably fresh)
- poppyseeds

Pie Crust

- rolled oats
- wheat germ
- whole wheat pastry flour
- ground sunflower seeds
- ground pumpkin seeds
- ½ t. herbal salt
- ½ t. ground cinnamon
- 2 T. honey
- 1 T. tahini
- 2 t. lemon juice
- 4 egg whites, well beaten

1. *Making the filling.* Bring the apple juice just to a boil. Sprinkle the agar-agar over the juice, then take the pot off the heat. Stir several times until the agar-agar has dissolved, then add the lemon juice. Return the pot to the heat and bring just to a boil once again. Simmer for 15 minutes, stirring occasionally. Set aside to cool.

*See Jelling and Thickening Agents, page 326.
†Unpeeled apples may be used, but the pie has a creamier consistency if the apple is peeled.

2. Mix the two yogurts together. Pour into a cheesecloth-lined sieve and allow the whey to drain from the yogurt for several hours or until the yogurt has a thick sour cream consistency.

3. After the mixture has cooled slightly, add the egg yolks, apple, lemon rind, orange rind, honey, and vanilla. Bring to a gentle boil once again, then remove from the heat and set aside to cool.

4. When the apple-lemon mixture has cooled, fold in the nutmeg, poppyseeds, and yogurt. Chill until set.

5. Preheat oven to 400° F.

6. *Meanwhile make the pie shell.* Combine enough oats, wheat germ, flour, and ground seeds to make 2 cups. (The proportions of each ingredient may be varied as desired.) This pie crust is similar to granola and will be crunchy rather than flaky. Add the remaining ingredients except the egg whites one at a time and work well into the grain and seed mixture. If the mixture seems dry or doesn't hold together well, add a tablespoon or two of cold water or a few teaspoons of oil or honey as needed. Press the mixture into a lightly greased pie pan, making a thin crust, and bake in the preheated oven for 10 minutes. Allow the pie shell to cool thoroughly before adding the filling.

7. Once the filling mixture has set and the baked pie shell has cooled, gently fold the egg whites into the apple-yogurt mixture. Pour into the pie shell, sprinkle the top lightly with more poppyseeds, then chill for several hours before serving.

Mandarin Oranges. Mandarins are more orange than an orange when ripe. Puffy or spotted mandarins are past their prime.

Mangoes. Mangoes vary in color, so don't be insistent about the beautiful rainbows some of them have. Instead, feel out their worth. Ripe mangoes yield but are not pillow soft.

Melons. All should have a warm, flowery aroma. Like most fruits, once a melon is cut, no more ripening takes place and the flavor and nutrients dissipate fast. So never buy half a melon that's been wrapped in cellophane. (For individual melons, see Cantaloupes, Honeydews, and Watermelons.)

Nectarines. Those that have been picked before they're ripe will never have any flavor, so don't buy a nectarine that's hard to begin with. A ripe nectarine has baby-soft skin and gives at the seams.

Oranges. Sometimes extra chlorophyll tinges the orange's skin, turning it slightly green. This is perfectly normal—a good sign in fact. Oranges should not be swollen or shrunken.

Stuffed Peaches

- 6 large peaches
- 1 T. milk
- 2 T. carob powder
- 1 egg yolk, beaten
- 1 T. vanilla extract
- ½ t. honey
- ½ t. ground cinnamon
- 1 t. grated lemon rind
- ⅓ c. shredded unsweetened coconut
- ½ c. finely chopped almonds
- 1 c. sweet white wine
- peach yogurt (optional)

1. Drop the peaches into boiling water for 30 seconds to loosen their skins. Drain, peel, cut in half, and remove the pits. Hollow out about a third of the fruit pulp. Chop this and set it aside.

2. Preheat oven to 375°F.

3. Add the milk to the carob powder and blend to a paste. Beat in the egg yolk, vanilla, honey, cinnamon, and lemon rind. Fold in the coconut. Fold in the chopped peach pulp. Mix well.

4. Stuff each peach half with a generous amount of the mixture, then top liberally with the nuts. Place them in a small baking pan. Pour the wine over the peaches and bake for 30 minutes in the preheated oven. Serve either warm or cold with a dollop of peach yogurt, if desired.

Papayas. Ripe papayas are creamy yellow, smell tropically sweet, and give readily.

Peaches. Ripe peaches have the smell of fresh-churned butter. Their background color is yellow (not green), and over the yellow there is a pink blush. Peaches should be delicate but firm. Fuzziness has nothing to do with anything.

Pears. Press the flesh near the stem end—it should give. Pears should also have a noticeable pear aroma.

Persimmons. Ripe persimmons have a silky, lipstick-orange sheen and not one speck or scar of brown. The fruit should feel heavy, as though it's about to burst.

Pineapples. Without scratching yourself (this can be tricky), pull the centermost leaf from the pineapple's crown. If it gives way easily, if the pineapple is heavy for its size, and if the whole fruit is golden brown (not green brown), you've got yourself a good one.

Plantains. Many people buy plantains thinking they are bananas, then wonder why they never get soft. Ripe plantains are hard. They should always be cooked before being eaten.

Plums. Plums display a little resistance when ripe and are also tart rather than sweet. They should feel tight, but not be rock hard.

Watermelons. Give it a good rap. If the knock sounds hollow, you've got a good one. Try to buy a whole one, but if you must buy watermelon cut, look for shiny rose flesh (absolutely no whiteness) and an uninterrupted row of shiny black seeds.

Fruits and Seasons

	Jan	*Feb*	*Mar*	*Apr*	*May*	*Jun*	*Jul*	*Aug*	*Sep*	*Oct*	*Nov*	*Dec*
Apricots						▲	▲					
Avocados	⧗		⧗									⧗
Bananas			⧗	⧗								
Berries						▲	▲					
Blueberries						▲	▲	▲				
Cantaloupes						●	●	●				
Cherries						▲	▲					
Coconuts										⧗	⧗	⧗
Cranberries										●	●	●
Grapes								●	●	●		
Honeydews								●	●	●		
Lemons					⧗	⧗	⧗					
Limes						⧗	⧗	⧗				
Mangoes					▲	▲	▲					
Nectarines							●	●				
Papayas					⧗					⧗		
Peaches						▲	▲	▲				
Pears								⧗	⧗	⧗		
Persimmons										▲	▲	▲
Plums/Prunes							▲	▲	▲			
Pomegranates										▲	▲	
Strawberries				●	●	●						
Tangelos											▲	▲
Tangerines	▲										▲	▲
Watermelons						▲	▲	▲				

● For this fruit, more than 50% of the year's crop is available during the months noted.

▲ For this fruit, more than 75% of the year's crop is available during the months noted.

⧗ Some percentage of this fruit is available all year. Highest peak months are noted.

Apples

Variety	Appearance, Flavor, and Texture	Uses: Fresh and Salad	Uses: Pie	Uses: Sauce	Uses: Baking	Season and Availability	
Cortland	Red and green tones. Flesh is white with a mild, tart flavor and tender texture. Cooks rapidly.	Excellent	Excellent	Very Good	Good	Oct.–March	Eastern and upper central States
Delicious, Golden	Greenish yellow to bright yellow. May have some russeting. Sweet. Semifirm texture.	Excellent	Excellent	Very Good	Very Good	Sept.–June	Throughout U.S.A.
Delicious, Red	Bright red color. Sweet taste. Mellow texture.	Excellent	Fair	Fair	Poor	Sept.–June	Throughout U.S.A.
Granny Smith	Bright lime-green color. Tart. Crisp texture.	Excellent	Very Good	Very Good	Very Good	October–July	Throughout U.S.A. mostly imported; increasing U.S. production, mostly in western states.
Jonathan	Bright red. Tart. Tender and juicy.	Very Good	Very Good	Very Good	Poor	Sept.–Jan.	At beginning and end of season not readily available in Northeast and Southwest, but generally available throughout U.S.A.

		Uses					
Variety	*Appearance, Flavor, and Texture*	*Fresh and Salad*	*Pie*	*Sauce*	*Baking*	*Season and Availability*	
McIntosh	Red and green in tone. Slightly tart. Tender. Intense flavor and aroma.	Excellent	Excellent	Good	Fair	Sept.–June	Available throughout U.S.A. during height of season. Less generally available in western and southern U.S.A. during rest of season.
Newton Pippin	Yellow green to green color. Slightly tart taste. Firm texture that is slightly mealy.	Very Good	Excellent	Excellent	Very Good	Sept.–June	Western states and Virginia. Most of crop is used for commercial processing.
Rome Beauty	Bright red with occasional yellow streaks. Firm texture. Slightly tart.	Good	Very Good	Very Good	Excellent	Oct.–June	Throughout U.S.A.
Stayman	Bright red color. Tart. Semifirm.	Very Good	Good	Good	Good	Oct.–Mar.	Mid-Atlantic and Southeast.
Winesap	Dark red. Winelike flavor. Somewhat tart.	Excellent	Good	Good	Good	Oct.–June	Throughout U.S.A.

Courtesy International Apple Institute.

Dried Fruits

The first Americans to land on the moon ate dried peaches for dessert. In a small way it was the culmination of an American tradition, for the first colonists dried every wild fruit they found here, by cutting each into rings, then spreading the fruit on mats in the sun to dry. At night the fruit was taken indoors and hung—like on a clothesline—near the fireplace; if it were left outdoors, it would be wet with dew by dawn. In every culture dried fruit and other dried foods have been a necessity. In fact, drying food has been so important and pervasive that the practice has lingered even though the need is gone.

A raisin doesn't taste like a grape. A prune doesn't taste like a plum. Drying concentrates the flavor and sweetness of a fruit. That's why breads, stuffings, puddings, stews, casseroles, and loafs call for dried apricots, currants, figs, raisins, and so on. A fresh grape just wouldn't survive inside a rugged Irish soda bread.

Drying is simply taking water away. Nutrients are lost in the process—but not many. Vitamins A and C seem to be the most susceptible. Still, drying usually beats freezing and is certainly pref-

Stuffed Figs

½ ripe avocado
2 T. plain yogurt
1 t. honey
1 T. raisins, softened*
½ t. ground cinnamon
½ t. dried basil
¼ t. sweet paprika
10 large fresh figs
½ c. or more chestnut or whole wheat flour
safflower oil

1. Remove the skin from the avocado, mash and mix well with the yogurt, honey, raisins, cinnamon, basil, and paprika.
2. With your thumb, make a well in each fig. Stuff the figs with the avocado mixture.
3. Dredge the figs in the flour. Chestnut flour is preferred, but whole wheat works fine.
4. Generously coat a medium-size skillet with safflower oil. Heat over a moderate flame, then sauté the figs for 3 to 4 minutes on each side. Drain on paper towels and serve as an appetizer, dessert, or snack.

*To soften raisins, let them sit in very hot water for several minutes.

erable to canning as a way of preserving nutrients in foods that can't be eaten fresh.

Commercially dried fruits and vegetables are either dehydrated mechanically or dried in the sun. Although drying in the sun is the most natural and least expensive method (and most fruits are dried this way), sun-drying results in greater nutrient losses than does mechanical drying. While mechanical drying never takes longer than twenty-four hours, sun-drying may take days; nutrients, of course, are lost through heat and over time.

Fruits and vegetables that are earmarked for drying are allowed to ripen as much as possible, since most of the natural sugar in a plant develops inside the fruit or vegetable during its last ten days on the tree or vine. Fruits and vegetables to be dried also must be in optimal condition, since a bruise or two will keep the food from drying evenly, causing the whole food to spoil. Until recently, most fruits and vegetables to be dried were handpicked; the most delicate still are.

Before drying, fruits and vegetables are washed, often peeled, and sometimes sprayed with sulfur dioxide gas. Sulfuring is a point of contention, for while it is an added chemical, not a natural component of the food being dried, sulfur dramatically preserves the vitamins and minerals in dried foods. With the exception of thiamine, a greater proportion of virtually every other vitamin (especially A and C) is preserved when fruits and vegetables are sulfured.[1]

Exhaustive clinical research has shown no negative effects from sulfur intake. This may be explained in part by the fact that sulfur is formed normally in the body and is routinely excreted in the urine. In any case, the average daily intake of sulfur in all of its different forms is very low—2 milligrams in the United States.[2]

The United States is a major producer of prunes, dried plums that have a high sugar content, and raisins. The most commonly used grapes for raisins are wine grapes, since these contain the most sugar. The best, largest, juiciest raisins—Malaga raisins—come from muscat grapes. Currants, dried small black grapes, are more tart than raisins, even though both are roughly 70% sugar.

Much of the dried fruit found in natural food stores is imported. Apricots, figs, and the best golden raisins come from Turkey. Deglet Noor dates—amber brown, very juicy, and the sweetest dried fruit

[1]"From Tree to Table," *Whole Foods* (September 1978), p. 30.

[2]The acceptable daily intake set by the United Nations FAO/WHO is .7 milligram for every kilogram of body weight—or 50 milligrams for a 155-pound person.

of all—come from North Africa. Dried mangoes and bananas come from the Philippines. Dried pineapple comes from Taiwan.

Dried pineapple is often labeled honey dipped. Actually, like many other dried fruits both imported and domestic, it is dipped in a sugar-water solution. Dried fruit found in natural food stores is more likely to be sprayed with a honey-water solution.

By law, all imported dried fruit must be fumigated. The fumigates in use today are gaseous chemical pesticides used to disinfect boxcars, grain elevators, food-processing plants, and other areas where foods are stacked or stored. All fumigates are toxic to humans; and toxic residues do remain on the food.[3]

Some of the domestic dried fruit available in natural food stores is labeled organic. Most of the companies that market organic dried fruit back up the claim with grower certifications.

Apricot-Pecan Tea Ring

Dough

- ¼ c. warm water
- 1 pkg. dry yeast
- ½ c. milk, scalded
- 1 T. honey
- 1 T. butter
- 1 t. herbal salt
- 1 egg, well beaten
- 1 t. finely grated lemon rind
- 1½ c. whole wheat flour sifted together with 1 c. white flour
- softened butter or safflower oil
- ½ t. grated nutmeg

Filling

- 1 c. finely chopped dried apricots
- ½ c. apple juice
- 1 c. pecans, chopped

1. Put the warm water in a large bowl. Sprinkle the yeast over the water and set aside.

2. Combine the milk, honey, butter, and salt. Cool to room temperature. Add to the yeast mixture.

3. Add the egg and lemon rind, mixing well.

4. Beat in the flour, making a soft, manageable dough. Turn the dough out onto a floured surface and knead for at least 10 minutes, or until the dough feels full and elastic. Rub the dough lightly with butter or safflower oil and place it in a cloth-covered bowl until doubled in volume.

[3]Donald A. Wilbur, "Fumigant," *McGraw-Hill Encyclopedia of Food, Agriculture, and Nutrition* (New York: McGraw-Hill, 1977).

5. Punch the dough down. Knead for a few minutes. Allow to rest for 10 minutes.

6. On a well-floured surface, roll the dough out into a rectangle no more than ¼ inch thick. Spread lightly with softened butter and sprinkle with nutmeg.

7. In a saucepan, heat the apricots and apple juice slowly over low heat until the apricot bits have swelled. Blend in a blender to a thick, lumpy pulp.

8. Spread the dough evenly with the apricot pulp. Sprinkle the chopped pecans over the apricot. Roll the dough up, jelly-roll style, beginning with one of the long sides of the rectangle. Transfer to an ungreased baking sheet, seam side down.

9. Bend the roll into a ring, tucking one end into the other. Pinch the seams closed. Using scissors, make V-shaped cuts, ½ inch deep, in the ring every 2 inches. Turn the points of the V outward, exposing a bit of the filling. Cover with a cotton towel and allow to rise a second time until doubled in volume.

10. Preheat oven to 350°F.

11. Bake in the preheated oven for approximately 30 minutes.

Drying Your Own Fruits and Vegetables

Drying fruits and vegetables is easy, inexpensive, ecological, and requires few tools.

Virtually all fruits and vegetables can be dried. Fruits are easier than vegetables, and dried fruits taste better than dried vegetables. In fact, you may want to skip vegetables entirely. Dried vegetables must always be reconstituted before they can be eaten. By the time they're picked, dried, reconstituted (soaked until soft and plump), then cooked, many dried vegetables have lost their vitality and flavor.[4]

The best fruits for drying include the following:

Apples and Pears. Pare, core, and cut into rings ⅛ to ¼ inch wide.

Apricots and Peaches. Cut in half; remove pit.

Bananas. Use very ripe, brown-spotted ones. Remove soft spots. Cut into ¼-inch slices.

Berries. Halve strawberries. Pit cherries. Give cranberries a 30-second dunking in boiling water, then in cold water to crack skin. All other berries leave whole.

[4]Mushrooms are an exception. Not only do mushrooms dry well, but their flavor is intensified.

Grapes. Use seedless variety. Dunk in boiling water to crack skins. Drain juice away (save it and drink).
Plums. Pit or leave whole. Quickly dunk in boiling water to crack skins.
Pineapple. The riper the fresh pineapple, the less sour the dried pineapple will be. Dice or slice into ½-inch pieces or rings. Dry on a very fine mesh material so the juicy pulp doesn't slip away.

The goal in drying is to remove as much moisture from the food as possible. This requires heat and air movement. Heat, of course, causes the water in food to evaporate. But the right balance of heat must be struck. Too much heat will cause the outer surface of the food to dry as hard as a rock very quickly, leaving moisture locked in the center. You end up with leather outside and mush inside. On the other hand, too little heat will allow the food to spoil before it dries. Food dries best at temperatures between 90° and 110°F.

Air movement is important because without it, drying fruit is surrounded by a halo of humidity from the evaporating water. Humidity slows down the drying process and may cause the fruit to spoil before it can dry completely.

If you live in a hot, dry climate, you can dry enough fruit for family and friends outdoors in the sun.[5] Your only problem will be insects, so unless you have a screened-in porch, you'll have to cover your drying trays with wire mesh or cheesecloth to protect the fruit.

To construct a tray, stretch wire mesh or cheesecloth tightly across the bottom of a wooden picture frame. Or simply buy a cheap window screen and use it as a drying tray. Anything that will allow a maximum amount of air to circulate around the fruit will do.

If you're drying outdoors, make sure the trays are placed in a dust-free spot and elevate them above ground so that air can circulate easily. On very hot days dry in the shade. Hot sun may harden the fruit's surface too much—especially in the beginning. Sun-dried fruits take about two days. Do not leave the trays out overnight, since the fruit will be soaked with dew by morning.

Choose only the best unblemished ripe fruits and arrange them skin side down with plenty of room on the tray; never stack fruits. Rotate them every now and then to prevent sticking.

All sun-dried fruit should be pasteurized after drying to kill insects, which may not be visible. Simply place the dried fruit on baking sheets and put in the oven at the lowest possible setting for 15 minutes.

Oven-drying is perfect for small amounts of fruit. It can be done

[5]Elaborate box driers, capable of drying many pounds of food at the same time, are expensive —$65 to $130—and are worth the expense only if you own a natural food store. For everyone else, most books on food drying include instructions for building a perfectly suitable substitute.

Strawberry Cheesecake

2 c. strawberry yogurt

Pie Crust

2 c. homemade granola or 2 c. crushed graham crackers
2 T. butter, softened
2 t. honey
2 T. apple or lemon juice
1 t. grated lemon rind

Filling

3 large (Japanese) cakes tofu, well drained
1 lb. ricotta cheese
2 or more T. apple juice
1 T. vanilla extract
1 T. tahini
2 eggs, well beaten
1½ t. grated lemon rind
1½ t. grated orange rind
3 T. honey
1 pt. fresh strawberries

1. Drain the yogurt through a cheesecloth-lined sieve for several hours (6 to 8). The yogurt should have the consistency of heavy whipped cream.

2. Meanwhile, combine all the crust ingredients together and mix well, adding more juice to moisten if necessary. Press into a lightly buttered 9-inch pie pan. If graham crackers are used, bake the crust in a preheated 400°F oven for 5 minutes, then allow to cool.

3. Preheat oven to 350°F.

4. In a blender, combine the tofu, ricotta, apple juice, vanilla, tahini, eggs, lemon rind, orange rind, and honey. Puree until smooth. The mixture should be quite thick.

5. Pour the filling mixture into the piecrust. Bake in the preheated oven for 25 to 30 minutes. Allow to cool completely, then chill in the refrigerator for 1 hour.

6. Wash, dry, and remove the green caps from the strawberries. Holding each strawberry pointed side up, make a ring of strawberries around the outside edge of the cheesecake. Firmly press the cap side of each strawberry down into the cheesecake, so that it's secure.

7. Spoon the strawberry yogurt into the center of the cheesecake and chill for an additional 2 hours before serving.

winter or summer and takes 6 to 12 hours, depending on the water content of the fruit.

Place the fruit directly on the oven racks or on a baking rack if the slats are too far apart. If you use both oven racks, make sure they're at least 3 inches apart. The oven should be set at 150°F and lowered slightly as the fruit dries. Keep both electric and gas ovens propped open at least 8 inches for the entire drying period so that the evaporating water can escape. It's also good to create air movement in the kitchen by opening the window or setting up a small fan. Oven-dried fruit can be pasteurized (if you want) simply by turning the oven up to 175° for the last ten minutes of drying.

Fruit is completely dry when it feels leathery outside but slightly soft inside. Hot fruit always feels more moist than it actually is, so cool the fruit before you test it for doneness.

Store dried fruits in clean, dry glass containers. For four to five days after the fruit has been dried, stir it around a bit every day so that any remaining pockets of moisture are exposed to air. If the fruit seems too moist, simply put it in the oven for a bit more drying.

Always store dried fruit in a cool, dark place. In the summertime, that means in the refrigerator.

Growing Your Own Fruits and Vegetables

The best, least expensive way to have extremely fresh, nutritious, organic produce is to grow your own. With a few tips, anyone—from city dwellers to country people—can grow his or her own food. And you can do it to whatever extent your life-style allows, from growing sprouts or tending a windowsill herb garden to planting a full-fledged vegetable patch.

There are many excellent books on growing vegetables, but one of the simplest ways to get started is by writing to the USDA and requesting a booklet from them. *Growing Your Own Vegetables,* Bulletin 409, is a clear and easy-to-use book with step-by-step directions for growing everything from rhubarb to okra. *Minigardens for Vegetables,* Bulletin 163, is a beginning booklet for city people living in small spaces. Both are available by writing the Superintendent of Documents, U.S. Government Printing Office, Washington, D.C. 20402.

Growing food is also something you can do year-round. Small vegetables, especially salad greens, as well as all varieties of herbs can be grown in containers indoors. But for large vegetables, you'll need a hydroponic garden.

Hydroponic gardens contain no soil. Instead, the plant's roots are fed directly with measured amounts of water, minerals, and nutrients. Because the roots do not have to grow in search of food, they stay small, while the plant, or plants, grow quite large. A three-foot-square hydroponic garden can yield as much produce as a thirty-foot-square soil garden. Commercial hydroponic gardens are easy to use, not messy, since no soil is involved, and require little attention.

One of the best and most reasonably priced (approximately $50) is the Living Green Garden. Living Green, 1146 Garret Avenue, San Diego, California 92109, will send you more information on request.

Whatever type of garden you plant, you'll need good-quality seeds. You can purchase seeds from a grocery or hardware store, but requesting seed catalogs from several seed companies is a better idea. Seed catalogs themselves often give planting directions; seeds purchased mail order are usually less expensive than store-bought seeds; and a catalog will give you a better idea of the planting options you have, plus offer you choices among different varieties of fruits and vegetables.

Seeds, like foods, aren't what they used to be. Today, most seed companies live as branches of massive companies. General Foods owns Burpee Seeds, for example. Purex owns Ferry-Morse Seeds; Union Carbide owns Keystone Seeds.

There is nothing defective about the seeds large companies produce. However, large companies do focus on hybrid seeds that produce large crops when grown with plenty of water, pesticides, and

Persimmon-Rice Loaf

- 1½ lb. ripe persimmons
- ¾ c. cooked brown rice
- ⅓ to ½ c. plain kefir
- 2 eggs, well beaten
- ⅓ c. safflower oil
- ¼ c. honey
- 2 t. vanilla extract
- 2 c. whole wheat pastry flour
- 1 t. baking powder
- 1 t. ground cinnamon
- 1 t. grated nutmeg
- ½ c. grated raw sweet potato (optional)

1. Peel the persimmons and cut each into quarters. Puree the persimmons in a food mill or blender. You need approximately 1½ cups of pureed fruit.

2. Preheat oven to 350°F.

3. In a small bowl, combine the rice with the kefir. Set aside.

4. In a large bowl, combine the eggs, oil, honey, and vanilla. Mix well. Add the persimmon pulp.

5. Sift together the flour, baking powder, cinnamon, and nutmeg. Slowly add this to the persimmon mixture. Stir in the rice and kefir. Fold in the sweet potato.

6. Pour the batter into a greased 9 × 5-inch loaf pan and bake in the preheated oven for 1 hour or until a cake tester, inserted into the loaf, comes out clean.

fertilizer. The varieties that are marketed are usually those that yield vegetables and fruits that can stand up to brutal harvesting machinery. These aren't necessarily the same varieties of seed that yield the best-tasting, most nutritious vegetables and fruits.

There follows, then, a list of several small, single-person or family-run companies that offer old-fashioned and rare varieties of seed. A complete list of companies such as these can be found in the *Graham Center Seed Directory.* The directory costs $1 and is available by request from the Frank Porter Graham Center, Route 3, Box 95, Wadesboro, North Carolina 28170.

Since the companies listed below are small and generally operate on tight budgets, please try to pay for catalogs in advance and even send stamps to defray postage costs.

Seed Companies

Vegetables, Fruits, and Nuts

True Seed Exchange
c/o Kent Whealy, R.R.1
Princeton, Missouri 64673

TS Exchange is a group of about three hundred people who trade among themselves old, foreign, and unusual seeds. Each February the exchange publishes a list of the names and addresses of its members and the varieties of seed each member would like to trade. Seeds are traded between members for postage; other persons must enclose $1 and a self-addressed stamped envelope. Send $2 to the exchange for a membership application and the latest exchange list, which includes a seed-saving guide.

Johnny's Selected Seeds
Organic Seed and Crop Research
Albion, Maine 04910

Organically grown seeds and special varieties developed for short growing seasons. The excellent catalog is 50¢. One of the clearest descriptions of how to save your own seeds can be found in Johnny's small book, *Growing Garden Seeds,* $2.30 postpaid.

Abundant Life Seed Foundation
Gardiner, Washington 98334

Regional plants for the North Pacific. Their 50¢ catalog includes vegetables, trees, shrubs, herbs, and flowers.

Lemon Crepes

Filling

2 c. lemon-flavored yogurt
4 t. finely grated lemon rind

Crepes

2 eggs
½ c. whole wheat pastry flour or ¼ c. whole wheat pastry flour plus ¼ c. chestnut flour
½ c. milk
¼ t. honey
¼ t. vanilla extract
pinch of herbal salt
butter

1. *Making the filling.* Spoon the yogurt into a sieve lined with cheesecloth or a paper filter and allow the whey to drain off for 20 minutes. Then combine it in a bowl with the lemon rind, mix well, and place it in the refrigerator to chill.

2. *Making the crepes.* Combine all of the remaining ingredients except the butter in a blender and blend until the batter has a buttermilk consistency. (It may be necessary to add more flour or milk.)

3. Butter a small omelet pan well. Place the pan over medium heat. In one movement, pour a good amount of crepe batter into the pan, then immediately pour any excess batter back into the blender. This will leave a thin coating of batter in the pan. Place the pan back over the heat, and in less than 30 seconds the crepe will be done. You will be able to tell because the edges of the crepe will begin to curl away from the pan.

4. Continue making crepes until all the batter has been used, keeping the first ones warm in the oven as you go.

5. Spoon the chilled lemon yogurt onto the warm crepes, fold up like a letter, and serve immediately. Makes about 6 crepes.

Nichols Garden Nursery
1190 North Pacific Highway
Albany, Oregon 97321

Oriental vegetables including seeds for burdock, bok choy, Yamato Japanese cucumbers, miniature flowering kale, Japanese pickling eggplant, snow peas, *mitsuba,* and *daikon.*

Beans

Wanigan Associates
262 Salem Street
Lynnfield, Massachusetts 01940

Four hundred heirloom bean varieties. Send $2 for the catalog or $5 for the catalog plus four varieties of beans and a year's subscription to *Wanigan—A Bean Newsletter.*

Corn

Alston Seed Growers
Littleton, North Carolina 27850
Old-time field corn: white, red, yellow, purple, and mixed.

Steinbrown Seed Farm
Route 2
Fairbank, Iowa 50629
Open-pollinated corn and oats. (Open-pollinated varieties can be saved and replanted.)

Fruits, Nuts, and Berries

North American Fruit Explorers
c/o Robert Kurle
10 South 55 Madison Street
Hinsdale, Illinois 60521
Traditional fruit and nut exchange, with members all over the country testing old varieties in local areas. The NAFE's purpose is to develop disease-resistant varieties. Send $5 for a subscription to the quarterly journal.

Pear-Currant Blintzes

These blintzes freeze very well. Cooking several fresh and freezing the remainder is recommended. To freeze, wrap them in batches—three or four together in a single paper towel—before wrapping all the batches snugly together in plastic wrap.

Filling

- 3 lb. farmer or pot cheese
- 3 ripe pears (Bartletts work well; apples may be substituted)
- 1 c. currants
- 1 t. ground cinnamon
- ½ t. ground cloves
- ½ t. grated nutmeg
- ½ t. salt

Blintzes

- 6 eggs
- 2 c. whole wheat pastry flour
- 1½ c. skim milk
- ½ t. honey
- ½ t. herbal salt
- butter or butter plus safflower oil

1. Divide the cheese into 3 roughly equal portions and wrap each in a clean cotton towel. Refrigerate overnight. (The towels will absorb much of the whey, leaving the cheese dry and lessening the risk of soggy blintzes.)

Bountiful Ridge Nurseries
Princess Ann, Maryland 21853
A fourth-generation family business with a free catalog of apples, cherries, persimmons, berries, and nut- and shade-tree seeds.

Stronghold, Inc.
1931 Upton Street NW
Washington, D.C. 20016
A pervasive chestnut blight in the early 1900s made chestnuts virtually extinct in America. Stronghold is dedicated to saving the American chestnut by growing and encouraging others to grow as many chestnut trees as possible while disease-resistant varieties are being developed. Seeds and seedlings are available.

Suter's Apple Nursery
3220 Silverado Trail
St. Helena, California 94574
Relief from the not-so-delicious Delicious apple at last! Seventy old apple varieties are available. Send a self-addressed stamped envelope for the first list.

2. Peel and core the pears. Chop them into small pieces and combine with the cheese. Into this, mix all of the remaining filling ingredients. Set aside.

3. Combine all of the blintz ingredients except the butter in a blender. Blend well to achieve a uniform batter with the consistency of buttermilk. More milk or flour may be added as needed.

4. Butter a small omelet pan and place over medium heat. Quickly pour a good amount of blintz batter from the blender into the pan. Tip the pan back and forth to coat the bottom evenly with a thin layer of batter. Pour any excess batter back into the blender.

5. Return the pan to the heat. In approximately 30 seconds, the blintz will be done (the edges will begin to curl away from the sides of the pan). Flip out onto a cotton or paper towel. Make the remaining blintzes in the same way.

6. When all of the blintzes are made, spoon a generous amount of filling onto each. By placing the filling more toward one end rather than in the center, you'll be able to roll the blintz up securely, tucking the flaps in as you go.

7. Sauté the blintzes in a small amount of butter or butter plus safflower oil over very low heat for about 12 to 15 minutes on each side. Serve piping hot.

Boston Mountain Nurseries
Rt. 2, Highway 71
Winslow, Arkansas 72959

Blackberries, dewberries, youngberries, wineberries, raspberries, gooseberries, and strawberries. Send a self-addressed stamped envelope.

Gourds

American Gourd Society
P.O. Box 274
Mount Gilead, Ohio 43338

Information and exchange for unusual gourd varieties. Send $2.50 for a subscription to the newsletter and membership.

Of Special Note

USDA National Seed Storage Laboratory
Colorado State University
Fort Collins, Colorado 80523

In 1912 the USDA distributed 63 million packets of seed—free—to American farmers and gardeners. "Too much of a good thing" has never been a government credo, though, and after 1923 there were no more seed handouts. Recently, however, the Frank Porter Graham Center, a nonprofit organization and experimental farm, petitioned the USDA to make seeds, especially old varieties of seed, available to citizens again. Thanks to the Graham Center's hard work and gentle prodding, the USDA's NSSL decided to comply on a limited basis.

The NSSL is willing to provide small amounts of rare seed to concerned citizens provided that (a) the person save seeds from the crop and return the original amount of seed to the NSSL; and (b) the person be willing to share his or her seed with other people interested in growing the same variety.

The Graham Center suggests that you request unusual seed varieties from the NSSL laboratory only after you've exhausted other sources.

Dairy Products

Milk

Pasteurized milk is conspicuously absent from natural food stores across the country despite its image as a pure, natural food. In truth, pasteurized milk is neither pure nor natural. It is, in fact, a mixed blessing. Both pasteurized and raw milk contain high-quality proteins and fat and are strong sources of calcium, but these pluses must be weighed against the following negatives.

Many of us outgrow our ability to digest milk sugar—lactose—at three or four years of age, when our bodies may stop producing the enzyme that breaks up milk sugar so that it can be digested and absorbed. In the late 1960s investigators at Johns Hopkins School of Medicine reported that 15% of all whites and 70% of all blacks tested could not digest milk.[1] Since that time it's been shown that between 8% and 20% of northern European whites; 70% of American blacks, Indians, and Jews; and 80% of Asians and Middle Easterners cannot digest milk.[2]

The milk that lactose-intolerant people drink passes through the stomach and small intestine and collects in an undigested lump in the colon. Here bacteria ferment the milk, producing gas and acid. The result is bloating, cramping, flatulence, diarrhea, a distended abdomen, and possibly gastrointestinal bleeding.

The American Academy of Pediatrics in a 1974 statement, "Should Milk Drinking by Children Be Discouraged?," concluded that a limited amount of milk would not be seriously detrimental for most children, though the research they cited showed that among nonwhite or impoverished or ill children, milk drinking produced gastrointestinal problems. According to the academy's report, healthy, well-nourished children seemed to adjust better to milk, although

[1]D. M. Paige, "Lactose Malabsorption and Milk Rejection in Negro Children," *Johns Hopkins Medical Journal,* Vol. 129 (1971), p. 163.

[2]Jane E. Brody, "Personal Health," *New York Times,* October 12, 1977. See also: *Background Information on Lactose and Milk Intolerance,* Food and Nutrition Board, National Research Council/National Academy of Sciences, May 1972.

after three years of age, even these children began to show digestion difficulties.

Children and adults who are lactose intolerant are generally able to digest milk products such as cheese, yogurt, kefir, sour cream, butter, and buttermilk, even though they cannot digest milk. The reason for this is that these dairy foods are made from cultured milk; that is, milk that has had the sugar in it broken down and predigested by bacteria.

To counteract the digestion problems so many people have with milk, sweet acidophilus milk was developed. Sweet acidophilus milk is pasteurized low-fat milk that has had acidophilus bacteria added to it while the milk is cold so that the acidophilus doesn't go to work or change the flavor of the milk. Theoretically, once the milk and bacteria are warmed in the intestines, the acidophilus bacteria can implant and help the digestion process by promoting the growth of beneficial bacteria and effectively destroying some of those harmful bacteria that cause partially digested food to putrify in the intestines. The effectiveness of sweet acidophilus has not been confirmed, however. It is not known, for example, whether enough of the acidophilus does implant, and if it does, whether it can act quickly enough to make the milk easily digestible by lactose-intolerant people. The Mayo Clinic is currently conducting a study on this.

Acidophilus bacteria are killed by heat, so even if sweet acidophilus milk is effective, it cannot be used in cooking (or in coffee) and still promote bacterial growth in the intestines.

Another problem with fluid milk is that it is one of the best mediums for the growth of harmful bacteria. Before pasteurization, fluid milk was a major cause of typhoid, tuberculosis, diptheria, scarlet fever, and fatal attacks of diarrhea. At that time milk was supplied by local farmers, who housed their cows in wet, feces-strewn sheds, then transported the thin, watery milk in open buckets through the streets, where it was soon inundated with disease-producing organisms.

After pasteurization became a standard practice, milk no longer precipitated diseases that could end in death. Still, pasteurization did not—and does not—guarantee absolute purity.

Milk left unopened in the refrigerator will support a bacterial population that will double every thirty-five to forty hours. In January 1974 Consumers Union tested three samples each of twenty-five different brands of pasteurized milk. The bacterial counts in many samples far exceeded the permissible level of 20,000 bacteria per milliliter (about ⅕ teaspoon). Seven samples contained more than 130,000 organisms per milliliter, with some samples in the 400,000 to

Pasteurized Milk

The International College of Applied Nutrition considers raw milk nutritionally superior to pasteurized milk. According to their findings:

1. Pasteurization causes a loss in the soluble calcium and phosphorus contents and thereby affects the metabolism of calcium, phosphorus, and nitrogen. There is 6% less calcium available after pasteurization. The heat alters the absorption of the remaining calcium so it is not readily available.
2. Pasteurization causes the disappearance by volatilization of 20% or more of the total iodine.
3. Pasteurization destroys 50% of the vitamin C in milk.
4. Pasteurization destroys up to two-thirds of the B-vitamin-complex components.
5. Pasteurization reduces the levels of natural enzymes in milk.
6. Pasteurization destroys an unidentified growth-promoting substance in milk. When laboratory animals are fed exclusively on pasteurized milk for several generations, they show degenerative changes—including a reduced ability to reproduce—not found when laboratory animals are fed raw milk exclusively.

Reprinted, with permission, from *Nutrition—Applied Personally* (La Habra, Calif.: International College of Applied Nutrition, 1973).

2.9 million range. Consumers Union tasters didn't like the taste of those milks that were later shown to contain more than 57,000 organisms per milliliter.

Since there is such potential for bacterial growth in milk products, a dairy's sanitary practices are crucially important. Inside the cow, milk isn't sterile, but it does have a low bacterial count and contains a natural germicide that keeps bacterial growth initially in check. Because milk becomes contaminated with bacteria that originate in fecal matter, cows in the best dairies have their udders and flanks washed before milking, as the first measure in producing clean milk. A dairy that doesn't take strict sanitary measures, however, will find that its milk contains large numbers of harmful bacteria even if the milk is pasteurized. For although pasteurization destroys disease-producing organisms and reduces the number of bacteria that have grown up until the point of pasteurization, bacteria will begin to multiply again after pasteurization unless the milk is thoroughly protected and kept quite cold until it's drunk.

Besides killing harmful bacteria, pasteurization destroys some vitamins, enzymes, and minerals, may impair milk protein, and kills the flavor components in milk.[3] Pasteurized milk also often tastes cooked and flat and has picked up the metallic flavor of the pasteurizing machinery and the waxy flavor of the plastic packaging carton. Raw milk, by comparision, tastes distinctly sweet, fresh, and alive, and it contains all of the nutrients that are destroyed in pasteurized milk. If you can digest milk easily, raw milk is the milk to buy for both flavor and nutrition.

The manner in which raw milk is sold commercially depends on a state's regulations, and every state has somewhat different rules. Some states do not allow raw milk to be bottled and sold commercially at all, although these states do permit consumers to purchase small quantities of raw milk directly from farmers. The consumer brings a container to the farmer and assumes all liability for the milk.

Other states do allow raw milk to be bottled, sold, and transported, but the milk must be certified by the American Association of Medical Milk Commissions. The sanitary standards of this commission are so stringent that dairies under their supervision produce milk with consistently lower bacterial counts than dairies producing pasteurized milk. Consumers Union, in fact, has recommended that pasteurized milk be produced under the same strict sanitary conditions required for the production of certified raw milk. Raw milk that has come from an AAMMC certified dairy will always be labeled certified raw milk.

And finally, some states allow raw milk to be sold if the milk meets the state's own milk commission's sanitary standards.

In all honesty, raw milk can be contaminated with disease-producing bacteria—especially dangerous salmonella—so it's important to make sure the dairy from which you buy raw milk has a solid history of contaminant-free milk. Although certified raw milk sold in natural food and specialty stores is generally considered safe, you may want to call your state department of health (food and agriculture division) for complete background information on the dairies certified to sell raw milk in your state. If you purchase raw milk directly from a local dairy, check with the health department beforehand to make sure the dairy has not had contamination complaints lodged against it and make sure the container you bring for the milk is sterilized.

A third problem with pasteurized milk is the pesticides and antibiotics it may contain. In the Consumers Union study of pasteurized

[3]Nutritional losses due to pasteurization vary. *Nutritional Evaluation of Food Processing,* edited by Robert S. Harris and Endel Karmas (Westport, Conn.: Avi Publishing, 1975), reports minor losses of thiamine and vitamins C and B_{12}, but no destruction of protein (p. 225).

milks bought in supermarkets, only four out of twenty-five samples of milk contained no determinable amount of chlorinated-hydrocarbon pesticide residues. Half the samples showed low levels of DDE, a breakdown product of DDT. The exact extent to which pesticides pose a long-term threat of birth defects, mutations, and cancer is not known.

Cows are also injected with penicillin and aureomycin—two antibiotics used to treat mastitis, an inflammation of a cow's udders. These antibiotics can lead to allergies and, something even more serious, antibiotic immunity. For the more we injest antibiotics in food, the less effective against disease-producing bacteria they be-

Mother's Milk

Milk is treasured because it is the food that links us to our birth, the food that we, in turn, nourish our children with. Through milk the process of evolution takes place, with each generation feeding the next, insuring that life continues.

Mother's milk is the most valuable milk. It is chemically structured with specific nutrients in specific proportions to fulfill the needs of a human baby. Cow's milk is structured quite differently. For example, it has nearly three times more protein than human milk. This is a massive amount of protein for a human baby's immature digestive system to handle, and many babies develop mild to extreme allergies to cow's milk as a result.*

Breast-feeding is not without problems, however. Agricultural and industrial toxins that find their way into a mother's body through her food are passed on, at concentrated levels, to her child. In a 1975 nationwide survey of 1,436 women, the Environmental Protection Agency found frightening levels of cancer-causing pesticides in mother's milk. Mothers, therefore, need to be extremely cautious about feeding their children, for, sadly, all milks are becoming less wholesome and safe. An excellent sixty-six-page booklet presenting the benefits and risks of breast-feeding with recommendations for nursing mothers is "Birthright Denied: The Risks and Benefits of Breast Feeding" by Stephanie Harris. It is available for $1.50 from the Environmental Defense Fund, 1525 18th Street, NW Washington, D.C. 20036.

*J. D. Gryboski, "Gastrointestinal Milk Allergy in Infants," *Pediatrics,* Vol. 40 (1967), p. 354. See also: S. R. Halpern et al., "Development of Allergy in Children Fed Breast, Soy, or Cow Milk in the First Six Months of Life," *Journal of Allergy and Clinical Immunology,* Vol. 51 (1973), p. 139.

come when we take them orally. Bacteria simply become resistant to the high levels of antibiotics already in the body.

Like pasteurized milk, certified raw milk usually does have pesticide and antibiotic residues, but at much lower levels, since the cows are fed a higher quality, less chemicalized feed. Certified dairies usually don't sell a cow's milk if the cow must be treated with antibiotics.

Milk contains high-quality proteins and a significant amount of minerals, especially calcium.[4] But whole milk is also high in saturated fat, and too much saturated fat in the diet has been shown to have potentially negative effects, such as speeding the clogging of arteries, increasing the level of cholesterol in the blood, and possibly being a contributing factor in heart disease and some cancers.

Whole milk is roughly 3.25% fat, 60% of which is saturated. After high saturated fat consumption was found to correlate with incidence of heart attack, the dairy industry itself began to promote low-fat milk products. Between 1963 and 1973 we drank 20% less whole milk and 571% more low-fat milk! Unfortunately the switch to low-fat milk alone has not reduced the incidence of fat-related diseases.

Low-fat milk has had enough milk fat removed to bring the fat level down to between .5% and 2%. It also contains at least 8.25% milk solids-not-fat. In addition, 2,000 IUs of vitamin A are added to offset the vitamin B loss caused by removal of some of the milk fat. You will find milk in this category labeled low-fat, 2% milk, and 1% milk. Certified raw low-fat milk is also available.

Skim milk, also called nonfat milk, has had enough milk fat removed to bring the level to less than .5%. It also must contain not less than 8.25% milk solids-not-fat and must be fortified with vitamin A.

Nonfat dry milk is obtained by removing water from pasteurized skim milk. It therefore has the same amount of nutrients as skim milk and the same low fat content. Nonfat dry milk is a concentrated source of milk protein—the most accessible and least expensive source. It's really the ideal form of milk for cooking, since one to two tablespoonfuls can be mixed dry into other foods to boost the protein content appreciably. Nonfat dry milk also makes a creamier, more solid homemade yogurt than does fluid skim milk. For reconstituting

[4]According to the Expert Group of the Food and Agriculture Organization of the World Health Organization (Technical Report Series No. 230, 1961), no optimal calcium requirements can be stated. The group cautiously suggested practical allowances of 500 to 700 milligrams per day. The American Association of Pediatrics noted that the amount of milk that is popularly recommended for children and adolescents would provide much more calcium than is needed for normal skeletal and dental growth given the WHO's recommendations. Even people who drink no milk can get more than enough calcium from other very high sources: spinach, almonds, fish, kidney beans, broccoli, and cassava.

to skim milk, one part dry milk powder should be combined with four parts water. If the milk is going to be drunk plain, I like to combine reconstituted nonfat dry milk with exactly the same amount of fluid skim milk, since I've found that reconstituted nonfat dry milk alone tastes a bit chalky.

"Instant" nonfat dry milk is made of larger particles than noninstant nonfat dry milk. These particles are meant to dissolve more easily in water, which is exactly what happens in cooking. Instant nonfat dry milk added as a dry ingredient to flour, for example, will form chalky lumps in a batter. Simple noninstant nonfat dry milk is always better for cooking.

Goat's Milk

Goats that feed on the wild shrubs and grasses that grow along the rocky ledges of mountains here and in Europe produce a milk that tastes markedly different from cow's milk. The flavor can't be generalized, however, because fresh goat's milk will taste different depending on the goat. In fact, when a farmer buys a goat with the intention of milking her, the farmer will usually taste the milk before buying the goat to make sure the milk has a good creamy flavor.

Raw goat's milk, goat's milk cheese, and goat's milk yogurt are all available in natural food stores. The companies that produce these products here are usually small and often family owned. Sometimes I think that I love the taste of goat's milk and yogurt—but especially cheese—as much because I trust these small family dairies as the fact that goat's milk foods really are delicious.

The fat particles in goat's milk are smaller and more evenly distributed throughout the milk, making it easier to digest than cow's milk for some people. The protein content is higher than cow's milk and the iron content ten times higher.

Buttermilk

Buttermilk was originally the liquid leftover in the churn after the butter was removed. Today, commercial buttermilk is made by adding a bacterial culture to pasteurized skim milk. The culture gives the milk a thicker, creamier texture and a more dominant taste. In natural food stores you can still buy a natural tart buttermilk made after butter has been churned from raw, unpasteurized cream.

Buttermilk gives muffins, pancakes, and breads a sourdough kind of flavor, and in recipes for these foods it can be substituted for milk.

Soy Milk

Soy milk has the same amount of protein as cow's milk but roughly one-third the fat. And the fat that it does have is unsaturated.

Soy milk can be bought in natural food stores in a fluid state, either plain or flavored. The flavor of plain soy milk takes a bit of adjusting to. To some, it tastes "beany" initially, although when blended in a blender with fresh strawberries or blueberries and a drop of honey, everyone seems to love it. Soy milk can also be bought carob flavored. Carob soy milk is very caroby (chocolatey) sweet, and children especially like it. Note: It's difficult to make your own carob milk (cow or soy). Please see the section on carob in the chapter "Sugars and Sweeteners."

You can buy soy powder in a natural food store and mix up your own soy milk, flavoring it as you like with nut butters, honey, or fruit. The advantage here is that dry soy powder keeps well for long periods of time and having it on hand means you can add it dry to other foods to boost the protein content of the final dish.

Soy milk can, of course, be made directly from soybeans, but the process isn't as simple as pureeing cooked soybeans in a blender. Soybeans contain the enzyme lipoxidase—an enzyme that causes raw soy products to taste exceedingly bitter. To make a soy milk that does not taste bitter, the soybeans must be ground in *boiling* water, thereby inactivating the lipoxidase. If the soybeans are boiled, then ground, the protein in them will be altered enough so that it won't make milk. *Laurel's Kitchen* by Laurel Robertson, Carol Flinders, and Bronwen Godfrey has a good recipe for making your own soy milk with tips on how to grind the beans while keeping the water boiling.

Cream and Sour Cream

All cream is at least 18% milkfat. Light cream (coffee cream) ranges between 18% and 30% milkfat; heavy cream (whipping cream) between 30% to 36% and half-and-half, technically not a cream but a mixture of cream and milk, contains 10.5% to 18% milkfat.

Cream is so high in saturated fat, in fact, that it should be used sparingly. For desserts, a whipped tofu topping is more healthful and tastes delicious in its own right. For dressings, yogurt flavored with a drop of honey and herbs is a good cream substitute.

If cream is a must, though, you may as well eat the most superlative-tasting sweet cream you can find. Since commercial creams are always pasteurized and, by law, may contain emulsifiers, stabilizers, and flavors, I skim my own cream from the top of certified raw milk, which has not been homogenized.

Sour cream is light cream that has been pasteurized, homogenized, inoculated with a bacterial culture, then allowed to ripen. Very thick sour creams are often homogenized twice and may contain additives that produce a uniformly whipped texture.

In the old days sour cream was made by skimming the cream off raw milk and allowing it to sour on the back of the stove. Sometimes a souring agent was added to quicken the process. I have made my own sour cream in this old-fashioned way, sometimes adding a bit of plain yogurt to the souring cream to make it sour faster. My homemade sour cream isn't smooth and velvety like commercial sour cream, but a potato never had a more delicious topping.

Natural food stores carry a goat's milk sour cream that is creamy, tangy, and luscious. Like all sour creams, it is high in fat and should be used sparingly. Its advantage is taste and the fact that most goat's milk sour creams do not contain texture-improving additives.

Cheese

The first trick all beginning natural food cooks learn is: If you melt cheese over it, everyone will love it.

Who, after all, could dislike an honest croquette once it's dotted with melted cheddary softness? Even if the croquette tasted like a cork, no one would know the difference. For among foods, cheese is a politician with charisma.

In France, where you can eat a different cheese every day of the year, the *fromagers* say that good cheese cannot be made with assassinated milk. That is what they call pasteurized milk, and the cheese made from it, they say, shaking their heads sadly, is dead.

For a cheese to be good—and for it to be natural—it must be made with fresh, unpasteurized milk. The process is simple. Raw milk is encouraged to curdle either with rennet (the membranes lining the stomach of an unweaned calf) or with a bacterial culture (added in forms as simple as buttermilk). The coagulating milk separates itself into liquid whey, which is poured off, and solid curds, which are drained thoroughly, pressed into form, and allowed to age as cheese.[5]

[5]Pasteurized processed cheese, cheese food, and cheese spread are not natural cheeses. They're blends of inexpensive pasteurized cheeses that have been shredded, mixed with emulsifiers and artificial flavors, melded together with heat, then extruded into blocks and slices. Cheese food and spread contain less actual cheese and more nonfat milk solids, whey, and water. Compared with any true cheese, processed cheeses lack flavor and have a rubbery texture. Only in the United States are they popular; here, they comprise half of all the cheese sold each year.

The distinctive flavor and body of each different cheese are due to the following:

1. The kind of milk used. It's usually whole cow's milk, though some cheeses, by definition, must be made with milk from other animals: sheep (Romano), ewes (Roquefort), goats (chevre), even buffalo (which mozzarella was originally made from). Sometimes the flavor of whole milk is intensified with extra cream to produce a lusciously rich triple or double crème such as Fougeru and Explorateur. And some cheeses are made with mixtures of whole milk, skim milk, and whey (ricotta) or mixtures of milk from different animals (Gorgonzola).

2. The method used for curdling the milk. Rennet has been commonly used. But safflower seeds, thistles, and herbs were used centuries ago, and today vegetable extracts as well as cultures grown on grains are again being widely used in many different kinds of cheese, both because vegetable extracts and grain cultures are less expensive than rennet and because vegetarians won't eat cheese made with rennet. Vegetable- and grain-based curdlers are available in natural food stores for people who want to make their own cheese.

3. The method used for cutting, cooking, and forming the curd.

4. The amount of salt, herbs, spices, and other seasonings that may be added.

5. The length of time plus the temperature and humidity at which the cheese ripens. The longer a cheese ripens, the sharper its taste. Mild cheese is cured (allowed to ripen) two to three months. It emerges light in flavor with a soft, open texture. Medium aged cheese is cured up to six months. It has a mellow but richer, nutty flavor and a bit more body. Sharp or aged cheese is cured longer than six months. It has a stronger flavor and distinctive texture. Such cheeses make the best cooking cheeses because they can be shredded, grated, melted, and so on and still retain their dominant character.

There are six ripening classifications, and all cheeses fit into one of these categories. Generally, if you like one of the cheeses in a category, you like them all, since they'll all have similar characteristics.

Unripened. These fresh cheeses do not undergo any ripening. They include cottage cheese, farmer cheese, cream cheese, pot cheese, and ricotta, as well as firm unripened cheeses like gjetost and mysost.

Soft Ripened. Here is where the quintessential Bries and Camemberts belong. Soft ripened cheeses ripen from the rind toward the center. Molds and bacterial cultures that grow on the rind (the feathery Camembert molds are called cat fur) help the cheese ripen to its full flavor and body.

Semisoft Ripened. These cheeses ripen from the center out as well as from the rind in. They're not as moist as soft ripened cheeses but definitely more moist than firm cheeses. Brick, Münster, Limburger, and Port Salut belong here.

Firm Ripened. Everyone seems to love these long-curing cheeses. They include the true Swiss cheeses—Emmentaler (very large holes) and Gruyère (more delicate with smaller and fewer holes)—plus the Swiss cheeses, such as Jarlsberg, that are imported from other countries, plus the Cheddars and the English variations on the Cheddar theme: Cheshire and Lancashire.

Very Hard Ripened. These cheeses are very dry, grainy, and have a higher salt content than other cheeses. They're known as the great *grana* (grainlike) cheeses. They're cured extremely slowly, washed, scrubbed, turned often, and tapped with little hammers to determine if they're ready. Asiago, Parmesan, Romano, sapsago—all belong here.

Blue-Vein Mold Ripened. These cheeses, mottled with blue and green whorls, contain yeast and penicillin types of bacteria, making them among the tastiest and healthiest of all cheeses. The kings are Roquefort, Stilton, and Gorgonzola, and all of them require the patience and skill of a master cheese craftsman.

Cheeses made naturally by the methods just described are alive and must be watched over and skillfully handled.

In Europe, cheese shop proprietors are called cheese "finishers" because, ultimately, the quality of the cheese will depend on this person's ability to coax the cheese along to full maturity. Some cheeses need warmth, others need to be washed with white wine, beer, or salt water. All need to be turned again and again so that they age evenly. Cheeses have seasons a little like fresh fruits and vegetables, and only a good cheese finisher will be able to determine (by smell and touch) exactly when a cheese has come of age. Once the cheese is cut open, maturation stops, and, like a fruit, the cheese can ripen no more. If the cheese was not fully ripe, it is lost.

America has very few cheese finishers, for most of the cheese sold here is not alive; it is made with pasteurized milk, which doesn't retain the flavor or character of the original fresh milk. American laws forbid the importation of cheese unless it is made from pasteurized milk, and for many cheeses importation laws also require that the cheese contain salt, other chemicals, and a certain percentage of butterfat. The French Bries and Camemberts, the Swiss Emmentalers and Gruyères sold here, therefore, are not the same as those sold in France and Switzerland. Instead, they've been made especially for the American market. And the flavor has suffered.

American-made cheeses are not bound by the restrictions applied to imported cheeses, and as a result, cheeses made with fresh raw milk are luckily becoming more available here all the time. But you'll only find them in exceptional cheese and natural food stores.

There are about fifty American companies making cheese from raw milk and a few more falsely saying they do. Raw-milk cheeses are quite expensive; first, because raw milk itself is much more expensive than pasteurized milk and, second, because a raw-milk cheese, as alive as it is, must be made by a highly trained, experienced cheese maker.

To be assured of true raw-milk cheese, look for a cheese stamped

Cheeses for Melting

I remember my first days in the kitchen with whole grains. Even if I cooked that pot of brown rice for exactly the right amount of time, in exactly the right amount of water, I couldn't imagine brown rice tasting good alone. I wasn't taking any chances, either. The rice simmered not in water but in homemade vegetable stock. There were sautéed onions, a handful of fresh herbs, and before the rice was fully cooked, I grated in some fresh Asiago and let the cheese melt down through the nutty grains.

Almost any food tastes good with a sharp or buttery-sweet cheese melted over it. Not every cheese tastes good when melted, however, and some cheeses simply don't melt well, becoming glue-like or watery instead. Here, then, are some cheeses that melt well.

Cheddar. The finest creamy yet solid Cheddars are made by small family cheese makers, although many of the original cheese-making families in Vermont and Wisconsin stopped making their Cheddars in the 1960s when huge cheese factories began producing tons of bland Cheddar that was more acceptable to the American taste. But avoid bland Cheddar. Buy a regional Cheddar from a small producer if you can, and if you're melting the cheese over a grain or root vegetable, choose an aged sharp Cheddar (white or blood-orange), since, of all Cheddars, it will have the most intense flavor.

Colby. Colby, named for a small Wisconsin town, is really a form of Cheddar. It's softer and more delicate in taste than an aged sharp Cheddar, however, and can be used to heighten, but not change, the flavor of a dish. Grated lightly over fish or vegetables, it will begin

with the National Raw Milk Products Institute seal—a green-on-gold star. These cheeses must meet the USDA standards for raw-milk cheese, and the making of the cheese must be monitored by the institute. The institute was begun by people in the natural foods field whose specialties were dairy foods and who wanted to insure truthful labeling and honest production of truly natural cheese.

Storing Cheese

The best thing you can do for a cheese is give it a cool, moist environment in which it can retain its flavor. This involves more than leaving a cheese in its store wrapper on your refrigerator shelf. Instead, fold the cheese inside a cotton napkin or towel that's been

to melt of its own accord. But place the dish back in the oven for a second or two so that the Colby becomes really creamy.

Monterey Jack. Originally made in Monterey, south of San Francisco, Monterey Jack is still best melted over a fresh loaf of San Francisco sourdough with a good California wine to wash it down. Jack is excellent in omelets, and lacking feta cheese, you can use it to make a very good spinach pie with a bit of fresh nutmeg.

Leicester. Leicester is the flat lipstick-red rectangle cheese used in Welsh rabbit. It's a regal old English standby—crumbly in texture but custardy when melted, and the flavor is creamy and mild. Leicester can be used when you want cheesiness but not sharpness. Often the simpler the dish, the better. For example, melt Leicester over steamed or baked potatoes that have been slit open, then add toasted chopped walnuts or almonds and chopped fresh chives, parsley, or dill.

Gruyère. In Gruyère, the village high in the Alps where Gruyère cheese is made and fondue is famous, one of the best regional dishes is made by cutting Gruyère into thick slices, dipping the slices into a beer-and-egg-white batter, then frying the cheese until it's melting hot inside the batter. Whereupon baked eggs are spooned over the fried cheese and sautéed mushrooms spooned over the baked eggs. In America processed Gruyère is more common than natural Gruyère, so make sure the cheese you buy is stamped with the word *natural.* Processed Gruyère not only tastes awful but is glued together with additives and can't be melted.

moistened in a mixture of 2 cups water (preferably spring water), ½ cup dry white wine, and 1 tablespoon salt. Store the napkin-wrapped cheese in the crisper compartment of your refrigerator, rewetting the napkin about twice a week. The water, wine, and oxygen will allow the cheese to develop its full flavor. To stop the maturing process of any cheese, wrap it in plastic and place it under the meat compartment of the refrigerator, which is the driest and coldest part. Note: Hard grating cheeses such as Parmesan do require dryness. These cheeses are best kept loosely wrapped in waxed paper, stored on a main shelf in the refrigerator, and turned over every few days.

Comparing Cheeses

On the chart that follows, the term *milk* indicates whole milk, unless otherwise indicated. Most cheeses are in fact made from whole milk, which, ironically, doesn't mean they have more fat than cheeses made from decreamed or skimmed milk. The fat content of cheese depends on how much fat was contained in thee original milk and whether or not cream was added to the curds during the cheese-making process. Cheeses made from whole milk are often called full-fat cheeses, and they usually contain roughly equal amounts of fat and protein.

Cottage cheese is the most common low-fat cheese. It has more protein than fat—though not necessarily more protein than other cheeses. Of the partial-fat cheeses, Parmesan and Romano are the best known. They are made simply from milk that has been skimmed.

As you read the chart, remember, too, that the U.S. Food and Drug Administration requires that imported soft ripened cheeses such as Brie and Camembert be made from pasteurized milk. The FDA regulations also require such cheeses to have a minimum 50% butterfat content—a regulation not present in France, where soft-ripened cheese often has a lower butterfat content and is generally made from unpasteurized milk.

A final interesting note is that since 1955, cheese consumption has consistently risen in the United States. The consumption of Italian cheese has been especially high, and since 1970, the sale of mozzarella, in particular, has skyrocketed (due to pizza).

An excellent book on cheese, with histories, comparative descriptions, and numerous recipes, is *The World of Cheese* by Evan Jones (Alfred A. Knopf, 1978).

Cheese and Origin	*Source of Milk*	*Ripening Classification*	*Flavor, Body, and Color*	*What to Be Aware Of*
Bel Paese (Bel Pa-ā'-ze) *Italy*	Cow's milk	Semisoft ripened	Mild to moderately robust sweet flavor; soft to medium firm; creamy-yellow interior with a slightly gray or brownish surface	Look at the map on the label. Italian Bel Paese has a map of Italy. The American Bel Paese (a copy) has a similar-looking map—but it's of North and South America.
Blue, spelled *Bleu* on imported cheese *France*	Cow's milk is usually used, sheep's milk is frequently used, and at times a percentage of goat's milk may be present.	Blue-vein-mold ripened	Tangy, peppery flavor; interior streaked with blue veins of mold; semisoft, pasty, and sometimes crumbly	Most blue-veined cheese available is produced in modern factories. To distinguish between imported farmhouse blues and factory-produced blue-veined cheese, notice the pattern of the blue veins. If regularly uniform, the cheese has been injected with air pockets and commercial penicillium to allow the molding process to occur quite rapidly. Cheeses produced by scientific formulas lack the zesty flavor of the farmhouse blues and lie rather sharply on the taste buds.
Brick *U.S.A.*	Cow's milk	Semisoft ripened	Pungent yet sweet flavor, somewhat mild and nutlike; smooth, semisoft texture and pale yellow color	This American cheese was created in 1877 in Wisconsin. The texture should be slightly elastic.
Brie (Brē) *France*	Cow's milk	Soft ripened	Mild to pungent flavor; soft, smooth texture; creamy-yellow interior; edible thin brown and white crust	Because U.S. law requires the pasteurization of imported dairy products, it is impossible to buy a freshly matured French Brie in America. Cheese is a living substance. The minute Brie is cut, it loses its best qualities and will not continue to mature. If a Brie bulges against its cellophane constraint, it is so ripe it should be eaten immediately.
Caciocavallo (Ka-chō-ka-val' lō) *Italy*	Cow's milk	Firm ripened	Somewhat salty, smoky taste; firm texture; light or white interior; clay-colored surface	Caciocavallo means "cheese on horseback" because it looks something like saddlebags and was a cheese of nomads. The somewhat salty taste is usually rather lactic.

Information on source of milk, ripening classification, and flavor characteristics has been adapted from USDA Home and Garden Bulletins No. 112 and No. 193, U.S. Government Printing Office, 1966 and 1971.

Cheese and Origin	*Source of Milk*	*Ripening Classification*	*Flavor, Body, and Color*	*What to Be Aware Of*
Camembert (Kam'-em-bar) *France*	Cow's milk	Soft ripened	Distinctive mild to tangy flavor; soft, smooth texture—almost fluid when fully ripened; creamy-yellow interior; edible thin white or gray-white crust	Camembert should seem slightly plump to the touch, slightly springy, an indication that it does not have a heart of chalk. Once again, importation laws mean that all French Camemberts here have been pasteurized.
Cheddar *England*	Cow's milk	Firm ripened	Mild to very sharp flavor; smooth texture; firm to crumbly; light cream to orange	U.S. law restricts the importation of English Cheddar. Canadian Cheddar is usually superior, as is that of several Vermont and rural New York dairies. Cheddar should not be too dry or cracked.
Colby *U.S.A.*	Cow's milk	Firm ripened	Mild to mellow flavor, similar to Cheddar; softer body and more open texture than Cheddar; light cream to orange	Very popular American variant of Cheddar.
Cottage, plain or creamed *A cottage, obviously; where is unknown*	Cow's milk—skimmed, plain curd, or plain curd with cream added	Unripened	Mild, slightly acid flavor; soft, open texture with tender curds of varying size; white to creamy white	U.S. law requires cottage cheese to contain no more than 0% to 15% fat in the dry matter. Creamed cottage cheese must contain 4% or more milk fat.
Cream cheese *U.S.A.*	Cream from cow's milk	Unripened	Delicate, slightly acid flavor; soft, smooth texture; white in color	Cream cheese contains considerably more fat than other cheeses. Other similar high-fat cheeses are Boursin, Petit Suisse, and all double- and triple-crèmes.
Edam (E'-dam) *Netherlands*	Cow's milk, partly skimmed	Firm unripened	Mellow, nutlike flavor, sometimes salty; firm, rubbery texture; yellow to yellow-orange interior; red wax coating	If, on rapping your knuckles on ripened Edam, a hollow sound is produced, it means there are either too many air pockets or the cheese has been insufficiently cured. A dull thump means a perfect cheese.
Gjetost (Yēt'-ost) *Norway*	Whey from goat's milk or a mixture of whey from goat's and cow's milk	Firm unripened	Sweetish caramel flavor; firm, buttery consistency; golden brown color	When labeled *ekte* it is made of pure goat's milk. This uncheeselike cheese was originally made for those who spend a lifetime in the Artic ski regions. It is a combination of boiled goat's milk whey, caramelized lactose, added fats, and sometimes brown sugar.

Cheese and Origin	*Source of Milk*	*Ripening Classification*	*Flavor, Body, and Color*	*What to Be Aware Of*
Gorgonzola (Gor-gon-zō'-la *Italy*	Cow's milk	Blue-vein-mold ripened	Tangy, rich, spicy flavor; semisoft, sometimes crumbly texture; creamy-white interior with blue-green veins of mold; clay-colored surface	Gorgonzola is slightly fattier in texture than Roquefort and moister than Stilton.
Gouda (Goú-da) *Netherlands*	Cow's milk, whole or partly skimmed	Firm ripened	Mellow, nutlike flavor; semisoft to firm, smooth texture; creamy-yellow to yellow-orange interior	Gouda is similar to Edam, but much higher in fat content.
Gruyère (Grē-yar') *Switzerland*	Cow's milk	Firm ripened	Nutlike, salty flavor, similar to Swiss, but sharper; firm, smooth texture; light yellow in color; wrinkled rind	Gruyère is a holey Swiss, but because the cheese is fermented at a low temperature, less acid is produced and the holes are smaller than regular Swiss. The special fruity flavor and bouquet is the result of the briny, slightly moist rind.
Liederkranz (Lē'-der-krants) *U.S.A.*	Cow's milk	Soft ripened	Robust flavor; soft, smooth texture; creamy-yellow interior; russet surface	*Liederkranz* is a German word for "wreath of song." But the cheese is totally American, developed by German immigrants in New York at the end of the nineteenth century. When fully ripened, Liederkranz has an assertive aroma, but its taste is mellow.
Limburger *Belgium*	Cow's milk	Soft ripened	Highly pungent, very strong flavor and aroma; soft, smooth texture; creamy-white interior; reddish-yellow surface	Limburger is best eaten with pumpernickel bread and washed down with a beer.
Mozzarella (Mō-tsa-rel'la) *Italy*	Whole or partly skimmed cow's milk. In Italy buffalo milk is sometimes used with cow's milk.	Firm unripened	Delicate, mild flavor; slightly firm, plastic texture; creamy-white color	In Italy, mozzarella is increasingly made from cow's milk, but the authentic stuff is made with buffalo milk and is eaten moist, dripping in its own buttermilk. The plastic rubber balls of mozzarella here are insults.
Münster (Mun'-ster) *Alsatian area between France and Germany*	Cow's milk	Firm unripened	Mild to mellow flavor; semisoft texture; creamy-white interior; yellowish-tan surface	True Münster comes from the hilly Alsatian wine country and has a red rind. American Münster is lifeless and dull by comparison. It bears no resemblance to the original and is made in factories in Wisconsin and Illinois.

Cheese and Origin	*Source of Milk*	*Ripening Classification*	*Flavor, Body, and Color*	*What to Be Aware Of*
Parmesan (Par′-mē-zan) *Italy*	Partly skimmed cow's milk	Very hard ripened	Sharp, piquant flavor; very hard, granular texture; creamy-white color	When properly cured, this cheese has less fat but is slightly saltier than many other cheeses. Stick to Parmesans from legally defined areas of northern Italy, those stamped *parmigiano-reggiano.*
Provolone (Prō-vō-lō′-ne) *Italy*	Cow's milk	Firm ripened	Mellow to sharp, smoky, salty flavor; firm, smooth texture; light, creamy interior	There are two varieties: provolone dolce and provolone piccante. Mild provolone has a buttery flavor, and the other is piquant and can be biting. Provolone can be used as a table cheese for up to nine months after aging and then is good for grating.
Ricotta (Ri-cot′-ah) *Italy*	Whole or partly skimmed cow's milk or whey; in Italy, whey from sheep's milk.	Unripened	Soft, sweet, and nutty-flavored curds. Dry for grating	Ricotta is an aristocratic cottage cheese. It is made from the liquid residue of other cheeses, especially mozzarella and provolone.
Romano *Italy*	Vacchino Romano: cow's milk. Pecorino Romano: sheep's milk. Caprino Romano: goat's milk.	Very hard ripened	Very sharp, piquant flavor; hard, granular texture	Romano is Parmesan's close friend. Try to buy an Italian Romano, however. Other countries, including America, market Romanos with complete Italian names to fool you.
Roquefort (Rōk′-fert) *France*	Sheep's milk	Blue-vein-mold ripened	Sharp and peppery and often crumbly	Roqueforts spend three to six months in caves, and when they're finally let out, they're wanton. Authentic Roqueforts must be stamped in red with the picture of a sheep.
Stilton *England*	Cow's milk	Blue-vein-mold ripened	Milder than Gorgonzola. Just piquant enough to be zesty without being abrasive; creamy	Buy only naturally blue-molded Stilton. Those that have been injected with commercial penicillium are second best.
Swiss or Emmentaler *Switzerland*	Cow's milk	Firm ripened	Smooth, elastic body with large, famous holes; mild to nutty flavor	The holes or eyes are gas pockets that result as the cheese ferments. After ten weeks of continuous fermentation, washings, and salt treatments, the eyes are wide open and the cheese is ready for the world. Swiss cheese is made in many countries and labeled "imported Swiss." Only cheeses marked *Switzerland* are the true stuff.

Cottage Cheese

In colonial days a tray of milk would be set on the back of the stove. It would soon congeal, leaving ripe, shiny curds with a fresh, sweet dairy aroma sitting in a pool of milky liquid whey. The curds would be gingerly gathered into cheesecloth, the cheesecloth tied, then hung until all of the whey dripped off and only fat, creamy balls of cheese remained. In those days cottage cheese was truly cottage cheese.

Today about a billion pounds of cottage cheese are made a year by small regional dairies. Sometimes the cheese is fairly natural, the curds are soft and silky, and the flavor smacks of freshness. Sometimes, though, the cheese has been shot with enzymes that speed up coagulation, then doused with stabilizing gums to create a uniform texture and to retard spoilage. Even under heavy chemical manipulation, cottage cheese is still a delicate food, as are most dairy products. And so, what lines the shelves these days can be decidedly less wholesome and tasty than you'd imagine. When Consumers Union tested cottage cheeses in 1979, only twelve of the forty-two tested brands contained reasonably low levels of yeasts, molds, and unwanted bacteria. When it came to taste, the word CU used was *mediocre.*

A shame, really, for cottage cheese is one of the best dairy foods nutritionally. Half a cup has as much protein as two eggs (although less usable protein unless it's combined with a grain). It's also low in calories—from 80 to 120 per half cup, depending on the fat content of the milk it's made from and what those curds are dressed with. Standard cottage cheese has a tiny bit of sweet-cream dressing added to it. Low-fat cottage cheese is dressed with a skimmed cream. (Dry-curd cottage cheese is not dressed at all. It certainly has fewer calories than regular or low-fat cottage cheese, but the flavor is awful). Two final assets: Cottage cheese is much lower in fat than most ripened cheeses, and it's easily digestible.

When you do buy cottage cheese, here's what to look for:

- *First, a reputable store.* Small dairy markets, cheese shops, and conscientious natural food stores may be the best bet. It's important that the store handle dairy products carefully, always making sure that they're refrigerated well in closed cases. The big open refrigerated cases in supermarkets not only fail to keep dairy products cold enough so that they remain fresh, but those cases also allow dairy foods to pick up cigarette smoke and the flavors of foods stored nearby. (In my supermarket, tortilla chips hang over the dairy case.)

- *A good brand.* Supermarkets usually have their own private-label cottage cheese. A large supermarket will have its cottage cheese packed by several companies, so the cheese might vary each time you buy it. Among the highest quality brands I've found are Lucerne and Knudsen on the West Coast; Axelrod and Friendship on the East Coast. The first three were also rated superior in a Consumers Union testing (July 1979), and Friendship was found exemplary in a *New York Times* report (April 26, 1978).
- *An ingredient list that's only four words long.* The best cottage cheeses list milk, cream, salt, and culture and nothing more. Additives cover up staleness and make the cheese curds hard.
- *Creamy-white cheese fluffed high in the container.* You can actually sneak a peak in the store. When you lift the cover of fresh cottage cheese, some cheese should pull away with the cover. If the cheese has sunken into a hollow or seems crusty, dry, or yellowed, it's not worth eating. If the cheese has a little pool of whey in it, it's also far from the best. Pools of whey indicate that the cheese was not properly made and drained in the first place.
- *Shiny curds that have a uniform size.* Cottage cheese that's wholesome and fresh is not matted, mushy, runny, slimy, or hard.

A final thought: When you take the cottage cheese home, and after you've dipped into it a few times, transfer it into a smaller container or press some waxed paper or plastic wrap down over the cheese inside the larger container. Cottage cheese keeps best in a full container. As a large air space is formed, the cottage cheese spoils more rapidly, the creamy dressing plus drops of whey separate from the curds, and what you're left with is dry cheese in liquid that's fast going sour.

Homemade cottage cheese is very easy to make and deliciously creamy and sweet. If you use certified raw milk, the process is similar to the way cottage cheese was originally made: by pouring the raw milk left over from butter-making into a crock, setting this on the stove, and allowing the milk to clabber (curdle) by itself. If you use pasteurized milk, however, you must use a starter, because pasteurized milk doesn't clabber well alone.

The starter can be rennet, a vegetable "rennet" (sold in natural food stores), or any milk product that contains live bacteria: yogurt, buttermilk, or kefir.

Pour a gallon of milk (raw or pasteurized, skim or whole) into a clean crock, glass bowl, or enamel pot. Bring the milk to room temperature over low heat if it's cold. If you're using pasteurized milk, add ¼ cup plain yogurt or ½ cup cultured buttermilk, or 1 teaspoon rennet dissolved in ½ cup warm water. Mix the starter into the milk. Now cover the crock loosely with cheesecloth or a very thin cotton towel. Air must be able to circulate near the milk; the cover's function is simply to keep dust, insects, and airborne particles out. Let the crock sit, covered and undisturbed, in a warm place (75° to 85° F) until the milk is clabbered: 15 to 18 hours for milk with a starter; 2 days for raw milk alone.

You'll know it's done when the thick white curds have settled to the bottom and the thin, milky whey floats on top.

Now you must cut the curds so that even more whey can separate out. Ideally, curds should be cut into 2-inch squares. If you cut them smaller, too much whey separates out, and your cheese will end up hard and dry. To cut the curds, simply draw a ticktacktoe box in the crock with a long knife. If the curds are more than 2 inches deep, you can slice them in half horizontally with a spatula. (Note: You haven't drawn any of the whey off yet.)

After the curds have been cut, let them rest for an hour or two while more whey separates out. At this point, all that remains to do is to heat the curds briefly (to give them firmness and body), then strain the curds and store the cottage cheese.

To heat the curds, place the crock in a pan that's had a few inches of water added to it. Place the pan, with the crock inside it, over low heat. Heat the curd until it's warm to the touch but not hot (a temperature of about 115° F). Keep the curds at that temperature for ½ hour, stirring them occasionally.

After 30 minutes the curds will have completely settled to the bottom and the whey will be floating at the top of the crock. Pour both curds and whey into a colander lined with cheesecloth. Set the colander itself into a bowl that will catch the whey. (Whey is an important source of vitamins—especially B vitamins—and minerals. Rather than throwing it away, add it to soups, a vegetable stock, bread or pancake batter, cook rice in it, or water plants with it.)

When most of the whey has drained off, tie the four corners of the cheesecloth into a knot and hang the bag up to allow the whey to drip off completely. (You can hang the bag on the kitchen faucet, for example, and catch the whey in a bowl placed in the sink.) When no more whey drips from the curds, the cottage cheese is ready.

You can eat it on the spot. At this point the cheese's fresh, ripe flavor is at its peak. If you like your cheese a bit milder, simply rinse the curds gently in cold running water for a few seconds. If you like it creamier, stir in a bit of fresh cream and a dash of salt to bring out the flavor.

Butter

I remember the first time I saw tub butter in an old, rural New England store. It sat heavily inside an old-fashioned wood and glass icebox built into the wall. Although the sign above the icebox said tub butter, the butter was not in a tub. Instead, it stood alone—a stocky, forty-pound block that from a distance looked to me like the biggest chunk of white Cheddar cheese I'd ever seen. Each time a customer asked for some butter, the white-aproned butter-milk-and-cheese man behind the counter would whip out his ten-inch butter knife and whack off a square weighing several pounds. In the course of a few minutes he loped off square after square, carving a staircase out of the huge block.

Butter is the ultimate seducer—melting languorously into the very grains of toasted bread or dripping down the kernels of corn on the cob.

Unfortunately, too much butter isn't good for the body. In fact, it's distinctly bad for it.

The problem is saturated fat. Butter is made by churning pasteurized cream and draining off the liquids that separate out from the thick globules of cream. The liquid is natural buttermilk, and the thickened cream, once every bit of liquid is squeezed from it, is butter.

By law, butter must be at least 80% milkfat, but some of the richest, creamiest butters have even more fat than that, and 65% of that fat is saturated, since butter is an animal fat. And because butter is so fat concentrated, it's also high in calories—about 100 per tablespoon.

Be careful with butter; the stuff is really addictive. You may find that, without realizing it, you've grown fonder and fonder of butter's sweetness, plopping three or four pats into a baked potato, layering a muffin with miniature mountains of it. Although we think of bread and butter in the same mouthful, most of the world throughout most of history never put them together. In Italy bread was (and often still is) brushed lightly with olive oil.

So olive oil (and a sprinkle of cinnamon or toasted sesame seeds) is one butter alternative. Then, there are

Nut Butters. Almond and cashew butters are luscious, and even though, like butter, they're high in calories and fat, the fat at least isn't a saturated animal fat.

Fruit Butters. Pure apple butter—the kind that hasn't had sweeteners added to it—is naturally very sweet and is found in every natural food store.

Cheeses. The French eat bread with cheese, and although ripened cheese is certainly not low in fat, at least it's high in protein. Unripened cheeses, such as ricotta, cottage cheese, and farmer cheese, are the best choices, since they're much lower in fat and calories but still high in protein.

Butter isn't essential in cooking, either. Sometimes butter is needed to achieve a certain consistency, but with those exceptions aside, you can cook quite well using a flavorful unrefined vegetable oil. The chart on pages 254 and 255 lists all of the oils and the cooking purposes each is best suited to.

When you sauté foods in oil rather than butter, you need a bit less oil, since oil doesn't burn away as butter does. By cooking foods in a small amount of fresh, unrefined vegetable oil and adding a bit of homemade vegetable stock if needed to keep the food coated and moist, you'll find that the natural flavor of the food will be brought out more distinctly than if you'd coated everything with the heavy richness of butter.

Still, every summer there's always at least one basket of mammoth mushrooms or one huge zucchini right from the garden that demands to be sautéed in nothing short of the sweetest butter. What can a food lover do but give in?

Regular commercial butter is made with pasteurized milk. As a result, the butter can taste cooked, like boiled milk. Also, butter, more than any other food, picks up the flavors and aromas of anything it comes in contact with. Packaged commercial butter can taste brassy and metallic after it's gone through stainless steel cutting machines. It can also taste tin-foily or waxy, depending on what it's wrapped in.

The sweetest, purest-tasting commercial butters are the kind you buy cut on the spot from a bulk block or scooped from a huge tub. Unfortunately, tub butter is hard to find today. Dairies and specialty dairy stores are almost the only sources.

The best tasting butter of all is churned from certified *raw* cream. This butter is as thick and sweet as ice cream, and because the cream was not pasteurized, the butter has an extraordinarily fresh taste and more of the original nutrients. The thickness and intensity of flavor make raw-milk butters excellent in sauces and in delicate pastry breads.

Butter differs in flavor and color from season to season, depending on the cow and what it's been fed. In its natural state butter may range from milky white to yellow. Most commercial butters are colored yellow. Butters made from certified raw cream, however, are usually left their natural color.

Two of the best raw-milk butters are those made by Alta Dena and Shiloh Farms. Both are more sour and piquant than sweet, and both are thick, creamy, and expensive. They're found in natural food stores. The best pasteurized-milk butter is, I believe, Land O'Lakes. It contains no coloring, has a light, creamy, sweet flavor, and is well packaged to protect it.

Both commercially pasteurized and raw butter can be bought salted or unsalted. Salted butter has a lot of salt—1½% to 2%. The salt helps preserve the butter, but it masks the true flavor. Salt, in quantity, has also been shown to have medical drawbacks; it may elevate blood pressure, for example.

Unsalted butter, usually labeled sweet butter, is definitely a better choice than salted. Keep it as cold as possible and tightly wrapped inside a separate covered container. Both sweet and salted butter can be frozen with only a little loss of flavor. Butter, in fact, should be frozen if held more than a week. In the freezer it will keep well for a month.

Margarine

Margarine is not unconditionally more healthful than butter. Even though margarine begins with unsaturated vegetable oils rather than saturated animal fat, a large percentage of the vegetable oils in margarine are hydrogenated—or hardened—so that the margarine is solid or semisolid rather than liquid. Hydrogenation turns fats that were once unsaturated into saturated fats. This is a little known but extremely important fact, for most people buy margarine in the belief that the fat in it is somehow better than the fat in butter. This has not been substantiated. In fact, research indicates that fatty acids altered by hydrogenation may actually be more damaging than regular saturated fats.[6]

The extent to which the oils that make up different margarines are hydrogenated varies, however. While all margarines contain some hydrogenated oil, some oil is not hydrogenated or only partially hydrogenated. The less a margarine is hydrogenated, the fewer saturated fats it has, the more polyunsaturated fatty acids it has, and the better it is for you. In February 1979 Consumers Union tested margarines for their polyunsaturated fatty acid content and found that

[6]L. Thomas, "Mortality from Arteriosclerotic Disease and Consumption of Hydrogenated Oils and Fats," *British Journal of Preventive Social Medicine,* Vol. 29 (1975). See also: Beatrice Trum Hunter, *The Great Nutrition Robbery* (New York: Scribner's, 1978).

Promise margarine had the highest percentage, followed by Soft Fleischmann's, Soft Parkay, and Mrs. Filbert's. On the basis of fat content, these would be the best margarines to buy. Margarines, however, have other drawbacks.

To give margarine butteriness, manufacturers add artificial flavors. They also add stabilizers and preservatives to give the margarine a butterlike texture. Even margarines sold in natural food stores contain flavors and additives and are partially hydrogenated, which means that some of the fat is saturated. Natural-food-store margarines also have a flat, heavier, oily quality.

Like butter, margarine must be 80% fat by law, so butter and margarine are equal in calories.

Margarine's only advantage is that it's not an animal fat. Still, if you think about the total fat, about the hydrogenation, artificial colors and flavors, and about the preservatives and stabilizers, you can see that margarine is far from a wholesome food. Vegetarians might opt for fruit or nut butters instead.

Eggs

There is an old French woman still living in New York who, many years ago, secured a tiny space just off Fifth Avenue. She arranged it with tables and chairs and the bits and pieces of life she'd brought with her from the French countryside. Then out came her omelet pans, and into the miniscule kitchen she went.

She was devoted to eggs. Her menu listed only omelets, wine, and good bread, and she served these only from midmorning to midafternoon.

The little omelet restaurant was not well known, but anyone who loved eggs as much as she made it a point to have lunch there. Even though omelets were the sole offering, deciding what to eat wasn't easy, for there were over four hundred of them.

One day last spring I sat in the crowded omelet restaurant watching French girls carry white porcelain plates out of the kitchen. On each plate a huge, pillowy omelet rested on its side like a beached whale. But these were not made by the old woman. She had worked in the kitchen making every omelet until she was in her eighties, but a few years ago the heat had become too much for her. Now the omelets were made by her assistant—a man equally devoted to eggs. The omelets were very good. You could tell by the expression on each person's face. It said, "Nothing like a good old honest egg."

Flat Omelet with Almonds and Cheese

A flat omelet has no filling. Instead, various ingredients are folded into the eggs from the beginning, and the whole mixture is then cooked like one big, thick pancake.

1	c. farmer cheese	4	T. (½ stick) butter
3	T. freshly grated Parmesan cheese	½	c. almonds, slivered
		½	c. rolled oats
1	t. herbal salt	6	eggs
½	t. dried thyme	1	t. water
1	t. dried oregano	2	t. honey
⅓	c. raisins or currants	1	T. safflower oil

1. The farmer cheese works best if excess moisture is removed first. To do this, wrap the cheese in a cotton towel and place under weights in the refrigerator for several hours, or until the towel is damp.

2. Crumble the farmer cheese into a mixing bowl. Add the Parmesan. Also add ½ teaspoon of the salt, the thyme, the oregano, and the raisins or currants.

The truth, however, is that a good old honest egg is nearly impossible to find. The eggs we buy in supermarkets come from hens who are fed chemical dyes and their own liquid waste for food and are injected with hormones to make them fat, antibiotics to keep them disease-free, and tranquilizers to keep them calm. They're also debeaked to keep them from cannibalizing each other, which hens, under extreme stress from overcrowding, will do.

A typical hen's environment is completely mechanical and synthetic. She may never see natural light. She may never see much artificial light either, since a hen's reproductive system can now be completely controlled with flashes of light timed to her ovulation cycle.

Years ago a typical barnyard hen left to range about a large outdoor yard and feed herself on scraps, feed, and insects would lay about 115 eggs a year. She would lay one a day until she had as many as she could spread her feathers over, then she'd stop. Three weeks later, her chicks would hatch, and several weeks after that, once the baby chicks could fend for themselves, the mother hen would go back to laying eggs.

The modern, sexually manipulated hen now lays eggs continuously—more than three hundred a year. But current experiments designed to get hens to lay even more eggs have come to a standstill.

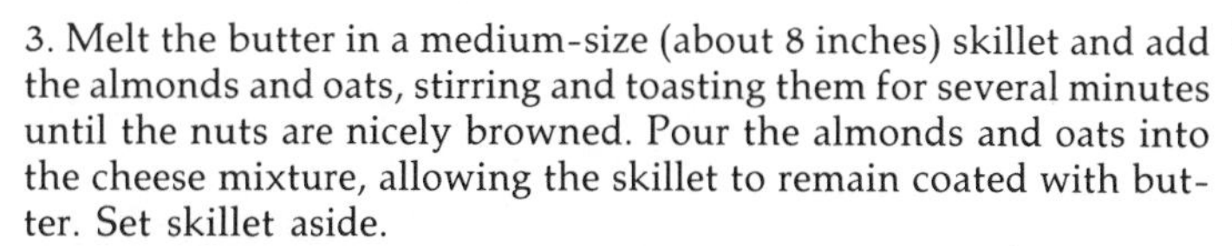

3. Melt the butter in a medium-size (about 8 inches) skillet and add the almonds and oats, stirring and toasting them for several minutes until the nuts are nicely browned. Pour the almonds and oats into the cheese mixture, allowing the skillet to remain coated with butter. Set skillet aside.

4. Separate the egg yolks from the whites. Place all of the whites in a blender and whip for a minute or two until they begin to foam. Add the yolks, water, honey, and the remaining ½ teaspoon salt. Mix in the blender for a mere second.

5. Pour the eggs into the cheese mixture and stir just enough to blend.

6. Heat the buttered skillet for a minute over medium-low heat. Add safflower oil and allow to heat again.

7. Turn the heat as low as possible and pour the egg-cheese mixture into the skillet. Cook until done, 5 to 8 minutes. To brown the top without turning the omelet over, place the skillet under the broiler for 1 minute just before serving. When done, slide the omelet out of the skillet onto a large platter and cut into wedges. This is a wonderful breakfast omelet, but cut into thin wedges, it's also a delicious before-dinner appetizer that will serve several.

The problem is that the more eggs a hen lays, the poorer each egg turns out to be. The shells become brittle, thin, and break easily because the hen's body cannot manufacture enough calcium to wrap three-hundred-plus eggs in a hard shell. Even now, many hens become so calcium deficient that their bones won't hold them up. They lie down in their cages and stay that way.

Poultry researchers say that thorough research has not yet been done on the nutritional quality of eggs laid by hens raised according to modern methods in factory farms. As an egg eater, I find it hard to believe that good-tasting, wholesome eggs could be laid by hens who are sickly enough to look like pieces of shag carpet.

Yet eggs are a very nutritious food—high in protein, fat, iron, and vitamins A and D. And to boot, they're low in calories—a large egg has about 90.

It does not make sense to give up eggs. It may make sense to give up factory-farm eggs, however. Natural food and other stores carry eggs laid by hens that are allowed to range freely and that are fed rations free of antibiotics and drugs. Eggs from free-ranging hens are sometimes called organic eggs, and they cost quite a bit more than the factory-farm eggs found in supermarkets. I feel they are worth the extra cost.

Eggs are graded by the USDA as AA, A, or B. AA eggs have a firm yolk that stands up well if the egg is cracked raw into a bowl. The white is thick, and the egg holds together tightly. Grade A eggs have a looser white that spreads out more thinly, and the yolk is reasonably firm. Grade B eggs have a white that is part liquidy, part firm. The yolk is somewhat flattened and enlarged.

Eggs also are characterized by different sizes. Jumbo, the largest, weighs twice as much as peewee, the smallest. Grade AA, A, and B come in all sizes, so the best egg in terms of quality, consistency, and size would be a Jumbo AA.

All birds' eggs are edible. On the coast of Africa you can have a three-and-a-half-pound ostrich egg for breakfast. Here, next to chicken eggs, duck eggs are the most popular. They're smaller, richer in fat, and, as you'd expect, have a light, gamey flavor that's delicious.

Brown eggs and white eggs do not differ in taste, though they do seem to differ in texture just a bit. Brown eggs are laid by Rhode Island Red hens and by Amber Links, while white eggs are laid by White Leghorns. Since brown-egg layers are bigger hens than white-egg layers, they eat more feed, and farmers charge more for their brown eggs to make up for it.

An egg contains 250 milligrams of cholesterol. This is lower than the amount of cholesterol in three and a half ounces of brains, kidneys, and liver, but higher than the amount in all other animal foods. (Plant foods contain no cholesterol.)

Sixty years ago the first experiments were conducted linking high-cholesterol diets in animals with the development of atherosclerosis. Since then the relationship between cholesterol and heart disease has become a scientific controversy.

At the core of the problem is whether or not cholesterol in the diet increases cholesterol in the blood, and whether cholesterol in the blood contributes to heart disease directly or whether it is simply a warning flag of abnormal arterial tissue growth. Once the blood—or plasma—level of cholesterol is high, the risk of heart attack has been shown by numerous studies to increase. Based on the significant body of research presented to it, the Select Committee on Nutrition (*Dietary Goals*) set a 300-milligram-per-day suggested limit on cholesterol intake (just above the amount one would get from one egg). However, the scientists reported in testimony that any set limit would, by necessity, be arbitrary, for it was impossible to determine a distinct value of cholesterol that separated the population at risk for coronary heart disease from those not at risk.[7]

[7]See: "Diet Related to Killer Diseases. Vol. II, Pt. I. Cardiovascular Disease." February 1, 1977, U.S. Government Printing Office, Washington, D.C., Stock No. 052-070-03987-6.

In fact, as pointed out here and in the chapter "Edible Oils," it's not even clear the extent to which cholesterol *in food* is related to cholesterol *in the blood.* Many studies show that eating eggs and other cholesterol-containing foods, for example, may have no effect on blood cholesterol levels. In a long-term cardiac-risk study (1977) headed by Margaret Flynn, professor of nutrition at the University of Missouri, one-half of a group of 114 men were asked to eat two eggs a day for three months. The other half of the group ate no eggs at all. At the end of three months there had been no change at all in cholesterol levels among any of the men.

In a study conducted in 1976, older men with an average age of fifty-one were fed an extra egg a day, whereas younger men, average age twenty-four, were fed two extra eggs a day. Both groups ate the eggs every day for eight weeks, yet, once again, no increases in blood cholesterol were found.[8]

It's important to point out that even though the factors behind elevated cholesterol levels have not been conclusively determined, once a person's blood cholesterol level *is* high, doctors do tend to assume that a greater risk of coronary disease exists.

Scientists hypothesize that there may be a cholesterol threshold.[9] In many of the studies that show egg eating to have no effect on blood cholesterol, the cholesterol level of the subjects was already high. The average American ingests 500 to 600 milligrams of cholesterol a day. In studies showing that cholesterol in food has no effect on cholesterol in the blood, the men tested already had daily blood cholesterol levels of 400 milligrams. For these men, one more or three more or six more eggs didn't matter.

Two other pieces of data must be factored in. First, the most famous population study in the United States, the Framingham study, failed to turn up any positive association between food intake and blood cholesterol levels.[10] Second, it's important to point out that only 30% to 40% of the people with atherosclerotic heart disease have elevated serum cholesterol levels; so how does one account for the remaining 60% to 70%?[11]

What should we do, then, about egg eating? Perhaps a good mea-

[8]J. G. Slater et al., "Plasma Cholesterol and Triglycerides in Men with Added Eggs in the Diet," *Nutrition Reports International,* Vol. 14 (1976), p. 249.

[9]Charles J. Glueck and William E. Connor, "Diet—Coronary Heart Disease Relationships Reconnoitered," *American Journal of Clinical Nutrition,* Vol. 31 (May 1978), pp. 727–37.

[10]The Framingham Study was begun in Framingham, Massachusetts, in 1948. A subject field of 2,283 males and 2,844 females between the ages of thirty and sixty-two years were enrolled and continue to be followed. (W. B. Kannel and T. Gordon, *The Framingham Study: An Epidemiological Investigation of Cardiovascular Disease,* Class No. HE20, 3002 F 84. 1970, Superintendent of Documents, Washington, D.C.)

[11]Dr. Michael De Bakey, interview, *Family Circle,* February 1977.

sure of simple common sense is warranted. One doesn't need to be a scientist to recognize the faulty logic behind the inference that an old food (eggs) is the cause of a new disease (heart disease). Diseases such as heart disease are generally a cumulative expression of life-style. Though diet is definitely a major component of life-style, the egg/cholesterol/heart disease connection is simply too sophomoric and unsubstantiated to warrant major changes in egg consumption.[12] Even the *Dietary Goals,* which has set a very conservative suggested limit on cholesterol, acknowledges that highly saturated fat foods (which eggs are not) present greater dietary risk than high-cholesterol foods. Furthermore, the *Dietary Goals* make an even stronger point: For children, the elderly, and women who have not yet reached menopause, eggs may have more benefits than risks, since eggs are an excellent, inexpensive, and low-calorie source of protein, vitamins, and minerals.

Finally, most of the cholesterol (and calories) in an egg are in the yolk, while most of the protein is in the white. For those who have been strongly advised against egg eating, one solution might be to use two egg whites but only one yolk in egg dishes and other recipes. Scrambled eggs made this way turn out fine—slightly lighter in consistency and flavor, but quite good if your mind's set on eggs.

Yogurt

Perhaps more than any other single food in America, yogurt is associated with healthfulness. Yet few people know why yogurt is healthful; and even fewer know why only some yogurts are healthful while others are not. In natural food stores and supermarkets across the country, we're presented with a bewildering array of options—everything from nail-polish-pink yogurt with sugary strawberries suspended throughout to ascetic plain yogurt injected with acidophilus bacteria. Just what are the differences among yogurts, and which actually do work positively in the body?

Yogurt, by definition, is the cultured milk product formed when *Lactobacillus bulgaricus* and *Streptococcus thermophilus* are added to pasteurized milk. As the two bacteria multiply, they work on the natural sugars in milk, breaking them down and culturing the milk into yogurt in the process. When you eat the cultured milk—the yogurt

[12]See: R. Reiser, "Oversimplification of Diet: Coronary Heart Disease Relationships and Exaggerated Recommendations," *American Journal of Clinical Nutrition,* Vol. 31 (1978), pp. 865–75. See also: Ross Hume Hall, "Cholesterol and Heart," *En-trophy Institute for Advanced Study Review,* Vol. 2, No. 5 (September–October 1979).

—you take in those millions of bacteria as well as the yogurt itself. It is primarily such bacteria that make yogurt healthful.

When live bacteria are introduced into the gastrointestinal tract, some implant in the intestinal wall and help other beneficial strains of bacteria already in the intestines to flourish. Beneficial bacteria aid digestion by working with enzymes and gastric secretions to create an optimal environment for the breakdown of food. Beneficial bacteria also destroy strains of harmful bacteria that, in the colon, putrify partially digested food, which causes sluggish digestion, cramps, bloating, gas, and sometimes diarrhea. When the colon is coated with beneficial bacteria, the whole process of digesting food and assimilating nutrients works more smoothly.[13]

Technically, a yogurt that does not contain live bacteria is not a yogurt at all. Still, many brands of yogurt do not contain live bacteria, and as a result they don't help digestion. For a yogurt to contain live bacteria, the manufacturer must add the bacterial culture to the milk *after* the milk has been pasteurized, then sell the yogurt right away. But some manufacturers add the bacterial culture to pasteurized milk, then *pasteurize the final yogurt.* They do this to extend the shelf life, since a pasteurized yogurt will last nearly three times as long (about two months) as one that has not been pasteurized (about twenty-five days). When yogurt is pasteurized, however, the live cultures in it are destroyed and so is the effectiveness of those cultures. The first rule when buying yogurt, therefore, is to buy only those that list live cultures on the label. Such a yogurt will be made with pasteurized milk, but the yogurt itself will not be pasteurized.

The second factor to consider when buying yogurt is the specific kind of bacteria the yogurt contains. All yogurts that contain live bacteria contain *Lactobacillus bulgaricus* and *Streptococcus thermophilus.* Recently, however, some of the yogurts sold in natural food stores have begun to list a third strain of bacteria on their label: *Lactobacillus acidophilus.* For a bacteria to be effective in the intestines, an extremely large number must be introduced and able to survive the intestinal environment. Some of the research on gastrointestinal bacteria also suggests that it is not sufficient for such bacteria merely to survive; they must actually implant in the intestinal wall to be effective.[14] Here is where the question of bacterial type becomes important, for research with *L. acidophilus* has shown that it is the most common

[13]For a complete overview, see: "Interrelationships of Diet, Gut Microflora, Nutrition and Health," *Dairy Council Digest,* Vol. 47, No. 4 (July–August 1976).

[14]"Acidophilus Food Products," reprint of a presentation by M. L. Speck, Department of Food Science, North Carolina State University, before the Society for Industrial Microbiology, East Lansing, Michigan, August 22, 1977.

strain of lactobacilli capable of surviving and implanting in the intestinal wall.[15] Unlike *L. bulgaricus, L. acidophilus* seems to be able to withstand, then implant in, the harsh intestinal environment, where bile salts, acids, sugars, and variations in temperature all conspire to destroy bacteria. Theoretically, then, a yogurt with *L. acidophilus* would aid digestion the most.

Most of the research on the benefits of yogurt, however—research that has shown that growth has been accelerated, gastrointestinal problems have been alleviated, and cholesterol levels have been reduced—has been conducted on patients fed *yogurt* per se.[16] The specific strains of bacteria were not identified in any of these experiments, yet the yogurt had positive effects on the body. And to go one step further, it's also true that in most of the studies showing the positive effects of acidophilus, *acidophilus yogurt* was not used. Instead, the benefits were produced when acidophilus was given in tablet form or in fluid milk.[17] Whether or not acidophilus bacteria exist in yogurt is actually up for question.

When *L. acidophilus* is added alone to pasteurized milk, it does not produce yogurt. Instead, a buttermilklike food is formed. As a result, *L. acidophilus* bacteria must be added to milk after it's cultured; that is, after it's already been made into yogurt. What manufacturers do, in effect, is make a good-tasting, good-textured yogurt with the two

[15]Statement of Walter L. Slatter, Department of Food Science and Nutrition, Ohio State University, for the USDA, Dairy Technology Division.

[16]J. Alford, Ph.D., Dairy Foods and Nutrition Laboratory, and R. E. Hargrove, Nutrition Institute, USDA, found that baby rats fed yogurt containing *L. bulgaricus* and *S. thermophilus* grew 15% to 20% more than baby rats fed buttermilk, acidophilus milk, kefir, or milk with lactic acid (*Journal of Dairy Science,* January 1978).

G. V. Mann, M.D., Ph.D., Vanderbilt University, and A. Spoerry, African Medical Research Foundation, conducted a study on Masai tribesmen with extremely low blood cholesterol levels despite a high-fat (dairy and meat) diet. Note was made that Masai also consumed large quantities of their own yogurt. Low levels of cholesterol were found to correlate significantly with yogurt intake: The more yogurt consumed, the lower the cholesterol level. A similar study conducted by the authors at Vanderbilt University on twenty-six men and women indicated that cholesterol levels dropped significantly when subjects consumed two quarts of yogurt per day (*Atherosclerosis,* March 1977).

K. Shahani, Ph.D., Food Science Department, University of Nebraska, fed yogurt to mice with tumor transplants and compared them to a control group. Mice fed yogurt averaged a 28% inhibition of tumor growth (*Journal of the National Cancer Institute,* March 1973).

[17]H. A. Rafsky and J. D. Rafsky treated thirty-nine patients with functional diarrhea and/or constipation with tablets containing *L. acidophilus* (total dosage: 100-billion-plus organisms daily). Clinical improvement: relief of gas, pain, constipation, and diarrhea in thirty-two of thirty-nine cases in one to three weeks ("Clinical and Bacteriological Studies on a New Lactobacillus Acidophilus Concentrate in Functional GI Disturbances," *American Journal of Gastroenterology,* [1955]).

C. Beck and H. Nichiles treated fifty-nine patients suffering from gastrointestinal disorders with *L. acidophilus.* Cases included postantibiotic diarrhea and epidemic diarrhea. Relief obtained in seventeen cases; improvement noted within twenty-four hours in most cases ("Beneficial Effects of Administration of Lactobacillus Acidophilus in Diarrhea and Other Intestinal Disorders," *American Journal of Gastroenterology* [1975]).

V. C. Harrison, M.D., and G. Peat reduced the level of serum cholesterol from 147mg/100 ml to 119mg/100ml in bottle-fed infants by introducing *L. acidophilus* into the infants' milk ("Serum Cholesterol and Bowel Flora in the Newborn," *American Journal of Clinical Nutrition,* Vol. 28 [1975]).

standard yogurt bacteria, then, right before the yogurt is packaged, an acidophilus culture is injected. The problem has been that even though *L. acidophilus* is known to be effective in the intestines, and even though manufacturers can put *L. acidophilus* into their yogurt, it's impossible to monitor how many of the *L. acidophilus* survive. The other two strains of bacteria, or any stray bacteria for that matter, are capable of destroying it. And if the *L. acidophilus* does not reach the intestines in sufficiently large numbers, it's simply not effective. In addition, it's not known how much acidophilus must be injected into yogurt in the first place, nor how much any one yogurt manufacturer adds. And finally, for *any* bacteria to survive in the intestines and implant in the intestinal wall, a certain nurturing environment must be provided. There must be a ready source of carbohydrates for the bacteria to feed on, for example, and other favorable bacteria must reside in the same location. So the type of intestinal environment you have also becomes a factor.

Considering all the variables, then, *L. acidophilus*-containing yogurts may not be any more effective than yogurts with live *L. bulgaricus* and *S. thermophilus* cultures. In the final analysis, what seems to be most important is that the cultures—whatever they are—be live.

Yogurt may contain many things other than milk and bacteria. The third and fourth factors to consider when buying yogurt, therefore, are what those other things might be.

Some yogurts—even some of those sold in natural food stores—contain cream in addition to milk. Cream makes the yogurt taste richer, more like ice cream rather than the true taste of yogurt, which is tart like sour cream. A plain yogurt that contains cream may have two-thirds again as many calories (240) as a plain yogurt made with low-fat milk and nonfat milk solids (150). In fact, in terms of calories, fat, and protein, yogurts made with low-fat milk to which nonfat milk solids are added are the best yogurts. Because they're made with low-fat rather than whole milk, such yogurts have less fat and fewer calories, and the nonfat milk solids that are added increase the protein, vitamin, and mineral content without adding extra fat.

Finally, some yogurts—especially the fruit-flavored ones—are doused with stabilizers, preservatives, sugar or corn sweeteners, artificial flavors, and artificial colors. Yogurts that have a glossy uniform color and fruit suspended throughout them always have a good share of additives; yogurts that do not contain additives (other than a single natural stabilizer such as the sea moss carrageen) are usually milky white in color and the fruit preserves added to them are put in the container first, so they're always at the bottom.[18] These are the best kind of fruit yogurts. They are usually sweetened only with fruit preserves, although fruit preserves, by nature, do contain sugar. Fruit preserves are made, in fact, by heating crushed fruit with sugar. Still, a fruit-flavored yogurt sweetened with fruit preserves will have less overall sugar than a fruit yogurt to which sugar *and* fruit preserves have been added. By buying a fruit-flavored yogurt that has fruit preserves at the bottom of the container, you also have the option of mixing in only as much fruit and sweetness as you like.

Like fruit-flavored yogurts, flavored yogurts (coffee, lemon, and vanilla) also contain some sugar, although a small amount. One way to get a bit of sweetness plus true fruitiness, then, is to add fresh fruit to vanilla or lemon yogurt—or one of these mixed half and half with plain yogurt.

In summary, the most healthful, nutritious yogurts

- Contain live bacterial cultures.
- Are made with low-fat milk that has nonfat milk solids added to it.
- If plain, do not contain preservatives, stabilizers, or refined sugar or sweeteners. If fruit flavored or flavored, do not contain preservatives, stabilizers, artificial flavors, or artificial colors and do contain a minimum of sweeteners, preferably fruit preserves.

Based on the above criteria, I have found some brands of yogurt to be consistently better than others. These aren't necessarily the yogurts found only in natural food stores. In fact, natural-food-store yogurts are often considerably higher in calories than yogurts found in supermarkets because they're made with whole milk; some are made with whole milk and cream, making the yogurt more caloric than ice cream.

Also, not all of the yogurts sold in natural food stores are additive-free. Often they contain stabilizers, preservatives, and sugar. Conversely, some of the yogurts sold in supermarkets *are* additive-free. Since yogurts sold in natural food stores usually cost twice as much as yogurts sold in supermarkets, I recommend buying the latter. But make sure such a yogurt contains live bacterial cultures, for some yogurts sold in supermarkets don't; they've been repasteurized.

All brands of yogurt taste slightly different depending on the quality of the milk, the degree of pasteurization, the number and type of bacteria, and the presence of other substances: sugar, gelatin, modified food starch, artificial flavors, and so on. Ideally, a plain yogurt should have a tart sweet/sour dairy flavor and should be creamy, though less thick and uniform in texture than sour cream. Below, in three categories listed in order of preference, are recommendations of several brands of plain yogurt based on my own research plus findings published by *Consumer Reports* in January 1978.

Dannon, Lucerne, Axelrod, and Carnation are all very good tangy yogurts made with low-fat milk. Dannon has one of the best creamy textures. Carnation can be a bit more lumpy and sour.

Knudsen, Continental, and Columbo are all reputable yogurts, but because they're made with whole milk and are more caloric, I've listed them as second choices. Continental has cream added to it, making it even more caloric and giving it a thick texture that isn't truly yogurtlike. Knudsen's flavor is good, not overpoweringly sour, while Columbo's flavor can vary between good and bland.

Maya, Erivan, and Erewhon are three yogurts found principally in natural food stores. Maya is thick, glossy, sharp in flavor, and in general not yogurtlike. It's higher in calories than almost all other plain yogurts. Also, *Consumer Reports* found Maya to have a higher yeast and mold content than other yogurts. Erivan and Erewhon don't have a true yogurt flavor and character. Both can be very sour, watery, and curdled.

Homemade Yogurt

Homemade yogurt can be excellent—rich, fresh, and creamy, particularly when it is made with very fresh milk. It is also easy to make, especially if you use a yogurt maker such as Salton or a Solait cultured food cooker, which is a more expensive machine but can be used to make several cultured foods in addition to yogurt (sour cream, cottage cheese, buttermilk).

In rural Greece a bucket of sheep's, cow's, or goat's milk is set over an open fire and heated until it's between 17 and 25 thumb-degrees hot (the person puts his or her thumb in the milk and begins to count. If the thumb is withdrawn before the person reaches 17, the milk is too hot; if the person can reach 25, it isn't hot enough). When the temperature is just right, a bit of starter is thrown into the bucket and the mixture is allowed to sit and thicken into a yogurtlike food that is eaten when cooled or is poured into a cloth bag and hung up to drain for a yogurt cheese.

Lacking an open fire and a bucket of goat's milk, you can make luscious, creamy yogurt simply by heating 4 cups milk (cow's or goat's, pasteurized or certified raw) in a heavy saucepan until the milk begins to bubble around the edges of the pan (about 180°F). If you're using cow's milk, whole, skim, or reconstituted noninstant nonfat dry milk can be used. I've found that noninstant nonfat dry milk makes a creamier yogurt than whole or skim milk. If you use dry milk, the directions on the label will tell you how much water and dry milk should be mixed together to equal 1 quart fluid milk. Always add ⅓ cup *more* dry milk than the directions call for and mix the milk in a blender so that it will be absolutely smooth.

After you heat the quart of milk, remove the pan from the heat, allow the milk to cool to about 112°F, and stir in 2 to 4 tablespoons of a good-quality plain commercial yogurt. You can also use a previously made homemade yogurt as a starter, but I've found that the culturing strength of homemade yogurts varies, and as a result, milk doesn't always "take" and turn into acceptable yogurt when these are used.

Stir the yogurt starter in the milk until it dissolves. Pour the inoculated milk into warm cups or a warm bowl and let it stand, covered, in a warm place for 8 to 14 hours, or until it has set. Yogurt will keep (covered) in the refrigerator for 2 weeks or more depending on your kitchen hygiene. If you've sterilized all utensils before making the yogurt, it will keep longer.

Frozen Yogurt: Commercial and Homemade

There's no better place than Wall Street around lunchtime on a hot New York summer afternoon to be convinced that people are trying to eat better food. The yogurt shop there sells more than seventy-five pounds of frozen yogurt a day to three-piece-suiters. But in fact, frozen yogurt is important only as a symbol of wholesome food. It's not a wholesome food itself, for it's not simply yogurt that has been frozen.

The purest of frozen yogurts contain a small amount of natural gelatin plus about as much sugar as a regular flavored yogurt. The gelatin gives frozen yogurt its consistent satiny smoothness and allows it to be twirled into peaks that don't collapse the instant they're formed. The thickest, creamiest frozen yogurts, however, may contain a serious array of chemicals, including sugar, corn syrup, sodium citrate, polysorbate 80, vegetable gum, carboxymethal cellulose, mono and diglycerides, and artificial flavors and colors.

Frozen yogurt is usually not sold by brand; it is sold in small restaurants, coffee shops, ice cream stores, and so forth that buy one of several frozen yogurt mixes, then pour it into their own soft-frozen-yogurt machine. Because of this, it's difficult for a consumer to determine whether the frozen yogurt he or she is buying contains a minimum of additives or is chock full of them. One frozen yogurt that is sold by brand and that contains live cultures and a minimum of additives is Dannon's Danny-Yo.

It's easy to make your own homemade frozen yogurt, and it's healthier because you can control the amount of sweetener you put in. Be creative. Try frozen carob-almond yogurt, frozen banana yogurt, frozen blueberry-apricot yogurt—there's no limit.

To make frozen yogurt from scratch you need a home ice cream machine. Follow the directions for making ice cream, just use very cold yogurt instead. You can use a fruit-flavored yogurt to begin with, but your final frozen yogurt will taste more fruity if you first whip a good plain yogurt in a chilled blender with chilled fruit and whatever amount and kind of sweetener you prefer before pouring it into the ice cream machine. This will fluff the yogurt out with air, making the frozen yogurt lighter and smoother in the end.

Kefir

A really tangy, smooth-as-silk, sweet peach kefir is one of the most luscious drinks in the world. It's as creamy and velvety as heavy cream, as sweet and rich as ice cream, and as zesty as yogurt—though it doesn't taste anything like yogurt. (It tastes better.)

Kefir is made from certified raw or pasteurized milk that has been cultured with several strains of bacteria and yeast. The bacteria are closely related to the bacteria used to culture yogurt, and kefir has the same positive effects on digestion that yogurt has. Like yogurt, kefir coats the intestines with beneficial bacteria, some of which implant in the intestinal wall, causing other beneficial bacteria there to flourish.

Around the Mediterranean and in the Middle East, yogurt and most fermented milks are made from a liquid starter. Kefir, however, is made from dried grains that contain bacterial cultures and several yeasts. Traditionally, the grains were dropped into a goatskin bag, the bag was filled with fresh milk (often mare's or goat's milk), then the bag was hung up—during summer on a tree limb, during winter in the doorway of the house, where it would be jostled back and forth by people leaving and entering. And so the grains were kept moving in the milk, and the fermentation was kept going.

During fermentation some of the natural sugars in the milk would be converted into alcohol, and the traditional kefir made by nomadic horse breeders in the Caucasus mountains had a slight alcoholic zing.

Kefir sold in the United States doesn't have the alcoholic properties of European and Middle Eastern kefir, but it's extraordinarily delicious and can be used in baking bread, muffins, and biscuits. It also makes a creamy, lightly sweet sauce combined with herbs such as tarragon or basil and poured over stuffed tomatoes or asparagus. In the summertime, kefir mixed with fresh mint and sliced almonds can be poured over vegetable and fruit salads. And one of the most supremely luscious of all simple natural desserts is a bowl of fresh sliced peaches in a pool of peach kefir, pineapple kefir poured over fresh pineapple, strawberries smothered in strawberry kefir, and, let's see, are you getting hungry?

Homemade Kefir

Kefir, like yogurt, can be made at home. Packets of kefir culture are available in most natural food stores or by writing to the mail-order sources listed below. After you've made your first batch, several subsequent batches can be made by simply adding 3 tablespoons of previously made kefir (as a starter) to a quart of milk. You may also want to add ¼ cup noninstant nonfat dry milk, which will give the kefir a thicker, creamier consistency. Please note that the first time you make kefir, it may turn out very liquidy, but later batches made from your own starter will be thicker.

To make kefir from raw or pasteurized milk, scald a quart of milk to about 180°F and pour into a glass jar that has been sterilized in boiling water. Let the jar of milk cool to room temperature. Add 3 tablespoons kefir or a packet of kefir culture, then cover the jar with a cotton towel and let it stand at room temperature for 24 hours, or until the milk has thickened. Again, stir, refrigerate, and serve when cold.

Kefir cultures are available in natural food stores and from: International Yogurt Company, Los Angeles, California 90069, and Rosell Institute Inc., Chambly, Quebec J3L 3H9, Canada.

Edible Oils

If you were to imagine a train made up of cars all the same size and shape linked to one another in the exact same mechanical fashion, carrying the same cargo to the same destination at the same speed, you'd have a good idea of what a fat molecule is like.

It is nothing more than a simple linear chain of carbon atoms. The length of the chain varies in different foods. To use the analogy, some trains are many cars long (beef), and some trains are comparatively short (butter).

Each car on the train has two windows, one on each side. As the train moves slowly along, these windows represent the only possibility a train jumper has to grab on for a free ride. In the analogy, train jumpers are hydrogen atoms. If every carbon car on the fat train has two hydrogen freeloaders—one hanging on to each window—then no other freeloaders can ride. The train is carrying its maximum—the fat, in other words, is saturated.

But sometimes there's an open window—no one hanging on. In this case, the fat is said to be unsaturated. The more open windows, the more unsaturated a fat is and the more likely it is to be liquid at room temperature. Fats that are liquid at room temperature are called oils. Highly saturated fats, on the other hand, are more likely to be solid at room temperature and are referred to as fats, or sometimes lard.

There are two ways that fats in food differ, then. First, by the number of carbon atoms that make up the chain; and second, by the number of open (unsaturated) positions along the length of the chain.

In general, plants store their fats in unsaturated chains—either mono-unsaturated or polyunsaturated, depending on whether one or many positions on the carbon chain are unfilled. Therefore, oils pressed from plants are mainly unsaturated. Animals, on the other hand, store their fats mainly in saturated form, so the fat in eggs, dairy products, and meat is saturated.[1]

Unsaturated fats (oils) look, taste, and serve different functions in

[1]The fat in fish is an exception. It is primarily unsaturated.

cooking than do saturated fats (solid fat and lard). But the biggest difference between unsaturated fat and saturated fat is the way each behaves in the body.

Both unsaturated fats and saturated fats are made up of specific fatty acids, of which there are about two dozen. Three primary unsaturated fatty acids—linoleic, linolenic, and arachidonic—are called essential because they are the only fats that cannot be produced in the body, and they have highly important bodily functions. They help carry the fat-soluble vitamins (A, D, E, and K) around the bloodstream, keeping the blood and circulation system in good condition, maintaining the nerves, and promoting normal growth, healthy skin, and other tissue. Unsaturated fats are also important contributors to the fatty tissue that surrounds, protects, and holds the organs in place.

Saturated fats, by comparison, make up the body's storage fat (adipose tissue).

But a more well-known distinction made between saturated and unsaturated fat is their relationship to coronary disease. In the section on eggs (page 235) the inconclusivity of the cholesterol/heart-disease link was presented. It was also pointed out that studies on which the *Dietary Goals* were based found that saturated fat played a more significant role in elevating blood cholesterol than cholesterol itself did, and furthermore, that unsaturated fat either decreased blood cholesterol or didn't affect it at all.

Unsaturated vegetable oils—especially the polyunsaturated ones—have gotten good press thanks to the *Dietary Goals* and other research. But once again, the data are actually conflicting and must be considered inconclusive. Just one small hint of this is the fact that between 1909 and 1978, the total daily calories derived from fat increased from 32% to 42%. However, what many of us never realized was that the increase was almost entirely due to increased consumption of processed vegetable oils. Consumption of animal (saturated) fat actually decreased slightly.[2] So if a parallel could be drawn between increased incidence of heart disease and increased consumption of fat, unsaturated fats would have to be considered, too. As was already pointed out, however, the complexity of heart disease has not been explained by this simplistic parallel.

More current research seems to suggest another variable—the quality of the unsaturated fat. It may be, for example, that un-

[2]Animal fat fell from 27% to 24%. The nature of the animal fat also changed: less butter, more chicken and beef ("Nutrient Content of the National Food Supply," *National Food Review,* USDA, December 1978).

saturated fats are modified during processing and that, in addition, some unsaturated fats are better than others. For instance, though commercial vegetable oils are widely publicized as beneficial because they're polyunsaturated, the fact remains that some of them are not made from the "essential" polyunsaturates the body needs.[3]

Let's look at the processing of unsaturated fat, or vegetable oils. All vegetable oils, with the major exceptions of coconut and palm kernel oil,[4] are polyunsaturated, although the degree varies, depending on what seed, nut, or bean the oil is pressed from. From the following chart you can see that safflower oil is the most polyunsaturated vegetable oil, whereas cottonseed oil is the least.

Vegetable oils differ in taste, viscosity, and smoking point—the temperature at which the oil will begin to smoke when it's heated. Deep-fat frying requires that oil be heated to very hot temperatures —often exceeding 375° F; otherwise the food cooks slowly, absorbs a large amount of oil, and in the end emerges soggy with grease. The oil that is used for deep frying, then, must be able to withstand severe heat before it begins to smoke.

Differences in both smoking point and taste depend on the extent to which the vegetable oil has been processed. In general, the less refined the oil, the more intense the flavor and the lower the smoking point. This is why a heavy, dark, unrefined corn oil—which may even have some sediment still in it—tastes powerfully good in a salad dressing but breaks down and begins to smoke quickly when you try to cook a batch of french fries in it.

Most of the oils sold in supermarkets have been highly refined to make them stable during cooking, to make them last for months without refrigeration—and specifically to make them taste bland. Oil manufacturers feel that oils without flavor are preferred by Americans, and the oils they manufacture therefore taste no more than slippery air. Such oils take nothing away from the flavor of foods cooked in them—but they don't enhance a food's flavor either.

Heavily refined oils have no taste because they have no nutrients. Unrefined oils, by comparison, contain chlorophyll, lecithin, vita-

[3]Margarine is a good example. Essential polyunsaturates may be altered by processing, when the polyunsaturated oil is "hydrogenated"—hardened—to turn the liquid oil into solid margarine. This changes the polyunsaturated fatty acids into saturated fatty acids, so margarine is actually a strong source of *saturated fat* (as butter is) and an unnatural saturated fat at that. The fats in liquid vegetable oils may also undergo structural modification, even though they remain unsaturated, based on the processing they've endured. It is thought that chemically modified nutrients may be metabolized in vastly different and unknown ways, since the body, throughout human evolution, has had no prior experience with them.

[4]Coconut and palm kernel oil are more saturated than meat. Both are used in many foods, including infant formulas, margarines, dessert toppings, and coffee creamers.

*Percentage of Saturated Fat in Various Foods**

	Coconut oil
80	
70	
60	
	Chocolate, lamb, butter, milk, cheese
50	Beef, veal
40	
	Pork, lard, bacon, chicken, turkey, eggs
30	
	Peanut butter, margarine, shortening, cottonseed oil, mayonnaise, salad dressing, fish
20	Avocado, peanuts, peanut oil, cashews
	Soybean oil
10	Olive oil, corn oil, safflower oil, walnuts
0	

*Figures indicate the percentage of saturated fatty acids in the total fat content of various foods.

From: USDA ARS Bulletin No. 361 (8).

mins E and A, copper, magnesium, calcium, iron, and other trace minerals originally in the plant and taste like whatever seed, nut, or bean the oil is pressed from.

Not all oils sold in natural food stores are unrefined, however. In fact, most of them are manufactured by the same large companies that produce supermarket oils: General Mills, Hunt-Wesson, Kraft, and so on. These large manufacturers produce both highly refined and unrefined oils according to the specifications of the company that will eventually sell the oil under its label. For one label, a manufacturer might simply press, filter, and bottle the oil. For another, they might adopt a multistepped process beginning with petroleum-solvent extraction and ending with deodorization.

All oil—refined or unrefined—must be extracted from the seed, nut, or bean that contains it. Oil can be extracted either by grinding the food, then heating and pressing it in a high-pressure expeller press, or by bathing the ground food in a petroleum solvent that is later boiled away.

Whether extracted through pressure or with a solvent, all oil is heated, since oilseeds give up their oil more readily under high temperatures. Technically, there are no "cold-pressed" oils. The term is simply a marketing phrase that health food companies began using in the 1950s to refer to oils that were expeller pressed. Nonetheless, oils that are expeller pressed come from heated seeds and reach temperatures of 150° to 160°F during pressing. "Cold-pressed" oil, then, has nothing to do with temperature. The term simply indicates an expeller-pressed oil.

Expeller-pressed oil can be either refined or unrefined, and the label may not indicate which. Thus, even "cold-pressed" oils sold in natural food stores may be refined.

The refining of oil begins when the oilseed is either pressed or mixed with a solvent that separates the seed oil from the seed meal. The most widely used solvent is hexane, a petroleum derivative that is flammable, toxic to humans, and must be very carefully controlled.

Solvents are capable of extracting more oil from a seed than could be pressed out. After the solvent draws the oil out of the seed, the solvent-oil mixture must be heated until the solvent boils off. The oil manufacturer knows that no solvent remains when the oil can be heated to an extreme temperature without igniting.

Technically, the actual refining now begins. The oil has been extracted and the meal filtered from it. Now the oil is "washed" by being mixed with lye or a caustic soda solution and agitated. The washing solution reacts with the unwanted substances in the oil (including the nutrients), which are separated out. The oil is then bleached and deodorized.

At this point the oil contains polyunsaturated fatty acids, but little else. The fatty acids, however, are perishable, and even an oil refined to this point can still turn rancid. As a result, some oils are further treated with preservatives, which stabilize the oil even more.

You can tell if an oil is refined by smelling it and/or tasting it. The more refined the oil, the less like food it smells and the more bland it tastes. But you can also tell by looking at it. A refined oil will range in color from straw to lemon yellow and will have a uniform, transparent sheen. An unrefined oil, by comparison, will be darker—almost murky—and may contain small bits of sediment.

Unrefined oils can have an intense smell and taste. To most of us,

Edible Oils

Oil	*Characteristics and Use**	*Flavor*	*Availability*	*% Saturated Fat†*	*% Linoleic Acid†*
Almond oil	Use in desserts and salads or brush lightly on bread. Also wonderful in homemade skin creams.	Nutty and faintly sweet	Refined: NFS and GS	5	17
Avocado oil	A very expensive oil, best used in salads and homemade skin creams.	Nutty and sharp	Refined: NFS and GS	unavailable	unavailable
Coconut and palm kernel oil	Both very high in saturated fat. Both used extensively in commercial crackers, cookies, cakes, other baked goods, coffee, creamers, and dairy substitutes. Recommended here only for homemade skin creams, not for eating.	Coconut adds flavor and crispness to fried and baked food	Refined coconut oil: NFS	Coconut: 91 Palm: 85	Coconut: 3 Palm: 2
Corn oil	Can be used in all types of cooking and with olive oil for salads. Corn oil withstands very hot temperatures.	Winy and toasted corn	Unrefined: NFS Refined: NFS and S	17	59
Olive oil Virgin olive oil: pressed from the olives themselves. Pure olive oil: extracted by solvents from olive pulp or pits. May be blended with other oils.	Imported brands have the best flavor. Domestic brands usually purchase imported oil and repackage it. Expensive and not well suited for cooking. Terrific with salads, where it can be mixed with other oil to lighten flavor and texture.	In a class by itself. Ripe, earthy flavor.	Unrefined: (usually labeled 100% virgin olive oil or raw green olive oil): NFS and GS Refined: NFS, S, and GS	10	15
Peanut oil	Frequently used by restaurants for frying. Inexpensive and unobtrusive in cooking. Alone, it's too bland for salads.	Bland to peanutty (imported French superior to all American peanut oils)	Unrefined: NFS and GS Refined: NFS and S	20	31

Oil	*Characteristics and Use**	*Flavor*	*Availability*	*% Saturated Fat†*	*% Linoleic Acid†*
Safflower oil	Highest in polyunsaturated acids. Also most prone to spoiling quickly. Light, oily oil—more suitable for cooking than salads.	Very little flavor	Unrefined: NFS Refined: NFS and S	6	78
Sesame oil	Strong-flavored oil, excellent and stable in cooking. Imparts a rich nutty flavor to sautéed food, sauces, dressings.	Oriental and Middle Eastern brands have the richest sesame flavor	Unrefined: NFS and Oriental groceries Refined: NFS and GS	13	44
Soy oil	Soybean oil is the major component of blended "vegetable" oils. It cooks well at high temperatures and has a very strong odor.	Bland to fishy. The best-flavored soy oils are Oriental.	Unrefined: NFS Refined: NFS and S	15	50
Sunflower seed oil	Difficult to find in America, but used throughout Mexico, Balkan countries, and parts of the Middle East. Fine for cooking. Well suited for salads and vegetables.	Light and delicate	Unrefined: NFS Refined: NFS and GS	8	75
Walnut oil	The French consider walnut oil one of the best salad oils. Buy in small bottles and use quickly. Expensive.	Rich and nutty	Refined: NFS and GS	16	51

NFS = Natural food stores GS = Gourmet stores S = Supermarkets

* The flavor of an oil becomes more intense when the oil is heated. Heavier and more strongly flavored oils, then, are better in cold dressings and uncooked sauces, and lighter oils are preferred for cooking. All oils can be mixed for special flavors and textures.

† Added together, the values for saturated fat and polyunsaturated fat will not add up to 100 because some amount of fat in a food is mono-unsaturated. With the exception of providing fatty acids and calories, mono-unsaturated fat works neither for nor against the body. All oils, no matter what the fat structure, have about the same number of calories (120 per tablespoon). The percentages of saturated fat and linoleic acid are from D. Swern, ed., *Baileys Industrial Fat and Oil Products,* 3rd ed. (New York: Wiley-Interscience Publishers, 1964).

conditioned by highly refined, no-aroma oils, an unrefined oil may smell rancid even if it's not. However, unrefined oils do go rancid considerably faster than refined oils. Unrefined oils, therefore should always be stored in the refrigerator, where they'll become more cloudy or even thickened as the natural substances in the oil are chilled. This doesn't mean that the oil is rancid, however, unless it smells objectionably strong.

What's the bottom line? For everything except extremely high-temperature frying buy an unrefined oil. You'll be buying nutrients and essential polyunsaturated fatty acids. They're worth it. (Buy smaller bottles of oil more often rather than larger bottles less often. Store oil in the refrigerator.)

Given the guidelines above for buying vegetable oils, are there brands that one can depend on to be as fresh and unrefined as possible? With certain qualifications, yes.

The oil industry is very complicated. As far as oils sold in natural food stores go, several large manufactuers (Agricom International, Cal Sesame Producers, PVO International, and others) make a variety of oils and sell them to many different natural food companies: Arrowhead Mills, Eden Foods, Erewhon, Westbrae, and so on. This means that Arrowhead Mills sesame oil could be virtually the same or the same as Erewhon sesame oil. It is true that certain natural food companies make similar demands of a manufacture: the lowest possible heat during processing, expeller pressing rather than solvent extraction, and a minimum of filtering with only natural filters, such as cotton or diatomaceous earth. These same natural food companies prohibit a manufacturer from bleaching and deodorizing an oil and request that no antifoaming agents or antioxidants (T–BHQ, BHA, BHT) be used. As a result, their oils are those I feel most comfortable recommending. The list includes: Arrowhead Mills, Eden Foods, Erewhon, and Westbrae.

Nuts and Seeds

The package said Alpine Munchies, but even if you couldn't see those amber brown almonds, roasted peanut halves, and nibbly bits of sunflower seeds through the cellophane, you'd have known anyway. What else would a naturalist with a case of the munchies snack on?

Nuts are powerfully nutritious—more like a main dish than a snack, in fact. Some of them are nearly as protein rich as meat, and most are good sources of minerals. But unlike most plant foods, nuts are high in fat. (The fat is unsaturated.)

Not everything nutlike is a nut. Peanuts, almonds, pine nuts, and Brazil nuts, for example, aren't nuts at all. Peanuts are a legume; almonds are a fruit; pine and Brazil nuts are seeds. Still, because they taste like nuts, feel like nuts, and can be used interchangeably with true nuts, they're included in this chapter.

In-shell nuts are less expensive than shelled nuts. If a recipe calls for one cup of shelled nuts, buy two cups of nuts in their shells. Or buy three cups of in-shell nuts and coax children (or friends) to help shell them. The extra cup's for unavoidable snacking along the way.

Nuts in the shell should feel heavy and solid. A nut that rattles loosely in its shell is probably stale. Also, nuts in the shell keep longer than shelled nuts, and the shell protects the nutmeat from pesticides and precludes it from being treated with preservatives. Shelled nuts (especially the packaged shelled nuts sold in supermarkets) are usually coated with a preservative, and often the packaging that the nuts come in has been treated as well.

The high fat content of nuts means that they spoil quickly. Untreated nuts spoil faster than those that are chemically treated. Chopped, sliced, and ground nuts also go bad more quickly than whole nuts. And roasted nuts go bad more quickly than unroasted. Therefore, the best nuts to buy are whole unroasted nuts in their shells. These will keep for a year, but only if they're stored in a cool, dry place. Shelled nuts will keep for about four months, but should be kept in a jar in the refrigerator or, even better, in the freezer, then taken out as needed.

For all their advantages, in-shell nuts are no easy job to crack. You can make shelling easier, however, by soaking the nuts in hot water for thirty minutes. Very-hard-shelled nuts can be soaked for hours. And Brazil nuts, which have the most stubborn shell of all, can be either frozen overnight or boiled for five minutes to make shelling easier.

When you do shell a nut, turn the jaws of the nutcracker around and crack the shell lightly in a number of places. If you crack a nut with one muscular crunch, more often than not the nutmeat will shatter into a bunch of uneven pieces.

The shelled nuts that you buy in the supermarket have usually been blanched (dipped in very hot water) to remove the paper-thin skin that surrounds the nutmeat even when the shell has been removed. Nut skins contain nutrients and are a part of the nut's flavor, so when you shell your own, leave the skin on.

Nuts bought in a supermarket or any store with a low nut turnover are often a poor option for another reason. Nut processors have not been able to persuade supermarkets and stores to hold nuts in cold storage, then sell them from refrigerated cases. By the time you buy shelled nuts, they may have been in a supermarket warehouse for a month or more, then on the shelf for several additional weeks. Shelled nuts held this long without refrigeration may be rancid.

If no market in your area stores nuts properly, you may want to buy fresh nuts directly from a nut processor. Shelled nuts purchased directly cost about the same as shelled nuts in a natural food store and less than the cost in supermarkets. The following two mail-order sources ship high-quality shelled raw nuts by United Parcel and will send a catalog on request.

Sunnyland Farms, Inc., Route 1, Albany, Georgia 31702
Mammoth pecan halves, extra-fancy black walnut pieces, whole almonds, Brazils, and filberts.

Torn Ranch Grove, 1122 Fourth Street, San Raphael, California 94901
Specializes in its own walnuts, also whole almonds, Brazils, filberts, mammoth fancy pecans, Eastern black walnuts; discounts for large orders.

Toasting Nuts

Toasting brings out a nut's nuttiness. Whenever you add nuts to anything, if you add toasted nuts, the flavor of the whole dish will be intensified.

Toasting nuts is so simple that it makes no sense to pay extra money for pretoasted nuts. Pretoasted nuts may also have been sprayed with oil (which is totally unnecessary) and are often sold so long after roasting that the oily nuts are rancid by the time you buy them.

You can toast about a month's worth of nuts at a time. They'll remain fresh if you store them in a clean, dry glass jar in a cool, dry cabinet.

To toast nuts, spread them on an ungreased baking sheet in one layer and toast in a 350°F oven for 10 to 20 minutes. The nuts must be stirred often and watched carefully, since they burn easily. Pull them out when they're toasted to your liking.

For tamari-roasted nuts, fill a plastic spray bottle or plant mister half with tamari and half with water. Spray the nuts well when they're about one-third toasted. Stir them around to turn them over and spray again. Continue roasting until done.

Curry-roasted nuts can be made in a similar way. Place a small amount of butter in a saucepan. Sprinkle the butter well with curry. Melt. (Melt enough butter to lightly coat nuts, but not enough to saturate them.) Stir untoasted nuts in the butter-curry mixture. Drain them on paper towels, then toast as before. Careful! Curry-roasted nuts are extra rich and addictive.

Toasting Seeds

Next to toasted nuts, toasted seeds are one of the most nutritious eating-out-of-hand foods (especially good for children, who quickly burn up the calories).

You can toast seeds along with nuts by adding them to the baking sheet five minutes after the nuts have already begun to cook, since seeds toast more quickly.

A better way—one that will make for tastier seeds—involves plunking the seeds (a mixture is fine) into a heavy skillet or pot, making sure the seeds are no more than an inch deep. Cook the seeds over medium heat, stirring constantly, until they become very light

Nuts and Seeds

			*Nutrients per Cup**				
Nut or Seed	*Characteristics*	*Cooking Ideas*	*calories*	*pr(g)*	*fat(g)*	*carb(g)*	*Notes*
Almonds	Fruit. Easily shelled.	Extremely versatile nut. Spread sautéed whole wheat bread rounds with almond butter. Top with crabmeat blended with yogurt. Broil momentarily.	775	24	70	25	Almond milk can be used as a substitute for cow's milk in desserts and casseroles. It adds sweatness. To prepare: Blanch nuts by dropping them into boiling water. Let rest 1 minute. Rinse in cold water. Blend in blender with water, juice, cider, etc. 1 cup nuts to 4 cups liquid.
Brazil nuts	Seeds of huge tropical tree, which grows wild.	Like chestnuts in flavor. A good, less expensive substitute for almonds in baking. Cut toasted Brazils into chips for salads.	185	4	19	3	
Cashews†	True nut. Cashew tree is a relative of poison ivy. Nut shell is toxic.	Sweet flavor; crunchy texture.	785	24	64	41	Cashews grow in an unusual way: A single kidney-shaped, olive-colored nut hangs beneath a cashew "apple."
Chestnuts‡	True Nut. Fresh are available from September to March. Dried available year-round and keep indefinitely.	Use along with or as a vegetable or dessert. Must always be shelled and skinned by making a crisscross cut on flat side of shell (not nut). Place in pan. Cover well with boiling water. Let stand 10 minutes, then peel off shell and skin.	310	4.6	2.4	67.4	Chestnuts used to grow plentifully in the U.S. until a chestnut blight in 1904 destroyed most of the trees. A pound of chestnuts in the shell equals 30–40 nuts, or about 2½ cups nutmeats.
Filberts (Hazelnuts)	True nut. Light when ground. Not as oily or heavy as many nuts.	Sweet. Perfect for baking.	730	14	72	19	
Peanuts†	Legume. Grows on a vine much like a pea.	Make an Indonesian peanut sauce for grains or vegetables.	840	37	72	27	There are two kinds: *Virginia*—the oilier variety; peanut is long, oval, and strong tasting. *Spanish*—shorter; milder in flavor.

Nut or Seed	*Characteristics*	*Cooking Ideas*	*Nutrients per Cup**				*Notes*
			calories	*pr(g)*	*fat(g)*	*carb(g)*	
Pecans	True nut. Rough texture. Sweet.	Best with rich foods. Bake into pies, cakes. Use in cream desserts.	810	11	84	17	
Pine nuts (Pignolias)	Seeds of pine tree.	European pine nuts have the best flavor. Use whole or chopped with vegetables, grains, and eggs or ground in sauces and soups.	468	27	40	9	There are two kinds: Pine nuts from small piñon pines, which grow in the American Southwest; and pignolias from pine trees, which grow in Italy and Portugal. The European ones are best nutritionally.
Pistachios	Green kernel nut encased in mottled, easily removed shell, which is often dyed red.	Excellent cooked with grains (especially rice); in pâtés, cakes, breads, stuffings, creamy desserts; or nibble with soft ripened cheese.	504	16	46	16	Iranian and Italian pistachios have the best flavor and are the most expensive.
Pumpkin and squash seeds§	Seed shells are thin, so shell and all can be eaten.	Of all squashes, Acorn and Hubbard have the best seeds. Scoop out. Spread on tray and allow seeds to dry for several days. When dry, remove stringy membrane and toast.	775	41	65	21	All seeds can be eaten raw, but they taste enormously better toasted. Also, hulled seeds should be refrigerated and used quickly, because oxidation causes the fat in them to turn rancid.
Sunflower Seeds§	Shells should not be eaten.	Add toasted seeds to blender drinks, cookies, muffins, puddings, salads, stuffings.	810	35	69	29	
Walnuts (English)	True nut. "English" walnuts actually originated in Persia. Currently the largest producers are USA, Italy, and France.	Walnuts and honey are delicious in all baked goods, from waffles to crust for apple pie. Also excellent in puddings, pâtés, and with soft fruits and cheeses.	780	18	77	19	Black walnuts are bitter tasting and difficult to shell, although they do contain more protein.

* Nutritionally, nuts are good sources of B vitamins, calcium, iron, phosphorus, and potassium. They also provide a high percentage of protein and fat (mainly unsaturated). The nutritional values listed are for 1 cup of chopped shelled nuts, except for Brazil nuts, where the values are for 6 to 8 large kernels; pine nuts, where the values are for 3 ounces; and pistachios, where the values are for 3 ounces.

† Nutritional values are for roasted nuts. ‡ Nutritional values are for raw nuts. § Nutritional values are for hulled seeds.

Adapted from: *Nutritive Value of Foods,* USDA Home and Garden Bulletin No. 72, rev. April 1977; and *Nutritive Value of American Foods,* Agricultural Handbook No. 456, USDA, November 1975.

in weight and nicely browned. The seeds will actually lose about half their weight in water, and you'll be able to feel this while stirring. Some of the seeds may pop as they toast. If too many do, the heat is too high.

Remove the pan from the stove momentarily. For every cup of raw seeds, mix a small amount (roughly ½ to 1 teaspoon) of herbal salt into no more than ¼ cup hot water and add quickly to the seeds. The seeds will hiss loudly as the salted water hits them and is drawn into the seed.

Return the pot to the stove and cook again over low heat, stirring until the seeds are dry and light again in weight.

This whole process can take 15 minutes. By the end, though, the seeds will be crisp, dry, and salted from the inside out, which gives them a unique flavor.

Nut and Seed Butters

First and foremost: peanut butter.

Why make your own when 250,000 *tons* of it are made commercially in America every year?

Because making peanut butter is easy, and it will taste infinitely better than commercial peanut butter, which has salt, sugar, hydrogenated (saturated) fat, and preservatives added to it and which is heated during processing to a temperature that destroys a good share of the peanut's nutrients and damages the roasted nutty flavor.

In August 1978 *Consumer Reports* investigated peanut butter. They found that commercial peanut butters were, on the average, 49% fat. Most had hydrogenated oil added to them as a stabilizer. They also found that both natural- and supermarket-brand peanut butters were very high in sodium unless the label stated that the peanut butter was specifically low in sodium. Also, in every two tablespoons of supermarket peanut butter there was, on the average, two-thirds teaspoon of added sugar. Some peanut butters sold as natural had one-third teaspoon of sugar in every two tablespoons of peanut butter.

Since most of us grew up on the commercial stuff, the first bite of a homemade nut butter is smackingly extraordinary. Peanut butter, almond butter, cashew butter, sesame butter, tahini, and sunflower butter can all be made the following way:

Toast 2 cups raw nuts, seeds, or a combination. Toasting the nuts and seeds gives the final butter a lightly roasted flavor.

For a sesame seed butter, either hulled or unhulled sesame seeds can be used. If hulled sesame seeds are used, the butter turns out milder and sweeter and technically is called tahini. If unhulled sesame seeds are used, the sesame butter that results is stronger in taste, has a slightly higher mineral content, and is called sesame butter.[1]

In a food processor fitted with the steel blade or in a blender, puree the nuts or seeds in batches with 3 tablespoons unrefined peanut oil. Puree sesame seeds, however, with 3 tablespoons of sesame oil only. Add herb salt to taste, starting out with just a pinch, since nuts and seeds already contain sodium. The juice from 1 lemon, 2 cloves of garlic, and 1 teaspoon vanilla extract or any dried herb can also be added for flavor. Blend until smooth.

Store nut butters in a clean jar in the refrigerator. Oil will rise to the top of natural nut and seed butters as the heavier solids settle. Simply give the butter a stir or two before using.

[1]Although unhulled sesame seeds are slightly more nutritious than hulled, unhulled seeds also contain a bitter-tasting substance called calcium oxalate. In very large doses, calcium oxalate has contributed to gastrointestinal difficulties, kidney stones, and poor mineral utilization. Hulled sesame seeds do not contain calcium oxalate, but the hulling process itself damages the nutritional quality of the sesame seeds. Vitamins and minerals are depleted, and the proteins in the seed may be damaged. Also, hulling is usually carried out with lye, acid, and enzyme solutions, followed by bleaching and high-temperature drying. If you purchase hulled sesame seeds, therefore, try to buy a brand that notes that the seeds have been hulled without the use of chemicals. Protein-Aide™ is one such brand, and is available in natural food stores or by mail-order from International Protein Industries, Inc., P.O. Box 871, Smithtown, New York 11787.

Meat and Fish

Meat

For people who are not vegetarians, fresh meat seems like a wholesome food. It comes from a natural source—animals—and when you're buying the meat, there isn't a label to read that might cause you to reconsider your decision.

Most of us know about meat's benefits. It is a strong source of protein, fat, thiamine, niacin, B_{12}, iron, phosphorus, potassium, sodium, and magnesium. But these benefits must be carefully weighed against the risks, which, year by year, are increasing. Prior to World War II few people thought about the amount of meat they consumed. Now meat eating warrants close attention.

It's important to note, from the beginning, that meat doesn't have a monopoly on protein. You can get more than enough protein eating no meat at all. In one of several studies reported in the *Journal of the American Dietetic Association,* the protein intakes of two hundred people on three kinds of diets were compared.[1] Twenty-six of the subjects were pure vegetarians, who ate no animal products at all. Eighty-six were lacto-ovo vegetarians, who ate milk and eggs but no meat. And the rest were meat eaters, who had standard diets. All three groups got much more protein than the recommended daily allowances suggest.[2] Interestingly, however, the pure vegetarians weighed, on the

[1]U. D. Register and L. M. Sonnenberg, "The Vegetarian Diet," *Journal of the American Dietetic Association,* Vol. 62 (March 1973), pp. 253–60.

[2]Protein needs vary dramatically depending on the individual. The National Research Council, which sets the recommended dietary allowances for healthy people living in the United States, recommends .42 grams of protein for every pound of body weight. A quick, approximate way to determine protein needs based on this formula is to divide body weight by two. A person who weighs 120 pounds, for example, would require 60 grams of protein based on the RDA recommendations. The council reports that the RDA for protein can easily be met on a no-meat diet.

Please remember that the RDAs are not the same as nutritional recommendations made by the United Nation's World Health Organization, and nutritionists in this country have criticized the whole concept of defining nutritional needs in terms of RDA numbers, saying that the RDAs grossly oversimplify the complex and little-understood process of nutrition. Rather than relying on the RDA standard, then, you may want to experiment with your protein intake just enough to see if you need a little more or less than the standard. The chapter "How to Plan Your Optimal Diet" will give you guidelines.

average, twenty pounds less than the others. The meat eaters weighed twelve to fifteen pounds over their ideal weight.

When chickens ran freely around a yard, scratching for worms and bugs, taking six to nine months to grow, and eating at least fifteen pounds of feed before they were ready for market, meat wasn't nearly the health risk it is now.

But today the sad truth is that chickens and other meat animals are so physically manipulated, their flesh so adulterated and contaminated with chemicals, that meat has less and less of a place in a book about natural food. Still, most of us in this country are not pure vegetarians, and because that's true, I feel it's important to address the issue of meat in this book. What exactly are the risks of eating meat? And, equally important, what are the viable options?

In the pages that follow I've attempted to present most of the problems associated with eating meat. As you'll see, the problem most people are aware of—ingesting too much fat—is only one of the possible dangers eating meat poses. There are also chemical dangers, and these are becoming more threatening all the time. In presenting such risks, I'd like briefly to describe how chickens are raised. It's not that modern methods of raising poultry makes eating chicken any more risky than eating beef, lamb, or pork, but the consumption of chicken has increased more than twice as fast as the consumption of other meats. Between 1960 and 1975 chicken consumption increased 50%, while beef and veal consumption rose by 22%.

The modern chicken never sees the light of day.[3] She is packed with five or more other chickens in a cage that is shorter in every direction than *one* chicken's wingspan. The cages are stacked one on top of the next, row after row, in a light-controlled, windowless building something like an airplane hangar. One building can contain as many as thirty thousand birds.

Soon after birth the chicken is debeaked and drugged to keep her from cannibalizing the birds pressed against her. She is heavily injected with antibiotics (as are 75% of cattle, 90% of calves, and 85% of hogs) to counter diseases that whip through the cages when chickens are packed together, unable to move, in a totally synthetic environment. The stress and crowding sickly birds experience may result in a cancer called Marek's disease. In 1971 a vaccine was developed to counteract Marek's disease, so few chickens now develop it, but in 1969, 37 million birds were exterminated because of it.[4]

[3]For a more comprehensive view of factory farming, see: Peter Singer, *Animal Liberation* (New York: New York Review Book, 1975), and Page Smith and Charles Daniel, *The Chicken Book* (Boston: Little, Brown, 1975).

[4]Stephen Singular, "Brave New Chickens," *New Times*, April 29, 1977.

The chicken is fed chemicals mixed with feed and her own recycled waste. The chemicals contain arsenic compounds and hormones powerful enough to fatten her in half the time on half the normal amount of feed. Other chemicals in her feed include dyes that will turn the chicken's flesh yellow—an unnatural color, but one that most of us associate with healthy poultry meat.[5]

What effect does the physical abuse and chemical manipulation of animals raised for meat have on the meat per se? Objective studies comparing the nutrient quality of such meat with the nutrient quality of meat from animals raised in a natural environment and manner are difficult to find. For the meat eater, though, other implications can be drawn.

For example, the hormone that has been most frequently used to fatten meat animals is the synthetic female sex hormone diethylstilbestrol (DES). In the early 1970s the FDA banned DES after carcinogenic residues were detected in animal livers. The hormone had been shown to produce cancer in test animals, and medical researchers had reported a high incidence of vaginal cancer in the daughters of women who had taken DES during their pregnancies to prevent miscarriage.

The DES ban was challenged and ultimately reversed, however, by DES manufacturers, who contended that they had not been given an adequate hearing. Throughout the seventies DES use (begun in the forties) continued.

In July 1979 DES was finally banned for a second time. The ruling was based on the fact that DES was consistently found to cause cancer at even the smallest levels and that the methods for detecting DES residues in meats were not effective enough to rely on spot-checking as a way of determining the meat's safety.[6] Livestock and poultry breeders now use other hormones to stimulate rapid bursts of growth in meat animals.

Animal feed contains chemicals other than ones intentionally put in it. Crop farmers use many agricultural chemicals including soil conditioners, seed-treating compounds, chemical fertilizers, insecticides, herbicides, fungicides, rodenticides, soil fumigants, and miticides. All of these are found in animal feed, and additionally, some get into the animal's body through the water supply. Insecticides are also sprayed directly on animals. The insecticide compounds seep into the animal through its skin. The metabolites that are formed in

[5]"Fresh Chicken," *Consumer Reports,* May 1978.
[6]"Kennedy Acts on D.E.S. and Cyclamates," *Community Nutrition Institute Weekly Report,* Vol. 9, No. 26 (July 5, 1979).

the animal's tissues are thought to be even more toxic than the original pesticide compounds.[7]

Industrial poisons like lead, mercury, and cadmium find their way into animal feed through pollution residues that settle on crops. Mercury is also used to treat grain seed. Although the plant grown from such a seed will not be contaminated with mercury, the mercury is ingested when the seed itself is eaten.

Industrial poisons like PCBs, PBBs, and DDT find their way into feed through contamination when the feed is being processed, through the water supply, and sometimes through components in the feed, such as ground fish meal. Fish have a tremendous capacity to store in their fatty tissues the industrial poisons dumped into rivers and lakes. The fish then pass them on in concentrated form to the animals that eat the fish.

One of the reasons meat eating carries with it the risks it does is due to the fact that toxic chemicals are bio-magnified in an animal's body.[8] As you move up the food chain, more and more chemicals become concentrated in fewer bodies. All of the grains of wheat in a loaf of bread, for example, will contain fewer pesticide residues than the liver of a beef animal that has been ingesting massive amounts of chlorinated hydrocarbon pesticides, industrial toxins such as the polychlorinated biphenyls, environmental pollutants, growth hormones, and antibiotics in the thousands of pounds of feed it will eat during its lifetime.

The antibiotics found in animal feed pose a different threat to health than the direct or indirect carcinogenic pesticides, industrial toxins, and growth hormones. In 1979 the Office of Technology Assessment presented the U.S. Congress with the finding that antibiotics such as penicillin and tetracycline are no longer as effective as they once were in treating human disease.[9] Physicians have found that bacteria in the body are becoming resistant to antibiotics, since the antibiotics have already found their way into human tissues through meat-based diets.

All of the chemicals talked about so far—animal drugs, pesticides, antibiotics, toxic industrial contaminants—are found in meat in alarming amounts. In 1979 the General Accounting Office issued a report that was sharply critical of the Food and Drug Administration, United States Department of Agriculture, and Environmental Protec-

[7]James A. Libbey, *Meat Hygiene* (Philadelphia: Lea & Febiger, 1975), p. 299.

[8]Ibid., p. 477.

[9]"Animal Drugs Pose Risk Benefit Issue," Report by the Office of Technology Assessment, U.S. Congress, June 1979. Reported in *Community Nutrition Institute Weekly Report,* Vol. 9, No. 25 (June 28, 1979).

The Politics of Meat

Imagine someone sitting in a restaurant eating an eight-ounce sirloin. Forty people with empty bowls are there, too—watching.

The steer that is now the steak ate twenty-one pounds of cereal protein for every pound of protein he ultimately provided in meat. That eight-ounce sirloin for one person could have been a bowl of grain each for forty.

Enough grain is produced each year to provide everyone in the world with 3,000 to 4,000 calories a day, not counting all the beans, vegetables, fruits, nuts, nongrain-fed meat, and fish that are also available and would provide even more food for all of us.

Why, then, do people starve?

In 1978 the U.S. General Accounting Office commissioned a report on world hunger. The report's findings confirmed earlier research: Hunger is *not* due to a shortage of food, but rather to the way our government and others control the agricultural production of underdeveloped countries by dictating economic policies there that support food consumption here. U.S. monies encourage other countries to plow under staple food crops and plant instead low-nutrition and feed crops for export to affluent countries like our own.

Brazil, for example, has replaced much of its black bean crop (for local human consumption) with profitable soybeans, which can be exported as animal feed.

tion Agency because of the high levels of chemical residues found in meat. Of the 143 drugs and pesticides the GAO identified as chemicals that leave residues in red meat and poultry, 42 are known or suspected of causing cancer; 20 of causing birth defects, and 6 of causing mutations.[10]

In addition to the risks of ingesting toxic chemicals, eating a lot of meat poses dietary risks. Beginning in the late 1950s, research linked diets high in meat to heart disease and colon cancer. The problems are, first, that meat, by nature, is high in saturated fat; and second, that chemicals in meat may be carcinogenic or may combine with other chemicals in the meat or in the human body to form carcinogenic compounds once the meat is eaten. This is what happens when nitrites are added to meat in the curing process.

In 1956 scientists discovered that nitrites react with compounds in meat to form carcinogenic nitrosamines. Recently the FDA ordered meat manufacturers to reduce the level of nitrite in bacon (not in all

[10]"G.A.O. Report Blasts Raw Meat and Poultry as Unsafe," *Food Engineering,* June 1979.

Soybeans render more usable protein per acre of land than any other known crop. An acre of cereal can produce five times the protein of the same acre devoted to meat production. An acre of beans, peas, or lentils can produce ten times the protein that would be produced if cattle were grazed on it. But Brazilians don't eat the soybeans they raise. It's earmarked for export and ultimately fed to animals.

Ironically, we are the world's leading producer of soybeans and one of the largest producers of other grain, pea, and bean crops. We export some of that. But of the grains and legumes that remain, 95% of the soybeans, 89% of the corn, 87% of the oats, and 64% of the barley is eaten by cows and pigs.

Every country must take individual responsibility for planting crops that feed its population. Still, hunger in other countries *is* exacerbated by what we choose to eat here. Since international economic policies are based on demand, we do have some power to make a difference in world hunger, as well as in the quality of our own nourishment.

Diet for a Small Planet by Frances Moore Lappé (New York: Ballantine, 1971) and *Food First: Beyond the Myth of Scarcity* by Frances Moore Lappé and Joseph Collins (New York: Houghton Mifflin, 1977) fully explore the relationship between food consumption and food needs here and abroad.

cured meats) so that nitrosamines would not be as readily formed in it. However, nitrites react with compounds in the human stomach to form nitrosamines there as well. But the nitrosamines that may form in the stomach were not taken into account when governmental regulations were issued. Cancer-causing nitrosamines are no longer permitted at *high levels in bacon,* but small amounts of nitrites are still allowed. Such regulations take no responsibility for what happens after bacon and other cured meats are swallowed.[11]

The relationship between meat eating on the one hand and heart disease and cancer on the other is more complicated. In both instances one of the problems seems to be that meat, by nature, contains a lot of saturated fat. Fat is interlaced throughout the muscle of beef, lamb, pork, and other animals. Animal fats, with the exception of the fat in fish, are always saturated. Saturated fat, in research study after

[11]Ross Hume Hall, "What Kind of Food Protection System Have We?" *En-trophy Institute for Advanced Study Review,* Vol. 2, No. 1 (January–February 1979). See also: the 1979 booklet on nitrites issued by Community Nutrition Institute, 1146 19th Street, N.W., Washington, D.C. 20036.

research study, has been linked to heart disease and some forms of cancer, although it's important to note that exactly how saturated fat may lead to these diseases has not been determined.[12] The point here, however, is that meat and animal products are the biggest sources of saturated fat in our diets. And as far as the fat in meat goes, you cannot cut it away, nor does it cook away. When every bit of trimmable fat has been cut from roast beef or a T-bone steak, for example, 40% of the remaining calories still come in the form of fat.

Now, what does one reasonably do with all of this information? Clearly, the dangers associated with meat eating are considerable. These dangers, however, must be looked at in relation to the very real and important position of meat as a leading source of protein.

First, we can cut down on meat and begin to get our protein from other foods. Many fish, for example, provide as much protein as an equal amount of meat, yet have half the calories and no saturated fat. If you're a big meat eater, you may want to begin trying some of the meatier fishes—swordfish and salmon, for example, rather than flounder or fillet of sole. In the next section I've included a chart that examines saltwater fish, freshwater fish, and shellfish. The chart may help you to determine some options. Of course, you can also get more than enough protein eating no meat or fish at all. See the chapters on grains and legumes and many of the recipes scattered throughout this book.[13]

Second, we can begin eating better quality meat that comes from animals that have not been treated with chemicals nor fed chemicalized feed. Small slaughterhouses, some butchers, and some natural

[12]Among the first studies that showed a connection between meat-based diets and colon cancer were those conducted with Japanese men. Japanese men who lived in Japan and ate very little animal fat rarely got colon cancer. By contrast, Japanese men who lived in the United States and were heavy meat eaters got colon cancer frequently. The initial research concluded that meat—and specifically the saturated fat in meat—was a major risk factor contributing to colon cancer (reported in A. M. Pearson, "Some Factors That May Alter Consumption of Animal Products," *Journal of the American Dietetic Association,* Vol 69 [November 1976], pp. 522–29).

But later research proposed another idea. Japanese men living in the United States not only ate a lot of meat, their diets were also very low in fiber. Research began connecting low-fiber diets with colon cancer (G. A. Leveille, "Issues in Human Nutrition and Their Probable Impact on Foods of Animal Origin," *Journal of Animal Science,* Vol. 41 [1975], p. 723).

Looking at all the research together, it appeared that the saturated fat in meat did not work alone in making people more susceptible to disease. But clearly, the combination of saturated animal fat plus low fiber (which would mean too few fresh fruits, fresh vegetables, and whole grains), plus a high intake of sugar and refined carbohydrates was consistently found to be destructive to bodily health. (See: Alexander R. P. Walker, "Colon Cancer and Diet with Specific Reference to Intake of Fat and Fiber," *American Journal of Clinical Nutrition,* Vol. 29 [December 1976], pp. 1417–26.)

[13]*Recipes for a Small Planet* by Ellen Buchman Ewald (New York: Ballantine Books, 1973) is a cookbook devoted specifically to high-protein meatless cooking.

food stores carry standard cuts of beef, lamb, veal, chicken, and turkey that have been raised on what is called organic feed or grazed on land that is managed organically.

The *Organic Directory* published by Rodale Press defines organically grown meats as cuts of meat from stock that are fed rations and raised in an environment free of pesticides, herbicides, growth hormones such as DES, antibiotics, and irradiation. If an animal requires drug treatment for an illness, the meat is not marketable until a chemical analysis proves that no traces of the drug remain in the animal's tissues. All animals are allowed to run free, to get physical exercise, and to be exposed to fresh air and daylight. Beef is raised with the goal of minimizing, not maximizing, the fat content.

Such meats cannot legally be labeled organic because neither the USDA nor state meat inspection boards have guidelines or standards governing meat animals raised in an organic manner. You'll have to rely on the reputation of the poultry farmer, livestock breeder, butcher, or store owner that the meat has been raised appropriately.

Third, when we do eat meat, we can always choose the leanest cuts. Not only does lean meat contain less fat, but the iron and vitamin-B contents of lean meats are usually higher than those of fattier meats.

Most of the meat sold commercially is graded USDA Prime or USDA Choice. Meat that is graded prime has lots of fat marbled throughout the muscle tissue. It's the most juicy and tender as a result. Choice-graded meat has less marbled fat, is more lean, still tasty, and the best choice in terms of health.

Pork chops and lamb are approximately equal to beef in fat content, while veal is much lower. Ham, the leanest cut of pork, is unfortunately cured with large amounts of salt and sodium nitrite.

In poultry most of the fat is concentrated in the animal's skin. Duck flesh plus skin, for example, has three and a half times the fat that the flesh has alone.

Of all poultry, chicken and turkey contain the least fat, duck and goose the most. Uncooked duck flesh (no skin), for example, has roughly three times the fat that uncooked chicken flesh has. All poultry flesh has a higher fat content after it's cooked, since some of the fat juices in the skin seep into the flesh. Once chicken and duck flesh are cooked, their fat contents more than double.

If you take the skin off any bird *before you cook it,* you can dramatically reduce the amount of fat you'll eat. Extra care must be taken in cooking poultry this way, since the meat (especially the white meat) will easily dry out. Basting the meat with a good stock helps.

Fish

The flesh of most fish is white, flaky, and easily digestible. Fish have almost no carbohydrate, extremely little fat (what fat they do have is unsaturated), and are high in protein, vitamins and minerals. Many fish, in fact, provide as much protein as an equal amount of lean meat, yet have half the calories.

Although any fish is a good choice in terms of nutrient density, some fish do provide more nutrients than others. These are the fish usually classified as fat fish. They provide more protein, more fat, and are cooked differently than lean fish. Fat fish include trout, whitefish, eel, herring, mackerel, pompano, salmon, and tuna. They can be brushed lightly with corn or sesame oil before cooking, but in general, fat fish are sufficiently moistened by their own fat so that they can be cooked simply as they are.

Lean fish, by comparison, require basting during cooking to keep them from drying out. Use a good vegetable oil or butter if broiling; a light sauce or stock if baking. Lean fish include sole, halibut, red snapper, yellow perch, flounder, sea and striped bass, catfish, and cod. Lean fish have fewer calories than fat fish, since they have less fat, but no fish has a lot of fat or calories to begin with. Also, in terms of overall fat, cooking method must be taken into consideration. A salmon broiled alone usually won't contribute any more fat than red snapper basted with oil or butter. And a final point: When buying canned fish, buy it packed in water rather than oil. Tuna packed in water, for example, has one-fifth as much fat as tuna packed in oil, even after the oil is drained.

Cooking fish is quite simple.[14] Begin with the freshest fish possible. If the fish is whole, the gills should be red, the skin pink and translucent, and the eyes clear. The flesh, whether you're buying a whole fish or a fillet or steak, should spring back when you press it lightly. Also, truly fresh fish doesn't smell fishy.

The simplest method of cooking fish is broiling it. To broil fish without overcooking it, it's imperative that your broiler be as hot as possible, so allow it to preheat for 15 minutes. To keep fish from sticking to the broiler pan, sprinkle the pan with cracker crumbs, bread crumbs, or cornmeal, and place the fish skin side down.

The Fisheries Council of Canada has developed a method for timing fish so that it is neither undercooked nor overcooked. By their method, you simply measure the thickness of the fish at its thickest

[14]For comprehensive descriptions of fish commonly eaten in the United States and accompanying recipes, see: James Beard, *New Fish Cookery* (Boston: Little, Brown, 1976).

part as the fish lies on its side. For every inch of thickness allow 10 minutes cooking time, whether you're broiling, baking, poaching, or steaming. This method applies to all fish and to steaks and fillets as well as whole fish.

The following chart describes most of the fish available for eating here. It is divided into saltwater fish, freshwater fish, and shellfish. Freshwater fish and shellfish deserve special attention:

Freshwater fish have been found to have high levels of industrial pollutants. The most serious pollutants are the polychlorinated biphenyls (PCBs). In 1979 the FDA reduced the allowable levels of PCBs in freshwater fish by more than half when continuing studies found PCBs to be more dangerous than was previously thought. Specifically, PCBs were linked to liver disease and reproductive failure in test animals. According to the FDA, restrictions on fishing in certain highly polluted waters around the Great Lakes have been imposed. The highest levels of PCBs are concentrated in salmon, trout, and catfish. Saltwater fish are much less likely to be contaminated.

Shellfish deserve special note because they are among the most nutritious of fish. They are extremely high in protein, iron, calcium,

Broiled Swordfish with Olive Butter

- 1 c. large black olives, pitted (preferably Greek)
- 1 T. fresh lemon juice
- 1 t. dried thyme
- herbal salt to taste
- 2 T. olive oil
- 1 T. butter
- ¼ c. white wine
- ¼ c. minced parsley
- 4 swordfish steaks (about 2 lb. total)

1. Puree the olives through a sieve, using the back of a wide wooden spoon. Add the lemon juice, thyme, and salt and mix well. Trickle in the olive oil, a drop at a time, beating vigorously. The mixture should be thick and smooth—almost like a mayonnaise.

2. Preheat the broiler for 10 minutes. In a small saucepan, combine the butter, wine, and parsley. With a pastry brush or spoon, brush each swordfish steak with the butter mixture. Broil steaks for about 6 minutes on one side. Turn and broil for 8 minutes on the other side. Turn again. Paint each steak generously with the olive mixture and place under the broiler for a final 2 minutes. Serve on a warm platter. Garnish with lemon slices.

Saltwater Fish

Name	*Description*	*Range*	*Season and Availability Fresh*	*What to Be Aware of*
Anchovy	Fish of the herring family. Available canned, salted in brine, smoked and kippered, or dried and salted.	Found in warm waters all over the world.	Season: Year-round.	5 anchovies have only 2.1 grams of fat and 35 calories.
Bluefish	Flesh is rich and oily with a sweet flavor.	U.S. Atlantic coast, Mediterranean Sea and Indian Ocean.	Season: Spring and fall. Fresh: Eastern Seaboard cities.	Bluefish is considered excellent eating but does not keep well.
Cod	Flesh is white and flaky with plain flavor. Available fresh, dry salted, shredded, pickled, smoked, or canned.	North Pacific and Greenland to Massachusetts and South of Great Britain.	Season: Year-round off Newfoundland and Massachusetts. Fresh: Northern Eastern Seaboard cities, Maine to New York.	Cod is lean and has few bones. Ounce for ounce, it equals lean sirloin steak in protein but has only ½ to ⅓ the fat. True for many white fish.
Flounder	Fish sold as sole are usually flounder. Gray sole is the best-flavored flounder. Lemon sole is the next best flavored. Blackback is the meatiest flounder with a very thick body. Sanddab is sweet flavored with a distinguishable texture. Summer flounder is a meaty fish with white, sweet-flavored flesh.	U.S. and European Atlantic coasts and Pacific coasts.	Season: Year-round. Fresh: Atlantic and Pacific coastal areas.	Flounder are lean and cook extremely quickly.
Haddock	Flesh is white and flaky with a plain flavor similar to cod.	Smoked haddock comes from the British and Norwegian coasts. The Atlantic coast, north of Massachusetts, supplies fresh and frozen haddock.	Season: Year-round. Fresh: Northern Eastern Seaboard cities, Maine to New York.	One of the highest protein-yielding fish and very lean—only 1.8 grams of fat in every ounce (raw).
Halibut	Flesh is white, firm, and of good flavor.	All northern seas; European, Atlantic, and Pacific coasts.	Season: Year-round availability on the Atlantic coast. Available on the Pacific coast from May to mid-July.	Another lean, high-protein-yielding fish, with only 2 grams of fat in every ounce (raw).

Name	Description	Range	Season and Availability Fresh	What to Be Aware of
Herring	Flesh has firm texture, and if fresh, the flavor is extraordinarily creamy.	U.S. Atlantic coast north of Cape Cod, though fished commercially as far south as Virginia.	Season: Year-round. Fresh: Northern Altantic cities.	One of the highest protein-yielding fish, a bit higher in fat than other fish. Plain canned herring has just under 4 grams of fat in every ounce.
Mackerel	Light, firm, oily flesh. Available fresh, smoked, kippered, salted, and canned.	Mediterranean, European, and U.S. Atlantic coasts. Pacific coast: between San Diego and the Galápagos Islands.	Season: April to November. Fresh: Eastern Seaboard and southern California.	High protein content; considered a fat fish.
Pompano	Flesh is moist with a rich but delicate flavor.	Found in warm seas around the world. Abundant in the South Atlantic from the Carolinas to the Gulf of Mexico.	Season: Year-round. Available January to April. Fresh: South Atlantic coast and South Pacific coast.	California pompano, which are extremely popular on the West Coast, are actually not members of this family but are closely related to butterfish. Florida pompano is available only locally or shipped north to better restaurants. Considered fat.
Perch (Ocean)	The flesh is spotted with either pink or reddish coloring and is firm and coarse. When cooked, flesh is white, flaky, and extremely delicate in flavor.	Atlantic coast from Cape Cod to eastern Nova Scotia.	Season: Usually sold only frozen in fillets with or without skin.	Well suited to sauces. Ocean perch are a bit more bland than yellow perch, which are freshwater lean fish.
Sardines	There is no one fish that is a "sardine." The name applies to any tiny fish with weak bones that can be preserved in oil.	First appear along New England coast in early spring. Also found in Maine, the Bay of Fundy, Nova Scotia, and on the West Coast.	Season: Sold all seasons in cans—salted, smoked, spiced, or in oils or sauces. Fresh: Available but not in great demand.	High in protein, minerals, and vitamins, but 1 ounce of canned sardines (drained) has 3.1 grams of fat—relatively high for fish. The most flavorful sardines are Portuguese and Norwegian, since they are packed in a higher quality oil.
Scrod	Scrod is a young cod weighing no more than about 2½ pounds.	North Pacific and Greenland to Massachusetts and south of Great Britain.	Season: Year-round off Newfoundland and Massachusetts. Fresh: Northern Eastern seaboard cities, Maine to New York.	Equals lean sirloin steak in protein but has only ½ to ⅓ the fat. Young haddock is also sold as scrod.

Name	*Description*	*Range*	*Season and Availability Fresh*	*What to Be Aware of*
Shad	Delicious with a sweet flavor, but extremely bony. Fresh, kippered, smoked, and boned fillets are available canned.	Pacific and Atlantic coasts. Also found in the Mississippi River and the Great Lakes.	Season: January through May. Fresh: Pacific and Atlantic coasts, Great Lakes and Mississippi area.	High in protein. Slightly higher in fat than most white fish.
Smelt	Flesh is lean, very sweet, and delicately flavored.	Great Lakes, Michigan, New England, Oregon, San Francisco, Alaska, and northeast Asia.	Season: September to May. Fresh: New England, North Pacific coast.	Pacific smelt is soft and doesn't keep well.
Snapper	The meat of most snappers is tender, lean, white, with a delicate flavor.	Found in warm seas north of Long Island to the coast of Florida and Key West to the Gulf of Mexico.	Season: Year-round. Fresh: South Atlantic and Gulf of Mexico.	Snapper keeps very well, and is considered the filet mignon of fish. Slightly higher in fat than white fish.
Sole	True sole is found in the English Channel (Dover sole). It is delicious and much differently flavored than the fish sold here as sole.	English Channel and surrounding waters.	Season: Frozen Dover sole is available in some East Coast restaurants.	In America, the name sole is used for any white-fleshed fish that are sold as fillets. These are usually members of the flounder family (dab, gray, lemon sole, yellowtail, winter flounder). Lean.
Squid	Sweet and rich when marketed fresh, squid average 1 foot in length.	Most abundant in the Atlantic Ocean from Labrador to the Carolinas.	Season: Year-round. Fresh: Atlantic seaboard.	Sweet taste, dominant texture. Fry or sauté. An elongated relative of the octopus.
Sturgeon	Fresh sturgeon flesh is firm and dry. Fresh, dry, smoked, and kippered.	Great Lakes, Mississippi Valley, and Lake Huron. The largest species of sturgeon, the Russian beluga, is found in the Caspian and Black seas.	Season: April to November. Fresh: Sturgeon is rarely seen in the markets fresh, but if you find them, lake sturgeon are superior in flavor to sea sturgeon.	High in protein, sturgeon requires frequent basting during cooking. The roe of sturgeon is considered the best caviar. Fish roe (eggs) have proportionately more protein than chicken eggs.

Name	*Description*	*Range*	*Season and Availability Fresh*	*What to Be Aware of*
Swordfish	The flesh is firm, meaty, and rich flavored.	Most coastal waters around the world; in Nova Scotia; from Cuba to Cape Breton; the South Pacific.	Season: In the Atlantic: April to September. In the Pacific: September to December. Imported swordfish is available frozen year-round. Fresh: Southern Atlantic and Pacific coastal regions.	Sold as steaks since fish itself can weigh as much as 600 pounds. Must be basted frequently during cooking or will become dry. Rich in vitamins.
Tuna	Several different species of fish are sold as tuna: albacore has the lightest meat and, when canned, is labeled white meat. All other canned species are labeled light-meat tuna. These species include bluefin, skipjock, and yellowfin in the Pacific; horse mackerel, little tuna, and white bluefin in the Atlantic. Light tuna tastes stronger than albacore.	All species are abundant in the Atlantic, Pacific, and Indian oceans and in warm seas all over the world.	Season: Atlantic coast: July to October. Pacific coast: May to December.	Tuna is packed in three different forms, which refer only to the size of the pieces in the can, not to the quality of the meat: (1) Fancy or solid pack: the most expensive and best cuts of white albacore; (2) Chunk style: second-best cuts; (3) Flake and grated style: the darker meat from one or more of the species other than albacore. All tuna is sold packed in either water or oil. Water-packed tuna has $1/5$ the fat that well-drained oil-packed tuna has.

Freshwater Fish

Name	*Description*	*Range*	*Season and Availability Fresh*	*What to Be Aware of*
Bass	Flesh is firm, delicious, and of a fine flavor. Sold fresh and frozen.	Almost every state in the U.S. and southern Canada.	Season: Year-round; warm-water streams and ponds. May through September best season in colder waters.	Freshwater bass should not be confused with sea bass (caught on both coasts, similar to a grouper) and striped bass, also caught on both coasts and known as rockfish. Freshwater and striped bass have better flavor than sea.
Catfish	Flesh is white, flaky, of a delicate texture and fine flavor.	Found in nearly every state.	Season: Year-round fishing in every state.	Catfish can live for hours without water. If you catch one, keep it alive until you are ready to eat it. Lean.
Salmon	Flesh varies from pinkish to deep red. Has firm texture and excellent meaty flavor.	Fresh salmon: Pacific coastal region and North American lakes. Smoked Salmon: Scotland, Ireland, and Canada.	Season: Available year-round, but summer best season.	Some varieties of salmon are twice as fatty as others, although no salmon is as high in fat as meat. The most fatty canned salmons are Atlantic, chinook (king), and sockeye. The least fatty are chum, coho, and pink salmon.
Trout	Includes lake trout, brook trout, and rainbow trout. All trout flesh is delicately delicious, firm, and white in color.	Large, deep North American lakes and streams.	Season: Available year-round. Fresh: Pacific coastal and mountain regions.	Trout loses its flavor faster than any other fish. It's best, then, when grilled on an open campfire, minutes after being fished out of a mountain stream. Also available from fish farms. Considered fat.
Whitefish	Flesh is lean and mild-flavored. Smoked whitefish is widely sold.	Found in the Great Lakes and other lakes in the U.S. and Canada.	Season: Available year-round. Fresh: Great Lakes area and various lake regions throughout the U.S.	Whitefish have been overfished, and the supply is currently very low.

Name	*Description*	*Range*	*Season and Availability Fresh*	*What to Be Aware of*
Abalone	Tough unless tenderized before cooking by pounding with a mallet. Light flavor, meaty texture.	Catalina Island and Monterey off the coast of California in the Pacific.	Season: Year-round. Fresh: Cannot be purchased in the U.S. outside of California.	Protective legislation prohibits the shipping of fresh abalone out of California because the supply is minimal. Mexican abalone is available in cans, in chunks, or in flake form. Reports of consumer fraud, in which cheaper fish are patched into abalone steaks that are then sold in restaurants, are well known.
Clam	There are hundreds of species of clams but only a few are sold commercially as food. Sold alive in shells, shucked, canned, or frozen.	Atlantic: hard-shelled clams —south of Cape Cod to North Carolina and from Florida to Texas. Soft-shelled clams—north of Cape Cod to the Artic Ocean. Pacific: along coast approximately 30 varieties of clams. The most popular is the razor clam. The famous Pismo clam is very succulent and is protected by law from overdigging.	Season: Peak season: October to April, but because of forced breeding, fresh clams are available in some form year-round. Fresh: Coastal regions.	Clams are extremely rich sources of proteins, minerals, and vitamins. The smallest hard-shell, under 2 inches, is called littleneck. Once the clam exceeds 2 inches, but not more than 3, it is termed a cherrystone. The larger clam, more than 3 inches, is a chowder clam and is used as such. Small sizes are referred to as steamers and larger ones as in-shells.
Crab	Salty flavor. Claw meat is white, the body meat a darker color.		Soft-shelled: always sold fresh. Peak season: July and August. Hard-shelled: available all year. Most plentiful during summer.	Canned crabmeat sold in stores is a combination of white and dark unless marked "white or deluxe."
• Dungeness Crab	Large Pacific-coast variety—extremely delicious and flavorful.	Pacific Coast		
• Soft-shelled Crab	Not a distinct species. The name applies to any young crab caught between the shedding of an old shell and the hardening of the new and larger shell.			

Name	Description	Range	Season and Availability Fresh	What to Be Aware of
• Stone Crab	Popular on the East coast. The male has extremely large claws.	Miami, Palm Beach, Key West, and Cuba.		
• King Crab	Largest edible crab; can measure 9 feet wide.	North Atlantic		Giant Alaskan king crab legs are sold at giant prices but are very delicious. Usually sold precooked and frozen in their shell or cleaned and canned.
Lobster	Opinion is divided. Some say the smaller the lobster, the more tender the meat and the better the texture. Other professionals disagree, saying the larger lobsters have the best taste and the most meatiness.	North and Middle Atlantic: in deep waters in winter and shallow waters during the summer. Most of the catch in the U.S. comes from the New England coast. Many lobsters from Florida and California are really crayfish.	Season: Year-round but most plentiful in summer, when they are in shallow water. Fresh: Northern and Middle Atlantic coast.	Canned lobster comes from Canada. Frozen lobster tails come from South Africa. A fresh lobster should be very active when you buy it.
Mussel	Meat is golden color, tender and sweet. Mussels must be tightly closed if alive when purchased. If partially opened, they are dead and must be discarded.	Abundant in cooler waters of the Atlantic and Pacific oceans.	Season: Year-round. Fresh: Most regions of the U.S., as they keep extremely well.	Mussel shells are thin, so there is more food per pound than in either oysters or clams. Mussels are also the least expensive shellfish.
Oyster	Many varieties; most are not large enough to use as food or, like the Japanese oyster, too large to eat on the half shell. Meat is dark gray-green and extremely succulent. Can be purchased alive in the shell, frozen, shucked, prebreaded, canned, or smoked whole.	Bluepoints and Rockaways come from Long Island, Coluits from Massachusetts, Lynn-Havina from Virginia. Half the supply of Atlantic oysters comes from the Chesapeake Bay and Long Island. The rest come from Delaware, the Gulf coast of Louisiana, and artificial beds in Maine and New Hampshire. Pacific oysters are found on the coast of Washington and Puget Sound.	Season: Most plentiful in September, but the best are available in October. Fresh: Alive in the shell predominately in the Atlantic and Pacific coastal regions; rarely seen fresh in mid-U.S. markets.	Extremely rich source of protein, minerals, and vitamins. The nutritional balance of oysters is superior to that of most foods. Six oysters supply more protein than milk, for example, and surpass the RDA for iron.

Name	Description	Range	Season and Availability Fresh	What to Be Aware of
Scallop	Meat is white and firm. Tiny bay scallop is extremely tender and more succulent than the larger sea scallop.	Bay scallops are found in shallow offshore waters and mudflats from Cape Cod to Texas and inshore waters around Long Island. Giant sea scallops are found offshore in deep waters from Labrador to New Jersey.	Season: Peak September to April, but marketed year-round. Fresh: Rarely found fresh inland or on the West coast.	The tiny bay scallop is so popular that the supply has greatly diminished. This has led to the creation of a "scallop puncher," similar to a paper puncher, used to "punch" bay-scallop-size scallops out of less expensive, less tasty giant sea scallops.
Shrimp and Prawns	All turn pink and white when cooked. Both have lean flesh, a firm texture, and a similar flavor.	Abundant in both fresh and salt waters, in temperature and tropical conditions. Large commercial catches are made on the coasts of Virginia, Louisiana, and the Gulf of Mexico.	Season: Year-round; peak season for average sizes is August through December; for jumbo sizes, March through June. Fresh: Virtually all shrimp sold in the U.S. are frozen. Experiments in 1978 raising shrimp in agricultural ponds were more successful than any previous year. If fish technology continues to improve, fresh farmed shrimp may be available in the future.	Shrimp should have a tight-fitting shell around the body. Any shrinkage of the flesh may be a sign of staleness. If there is the slightest smell of ammonia, the shrimp may have been spoiled, chemically bleached, refrozen, and sold. Shrimp are high in calcium, phosphorus, and protein; extremely low in fat: 0.3 grams per ounce.

and B vitamins and contain the least fat of all fish—generally no more than 3%. Shellfish are often thought to be high in cholesterol. Shrimp and lobster do have more cholesterol than beef (roughly 130 mg in 3 ounces of shrimp as compared with 75 mg in 3 ounces of beef or chicken), but this is still only half as much as an egg (250 mg) and a third as much as liver (370 mg). Crab contains less cholesterol than shrimp or lobster; it has, in fact, about the same amount as lamb and veal. Oysters and clams have less cholesterol than meat.[15]

Spiced Pears with Banana-Cream Topping

6	large Anjou pears, ripe but not soft
1	qt. apple juice
½	c. water
¼	c. honey
2	cloves
1	vanilla bean, split lengthwise
2-in.	stick cinnamon
1	bay leaf
	whole juniper berries (if available)

Topping

2	large (Japanese) cakes tofu, drained well
2	bananas
2	T. honey
2	T. safflower oil
½	c. pear nectar or apple juice
¼	c. almonds

1. Cut each pear in half. Remove the cores.
2. In a large saucepan, combine the apple juice, water, honey, cloves, vanilla bean, cinnamon, bay leaf, and juniper berries. Bring to a boil. Add the pears and cook for about 45 minutes over low heat, occasionally turning them gently so that they cook evenly.
3. Place 2 pear halves in each of 6 small bowls. Lightly spoon a bit of cooking liquid over them, let cool, then chill in the refrigerator.
4. Just before serving the pears, combine the topping ingredients in a blender and blend to a thick cream. Ring each pear with a generous amount of cream.

[15] As pointed out in the chapters on eggs and oils, a large body of evidence (especially the most recent studies) holds that cholesterol may not be a causative factor in heart disease. Please see those sections.

Juices, Waters, Teas, and Coffee

Juices

If any drink has an American heritage, it's apple cider. The early colonists drank bucketfuls daily—especially in the winter, when freshly pressed cider was warmed on the back of every family's wood stove. Each family pressed its own cider by hand using small cider presses and last autumn's apples that had been tucked away in the cellar.

Apples and other fruits were, of course, also used for cooking and eating. But the making of fruit drinks—mainly cider—was widespread here because early Americans brought their European distrust (and dislike) of water with them. In the old country, water was often undrinkable, if not poisonous.

Why apple drinks became the colonists' favorite is easily explained. Of all North American fruits, apples were not only the easiest stored for the longest period of time and therefore always available for juicing, they were also a source of both "soft" and "hard" drinks. For a few days after a load of apples was pressed, everyone drank sweet apple cider. After that everyone who could drank the naturally fermented applejack (sometimes called "essence of lockjaw") that formed when yeast, already in the cider, turned the sugar in the juice to alcohol. Unlike the hard cider from apples, the hard cider from most other fruits just didn't taste good.

Juices as we know them came about when a New Jersey dentist named Thomas B. Welch took Pasteur's discovery that heat kills bacteria and applied it to juice that had just been squeezed or pressed from fruit.

Today virtually all commercial juice (including juices bought in natural food stores) is pasteurized. If it weren't, spoilage and fermentation would eventually occur, and the result would be vinegar.

During pasteurization juices are run through a labyrinth of tubes that are heated until the juice reaches a temperature of about 190°F.

The juice is then bottled and the bottles cooled in cold-water baths to prevent the heat from inducing further chemical reactions. Pasteurized in this way, unopened juice has a shelf life of several months.

Pasteurization does destroy nutrients. Since both supermarket and natural-food-store bottled juices are pasteurized, the only way to get the full nutritional benefit of juices is either to make your own juice or find a store that squeezes and sells fresh, unpasteurized juice.[1] It's relatively easy to find unpasteurized apple juice/cider in the fall and unpasteurized orange juice year round from specialty greengrocers, roadside stands in the country, and farmers' markets in the city.

The difference between supermarket juice and natural-food-store juice is not in pasteurizing, but in the fact that supermarket juice is always clarified through filters, whereas natural-food-store juice is sometimes left unfiltered. Also, although this is not usual, some juice found in natural food stores is made with organic fruits and vegetables (the label will state this), whereas supermarket juice, of course, is not. Leaving the question of whether or not it's organic aside, however, what's the difference between filtered and unfiltered juice?

To produce a clear, uniformly transparent juice, bits of plant fiber and other particles must be removed from it. Some small bottlers simply allow the extraneous matter to settle, then pour off and bottle the clearest liquid. This juice is still unfiltered; it will look cloudy, and particles will continue to sink to the bottom of the jar in the store or at home.

For a clearer juice the liquid must be filtered. First, diatomaceous earth (skeletons of microscopic sea life) or enzymes are added to the juice to draw particles together at the bottom of the container. The juice is usually then filtered through a screen. Diatomaceous earth is a widely used inert material. Enzymes, on the other hand, are thought by some juice producers to take away from the juice's natural flavor and aroma. An extremely clear juice may indicate a heavy dose of enzymes, but there's no sure way for a consumer to tell. The bottom line, in any case, is that there's no *nutritional* difference between cloudy and clear (unfiltered or filtered) juice. Cloudy unfiltered juice does have a heavier mouthfeel and sometimes a fuller taste, but because the particles in it are just bits of plant fiber (cellulose), cloudy juice isn't any more nutritious than clear filtered juice.

Other points to be aware of when buying juice are as follows:

Juice makers add ascorbic acid (vitamin C) to juice in order to keep it from darkening due to oxidation. This seems to be a positive

[1]Juice manufacturers are not required to state the fact of pasteurization on the label.

practice, since vitamin C is a safe addition. Sodium benzoate is sometimes added also as a preservative.

Juice makers often add emulsifiers to juices that are made from fruits containing natural oils. The emulsifiers most often used are lecithin and carob gum—both have tested safe.

You may want to draw the line, however, with juices that are artificially colored. To spot artificial coloring, hold the bottle up to the light. No natural juice has a bright, plastic-colored sheen.

It's difficult to recommend fruit juices by brand, since the FDA's legal definition of a fruit juice is amorphous and poorly policed, making it nearly impossible to determine a juice's history. The juice you buy in a natural food store, for example, could be (a) a true juice (the liquid pressed from fruit); (b) a juice made from water plus a puree (the strained pulp of fruit that was frozen or canned); (c) a juice made from water plus a concentrate (the fruit juice solids left after the water in a juice is taken away by extreme heat or cold); or (d) a juice nectar (pulpy liquid juice made from fruit, water, sweeteners, and optional acidifiers).

In general it's best to buy a true juice, since true juice has been tampered with the least. Next best is juice made from a puree, then a concentrate. Erewhon, Knudsen, Mr. Natural, and Westbrae all bottle true apple juice made from *organic* apples. Several of Erewhon's and Westbrae's other fruit juices are also made from organic fruit. These four companies, along with most of the other companies that sell juice in natural food stores, bottle all four types of juices: true juices, juices made from purees, juices made from concentrates, and juice nectars. Virtually all are unfiltered and pasteurized.

How to Juice

It's almost impossible to juice vegetables without a juicer. Fruits, on the other hand, can be juiced without a machine. There's nothing like ice-cold raspberry or cranberry juice when those fruits first come into season.

With the exception of hand-pressed citrus juice, however, fruit juices made without a juicer must be made by heating the fruit. This will destroy many of the vitamins and some of the taste. Juicers, therefore, are worth their weight in nutrients and taste, as well as convenience.

Whether you use a machine or not, use fruits and vegetables as fresh and ripe as possible, since the nutritional quality of the juice will depend on the nutrients available in the vegetables and fruits you buy. To get maximum benefit and taste, juices should also be drunk immediately. If you make more than you can drink at once, store the juice in an airtight container in the refrigerator for no more than a day. Freshly squeezed juices spoil rapidly.

Juicing with a Juice Extractor

Wash the food and feed it (skin and all) into the feeder opening. Most fruits and vegetables can be fed whole but pitted. Tomatoes, apples, peppers, and so on don't need to be cored or seeded, though they may need to be quartered.

Vegetable juices are extremely concentrated and sharp. They're easier to digest and taste better if you combine strong vegetables, such as spinach or beets, with vegetables that produce lighter juices, such as celery or carrots. Juicing an apple along with any vegetable mellows and slightly sweetens the flavor of the final juice.

Leafy green vegetables should be juiced before root vegetables when making combinations. Greens juice better if you roll them into a tight ball, then feed them to the machine.

Process soft fruits before hard ones in fruit juice combinations. Soft fruits such as peaches, apricots, pears, and so on produce heavy, syrupy juices that taste better if they're lightened a bit with apple or orange juice.

Juicing Fruits Without a Juice Extractor

This will be a labor of love, so do it for someone who'll really benefit from all the nutrients and the easy digestibility. Fresh juice is excellent for newborn babies, children, and anyone who's ill.

The easiest fruits to juice are oranges, grapefruits, and pineapples. Oranges and grapefruits require an inexpensive plastic or glass hand juicer and a strong wrist. Pineapples simply need to be cut into cubes, pureed in a food grinder or blender, then strained. Since these fruits are not heated, the juices are strong on flavor and vitamins.

Berries, cherries, and grapes can be juiced by putting the ripest fruits into a heavy kettle and crushing them with a potato masher. Heat the mashed fruit slowly over a low flame, stirring constantly to soften the fruit and press out more of the juice. Cranberries should be cooked with water over moderate heat until their skins pop open. They can then be mashed and strained. Strain the juice into a container that can be put into a bowl of ice water so that the juice cools quickly and can be drunk right away.

Apricots and peaches can be juiced exactly like berries, cherries, and grapes, except that a bit of water must be added to the saucepan along with the fruit, since peaches and apricots are drier than berries.

A tomato juice that won't look supermarket smooth but will taste fresher, fuller, and have more vitamins can be made by coring and quartering tomatoes, then heating them with a bit of water and a stalk or two of celery just until the juice begins to boil. Press the tomatoes and the juice through a fine sieve to extract the juice. Cool quickly. Tomato juice tastes best flavored with a bit of sea salt or ground herbs such as basil, marjoram, and thyme.

Juicers

Throughout history a hammer has been a hammer and a pot has been a pot. It's really quite amazing that while advanced engineering has remodeled virtually every object in existence, kitchen and carpentry tools have remained essentially the same for centuries. Hardwood mortars and pestles, bamboo strainers, fired-clay casseroles—we're still using the same cooking instruments that were around before kitchens were.

Juicers are an exception. Only decades ago vegetable juices were being painstakingly squeezed by hand—pounded, pressed and strained through cheesecloth. It was an arduous, time-consuming process—like squeezing water from a stone. In the health resorts of Europe entire kitchen staffs worked all morning to extract one cup of freshly squeezed juice for every patron.

Today there are roughly a dozen major juicers on the market plus more comprehensive appliances that have juice attachments (sometimes these are only for citrus). The best juicers make juice exclusively. If you're considering a machine that also grinds peanuts and kneads dough, chances are it won't be a crackerjack juicer.

Juicers differ in price, how easily they can be used, how easily they can be cleaned, and how well they extract juice. All work on one of two principles: either *centrifugal force,* in which the vegetable or fruit is grated, then thrust forcefully against the sides of a revolving high-speed drum, which catches the pulp while the juice is extracted, or *mastication,* in which the vegetable or fruit is chewed and rubbed until the cell walls are so broken down that the juice can be pressed from the fiber. Both processes require a sturdy, well-built machine that has enough power to extract juice thoroughly from difficult vegetables like carrots, but has enough resiliency to withstand its own force without clogging, walking, or breaking down after a few months' use.

The best juicers also

1. Juice *any* vegetable or fruit from parsley to strawberries. Although most full-fledged juicers will claim to juice all vegetables and fruits, many of them process the food unevenly, leaving lumps of unground food in the container, and some juicers will miss difficult greens like parsley entirely.
2. Have a feeder opening that is large enough so that large or whole pieces of fruits and vegetables can be fed into the machine. A good-sized opening and strong plunger will allow you to juice rapidly. The juicer should also be able to juice enough vegetables and fruits for several glasses (as much as one-half gallon) of juice. Some juicers will only produce a glass of juice, at which point you have to stop and clean the machine if you want more.
3. Can be cleaned relatively easily, though don't expect cleaning to be a breeze.
4. Aren't noisy. Some juicers can outholler vacuum cleaners, which makes you think twice about using them the first thing in the morning.

Recommendations

The Acme Juicer is the samurai of juicers. It's extremely powerful, sturdy, and, compared with most other juicers, quiet. In a *New York Times* testing of the ten top juicers, Acme was rated the most professional and its juice was considered superior. The Acme works on centrifugal force. It has a special base and rubber feet that prevent it from walking. It's constructed from stainless steel, and the heavy steel cutting blade grates vegetables and fruits completely and evenly. The machine is quite simple to use, but time-consuming to clean. It's expensive, but comes with a ten-year guarantee on all parts except the blade. Restaurants and juice bars use Acmes daily for years without the machine breaking down. For further information write the Acme Juicer Manufacturing Co., 10 and Lowther Streets, Lemoyne, Pennsylvania 17043. Prices as of 1979 are $169.95 (steel container), $129.95 (plastic container).

Other juicers to consider include the Braun Multipress MP 50 Juice Extractor ($70), a compact, impressive-looking juicer, but slightly awkward to use and prone to missing difficult vegetables like parsley; the Oster Automatic Pulp Ejector Juicer ($70), a simple-to-use rectangular juicer that gives thicker juices and has an antifoam screen to take the head off juice; and the Invento Electric Vegetable Juicer ($60), one of the least expensive of all juicers and one that does a good job on all but the most difficult vegetables like parsley. None of these juicers should be relied on for heavy daily use, quietness, or swifter cleaning; only the Acme can meet all these requirements.

Waters

The story goes that it was Halloween in Mill Valley, California, and the kids were out dressed as witches and ghosts, trekking between redwood estates.

Upon reaching one of these homes and locating the correct door, the kids rang the Buddhist chimes loudly. The woman of the house appeared and was greeted by an enthusiastic chorus: "TRICK OR TREAT!"

"Oh," she said. "Is it really Halloween?"

Yes, obviously it was. But what to do? She never had sugar in the house, didn't *believe* in candy. An avocado would never do.

As the story goes, she went back inside and returned with four bottles of effervescent spring water, which she plopped with satisfaction in the outstretched bags.[2]

Water makes up 92% of the blood plasma, 80% of the muscle mass, 60% of the red blood cells, and 50% of everything else in the body. If any food warrants a closer look, then, it's the water that day in and day out we choose to drink.

There are over seven hundred brands of bottled water sold in the United States, and in the last few years consumption has burst through the floodgates. It's almost as though everyone, all at the same time, took a good look at their tap water. And all of them noticed the same thing: It wasn't clean. You couldn't even see through it, as a matter of fact. And as for taste, well, it's a good thing we have the taste of toothpaste to fall back on first thing in the morning.

But poor taste and filmy color are only fringe worries. At the core of the problem are urban and rural water systems that, on the one hand, are massively polluted with asbestos, heavy metals such as lead and cadmium, arsenic, nitrates, pesticides, detergents, fallout, and sodium—the salt runoff from snow removal—and are, on the other, highly chemicalized to counteract contamination. Currently, the Environmental Protection Agency is investigating chlorine, the major disinfectant added to tap water. Preliminary evidence indicates that chlorine has the ability to react and form carcinogens such as chloroform, carbon tetrachloride, and other chemicals collectively called trihalomethanes. In addition, and although most of us don't realize it, infectious diseases are still transmitted through tap water. About ten thousand Americans a year are affected, not counting cases of the flu.[3]

[2]Arthur Lubow, "The Perrier Revolution," *New Times,* May 15, 1978.

[3]Jane E. Brody, "Personal Health," *New York Times,* November 14, 1979.

Only about 20% of *bottled water* is *natural water.* The rest is tap water that has been reconditioned, bottled, and sold.

All natural water—water that comes directly from the earth—contains minerals and is therefore mineral water. The minerals in a water give it taste and character. And, wonderfully enough, natural mineral water—simple as it is—cannot be produced artificially in a laboratory. Minerals can be taken out of water (distillation), but all attempts to inject them back in fail. The minerals won't dissolve in the purified water. Because of the minerals it contains, natural water is preferable to reconditioned tap water for drinking.

Water is available in many forms. Besides natural mineral water, you'll see these labels and hear these terms:

Natural spring water is mineral water that is bottled directly from natural springs. The water comes to the surface of the earth on its own accord, and nothing is added to the water before it is bottled. The mineral content of different natural spring waters varies considerably. Natural spring waters are excellent for drinking.

Still water is water without bubbles. The water may come from the earth or from the tap.

Effervescent water, sparkling water, and *carbonated water* do have bubbles. The bubbles either come naturally from the water source along with the water or they're formed when water (earth or tap) is mechanically injected with a gas.

Well water must be pumped to the surface and usually purified with disinfecting chemicals before it's considered safe for drinking.

Distilled water is artifically produced pure water. It has no minerals and no taste. To make it, water is vaporized, then condensed back into a liquid. It's often used in machinery.

Hard water is natural mineral water that's high in minerals. Its taste is good (if unpolluted), but you can't make suds for washing the dishes. (Bottled spring water is usually hard.)

Soft water is natural mineral water that has had minerals removed and chemicals added so that you can make soapsuds. One way to tell what kind of water you have is by making ice cubes. Soft water makes cloudy ice cubes; hard water makes clear ice cubes that have one white dot in the center where the minerals have gravitated.

In the United States the best bottled drinking water is natural spring water. Bottled spring waters come from France, Italy, Sweden, Germany, Czechoslovakia, and Belgium, plus Arkansas (Mountain Valley), New York (Saratoga Vichy), Maine (Poland Springs), Pennsylvania (Ephrata Diamond) and Massachusetts (Sand Springs).

All of these bottled spring waters taste quite different. They have different pH factors, for example (pH is a measure of the alkalinity and acidity of a solution). Each of the waters has a different mineral composition. Some, for example, are naturally high in sodium, others in calcium, and so on. And each of the waters has different gaseous properties—some are light and soft in the mouth, others are volcanic. The following chart may help you decide which bottled spring water is best suited to your taste.

Two notes: Never pour an effervescent spring water warm over ice. The bubbles will burst, and the ice will eventually dilute the water, giving it a wishy-washy taste. Instead, make some ice cubes from the same spring water, and drop the ice cubes into the spring water after it's been chilled in the refrigerator. Also, never keep a spring water—effervescent or still—opened and uncovered in the refrigerator. The water will smell like an index of the whole refrigerator if you do.

Bottled Waters

Water	*Origin*	*Characteristics**	*Mineral Content*
Apollinaris	Bad Neuenahr, West Germany	Naturally effervescent; slightly alkaline; discernible aftertaste.	High: principally magnesium, sodium, and calcium.
Badoit	Saint Galmier, France	Naturally effervescent; lightly alkaline; springy bubbles.	Light: calcium, magnesium, and fluoride; sodium free.
Caddo Valley	Caddo Valley, Arkansas	Still; neutral pH; light taste.	High in calcium; low in sodium.
Deer Park	White Plains, New York	Still; lightly alkaline; soft, simple; bland flavor; also available carbonated.	Low in sodium.
Ephrata Diamond	Ephrata, Pennsylvania	Still; soft flavor.	Light mixture of minerals.

* Chemists use the term *pH factor* to describe acidity and alkalinity. Most water is either slightly alkaline or neutral—neither acid nor alkaline. Many waters come very close to the pH of the human bloodstream, which is slightly alkaline.

Adapted from *The Book of Waters,* by Steven Schwartz (A & W Visual Library, 1979).

Water	*Origin*	*Characteristics**	*Mineral Content*
Evian	Evian-les-Bains, France	Still; a touch alkaline; full, rounded, fresh flavor.	Moderate mixture of minerals; sodium free.
Fiuggi	Fiuggi, Italy	Still; flavor delicate to flat.	Low in minerals; sodium free.
Gerolsteiner Sprudel	Gerolstein, West Germany	Naturally effervescent; lightly bubbly; clean tasting.	High in calcium and magnesium; sodium free.
Mountain Valley	Hot Springs, Arkansas	Still; mildly alkaline; Good, clean flavor.	Moderate mixture of minerals; sodium free.
Perrier	Vergeze, France	Naturally effervescent; snappy, bubbly, clean tasting.	Calcium is dominant mineral, but overall content is low; sodium free.
Poland Water	Poland Springs, Maine	Still; neutral pH; full, soft, clean tasting.	No mineral tang due to complete absence of sodium and sulphur.
Ramlösa	Hälsingborg, Sweden	Slightly sparkling, but additional carbon dioxide added during bottling; lightly alkaline; clean tasting.	Moderate mineral content.
San Pellegrino	Bergamo, Italy	Carbonation added; slightly alkaline; clean taste; sparkly.	High in calcium, magnesium, chlorine, and sodium.
Saratoga Vichy	Saratoga Springs, New York	Naturally effervescent, strongly alkaline; aggressive bubbles; clean taste.†	High in sodium, calcium, magnesium, and potassium.
Vichy Célestins	Vichy, France	Slightly effervescent; salty, volcanic tang.	High in potassium and calcium.
Vittel	Vittel, France	Still; fairly neutral pH; soft, clean taste.	High in calcium and magnesium; low in sodium.

† Saratoga Vichy discontinued its use of additives in 1978. The water now tastes different, and many feel the flavor is better.

Teas

Historically, at the end of April, when the plants were at their best, traditional Chinese families climbed high into the mountains to pick the first fresh furled leaves of tea. They had already collected the spring rains in great jars placed around the outside of the house. This would be the special water used for brewing.

A place of "great tranquillity" would be chosen; then, with presence of mind, the tea would be made. The moment the steaming rainwater was poured, the tightly clasped leaves would twist and unwind their contorted bodies in a dance that the Chinese called the agony of the leaves.

Tea is the most universally consumed of all beverages. It comes from the leaves of the shrub *Thea sinensis,* which grows in China, Japan, Taiwan, India, and Ceylon. Left alone, a tea shrub would grow for nearly a century and during that time might grow to a height of fifty feet.

But tea shrubs aren't left alone, of course. Four times a year the shiny, spearlike leaves are picked. The first picking occurs in April, and the tender young leaves that are collected then are considered to make the best-quality teas.

Interestingly, in ancient China the tea pickers were always women —usually girls. For three weeks before the pickings they were not allowed to eat fish or certain kinds of meats so that their breath would not spoil the delicate scent of the tea leaves, and in addition they were required to take a thorough bath each morning before setting out for that day's picking.

To the eye, there are two major categories of tea: black teas and green teas. These come from the same *Thea sinensis* plant, but black teas result when the leaves are fermented, whereas green teas result if the leaves are left unfermented. There is actually also a middle category of semi-fermented teas. These are all called oolong.

Tea ferments naturally by withering. During fermentation, substances in the tea leaf called catechins are released, and the flavor of the tea emerges. Green tea, since it is not fermented (the natural withering is stopped by steaming the leaves), has 100% of its catechins and is a thin, bitter tea, green in color. Oolong tea looses about 50% of its catechins during fermentation, and black tea looses about 80%. Oolong and black tea give yellow, gold, and red liquid, and they have a richer, more flowery flavor than green tea. With black and oolong tea, the natural fermentation is helped along by mechanical fermentation—a simple process of rolling, twisting, and shaking the tea leaves. This makes the flavor elements in the catechins merge together. Almost all of this rolling, twisting, and shaking is done by precisely timed machines. But in China five young men a year are still trained to do the long, laborious process by hand.

Black Tea

Most of the green tea consumed in the United States is drunk in Japanese restaurants. Most of the oolong tea is purchased in gourmet shops. Clearly the tea most of us are accustomed to is black tea. But there are a lot of black teas, and that's why the differences among teas is confusing.

First of all, some black teas are named after the region where the plant itself grew. Darjeeling tea, for example, is from the tea-growing region of Darjeeling, India. Other black teas are named for the size or shape of the tea leaf. Orange pekoe and souchong tea, for example, are not names of areas or even flavors. Both teas come from India, but orange pekoe is a thin spiked leaf that grows at the top of the tea plant, whereas souchong is a rounder leaf picked further down on the stem.

Then there are all the tea blends, such as Earl Grey, English Breakfast, Queen Mary, Russian Caravan, Irish Breakfast, and so on. These blends are combinations of several teas put together by tea companies, such as Twinings, Jacksons of Piccadilly, and Bigelow. Once you begin experimenting with different teas, you'll find they have remarkably different flavors. Keep this in mind if you're a coffee drinker who wants to switch to tea (black tea has only about half as much caffeine as coffee). Coffee drinkers invariably love full, rich teas such as Russian blends, Ceylon tea, and Earl Grey.

Green Tea

Green tea was brought to Japan from China in the sixth century by Zen priests, who liked it because green tea kept monks awake through long hours of intense meditation. There is a great deal of confusion in the marketing of green tea, however. In Japan the finest quality green tea is made from the first pale, tender leaves of tea plants that have been cultivated in shade. Such tea is called matcha and is used in traditional tea ceremonies. Matcha—all tea, actually—should not be boiled, but allowed to steep in boiling water.

Bancha, the Japanese tea that is given prominence by many natural food stores here, is actually a lower grade tea. *Bancha* means "coarse" —the word does not indicate a particular flavor or a specific type of tea plant. Bancha is cultivated from the older lower leaves of any common tea plant, but usually those that have grown in the less-than-ideal sunny fields. Because of the plant's exposure to sun, bancha contains less caffeine than the higher quality green teas. The leaves and twigs that are sold as bancha are also roasted in iron kettles before they're marketed to help improve the bancha's flavor.

Herbal Teas

Herbal "teas" aren't really teas at all, but tealike drinks made when herbs are infused in boiling water. The correct name for them is *tisane,* and they're excellent drinks—delicious, yet calming and rejuvenating at the same time. Although most people begin drinking them as a caffeine-free substitute for coffee or tea, herbal teas are not simply neutral substitutes. They actually work *for the body.*

One of the most popular herbal tea blends, for example, is mu tea. The herbs it's composed of were first put together by George Ohsawa, founder of macrobiotics, who, after thirty years of studying Chinese and Japanese medicine, including traditional Chinese herbal medicine, blended together the sixteen different herbs for their balancing medicinal properties. The result is said to be a calming tonic for the nervous system and heart and an effective remedy for the weakness and dizziness caused by fatigue. The herbs Ohsawa used were licorice root, chinese cinnamon, ginger, rehmannia, Japanese tuckahoe, peach kernel, Japanese peony root, Japanese parsley root, ginseng, orange peel, cnicus, atractylis, cloves, coptis, and peony bark.

The best-known herbal blend of all—Red Zinger—was created in 1971 when a man named Mo Siegel (now president of Celestial Seasonings) mixed African hibiscus flowers, Bulgarian rosehips, Spanish orange peel, Mexican lemongrass, Wisconsin peppermint, and—for extra fruitiness—wild cherry bark together. Red Zinger continues to be so popular that it alone accounts for 30% of Celestial's sales.

Celestial Seasonings is a reputable herbal tea company, but the teas it markets are illustrative of an important point: You should not make assumptions about a natural foods company. For example, Celestial Seasonings, as well as many of the other companies that market herbal teas, has blends that contain caffeine (this is noted on the package). All matté teas, for example, contain caffeine. The real zinger is Celestial Seasonings' Morning Thunder tea—it has *54% more caffeine than coffee.* (The package calls it "the power of a thousand charging buffaloes.")

It's important to be creative with herbal teas. No one who has been a frequent coffee or tea drinker will find a lukewarm cup of sage water worth drinking. But a hot orange spice and sassafras tea flavored with honey or an ice cold mint julep with date sugar and lemon zest is another story. Please note that there are no rules when it comes to herbal drinks: They can be hot or cold (although if hot, they should be very hot; if cold, very cold); they can be made with dried herbs or fresh (a combination is often best); they can be drunk sweetened or unsweetened. Tisanes made with several different herbs turn out richer and have a more interesting flavor, although the specific combination is up to you. However, with the exception of mint, the major culinary herbs generally don't make the best-tasting herbal teas. Instead, try some of the more esoteric herbs available in natural food stores, specialty stores, or by mail from the sources listed in the chapter "Herbs and Spices."

Herbal teas are brewed the exact same way regular teas are, except that herbs should be allowed to steep for at least fifteen minutes. If the tea has cooled too much during this time, you can reheat it gently after straining away the herbs.

Often it's the final touch that makes an herbal tea delicious: a slice of fresh orange, a sprig of spearmint, half of a plump dried fig added to the teapot for a bit of sweetening.

How to Buy a Topnotch Tea

Black, green, or herbal, the most frequent pitfall is buying stale, dried-out tea. Just as a stale culinary herb is too withered and drawn to give flavor, so, too, dried-out tea leaves give a bitter, flat taste. By comparison, fresh tea leaves give a soft, rich flavor. Fresh tea feels resilient; it does not crackle and crush in your hand like autumn leaves.

Unless you actually peek into the tin or package, there's no direct way to ascertain a tea's freshness, although a deep tea aroma is a good sign.

Do not buy teas from open bins. Tea leaves pick up other odors and flavors easily and pick up moisture from the surrounding air as well. The best teas, therefore, are sold in tin cannisters. By comparison, cardboard boxes neither keep a tea fresh nor protect it from other elements. If you buy boxed or bagged tea, transfer it to a tin or sterilized glass jar when you get home. And always store tea in a cool, dry place.

Packaged herbal teas can be extraordinarily expensive even though the herbs inside usually aren't. Since packaged herbal teas and tea blends contain nothing more than the herbs themselves, you may want to buy herbs directly and mix your own blends. Individually, or with friends who use herbs for cooking and/or making teas, you can also place a bulk order with any of the herb companies listed in the chapter on herbs. Since many of these companies deal with small orders from small natural food stores, their ordering minimums aren't high.

Making a Good Pot of Tea

For anyone accustomed to flow-through bags, it's important to realize that making a very good pot of tea involves more than simply boiling water.

First, just as different waters give beers or wines different flavors, the water used for making tea is important. Try a taste test of teas made from an effervescent water, bottled spring water, hot tap water, and cold tap water.

The hot tap water will produce a flat, weak tea because hot tap water comes from your water heater, where it has sat for hours, gradually losing the bubbles of oxygen that give tea a picked-up flavor. The cold tap water, by comparison, will produce a much fresher cup of tea. The effervescent water, because of the bubbles of carbon dioxide, will make the liveliest, most refreshing cup of all.

To make tea correctly, you'll need two pots: a water kettle and a teapot. Boil the water in the kettle just until tiny bubbles (the Chinese call them crab's eyes) appear to stream from the sides of the kettle.

Pour some of this boiling water into the teapot to preheat it. Then, after swirling the water around and pouring it out of the now-warm pot, sprinkle in the tea and immediately cover it with boiling water.

Every cup of tea requires a teaspoonful of loose black or green tea leaves, or 1½ to 2 teaspoonfuls of herbs, plus an extra spoonful "for the pot." Allow the tea to steep for 3 to 5 minutes, then strain it into teacups, using a wire mesh or bamboo strainer to catch any leaves. If you like your tea strong, use more tea rather than letting the tea brew longer. When tea leaves are steeped for more than 5 minutes, they begin to release tea tannin, a bitter, bark-flavored substance that makes tea taste dry and acidic.

In the United States most tea is bought in tea-bag form, but tea experts say that a really good cup of tea can only be made from loose tea. When tea is put into the teapot loose, the leaves are allowed to writhe, twist, and unfurl completely, releasing their full flavor. Metal tea balls and tea bags, though they may be convenient, restrict the leaves' natural expansion and, in addition, give off a subtle metallic or wet-paper taste.

There is one exception to the loose-is-better rule, however: bringing tea to restaurants. It's amazing how few restaurants (including the expensive ones) offer a decent tea. But restaurateurs are beginning to understand that serious tea drinkers find low-grade, supply-house tea hard to swallow—literally. If you ask first, most restaurateurs won't mind if you substitute an herbal tea or blended tea for the supply-house sort the restaurant has on hand. If you make your own tea blends, you can buy empty tea bags with special paper seals from Nichols Garden Nursery, 1190 North Pacific Highway, Albany, Oregon 97321 (240 bags cost $2.50).

Two final notes: Teapots are structurally different from coffeepots. The best formed teapots have spouts set high on the pot, because here the least tannic tea is found (tea leaves, of course, settle to the bottom of the pot). The best teapot material is clay—whether it be simple earthenware or more elegant porcelain.

Hundreds of years ago the British popularized tea cozies—padded pouches into which the teapot was placed to keep it warm. A cozy is not essential, but it does work. In the United States, Crispin Jones Ltd. sells tea cozies handwoven in Wales of 100% wool, lined and padded. For their catalog, write: Crispin Jones Ltd., P.O. Box 83, Monticello, Iowa 52310.

Coffee

The summer that I finished this book, I spent a few days camping in the Rockies. The first morning I woke up under the Olympian wingspan of a ponderosa pine that sliced the sky into two blues. The biting mountain air crackled with two smells: pinewood and coffee, perking over an open fire. My friends were stamping around beside the campfire, waiting patiently for that first steaming cup.

Well, as usually happens, the coffee was delicious, but all morning long I felt rotten—headachy and nervous. Once again it was back to the drawing board for a good coffee substitute that contains no caffeine.

There are limits to how inventive you can be while camping, but I bought a coffee substitute, some dried figs, carob, and cinnamon. This brewed up into a delicious drink.

There are two options for coffee drinkers who don't want caffeine

Product	*Origin*	*Contents*
Cafix	West Germany	Roasted barley, rye, and chicory, and shredded beet roots.
Caphag	U.S.A.	Rye, oats, millet, figs, barley, chicory.
Pero	West Germany	Roasted, ground malted barley, barley, chicory, rye, molasses.
Pioneer	Switzerland	Barley, figs, chicory.
Postem	U.S.A.	Bran, wheat, molasses. Coffee-flavored Postem has artificial coffee flavoring added.
Roastaroma	U.S.A.	Crystal malt, roasted barley, carob, chicory, cassia bark, star anise, allspice.

but who want something more powerful than herbal tea. First, there are cereal coffee substitutes, such as Cafix. The major ones are listed here. Ceareal beverages actually have a flavor all their own; it's a good flavor, but not really coffeelike. For a diehard coffee drinker, switching to a ceareal beverage may not be easy in the beginning.

As you can see, the ingredients are similar, but the flavors of cereal beverages do differ depending on the principal ingredient and whether or not a sweetener, such as molasses, is added.

One trip to the natural food store for some grains and herbs and you can make a cereal beverage suited exactly to your taste. The process is simple: Wash and drain a cup of grain(s) (barley, rye, wheat) and spread the grain on a cookie sheet. Begin with a cup until you've experimented enough to develop your own favorite combination. At that point, you can make a lot of cereal coffee at one time. Put the grain into a 200° to 250°F oven and let it roast for 2 to 3 hours. The longer the roast, the stronger the coffee. Stir the grain while it's roasting to insure that it cooks evenly. Grind the grain, and there you have it.

Or almost have it. Most cereal coffees taste best if you flavor them further. Ground figs,[4] date sugar, or carob will add sweetness; cardamon, cinnamon, or nutmeg will add spiciness. And there are a number of herbs you can add: chicory root, cherry bark, dandelion root, sassafras, sarsaparilla root, juniper berries, and so on.

The second alternative to regular coffee is decaffeinated coffee.

[4]If you add ground figs, plan to use the coffee within two weeks.

Coffee is decaffeinated with steam and chemical solvents. The most common chemical solvent used is methylene chloride. Methylene chloride is related to the family of chlorinated hydrocarbons and is currently being tested by the National Cancer Institute for its suspected carcinogenic effects. The FDA has placed a limit on the amount of methylene chloride that can be used to decaffeinate coffee, but even the permissible level is thought to be risky. So while fresh roasted decaffeinated coffee beans make good coffee that won't speed up your nervous system, trading caffeine for chlorinated hydrocarbons isn't exactly reassuring.

There's a good ending, however. In 1979 a company in Switzerland —Coffex Ltd.—perfected a pure water process for decaffeinating coffee beans. The process uses no chemical solvents whatsoever. Professional coffee tasters rated the flavor of the water-decaffeinated coffee as very good and more coffeelike in flavor than solvent-decaffeinated coffee.

Production of the new water-decaffeinated coffee has, for the most part, been limited, and Europe has gotten most of the supply. In late 1979, however, shipments to specialty stores in the United States began. If none of the stores in your area carry it, however, Empire Coffee and Tea in New York ships around the country. Contact Empire Coffee and Tea, 486 Ninth Avenue, New York, New York 10018 (212-564-1460). Empire carries water-decaffeinated Columbian, Brazilian, and mocha coffee beans (Italian, French, and American roast on the Columbian).

Sugars and Sweeteners

Although the consumption of refined white sugar dropped by ten pounds per person from 1972 to 1978, most of us—natural and organic food eaters included—still eat our weight in sugar every year.[1] For giving up white sugar and giving up all sugar turned out to be two different things. In fact, giving up white sugar was easy for lots of people; they simply switched to honey cake and ice cream sweetened with maple syrup instead.

By now everyone knows the dangers of eating too much white sugar. Half the American population have no teeth left by the age of fifty-five. Five billion dollars a year are spent on dental problems—primarily the cavities that result when sucrose (found in white, brown, and turbinado sugar, as well as in molasses and maple syrup) is eaten.

White sugar has a devastating effect on blood sugar levels, causing them to peak and fall while insulin is shot through the body to help cope with the sugar overload. Although sucrose sugars have this effect on everyone, some individuals (hypoglycemic) are especially vulnerable.

About one-third of the American population is so fat that their life expectancy is diminished by their fatness. Obesity, due in large part to eating too much sugar and too much fat while getting too little exercise, is a causative factor in diabetes, hypertension, heart disease, gall bladder disease, liver disease, and hernia. Studies of diabetics, for example, indicate that 75% to 85% of diabetics are obese.[2] Alleviating the obesity, doctors feel, is the first step in combating diabetes.

An *American Journal of Clinical Nutrition* review of 186 studies on the relationship between sucrose and heart disease concluded that arte-

[1]U.S. Department of Agriculture, Economics, Statistics, and Cooperatives Service, *Sugar and Sweetener Report,* Vol 3, #9, September 1978.

[2]Ronald A. Arky, "Insulin and Fuel Metabolism: New Insights into Diet in Diabetes" (Report to the Western Hemisphere Nutrition Congress, V, Quebec, Canada, August 16, 1977).

riosclerotic and degenerative heart disease victims do consume more sucrose than control subjects. The review points out that on a worldwide scale, heart disease increases in rough proportion to increased sugar consumption.[3]

But the danger that is the most subtle and widespread of all is that sugar contains no or minuscule numbers of nutrients. Every hundred calories of sugar, therefore, is a hundred raw calories that contribute nothing to the body other than energy that is either expended or stored as fat. In fact, sugar not only fails to contribute vitamins and minerals, it also uses up vitamins and minerals as it's being assimilated, thereby robbing the body further of nutrients.

Yet despite these dangers, in sugar we are like unhappy lovers: miserable holding on, unable to let go. So while you probably couldn't find a snowflake of white sugar in any natural food store across the country, you could trip over all the turbinado, crystalline and liquid fructose, date sugar, molasses, maple syrup and maple sugar, barley malt, rice syrup, brown sugar, carob, and the most luscious sweetener of all—honey.

Is eating any one of these sugars different from eating white sugar? Well, yes and no.

How Sugar Works in the Body

Sugars in food are one of the two forms of carbohydrate, the major source of body fuel. The other form of carbohydrate is starch. Starches—grains, vegetables, legumes, and so on—are simply complex chains of several sugar units.

The body receives energy when carbohydrate sugars and starches are broken down into simple sugar molecules in the blood. When the blood sugar level drops, the appetite mechanisms in the brain are activated and the person feels hungry.

Under natural circumstances, a person satisfies hunger by eating carbohydrates in the form of starch. When starches are eaten, the individual sugar units are disassembled one at a time in the intestines and reach the bloodstream in a steady procession. As more and more of the starch is broken up into sugar and released into the blood, the blood sugar level rises and the person feels less and less hungry. Since starches contain concentrations of other nutrients in addition to com-

[3]Richard A. Ahrens, "Sucrose, Hypertension, and Heart Disease: An Historical Perspective," *American Journal of Clinical Nutrition,* Vol. 27 (April 1974), pp. 403–22.

plex chains of sugars, the digestion of starches also means that vitamins and minerals are gradually released into the bloodstream along with the sugar that provides energy.

When sugar is eaten directly, however, the whole process changes. Whereas starch provides bits of usable carbohydrate over long stretches of time, keeping the blood sugar level smooth and fairly even, large, direct sources of sugar—the kind and amount you'd get by eating a candy bar, for example—are absorbed immediately into the bloodstream. This causes the blood sugar level first to skyrocket, then to drop rapidly. Sugar, eaten directly, puts the whole metabolism under extraordinary stress as insulin and the adrenal hormones are shot through the system to keep the blood sugar level under control. The body has a roller-coaster response: first a temporary flight of energy, but following that, a letdown period of bodily exhaustion. We all know the feeling. It's the difference between the way you feel after eating a starch like rice and the way you feel after eating too much chocolate cake.

But what about the difference between eating rice and eating a sweet that doesn't contain white sugar—say, a honey fig bar. In the final analysis, is all sugar sugar?

Forms of Sugar and Their Differences in the Body

Sugar is naturally present in all vegetable foods and in two major animal foods: milk and honey. Sugar molecules, however, are structured in two separate ways: as monosaccharides and disaccharides.

The monosaccharides are the simplest sugar molecules. Glucose—one of the sugars in plants and the form that other sugars are broken down into in the body—is a monosaccharide. So is fructose, which is a major form of sugar in fruit and honey.

Disaccharides are more complex sugar molecules. Sucrose, the form of sugar in white sugar, is a disaccharide. So is lactose (the sugar in milk) and maltose (the sugar formed by fermented grain).

Glucose, fructose, sucrose, lactose, and maltose are all handled differently by the body. Even though the first two are monosaccharides and the last three disaccharides, each form of sugar presents the body with a different challenge, and each is metabolized in a slightly different way. It's the difference in the way sugars are metabolized that determines whether or not they evoke the energy exhaustion syndrome that's been nicknamed the sugar blues.

What follows is an examination of sucrose, fructose, and maltose, since these are the forms of sugar that are made into sweeteners: white, brown, and turbinado sugar, molasses, maple syrup, fructose sweeteners, honey, barley malt, and rice syrup. I've left lactose out of this chapter, since lactose only occurs in milk and is not eaten as a sugar per se. I've left glucose out because it usually does not occur in food alone. Instead, glucose is usually bound to fructose, and glucose-fructose molecules are what sucrose molecules are.

Before moving on, please note that the different forms of sugar also have different sweetening powers. If, for example, sucrose were given the sweetening value of 100, then the other forms of sugar would compare like this:

Form of Sugar	*Food Sources*	*Sweetening Power*
Fructose	Fruit, honey	173
Sucrose	White sugar, brown sugar, turbinado sugar, maple syrup, molasses	100
Glucose	Honey	74
Maltose	Barley malt, rice syrup	32
Lactose	Milk, milk products	16

This means that fructose is about 75% sweeter than the same amount of sucrose; glucose is only about 75% as sweet as sucrose, and so on.

Sucrose

White table sugar is 99.9% sucrose. The sucrose is obtained by processing the juice from sugarcane, sugar beets, sugar maple, sorghum, and sugar palms into tiny crystals, then refining the crystals until all of the trace minerals, molds, yeasts, and bacteria have been removed.

For sucrose to be used by the body it must first be broken down into its constitutent sugars: glucose and fructose. During this breakdown, the pancreas secretes the hormone insulin to monitor the amount of sugar being released into the bloodstream. Sucrose sugars are broken down quickly. Depending on the amount of sucrose taken in, excessive amounts of insulin may be triggered. The result is the syndrome of intense energy followed by bodily exhaustion described earlier.

When refined sugar is made from sugarcane or sorghum, the liquid that is left behind after the molecules of sucrose are extracted is molasses. As molasses liquid is processed again and again, more and more of the sucrose is extracted and the liquid that remains gets heavier and darker. The thickest, darkest remaining liquid is blackstrap molasses, a name rooted in the Dutch word for syrup—*stroop.*

Molasses is 50% to 70% sucrose, the rest water. It has the same energy exhaustion effect on the body that white sugar has; molasses is just a bit less intense. As a white-sugar substitute, molasses' advantage is that it contains all of the minerals that have been refined out of white sugar. These include small amounts of thiamine, riboflavin, and niacin, plus generous amounts of calcium, iron, magnesium, potassium, zinc, copper, and chromium. Molasses, however, contains concentrated amounts of all the other substances that may have been on or in the sugarcane, such as pesticides and industrial toxins. If sulfur was used in the original processing of the white sugar, the molasses will contain that as well.

The lighter grades of molasses are sweeter and less nutritious than blackstrap, since they contain a larger proportion of sucrose. The flavor of blackstrap is rich and smoky, and because it does contribute some nutrients, it's certainly preferable to white sugar. But it's still sugar—and still sucrose.

Brown sugar and turbinado sugar differ even less from white sugar than molasses does. Brown sugar is about 96% sucrose. In fact, it's simply refined white sugar that has been colored brown with a small amount of molasses. Adding the molasses returns some amount of nutrients back to the sugar—but an extremely insignificant amount.

Turbinado sugar, sometimes called raw sugar, is 99% sucrose. It has skipped the final stage of white sugar purification, so it contains minute amounts of some trace minerals, again insignificant amounts. With 99% sucrose, the effect of turbinado sugar in the body is exactly the same as that of white sugar, yet more than one-fourth of the approximately ninety companies manufacturing natural food snacks use brown or turbinado sugar in their nut and raisin mixes, cookies, brownies, cakes, and "nutritional" candy bars.

Maple syrup is about 65% sucrose. When the sap is first drawn from the huge maple trees in the backwoods of Vermont and New York, it is colorless, flavorless, and about 3% sucrose. Curiously enough, it's only by heating and concentrating the sap that the maple flavor and rich auburn color appear.

The first thirty-eight gallons of sap that are tapped will go to make one gallon of Fancy maple syrup. After Fancy come grades A, B, and C. One gallon of grade-C syrup will require more than forty gallons of sap, which will be boiled for a considerably longer period of time than the sap that becomes a better grade maple syrup. To bring out an intense maple flavor, grade-C syrup is boiled at temperatures as high as 248° F.

The production of true maple syrup in America is about one-fifth what it was in 1900, since pure maple syrup made from tree sap is so costly to produce and man-made sugar-syrup substitutes are so cheap. These substitutes, labeled maple-flavored syrup, usually contain corn syrup (the refined sweet juice of corn stalks), water, refined sugar, and artificial coloring and flavoring.

The first such substitute contained 45% pure maple syrup. Substitutes today, by law, need only contain 2% maple syrup. These substitutes, as well as better-tasting pure maple syrup, are still concentrated sucrose. And maple sugar—the crystallized form of maple syrup—is 95% to 98% sucrose.

Fructose

Fructose is found naturally in fruit and honey. As a form of sugar, it is very different from sucrose and is metabolized differently in the body. Sucrose—and its related sugar, glucose—are metabolized in the small intestine by the enzyme invertase, which triggers insulin. Fructose, however, is metabolized in the liver by the enzyme fructokinase, an enzyme that requires insulin in very small amounts if at all. Fructose is also absorbed more slowly into the bloodstream than sucrose. The combined effect of less insulin plus a slower rate of absorption makes fructose much less likely to set off wide fluctuations in blood sugar levels. In other words, fructose does not trigger the energy exhaustion sugar blues.

We eat fructose in three forms: in fruit, in honey, and in commercial crystalline and liquid form. The best way of consuming fructose is by eating fresh fruit, for not only do fruits contribute sugar for energy without causing blood sugar fluctuations, but they also contribute considerable amounts of vitamins and minerals. In addition, when fruits are eaten raw, their fiber has a natural cleaning action that scraps much of the sugar away from the teeth as the fruit is chewed. Eating one apple, for example, removes over 30% more bacteria from the mouth than brushing the teeth or gargling does.

Honey is currently the most popular alternative to white sugar. It is about 40% fructose, 35% glucose, 18% water, and 3% other substances. Because it contains glucose, honey is more likely than fruit to produce rapid fluctuations in blood sugar levels. So even though honey is considered a fructose-based sugar, in large quantities it will have the same effect in the body that white sugar and other sucrose sugars have. And whether you're eating white sugar (sucrose) or honey (fructose), you're still eating a concentrated source of calories. I've devoted a special section to honey at the end of this chapter, since honeys themselves vary and choosing a good one is dependent on knowing the manufacturing techniques involved.

Although fructose is sometimes called a fruit sugar, the commercially available crystalline and liquid forms of fructose are derived from corn, sugar beets, and sugarcane. Since corn is a major cause of allergies in the United States, many people develop allergic reactions to these fructose products. Liquid fructose is produced in this country through extensive refining of regular corn syrup. Crystalline fructose is made in Europe from refined cane and beet sugar.

Commercial fructose is all calories, no nutrients. But since it's about 60% sweeter than sucrose, a possible advantage is that you'll use only two-thirds the amount. At least in theory. In reality, the more you use sugar, the more sugar you use every time. When the ban on saccharine was enforced in Canada, the Ottawa Health Protection Agency presented research showing that people who eat and drink saccharine-containing foods consume more calories in sugar than do those who do not eat these foods, despite the fact that by using saccharine they should have been consuming less.[4] Sugar eating perpetuates itself, and the only real way to limit sugar in your diet is to stop eating it in any refined or processed form.[5]

Maltose

The malting of grain with natural enzymes breaks the grain's starch molecules down into sugar.[6] The two most popular forms of maltose—barley malt and rice syrup—are simply that: the cooked liquid of fermented grain.

Like fructose, maltose is metabolized by enzymes that do not require insulin. As a result, barley malt and rice syrup do not create fluctuations in the blood sugar level. Both are also absorbed more slowly and evenly than sucrose sugars. As far as sweeteners go, then,

[4]Ross Hume Hall, "Overweight: Clue to Decline in Quality of Nourishment," *En-trophy Institute for Advanced Study Review,* Vol. 1, No. 5 (July–August 1978).

[5]In some texts, sugars are divided into three categories depending on the amount of processing they've undergone: (a) naturally occurring sugars such as the sugar in fruit or milk are naturally a part of a food and have not been processed; (b) processed sugars (honey, molasses, maple syrup) are the natural sweet by-products of animals or plants that have been processed just enough to be used as sweet foods; (c) refined sugars (white, brown, raw, turbinado, commercial fructose) do not occur in nature, but have been made through the extensive refining of sugarcane and sugar beet crops.

[6]The enzymes that are used belong to the same family of enzymes used to make miso and soy sauce.

barley malt and rice syrup are among the best.

Barley malt is about 65% sugar—all of it maltose. Rice syrup is 33% sugar (maltose). Since maltose is only about 40% as sweet as sucrose to begin with, both of these sweeteners are much less powerful than white sugar or other sucrose sugars, and in flavor, both are much more subtle than honey. In fact, people who begin to use barley malt or rice syrup regularly soon find honey to be objectionably cloying.

Honey

The Book of Honey points out that honeybees are not native to America but were brought here by the early colonists. At the time, the Indians, having no word for these buzzing curiosities, called the bees the "white man's flies." It seems that the Indians found the colonists, their possessions, and their daily habits a bit unsettling, for a popular native saying went, "White man works, makes horse work, makes ox work, now makes fly work."

But the fruits of such labor were rich. The Indians, who had pressed the juice from corn stalks and had, in New England, tapped maple trees, had never tasted such a lusciously rich sweetener. In Europe, however, honey had been ladled over and into everything for centuries.

Honey's advantage over white sugar and other sucrose sweeteners is, first, that it is, in part, fructose; and second, that it has medicinal benefits.

Honey breaks down, on the average, to 40% fructose, 35% glucose, 18% water, and 3% other substances. However, the amount of fructose varies greatly depending on the plant the bee has collected nectar from. Tupelo honey has twice as much fructose as glucose, while alfalfa honey has relatively little fructose.

But no matter what the percentage of fructose, no *pure honey,* according to USDA and FDA standards, may contain more than 8% sucrose, and most contain less than half of that. Some honey producers, however, have been accused of adding corn syrup to their light honeys during bad years when the honey crop is small. There is no way for you to guarantee yourself a truly pure honey except to buy from a producer you believe has integrity.

Virtually all of the honey marketed in natural food stores is pure (as opposed to imitation honey, which is also marketed), and the label will state this. Pure honey does not mean that the honey hasn't been blended, however. Almost all honeys are naturally a blend of several floral nectars, and in addition the honey packer may blend

Cranberry–Coconut Corn Muffins

The tartness of the cranberries is balanced in these corn muffins by the sweetness of the coconut.

1	small ear of fresh corn (optional)*
1	c. undegerminated cornmeal
1	c. whole wheat flour
2½	t. baking powder
¼	t. herbal salt
3	T. butter
1⅓	c. milk plus a little extra if using dried coconut
¼	c. safflower or corn oil
2	eggs, lightly beaten
3	t. finely grated lemon rind
2 to 4	T. honey, to taste
1	c. fresh cranberries, chopped
½	c. shredded fresh coconut (or, if dried, unsweetened)*

1. Preheat oven to 500°F.

2. Shuck the ear of corn and place it on a baking sheet in the preheated oven. Allow the corn to roast for 15 to 20 minutes, turning it often. When done, it should be lightly browned on all sides. When the ear has cooled, cut the kernels from the cob with a sharp knife. Chop the kernels finely and set aside.

3. Reduce oven to 350°F.

4. Combine the cornmeal, flour, baking powder, and salt. Mix well; set aside.

5. Melt the butter. Add it to the milk, stirring well. Add the oil, eggs, lemon rind, and honey.

6. Pour the liquid ingredients into the dry ingredients, mixing well. Carefully fold in the chopped roasted corn, chopped cranberries, and coconut (in that order).

7. Spoon the batter into greased muffin tins and bake in the preheated 350° oven for 25 to 30 minutes. When the muffins are done, a cake tester inserted in the center should come out clean and the tops should be golden brown.

Makes 8 to 12 muffins.

*You can heighten the flavor of these muffins by using fresh coconut rather than dried and by adding chopped, roasted fresh corn to the batter as an additional ingredient. Both coconut and corn are available in early autumn. At other times of the year, unsweetened dried coconut can be used and the muffins will still turn out fine. Just pour a small amount of milk over the shreds in a bowl, place it in the refrigerator, and allow the coconut to absorb the milk. I don't recommend using canned corn, however, since it will make the muffins mealy and won't contribute much to the flavor.

different types of honey to achieve specific flavors. For example, orange blossom, a relatively bitter honey in its natural state, is often blended with a milder honey to make the delicate orange blossom we buy. By law, honey labeled as a specific type—orange blossom, clover, sage, alfalfa, and so forth—must contain 51% of that type of honey.

Because honey has a good share of fructose, it's less likely to lead to the jolting energy-to-exhaustion effect that white sugar and other primarily sucrose sugars have. Also, because fructose is sweeter than sucrose, a calorie's worth of honey will be sweeter than a calorie's worth of white sugar. In various taste tests, honey is judged to be from 20% to 50% sweeter than white sugar. It also contains more calories than white sugar: 64 per tablespoon as compared with 46 per tablespoon for white sugar.

Honey's nutritional assets include B vitamins and a number of trace minerals (especially true for the darker honeys); but the amounts of these are so small that by itself, honey, like all sugars, is nutritionally insignificant. (The only exception nutritionally might be blackstrap molasses because of the iron and calcium it contains.)

Honey's medicinal value comes from the floral substances it contains. These operate in the body as anti-allergens. It's known, for example, that people who suffer from an allergy to local pollen, such as hay fever, can be helped by eating small amounts of local comb honey before the pollen begins to disperse in the air. The comb honey contains tiny bits of pollen that act as immunizers later on.

Honey has also been a traditional dressing for external wounds and sore throats, since it relieves pain, dryness, and itching, and is thought to be an unfavorable medium for bacterial growth.

"Organic" honey, like "cold-pressed" oil, is a misnomer. No honey is treated with chemicals, although even honeys labeled "old-fashioned," "country style," or "natural" may have been extensively heated, filtered, and clarified. The best honey is one that has nearly escaped all three.

Almost all honey is heated to some degree. Honey packers heat honey to make it flow more quickly and to make bottling easier. This is even true of honeys labeled "raw."

Because honey is a highly saturated sugar solution, the natural sugars in it will crystallize or granulate over time.[7] Honey is therefore also heated to keep it uncrystallized and in a liquid state. If you've bought honey that *has* crystallized, you know you've found a honey that has *not* been heated for hours at high temperatures (as much as

[7]Honeys that are higher in fructose take longer to crystallize. Alfalfa honey, for example, crystallizes quickly because it's low in fructose, high in glucose.

150°F for six hours). Crystallization is unconditionally a good sign and doesn't mean the honey's damaged in the least. Just the opposite is true: Because the honey has not been heated extensively, it contains all the enzymes, vitamins, minerals, and proteins that heating may destroy or denature. To liquefy crystallized honey, simply put the jar in warm water for a few minutes.

When honey leaves the comb, it contains bee pollen and bee parts. Extensive filtering removes these, taking away the honey's anti-allergenic properties and its small amounts of protein. A honey that is clear and shiny has necessarily been highly filtered. Note: Because a jar of honey has a honeycomb in it does not mean that the honey has not been highly filtered. Some commercial packers pour filtered honey over a clean comb, since comb honey has an "old-fashioned" appeal.

Many honey producers market two types of honey—one for natural food stores (some heated up to 120°F, others not heated at all; lightly filtered and unfiltered) and the other for supermarkets (heated for longer periods at higher temperatures and highly filtered). Natural food stores sometimes carry honey from small local apiaries as well. This is often the best honey to buy. It's less expensive, minimally filtered, and heated only enough to make bottling easier. You can distinguish honey from a large producer and honey from a small independent apiary by looking at the honey itself and the types of honey available. A large producer bottles many different types of honey: clover, sage, orange blossom, rosemary, linden, eucalyptus, buckwheat, and so on. A small independent apiary usually has no more than two or three types because those are the only varieties the bees make in one area.

Carob

Carob powder is ground from bean-shaped pods that grow on locust trees around the Mediterranean. It has a sweet mocha-chocolaty flavor and can be used in place of chocolate or cocoa.

Why would you want to replace chocolate or cocoa? First, because they contain caffeine and are very hard to digest. A second reason is that chocolate and cocoa powder are made from the bitter seeds of the cocoa plant, which have no chocolate flavor but must be roasted, milled, and mixed with copious amounts of refined sugar to produce the chocolate flavor. And finally, chocolate, mixed in milk, is thought to inhibit the metabolism of the milk's calcium.

Chocolate and cocoa are also high in fat. Breakfast cocoa, by law, must be 22% fat. Bitter chocolate must be 50% fat. Carob, by com-

Sugars and Sweeteners

Sweetener	Principal Sugar	Effect on Body	Flavor and Sweetening Power	Conversion	Cooking Notes
Honey	Type of sugar depends on honey: clover = 60% sucrose; orange blossom = 70% fructose.	If eaten in large quantities, will produce adverse fluctuations in blood sugar level.	All honeys are blends of floral nectars. From 20% to 60% sweeter than ws.	Varies according to what the principal sugar and the moisture content of the honey is. As a start, substitute ½–⅔ cup honey for 1 cup ws. Reduce liquids by 3 tablespoons.	Honey makes breads and cakes moister and heavier and keeps them fresh longer. Honey gives food *flavor* as well as sweetness. It should not be used in delicate desserts where the weight of the honey would collapse the dessert. Also, foods brown more quickly when honey has been added.
Maple syrup	65% sucrose	Same adverse effect as ws on blood sugar. Also absorbed quickly.	Very sweet; nutty. Grade Fancy has richest flavor. About 60% as sweet as ws.	Substitute ⅔ cup maple syrup for 1 cup ws only in recipes where a maple flavor works well. Reduce liquid by at least 4 tablespoons.	Maple syrup's flavor is intense. It's especially good in breads, muffins, puddings, and sweet sauces and poured over homemade pancakes and waffles. Adds moisture and denseness.
Molasses	Light: 70+% sucrose; blackstrap: 50%–70% sucrose	Same adverse effect as ws on blood sugar. Does contribute more nutrients than other sugars.	Light: very sweet and smoky. Blackstrap: rich, deep, almost bitter-smoky. From 50% to 70% as sweet as ws.	Use ½ cup of light or ¼–½ cup of blackstrap (and no other sugar) in recipes where a molasses flavor is appropriate. Or substitute ¼ cup of molasses and ⅓–½ cup of honey for 1 cup ws in recipes that require strong sweetness and strong molasses flavor. Adjust liquids as necessary.	Light and blackstrap molasses should be used for their flavor; not for their sweetness. Light works well in all but very delicate foods. Blackstrap should be used only with strongly flavored or spiced foods—baked beans, gingerbread, pecan pie. Time the baking precisely. Overcooked molasses is gummy and bitter.
Barley malt syrup	65% maltose	Does not have adverse effect on blood sugar. Absorbed slowly.	Delicate, nutty flavor. From 25% as sweet as ws to 70% as sweet as ws (for those that have corn sweeteners added).	Substitute 1½ cups pure barley malt syrup for 1 cup ws. Substitute 1 cup barley–corn syrup for 1 cup ws. Use less liquid as necessary.	Barley malt is not an intense sweetener. Pure maltose is roughly 40% as sweet as sucrose. Barley malt adds denseness, but not so much as honey.

Sweetener	*Principal Sugar*	*Effect on Body*	*Flavor and Sweetening Power*	*Conversion*	*Cooking Notes*
Rice syrup*	33% maltose	See Barley malt syrup.	Very delicate. The mildest of sweet flavors. About 15–25% as sweet as ws.	Use 1–1½ cups in baking. In blender drinks, tea, and so on use 2 teaspoons. Neither of these conversions will bring the sweetness up to ws level. Good for tapering down.	Rice syrup also has a very light quality of sweetness to it. You can lick it off your finger, for example, without getting an intense sugary sensation on the tip of your tongue. Rice syrup bakes well. It is strongly recommended precisely because of its mildness.
Date sugar	Fructose and other sugars: 65% total	If eaten in very large quantities may have same effect as ws on blood sugar. Contributes same nutrients as dates.	As you might have guessed, flavor just like dates. About as sweet as ws.	Substitute 1 teaspoon date sugar for 1 teaspoon ws in hot and cold drinks. In baking, substitute ½ cup date sugar softened in as much boiling water or very hot liquid as needed to make a smooth paste. Combine with ⅓ cup honey. Together, date sugar and honey will approximate 1 cup ws in sweetness. Adjust other liquids.	Date sugar is really not a sugar. It is simply pitted, dried dates that have been ground to the consistency of coarse sugar. No refined sugar is added. Date sugar will not dissolve well unless it's mixed with liquids in a blender or a paste is made with it and hot to boiling liquid. It is best used sprinkled over food.
Commercial fructose	Crystalline and liquid: 90% fructose	Does not have adverse effect on blood sugar. May cause allergic reactions.	Intense sweetness. Commercial fructose is about 60% sweeter than ws in most cases.	Substitute ⅓–⅔ cup crystalline fructose for 1 cup ws. If using liquid fructose, note the exact sweetness equivalent on the label. Liquid may be 30%–60% sweeter than ws.	Fructose is a humectant, which means that it retains moisture. Note this in baking. The sweetness of fructose varies depending on how it's used. It is sweetest in foods that are acidic or cold and only a little sweeter than ws in hot foods. Crystalline works better in boiling and baking.
Brown and turbinado† sugar	96% and 99% sucrose	Same adverse effect as ws on blood sugar. Absorbed as rapidly.	Very sweet; slightly nutty. Same sweetening power as ws.	Substitute on a 1:1 basis.	Brown sugar does give food a slightly different flavor and color than ws because of the molasses in it.

ws = white sugar. * Trade name: Yinnie Syrup. † Turbinado sugar is sometimes called raw sugar.

parison, is only 0.7% fat. In practical terms, 3½ ounces of carob has 180 calories and 1.3 grams of fat, while the same amount of semi-sweet chocolate has 507 calories and 35.7 grams of fat.

All of the carob in this country is imported as kibble, which are broken carob pods that have had the internal seeds removed. The carob kibble is then roasted and ground into carob powder here.

Carob is roasted at about 325°F. The longer it's roasted, the darker it becomes and the more chocolaty the flavor. Most of the carob powder sold in natural food stores is the dark-roast variety, since carob is still used primarily as a flavor substitute for chocolate rather than as a natural sweetener.

Carob is 42% to 49% sugar by nature (a mixture of sucrose, fructose, and glucose). No refined sugar is added to carob powder, but extra sugar is added to carob products. Carob ice cream, for example, is further sweetened with sugar, maple syrup, or honey. Carob drops or carob-coated candy bars necessarily have added sugar.

Carob has a thin, inseparable husk that becomes part of the powder when carob is roasted and ground. Carob powder, therefore, is about 30% cellulose or fiber. While the fiber is excellent for digestion, it presents one problem: It won't dissolve in liquids.

If you've ever added a teaspoon of carob to a glass of milk, you've noticed that what you end up with is not the chocolate milk you'd been hoping for. Rather than dissolving in the milk, the grains of carob fiber float around like tiny shredded chocolate chips and eventually precipitate out. You can, however, sidestep this problem by first making a wet paste with the carob and a tiny bit of milk. Slowly add more milk to the paste while blending the mixture in a blender, which will literally cut the carob into the milk. A small amount of liquid lecithin worked into the carob paste in the beginning may also help, since lecithin is a natural emulsifier. In fact, carob drinks sold in natural food stores are simply mixtures of carob and milk (or soy milk) that have been emulsified with lecithin, then stabilized with natural stabilizers so that the minuscule bits of carob never precipitate out.

Cooking with Sweeteners

Cooking with sweeteners other than the major sucrose sugars (white, brown, and turbinado sugar) requires special attention. Other sucrose sugars such as molasses and maple syrup, plus fructose sugars and maltose sugars, all have specific characteristics in terms of texture, flavor, moisture content, power of sweetness, browning time and so on. (See the chart of relative sweetening power on page 304.)

Molasses or honey, for example, can't be substituted for white sugar at whim; their flavor must first be taken into account. Also, an adjustment in the amount of liquids used in the recipe must be made, since molasses or honey, like most sugars other than refined sugar, are liquid.

In order to cook with carob you should know that 3 to 4 tablespoons of carob worked into 2 tablespoons of milk (or 1 teaspoon of oil) will approximate 1 square of chocolate. Carob can also be used simply as a sweetener—especially in baked goods, where you want to avoid the heaviness and moistness that a liquid sweetener like honey would impart. If you use lightly roasted carob, almost no chocolatelike flavor comes through. Either light- or dark-roasted carob is an excellent sweetener and flavoring for grain coffees.

Use the chart on pages 312–313 as a guide, but experiment according to your own tastes. A little less sugar every time is an ideal to aim for.

Herbs and Spices

A plant's aroma is its personality. Just as you can tell a lot about an animal by its behavior, you can get an immediate feeling for an herb or spice based on the power, the delicacy, the pungency of its scent.

Herbs and spices work one of two ways in cooking, so before you use them, stop a minute and decide what you want to accomplish. A well-chosen herb has the magical power to transform a dish that's wholesome, but missing something, into a dish with extraordinary flavor by drawing out the natural flavor of the food by complementing it. Herbs, the leaves of low-growing plants (basil, thyme, and rosemary, for example) are usually better at this than spices, since they're more subtle. Spices—the bark, roots, fruit, or berries of shrubs and trees (cinnamon bark and gingerroot, for example)—work somewhat differently. They tend to transform basic foodstuffs, imparting so much character that a new food is created. Add ginger, cinnamon, nutmeg, cloves, and a sprinkle of allspice to flour and all of a sudden you've got gingerbread. This is different from whole wheat herb bread, where parsley, basil, and tarragon might be used to give the bread character without changing its essence.

Spices should be bought whole or unground, because once they're ground, they lose their flavor and aroma rapidly. When a recipe calls for a crushed or powdered spice, break it down yourself with a mortar and pestle or use a food grinder such as the Varco Multi-Use dry-food grinder.

Ideally, herbs should be pinched right from the plant on your kitchen windowsill. An entire herb garden is actually less work than three houseplants, so you may want to look up sources of herb seeds on page 318 and try planting a few herbs. The seed packets will give planting directions.

If you buy fresh herbs in the market, be sure to choose robust bundles, full of color and scent. At home cut ¼ to ½ inch off the root ends and place the herbs standing up in a cup of water in your refrigerator. Continue to clip off just a bit of the root every other day. Fresh herbs will stay fresh for about a week this way.

Prepackaged and loose dried herbs and spices can be found in natural food stores, gourmet shops, and specialty herb shops, although dried herbs are often freshest and least expensive if you buy them directly from herb companies. A mail-order list of sources follows. Please don't buy the small tins of herbs and spices in grocery stores and supermarkets. Unfailingly, they're stale—and are never worth the three to four times higher cost.

Dried herbs and spices should be stored in a cool, dry place, away from intense heat or direct sunlight. (This may rule out the spot right over your stove—a logical but deadly place, especially for delicate herbs.) Both spices and herbs lose their potency over time. Once they're six or so months old, you may want to use them for something other than cooking—potpourris, pomanders, a good herbal bath, or thrown in the fireplace. What smells fill the room!

The chart beginning on page 320 is given over to twenty-seven major culinary herbs and spices for which culinary notes have been provided. Interestingly enough, because of volatile political situations, wars, and natural disasters, America no longer imports herbs

Curried Corn with Yogurt

- 1 c. plain yogurt
- 8 fresh ears of corn
- 2 T. butter or 1 T. corn oil
- 1 small red pepper, finely chopped
- 1 t. curry powder
- ½ t. ground cumin
- 1 T. corn oil
- 1 small onion, finely chopped
- ¼ c. cilantro or parsley, minced

1. Spoon the yogurt into a sieve lined with cheesecloth or a paper filter and allow the whey to drain off for half an hour.

2. Shuck the corn and drop into boiling water. When the water returns to a boil, turn off the heat, cover the corn, and let it steam for 5 minutes. Drain. With a sharp knife, scrape the corn from the cob.

3. Melt the butter or heat 1 T. of corn oil in a saucepan. Add the red pepper and sauté for 1 minute. Add the curry and cumin and sauté for another minute. Add the corn, mix well, and remove to a warm serving bowl.

4. To make the sauce, heat the corn oil in a small skillet, add the onion and sauté until transparent. Add the cilantro. Remove from heat and stir in the yogurt. Serve the sauce, slightly warm, on the side.

and spices from many of the countries that supplied us just a few years ago. For example, until 1979 Iran was our major source of cuminseed. Now we buy most of our cumin from India. Before the Vietnam War, America purchased top-notch cinnamon from Saigon. Now China supplies us with the top grades. In the last few years nearly all the major herb and spice markets have shifted. In fact, for the first time in history the United States has become its own major supplier. In 1979 the United States met 35% of its spice needs (California is by far the largest producer), and if Mexico and Canada are included as regional suppliers, a full 60% of the spices and herbs we used in 1979 could be considered "locally grown."[1] Changing suppliers have meant changing products. Just as the same grape grown in different parts of the world will produce different wines, the characteristics and flavors of herbs and spices change depending on where they're grown. You may find, as a result, that the pepper you buy today has a flavor you're not accustomed to.

In addition to culinary uses, herbs and spices have powerful medicinal uses. In fact, only during this century did their primary status as medicines change. Formerly, medical information could necessarily be found in herbal and vegetable texts.

When an herb is used for its medicinal value, it's generally made into a tea and drunk rather than used in cooking. The medicinal values listed in the chart are those commonly presented in herb texts and are based on historical usage. In particular, I have relied on *Herbs & Things* by Jeanne Rose (Grosset and Dunlap, 1972) and *Back to Eden* by Jethro Kloss (Woodbridge Publishing Company, 1972).

The following companies offer herbs in bulk. Costs can be substantially less than herbs purchased in small quantities at retail prices.

Aphrodisia
28 Carmine Street
New York, New York 10014

Attar Herbs & Spices
Playground Road
New Ipswich, New Hampshire 03071

Indiana Botanic Gardens
Hammond, Indiana 46325

Meadowbrook Herb Garden
Wyoming, Rhode Island 02898

Nature's Herb Company
281 Ellis Street
San Francisco, California 94102

In addition, *The Herb Quarterly* magazine is an excellent source of herbal information, products, and further sources. Write P.O. Box 576, Wilmington, Vermont 05363. For specific information, you can also contact the Herb Society of America, 300 Massachusetts Avenue, Boston, Massachusetts 02115.

[1]Kevin J. Hannigan, "Spices: Changes Ahead," *Food Engineering,* June 1980.

Whole Wheat Muffins with Orange Cream Cheese

These spicy whole wheat–orange muffins are great toasted and served warm with sweet orange cream cheese made from yogurt. (The cream cheese must be made the day before.)

- ⅓ c. vanilla-flavored yogurt
- ⅔ c. orange-flavored yogurt
- 1 c. plain yogurt
- 1 T. orange marmalade (optional)
- 2 c. whole wheat flour
- 2 t. baking powder
- ½ t. herbal salt
- ¼ t. ground cinnamon
- ¼ t. grated nutmeg
- ¼ t. finely crushed cardamom pods or ground cardamom
- 1 large orange
- ⅓ c. milk (approximately)
- 2 eggs, beaten
- ½ t. finely grated lemon rind
- ½ t. vanilla extract
- 3 T. honey
- 2 T. butter, melted
- ½ c. chopped walnuts or pecans (optional)

1. Mix the yogurts together well and drain in a cheesecloth-lined sieve for 15 to 24 hours, or until you have a thick ball of yogurt "cream cheese." To add an extra orange flavor and sweetness, mix the cream cheese well with a tablespoon of good marmalade. This keeps well, covered, in the refrigerator.

2. In a large bowl, mix together the flour, baking powder, salt, cinnamon, nutmeg, and cardamom.

3. Into a separate bowl, squeeze the juice from the orange and add enough milk to make 1 cup. Reserve the orange shell.

4. Preheat oven to 350°F.

5. Cut the orange shell into 6 pieces. Flatten each piece on a cutting board and, with a very sharp knife, remove the membrane and the pith completely from each piece of shell. When you've done this successfully, the orange shell pieces will be thin enough for you to almost see through and all of the white pith that coats the inside of the pieces will be removed.

6. Put the orange shell pieces, the orange-milk mixture, the eggs, lemon rind, vanilla, honey, and butter into a blender. Blend until the pieces of orange shell are finely chopped.

7. Pour the blender mixture into the dry ingredients, stir in the nuts, and mix just enough to create a uniform, lumpy batter. Spoon into oiled muffin tins and bake in the preheated oven for about 20 minutes.

Makes about 8 muffins.

Herbs and Spices

Herbs and Spices	*Characteristics*	*Culinary Notes**	*Medicinal Uses*
Allspice	Ground berry native to West Indies, Mexico, and Central America.	Flavor combination of cinnamon, clove, and nutmeg. Best in fruity or nutty recipes.	As an anaesthetic when used in baths.
Anise	Oldest known aromatic seed. Native of Asia Minor, India, China, and Spain.	Sharp, tangy licorice flavor. Best in cookies, cakes, spicy pancakes. Blend with other spices in tea, warm milk, blender drinks.	In tea or milk for insomnia. Oil used to relieve flatulence.
Basil	Herb native to India and Persia. Now grown worldwide, including USA. ETG.	Thyme-peppermint-licorice-like aroma. Strong flavor. Use as dominant herb, especially with tomatoes, pasta, fish, vegetables, eggs, and any recipe calling for olive oil.	Infusion mixed with honey and nutmeg for diarrhea.
Bay	Leaf herb of the laurel tree. Supplied by Turkey and Greece.	Woodsy flavor, faintly like cinnamon-sarsaparilla. Bitter when overused. Best with fish, veal, soups, part of bouquet garni.	Decoction mixed with honey for coughs, colds, and lung disorders. Bay oil used to relieve pain of bruises. Always add a leaf when cooking grains or legumes.
Capers	Flower buds of Mediterrean caper bush.	Tart flavor. Tiniest ones superior. Rinse in cold water before using with eggs, fish, salads.	
Caraway	Crescent-shaped aromatic seeds from Holland, Poland, and Egypt.	Licorice-dill flavor. For rye bread, pressing into soft cheese. Grind and cook with carrots, cabbage, turnips.	Aromatic. Stimulant.

Herbs are noted here as mixers (the herb blends well with other herbs), dominant herbs (those that should only be used with mild, less assertive herbs), or pungent herbs (strongly flavored herbs to be used to achieve a strong flavor).

ETG = extremely easy to grow at home. The advantage of having fresh herbs for cooking is inestimable, since dried herbs can't compete with the flavor of fresh. An excellent text for growing herbs is *The Complete Indoor Gardener,* ed. by Michael Wright (Random House, 1975).

*Use twice as much of a fresh herb as a dried. With both herbs and spices, a longer cooking time brings out more of the flavor.

Herbs and Spices	*Characteristics*	*Culinary Notes**	*Medicinal Uses*
Cardamom	Spice seeds native to India. Guatemala supplies the U.S.A.	Powerful peppery-nutty-lemony-ginger flavor. Buy in pod. Remove pod and crush seed before using (sparingly). Excellent added to tea. Also in grain dishes, breads, and cookies.	Stomachic.
Chervil	Herb of parsley family. ETG.	Mixer herb. Faint tarragon-licorice flavor. Best with cold vegetable dishes, salads, cream soups.	
Chives	Mildest member of onion family. ETG.	Mixer herb. Use generously in cheese, egg, and vegetable dishes.	
Cinnamon	Spicy inner bark of cassia tree grown in Ceylon, Indonesia, Southeast Asia, and China.	Sometimes bitter used alone. Combine with nutmeg, cloves, ginger, allspice in cakes, puddings, grain stuffings, drinks.	Oil is used as an aromatic and stimulant. In tea, beneficial for the stomach; helps relieve diarrhea and nausea.
Cloves	Spice flower buds of clove tree. Grown in Zanzibar, Madagascar, and Brazil.	Crush well before using unless they can be removed. Good in spicy drinks, baked fruit desserts, cookies, muffins.	Antiseptic. Cleanses kidneys, liver, lungs. Mixed with mint in tea to aid sleep.
Coriander	Aromatic seed of plant of the parsley family. Suppliers: Morocco and Canada.	Round seeds have tough shell and must be ground before using. Fresh leaves of coriander plant are called cilantro. These are excellent chopped in grain dishes, with eggs, and with avocado.	Carminative. Aids in stomach problems.
Cumin	Aromatic seed similar to caraway. Grown in Iran, Turkey, Egypt, and India.	Chief ingredient in chili spices and curry powder. Excellent in bean-grain casseroles when mixed with parsley, garlic, and lemon juice.	Used in veterinary medicine.
Dill	Seeds and weed. Grown in India and U.S.A. ETG.	Weed has a finer lemony-spice flavor than seed, which is	Seeds and seed oil used to treat flatulent colic.

Herbs and Spices	*Characteristics*	*Culinary Notes**	*Medicinal Uses*
Dill (continued)		tart. Dominant herb. Excellent with yogurt, cheese, eggs, cold vegetables.	
Ginger	Root spice of Asian plant. Suppliers: China, Nigeria, Jamaica.	Dried or crystallized ginger has nowhere near the flavor of fresh. Should be very finely minced and used anytime with garlic and/or tamari in vegetable, grain, egg dishes. Pungent and biting flavor.	In tea, hot, for suppressed menses. Chew root for sore throat. Good for diarrhea.
Marjoram	Herbal cousin of oregano. France. ETG.	Mild, musky aroma. Mix with chervil, parsley, and savory in chicken, veal, grain dishes, potatoes, tomatoes.	Used in foot baths and in tonics to revive and strengthen the body.
Mint	Herb found in 30 varieties. Spearmint and peppermint most popular. Grows plentifully in U.S.A. ETG.	Dominant herb. Excellent in fruit salads, blender drinks, cold grain dishes, teas.	Carminative. Appetite stimulant. Used to treat women's complaints and as a douche.
Nutmeg	Spice seed of nutmeg tree. Grown in East and West Indies. Mace, a related spice, is the outer bark of nutmeg and is stronger.	Best to buy whole seeds and grind. Excellent in vanilla desserts and dairy dishes: quiche, yogurt drinks, blintzes.	Carminative. Promotes digestion.
Oregano	Wild majoram herb. Marigold aroma. Greek oregano stronger than other varieties. Turkey, Mexico, U.S.A. ETG.	Pungent. Use as dominant flavor for pasta, grain, and egg dishes.	
Paprika	Ground pods of Capsicum peppers native to Latin America. Major suppliers: U.S.A., Hungary, Spain.	The reddest, sweetest, mildest is Hungarian rose paprika. Good for vegetables, sauces, salads.	High in vitamin C.

Herbs and Spices	*Characteristics*	*Culinary Notes**	*Medicinal Uses*
Parsley	Herb grown in many varieties. Best known: curly leaf and flat Italian leaf. Both grow in U.S.A. ETG.	Italian flat leaf is stronger than curly. Both can be used in everything with any other green herb.	High in vitamins A and C, iron, iodine, manganese. Improves digestion. Cleanses kidneys and spleen.
Pepper	All varieties are berries of same tropical vine grown in India, Indonesia, Brazil, and Malaysia.	Black (strongest) are dried unhusked immature berries. White are dried inner cores of ripe berries. Green (mildest) are unripe whole berries.	True pepper is a strong irritant to the stomach. Cayenne pepper,* however, has a healing and stimulating effect. Good for digestion and respiratory system.
Rosemary	Needlelike herb leaves. France and Spain. ETG.	Pungent herb. Buy whole and crush well. Excellent in grain croquettes, vegetable pâté, and with chicken and lamb.	As a tonic for nervous disorders and headaches. Boiled in wine for colds and coughs.
Saffron	Crushed stigmas of Spanish crocuses. ETG.	Soak strands in tepid water, then use water to flavor and color rice, fish, sauces.	Carminative. Diaphoretic.
Sage	Herb leaves of sage plant. Belongs to mint family and grows in Yugoslavia, Turkey, and Albania. ETG.	Pungent herb. Excellent for grain stuffings and sautéing vegetables.	Sage water used as body wash for itchy skin and aching muscles. As tea for fevers and colds.
Tarragon	Herb leaves of tarragon plant. France. ETG.	Mixer herb, licorice-flavored leaves. Mix with sliced almonds and add to green vegetables, grain casseroles, cold fish dishes.	In tea to promote menses and help sleep.
Thyme	Herb leaves of thyme plant. France and Spain. ETG.	Dominant herb with woody-mint flavor. Use with roasted nuts and garlic in egg dishes, grain stuffings, soups.	Thyme tea with honey for hangover. Carminative, external antiseptic, and tonic for all skin conditions.

*Cayenne (red pepper) is not from the true pepper plant, but a ground spice from Capsicum pepper pods. This family of pods includes the Latin American Serrano and Jalapeño green peppers.

Salts, Seasonings, and Special Cooking Aids

The following chart capsulizes the special salts, seasonings, jelling agents, thickeners, and nutritive substances that form the underpinnings of natural foods cookery. Many, such as miso, shoyu, tamari, dulse, and kelp, are new to American cooking but have been used in traditional Oriental cooking for centuries.

All of the food substances listed are plant products that have undergone a minimum of processing—a statement that, in many cases, is not true of their American counterparts. For example, agar-agar, used like unflavored gelatin, is a colorless ground sea vegetable that readily dissolves in hot liquid foods and jells them without either adding to or subtracting from the food's flavor. By contrast, unflavored gelatin is a proteinlike substance derived from frozen edible-grade pork skins as well as the skin, white connective tissue, and bones of other animals. These are treated with acid or lime, washed to extract a gelatin solution, filtered, concentrated in vacuum evaporators, dried, and ground.

All of the food substances listed are available in natural food stores and specialty shops.

Salts

Food	*Form(s)*	*Source*	*Use in Cooking*	*Special Notes*
Sea salt	Refined and unrefined	Sun-dried and oven-dried sea water	All salt draws nutrients out of food. Use at the very end of cooking.	Truly unrefined gray sea salt is illegal in the U.S.A. All other sea salt is refined and has the same chemical composition as regular table salt. French sea salt is also refined but contains fewer anticaking agents.
Herbal salt	Fine granules	Herbs and refined sea salt	Use in place of sea salt. Much of the sodium chloride is replaced by herbs.	Preferable to sea salt in terms of health; adds flavor in cooking. Herbs include celery, leek, onion, parsley, kelp.

Food	Form(s)	Source	Use in Cooking	Special Notes
Gomashio (sesame salt)	Small granules	Toasted sesame seeds and refined sea salt	Use sprinkled over food in place of sea salt.	To make your own: toast 7 parts sesame seeds to 1 part sea salt in 350° F oven for 8 to 10 minutes, stirring often. Grind in blender.
Dulse and kelp	Powder and flakes	Dried sea vegetable	Use as a salt in salads, casseroles, baking. Adds mild spicy flavor.	An excellent substitute for sea salt. Kelp is more strongly flavored than dulse.

Seasonings

Food	Form(s)	Source	Use in Cooking	Special Notes
Miso	Creamy paste	Hatcho: fermented soybeans, salt, water, special culture Barley: more barley than soybeans, salt, water, culture Brown rice: 50% brown rice, 50% soybeans, salt, water, culture	Use alone to make miso soup. Add to sauces and toppings for grains. Sauté with oil, herbs, and nut butters for an excellent spread.*	Hatcho miso is considered the best. It is allowed to age the longest—2 years. Rice miso is the sweetest. Rice miso is often pasteurized; other flavors may not be. Unpasteurized is preferable.
Shoyu	Liquid. Naturally fermented soy sauce.	Soybeans, whole wheat, water, sea salt, culture	The wheat sugars in shoyu give it a subtle, light flavor that blends well with any food.	Most of the tamari sold in America is, in fact, shoyu. Look for a naturally aged shoyu (18–24 months).
Tamari	Liquid. Naturally fermented soy sauce.	Soybeans, water, sea salt, culture	True tamari is strongly flavored and thick. It should be used as a dipping sauce.	Only a small proportion of true tamari is produced naturally. Most of the available commercial brands have been artifically fermented and contain preservatives and coloring agents.

* An extraordinary text with hundreds of excellent miso recipes is *The Book of Miso* by William Shurtleff and Akiko Aoyagi (Brookline, Mass.: Autumn Press, 1976).

Jelling and Thickening Agents

Food	*Form(s)*	*Source*	*Use in Cooking*	*Special Notes*
Agar-agar *(kanten)*	Sticks, flakes, powder	Sea vegetable	Use in place of unflavored gelatin. 1½ tablespoons agar-agar to 1 quart fruit juice or stock.	Since it is a sea vegetable, agar-agar is high in minerals. Powder is more concentrated than sticks. Excellent for fruit desserts and vegetable aspics.
Arrow-root	Fine powder	Root starch of several tropical plants	Use 1½ teaspoons arrowroot in place of 1 tablespoon flour or cornstarch.	Arrowroot is clear when diluted. It does not have a chalky taste like cornstarch. It is more acid-stable than flour and therefore excellent in fruit sauces.
Kuzu (kudzu)	Chunky powder	Huge root of the legume *Pueraria thunbergiana*	Dissolve 2 tablespoons kuzu in ¼ cup *cold* water or juice. Pour through a strainer into food to be heated and thickened.	Can be used like arrowroot to thicken sauces and soups. Kuzu added to a batter makes food more crisp. Can also be used with agar-agar for a firm jell.

Chicken Breasts with Almond Sauce

- 2 lb. chicken breasts, skinned and boned
- 1 cup almonds
- ½ lb. mushrooms
- 1–2 c. fresh peas, 1 ripe avocado, or other fresh green vegetable
- 2 T. butter
- 2 T. safflower oil
- herbal salt to taste
- 4 large shallots, finely chopped
- 1 small fresh green frying pepper, finely chopped
- 3 T. brandy (optional)
- 2 T. fresh parsley, minced
- pinch cayenne pepper
- 1 c. chicken or vegetable stock

1. Trim away all bits of fat and sinew from the chicken breasts and cut into small cutlets about 2 inches long.

2. With ½ cup of the almonds, make almond milk as follows: Boil the two cups of water. Drop in the ½ cup of almonds. Allow almonds to blanch for one minute. Place almonds and 1 cup of the blanching liquid in a blender and blend until smooth. Makes 1 cup.

3. Place the other ½ cup of almonds on a cookie sheet and toast in a 400° oven for about 20 minutes. Chop coarsely.

4. Cut the caps from the mushrooms and slice in half, or leave whole if the caps are small. Reserve the stems for another use.

5. Steam the peas just until tender. Or if you are using avocado, slice the avocado in half, remove the pit, slice the halves into eighths, then trim away the skin. Set the vegetable aside.

6. In a large heavy skillet, heat the butter and oil together. Add the chicken cutlets and sprinkle with herbal salt. Sauté over moderate heat for about 2 minutes on each side. Remove to a warm flameproof serving dish.

7. Add shallots and green pepper to the skillet. Cook, stirring, for 1 minute. Add the mushrooms. Cook, stirring occasionally, for another 3 minutes. Add the brandy, the almond milk, and the stock and cook, stirring, for 10 minutes, or until the liquid is reduced. Add the parsley and cayenne to taste.

8. Gently add the peas or the avocado slices to the sauce, reduce heat and cook for 1 minute. Pour carefully over the chicken cutlets, then heat the whole dish for another minute on top of the stove and serve garnished with the toasted almonds.

Note: This dish is very good served with rice.

Supplements

Food	*Form(s)*	*Source*	*Use in Cooking*	*Special Notes*
Yeast (nutritional, brewer's, torula)	Powder, flakes	Commercially grown yeast cultures	Begin with 1 teaspoon added to fruit juice or blender drinks to add protein and B vitamins to the diet.	All yeast supplements differ in flavor. Some brands are bitter and unpalatable. The flavor of other brands grows on you, but it's never a flavor you'd look forward to.
Bran	Flakes	Wheat berries	Use in baking and over cereals to add fiber.	Bran is not a whole food. If your diet is high in whole grains, fresh fruits, and fresh vegetables, you don't need it.
Wheat germ	Flakes	Wheat berries	Toast wheat germ and add to cereals, breads, and fruits for a nutty flavor.	Wheat germ is also not a whole food, but it's one of the most direct methods of obtaining vitamin E. Buy fresh and use within 10 days of milling, otherwise the natural oils turn the wheat germ rancid. Always refrigerate.

Mussels Marinière Baked with Mushrooms in Miso

Mussels

1½ lb. fresh mussels
1 onion, chopped
3 cloves garlic, minced
2 T. safflower oil
⅓ c. chopped parsley
1 bay leaf
3 T. butter
1 c. dry red wine
⅓ c. sherry
2 T. arrowroot

Stuffing

3–4 slices stale whole wheat bread, thinly sliced
safflower or olive oil for brushing
dried oregano (optional) to taste
2 cloves garlic, minced
2 T. safflower oil
½ lb. mushrooms, chopped
1 bunch watercress, stems removed
2 T. miso (preferably hatcho)
½ c. hot water
1 c. whole wheat bread crumbs, toasted

1. Wash the mussels well in several changes of cold water. Scrub them with a brush until the shells are smooth and clean. Snip off each mussel's "beard" with scissors or a sharp knife. Set aside.

2. In a saucepan, sauté the onion and the 3 cloves of garlic in the safflower oil, until the onion is softened. Add the parsley, bay leaf, mussels, butter, and red wine. Steam covered for 3 to 5 minutes over low heat, or until the mussels open.

3. Remove mussels with a slotted spoon. Set aside to cool.

4. Add the sherry to the mussel broth and bring to a gentle simmer. Thicken broth by dissolving the arrowroot in some of the broth first, then pouring this back in. Simmer gently for 10 minutes, or until thickened, stirring constantly. Remove the bay leaf. Set the sauce aside.

5. *Making the stuffing.* Lightly brush both sides of the bread slices with safflower or olive oil, sprinkle lightly with oregano if you like, then toast under the broiler. Allow to cool, stack the slices, then cut them into small cubes. Set aside.

6. In a separate pan, briefly sauté the two remaining cloves of garlic in the 2 tablespoons of safflower oil. Add the mushrooms and cook until soft. Chop the watercress and add. Sauté for 1 minute more.

7. Preheat oven to 450°F.

8. Dissolve the miso in the hot water. Add to the mushrooms and watercress. Simmer for 1 minute. Remove the pan from the heat.

9. Add the bread crumbs to the miso-mushroom-watercress mixture. Mix until the bread is evenly moistened.

10. Remove the mussels from their shells. Chop the mussels and

add to the mushroom mixture. Mix well. This stuffing should be fairly moist. If necessary, moisten with some of the mussel sauce.

11. Fill each mussel shell generously with stuffing and place in a shallow baking pan. Discard any unused shells. Dribble half the mussel sauce over the stuffed shells, then bake the mussels in the preheated oven for about 20 minutes, or until they're lightly browned.

12. Just before serving, heat the remainder of the mussel sauce and pour over mussels.

Part Four
Eating Out

How to Eat Healthfully in a Restaurant

A *Washington Star* editorial in June 1976 made the point that if you eat enough precooked, frozen, and reheated packaged meals, part of you will starve to death. In this country 46 million of us eat out every day.[1] By the mid-1980s we'll be spending half our food money in restaurants. Although some of these meals may be as wholesome as the home-cooked variety, the vast majority are far less satisfactory.

For while elegantly arranged dinners may be served from gueridons in the dining room, that's no guarantee the kitchen isn't a frantic assembly line where precooked frozen chicken Kievs are bounced in and out of microwave ovens like Pop-Tarts.

I'm convinced, however, that you don't have to abandon eating out in order to eat well. You simply have to know something about how restaurants are run and how to read between the lines of a menu. If you're in a sandwich and omelet restaurant, for example, there's a good chance the lasagna special was precooked, frozen, then microwave heated. If you're in a French restaurant, it helps to know which dishes are filled with sugar, salt, and heavy cream. Given any menu for any restaurant anywhere, it is possible, to a certain extent, to anticipate which dishes will be the most healthful and which dishes you'd definitely avoid if you had a label to read or could see how or when the dish was prepared.

It's important to understand from the beginning that generalizations about restaurants can't be made. Not all expensive restaurants provide high-quality food. Not all natural food restaurants provide healthful food, and so on. Restaurants are orchestrated by thousands of independent owners and chefs, all of whom have different values and motivations. Whether an omelet is made with spray-dried eggs or fresh ones often depends more on the integrity of the person running the restaurant than it does on the kind of restaurant or how expensive it is.

One thing you can count on is that all restaurants are businesses at heart—not extensions of a grandmother's kitchen. In a restaurant

[1]Gallup Poll, 1978. In 1979 we spent $105 billion in the 535,000 restaurants here.

where a chef makes most of the dishes, food costs alone run between 30% and 40% of the restaurant's total costs. Once food costs inch up toward 40%, however, a restaurant owner (given fixed costs: labor, rent, utilities, equipment, etc.) has to cut back someplace in order to stay in business. Invariably, it's in the kitchen.

It is through buying fewer expensive vegetables, meats, fish, and other ingredients, using every scrap of food, and buying from commercial sources that restaurants cut their costs.[2] For example, the reason most restaurants do not make their own cheesecake (even though 25% falsely claim they do) is that the ingredients for one good cheesecake can cost more than six dollars. Cheesecake also involves high labor costs: A chef can easily spend one-quarter of a day making cheesecake alone. Since most restaurants are convinced that you as a customer won't pay the four dollars per wedge they would have to charge to cover their costs, their only option is to buy cheesecake from a commercial bakery that mass-produces them with cheaper or substitute ingredients.

For anyone who is not a restaurant owner or professional chef, ordering a meal—especially in an expensive restaurant—has been compared to buying a car without taking a test drive: You have no idea what you're getting into. This makes it nearly impossible to order wisely and eat healthfully, unless you're armed with a knowledge of what goes on behind the scenes in a restaurant; that is, what goes into certain dishes, how they're prepared, when and how restaurants take shortcuts, and so on. What follows, then, is precisely that information. I've also suggested ways of sidestepping particularly unhealthful dishes and have indicated what the best restaurant food options and alternatives might be. The information presented has been gathered from chefs, restaurant owners, food consultants, and food-service industry texts. In addition, some of the recommended strategies are based on my own experiences as a restaurant reviewer in New York.

To begin, there's a limit to what you can tell about a restaurant's food from the restaurant's decor. The person who designed the menu may not be the person who designed the dining room. The person who cooked the food may not be the person who purchased it. Admittedly, all of these individuals may have similar philosophies, but unless you know that one key person has been responsible for every facet of a restaurant, don't base your expectations of the food on the physical surroundings.

[2]According to the Los Angeles County Health Department, the reuse of food is one of the biggest restaurant violations.

A restaurant with too long a menu should be approached cautiously. Often, elaborate menus with lengthy descriptions cover up psychologically for what the food itself lacks in terms of quality. In American restaurants, menus are often written in French to make the food seem more sophisticated. Avoid restaurants that are trying to pull the wool over your eyes. Keep in mind that no restaurant can keep fresh and prepare well dozens of different foods and complicated dishes in many ethnic categories. A blackboard menu, which indicates that a menu is changed frequently, is a good sign. Cooked-to-order items listed on a menu are another good sign. And if you order a dish only to find that the restaurant has run out of that item, be happy! You've found a restaurant where, chances are, food is fresh and certain dishes have a high turnover.

No matter what form the menu takes, you usually can't rely on it to be completely accurate. In 1977 Dr. Bailus Walker of the Environmental Health Administration in Washington, D.C., conducted a survey of 350 menus representing 141 restaurants in the District of Columbia. He found that

- 100% of the shrimp listed as fresh was previously frozen.
- 90% of restaurant prime rib was actually choice-grade meat.
- 95% of the restaurants used ground beef, even when their menus listed chopped sirloin, chopped tenderloin steak, Salisbury steak, and chopped sirloin steak.
- 75% of the restaurants substituted a commercially made turkey roll (containing additives and possibly extenders) for sliced chicken and chicken salad on the menu.
- 50% of the foods listed on menus as kosher were not kosher.
- 75% of the restaurants substituted domestic blue cheese for Roquefort.

Walker also noted that the word *fresh* was used in misleading ways. For example, it was used in the term *fresh-baked bread,* which did not mean that the bread was freshly made that day, only that when it was made, the bread dough was fresh. Actually, the "fresh-baked bread" could have been delivered to the restaurant frozen. Second, *fresh* was used to describe foods that, in their original form, were fresh because they were grown or harvested rather than manufactured. Howard Johnson's "fresh garden vegetables," for example, were, by nature, fresh at some point, but they come frozen and heated on the plate.

- Fines may be levied against restaurants that misrepresent the food they offer.[3] McDonald's was heavily fined for describing frozen

[3] "Truth in Menu" legislation is underway in a number of states because of the gross misrepresentations that have been found on so many menus.

concentrated orange juice as "fresh orange juice," and imitation hotcake syrup as "maple syrup."

- It's always a good idea to ask the waiter for more specific information about the foods listed on the menu. It may not matter in terms of health whether or not the Maine lobster you're about to order is really from Maine. On the other hand, if the sliced chicken in your chef's salad is really imitation turkey glued together with additives, sugar, and salt, you may want to substitute cucumbers for the "chicken."

Many of the foods used in restaurants come from commercial sources—that is, they were not made by the restaurant itself. For example, most of the breads, muffins, cakes, pies, and puddings served in restaurants are made by commercial bakers. Commercial bakers use a lot of sweetener—white sugar, malt syrup, corn syrup, molasses, and grade-C (the lowest) maple syrup—as well as large amounts of stabilizers and preservatives that help baked goods survive through freezing, transporting, thawing, and "finish baking." In place of butter, which is extremely expensive given the quantities they need, bakers may use a lard-based (saturated fat) butter substitute.

Most commercial bakeries also use frozen or dried eggs for convenience. When eggs are collected, the imperfect ones are candled out, and the remainder are inspected and graded for market. There are flagrant examples of inadequate inspections, however, and the largest egg producers salvage eggs, even cracked "floor eggs." These are the broken eggs squashed by poultry confined on a crowded floor. The eggs are pooled together, "washed" (a measure to combat bacterial contamination), then frozen or dried to be used by bakeries or in processed foods.

Of course, restaurant breads and baked goods from commercial sources are no less wholesome than the commercial breads and baked goods found in supermarkets. Still, in a restaurant, the goal is to have the best bread or dessert available. So always specify the kind of bread you'd like for toast or on a sandwich. Very few restaurants offer true whole wheat bread, but you may find rye or pumpernickel, and both are preferable to white. Fresh French or Italian bread—especially if the restaurant purchases it from a small reputable bakery—is also preferable to sliced white sandwich bread. The round peasant bread that is sometimes served warm on a cutting board is usually bought frozen and served to give the illusion of wholesomeness and country hospitality.

Also, ask that the butter for your bread or toast be brought on the side. Coffee shops and restaurants sometimes paint toast and almost always paint garlic bread with a margarine-oil mixture to cut down on butter costs. In more expensive restaurants you may be able to ask for sweet butter in place of salted butter.

In the last few years restaurants have begun to use more frozen commercial desserts. From 1972 to 1974 the use of frozen cakes rose more than six times—from 3.2% to 20.5%.

Both breads and desserts may be listed on a menu or described by the waiter as "baked on the premises." Restaurants that finish-bake frozen commercially bought cakes and pies feel that the term *home-baked* is not deceptive, even though the food was not *made* in-house. When you ask about a dessert, therefore, ask if the restaurant chef made the dessert from scratch. Chances are, he or she did make some of the desserts but purchased others, so you'll have a choice. Be wary of restaurants that offer a lot of ice cream, custard, cream pie, and mousse desserts. There's a good chance they're from a commercial source.

A note about ordering fruit for dessert. If you want to avoid refined sugar completely, order a whole apple or pear with cheese. Fresh fruit salads are often made with sweetened canned fruit, then mixed with sugar and lemon juice to keep the fruit from turning brown. Fresh blueberries or strawberries are often glazed with a sugar syrup to make them shiny and extra-sweet. Fruit tarts are made to glisten by being coated with apricot preserves and food coloring.

In addition to commercial baked goods, restaurants often purchase commercial salads: tuna, macaroni, chick-pea, potato, and so forth. Such salads have a shelf life of approximately twenty days and are made with fresh, frozen, or canned vegetables and salt, sugar, stabilizers, and preservatives. The mayonnaise-based salads are often "cut"—that is, mixed with a formula of spices and liquid—to save on costly mayonnaise. Commercial salads are used mostly in inexpensive restaurants, although in an expensive restaurant a commercial tuna salad, for example, might be jazzed up with capers or chopped egg and surrounded with radishes or carrot strips. Commercial salad companies also provide restaurants with processed, preshredded lettuce, spinach, and cabbage for salad bars. These greens have been coated with a preservative to keep them from becoming mushy and brown. They have lost copious amounts of vitamins, since vitamins are lost over time and by exposure to air due to cut surfaces.

Find out what's in a salad and whether mayonnaise-based salads are made in-house before you order them. An innocent spinach salad may be sprinkled with imitation bacon bits and stale white-bread croutons; salads are often topped with processed cheese. If you ask, you may have the option of substituting another kind of cheese or a fresh vegetable.

Restaurants can also buy prepeeled hard-boiled eggs for use in salads. Such eggs have been dipped in a citrus acid solution that extends their shelf life to sixty days. There's no way to get around these eggs except to ask the waiter, before you order, if the restaurant boils its own eggs. You can also choose restaurants where you can watch the eggs being cracked over an open grill.

Restaurants may use frozen or spray-dried eggs in place of or in addition to fresh eggs for omelets. Eggs are spray-dried by a conveyor system that separates the yolks from the whites, pasteurizes the eggs in holding tanks, then sprays them into a hot air chamber. As the liquid eggs drop from the top of the tank to the floor, solids form and can be packaged and then shipped.

So much of the food served in restaurants is frozen that it's a good idea to become familiar with the seasons for various fruits and vegetables and, as a double check, ask the waiter which of those on the menu are fresh. Some restaurants use frozen or canned fruits and vegetables year-round for convenience. Creamed spinach, for example, is easier to make from frozen spinach, and few customers can tell frozen spinach from fresh in creamed spinach. To be absolutely sure of freshness, order simple vegetable dishes that can't be disguised.

The fish used in restaurants is often frozen. Even if you live in a seaport city, fish on a Sunday is either frozen or old, since fishing boats do not go out or deliver their catch on the weekends. Fish on a Monday is either frozen, very old, or very fresh.

Fish may be the only exception to the fresh-is-always-better rule. Which fish, for example, is "fresher" and which contains the most nutrients, the fish that has been squashed under a ton of other fish at the bottom of a boat's hold for five days, spent a day or two more being juggled into crates and loaded on trucks, then spent perhaps another day being shuffled around in the restaurant's kitchen—or the fish that was immediately cleaned and frozen on board ship and kept in a deep-frozen state until it was cooked?

Since nutrients are lost over time and are also lost through rough handling that damages the food's surface, the answer is clear.

Frozen fish can be mishandled, too, however, and if it is, the result is usually a bland, watery fish dish. If you want to know whether a fish is fresh or not, ask to see it before it's cooked. In an expensive restaurant, this is quite proper. The fish should have protruding eyes, red gills, and firm flesh that doesn't look slimy.

A final note on fish: Ask the waiter how the fish will be brought to the table. Broiled fish is usually cooked in the kitchen on a sizzli platter. If it's also brought to you on that platter, it will necessar be overdone, since the fish will continue to cook until the platte cool. Ask to have the fish served on a regular plate.

The high cost of fresh ingredients and the even higher cos trained and talented chefs have resulted in the counterfeitin whole dishes, such as beef Stroganoff or seafood wrapped in pastry. For a precooked, frozen chicken Kiev, for example, a preci weighted piece of chicken is cooked in an infrared oven, cryogenically frozen with vaporized liquid nitrogen at 300°F b zero.[4] Finally, the Kiev is packaged and shipped out to be "rest in a microwave or convection oven.

Apparently, there is virtually no dish that can't be preco ultrafrozen, then reheated this way. But the precooked frozen restaurants use most are those well-known, ambitious entrée only a skilled chef with time could produce: coq au vin, chicker beefs Wellington and Stroganoff, veal Cordon Bleu, Rock C game hen, clams casino, crab imperial, coquilles Saint-Ja shrimp/lobster/crab Newburg, stuffed cabbage, dim sum stuffed pheasant, lasagna, quiche, shrimp scampi, and a nur tomato-based ethnic specialties.

FREDERICK B. EMERSON JR., M.D.
Student Health Service

I've watched food being ferried along conveyor belts, dipped into acid solutions that retain color and delay molding, snipped and patched into exact portions, rolled into enormous computer-operated ovens, then frozen in air tunnels that seem as long as airplane hangars.

Something happens to food that is assembly-line-produced. It is what a French chef would call *sans coeur*—without heart. If it is "without heart," it's almost sure to be without nutrients. There is a close relationship between color/flavor/texture and nutrients, and even if

[4]When a food is frozen, the water in it freezes, producing ice crystals with sharp edges. Large ice crystals are formed when the food is frozen slowly and at relatively high temperatures (0° to 32°F). Nutrients are lost when large ice crystals rupture cell walls, allowing vitamins, minerals, protein molecules, and other nutrients to be lost.

Cryogenic freezing is very low-temperature freezing: below −70°F. Most cryogenic freezing is accomplished at temperatures even lower than that, however, by using liquid nitrogen gas (LNG), which can bring the surface temperature of a food down to −320° in a matter of moments. Droplets of the liquid nitrogen are vaporized on contact with the food. The droplets form a cold gas, which is blown at a high velocity over and around the food so that small ice crystals are produced within as well as around the cells. These small ice crystals do not damage cell walls to the extent that large ice crystals do.

As a result, cryogenic freezing is not nearly as damaging to nutrients as higher temperature freezing is and can be used with fairly delicate foods, such as avocados, asparagus, cherries, pears, strawberries, and mushrooms.

you never knew what processes were involved in cooking a given food, you could still come to some assessment of its nutritional worth by its appearance, taste, and texture.

How can you tell if an entrée has been frozen, then microwave-cooked? Or precooked frozen, then microwave-reheated? There's no sure method, but you can concentrate on items that are generally cooked to order: sautéed, grilled, or poached dishes rather than baked, stewed, or braised. Also, expensive restaurants may use precooked items less often because an expensive restaurant has a reputation to protect. Watch out for a highly sophisticated menu in a restaurant that doesn't seem quite up to the challenge. No middle-class suburban restaurant can make fifteen different international entrées from scratch every day unless they're charging a fortune for them. Also, restaurants in certain parts of the country have a difficult time finding top chefs capable of cooking complicated dishes. So assess a restaurant and the logic of its menu before choosing to eat there, and then stay away from menu offerings like quiche and chicken Kiev unless they are specialties of the house.

Always be wary of fried foods in restaurants. The fat that a restaurant uses in its fryolater may be all refined vegetable oil, all animal fat, or a blend of both. Animal fat is cheaper than vegetable oil (and is also completely saturated).

Fryolater oil, whether it's liquid vegetable oil or melted-down animal fat, is rarely, if ever, changed. It may be regularly filtered and replenished with new oil, since the old oil is constantly being absorbed by food cooked in it.

Many different kinds of food may be cooked in the same fryolater in the same oil. Such foods will pick up all kinds of stray flavors. If the oil is not filtered regularly, the food and miscellaneous stray particles that drop into it will cause the oil to smoke when it's heated. The fryolator cook may decide to turn down the temperature of the smoking oil rather than attempt to filter or replace it. Foods that are cooked in oil that is less than crackling hot take longer to cook and absorb more oil. Overly fried oily foods (high in saturated fat) are all too often the result, even in expensive restaurants.

Under good conditions, the fat in fryolators is kept at 400°F. Heating oil to this severe a temperature and keeping it this hot day after day for perhaps eight to ten hours a day changes the oil's chemical composition. Long-chain fatty acids are broken down, rendering compounds that may be carcinogenic.

In general, fried foods in restaurants just aren't worth the health risks. With one exception: reputable Chinese and Japanese restaurants. Such restaurants may not use fryolaters at all. Instead, foods are stir-fried or deep fried in woks, and every dish is made to order. Oil is not saved and reused. The oil itself is usually peanut oil (unsaturated).

Some dishes are, by their nature, more healthful than others. In a Chinese restaurant, compare a steamed sea bass, served in its own juices and topped with shredded fresh vegetables, to sweet and sour pork, in which (high-fat) pork is first deep fried (extra fat), then mixed in a sauce of catsup (456 mg salt per teaspoon, 28% sugar), cornstarch, canned pineapple (high in sugar, low in vitamins), sugar, salt, vinegar, and grenadine or red food coloring (possibly carcinogenic).

In addition, some foods—even within the same food category—are more healthful than others. Among dairy foods, for example, compare milk and cream:

One ounce of whole milk is 3.7% fat (20 calories).
One ounce of half-and-half is 12% fat (41 calories).
One ounce of coffee cream (light cream) is 21% fat (64 calories).
One ounce of whipping cream (heavy cream) is 37% fat (104 calories).

If the taste difference between milk and cream is not as important to you as the fat-calorie difference, you may want to request milk with your baked apple or bread pudding rather than cream.

If you eat meat, note that restaurants are supplied with the juiciest, most tender cuts of prime meat. These are also the cuts that have the most fat. The meats with the least fat are veal, chicken, and turkey. Beef, pork, lamb, and duck are all considerably higher. Sausage—whether veal, pork, or beef—can legally be 50% fat. Fish is always one of the best options in restaurants, since it's virtually fat-free.

To really cut down on fat, order all sauces and salad dressings on the side. If the waiter says that the fish/meat/vegetable cannot be prepared with the sauce on the side, you have a legitimate reason to suspect the food's quality, since the chef may be trying to disguise the food with the sauce. Ordering sauces and dressings on the side allows you to control how much of a creamy, buttery, salty, oily, or sugary dressing or sauce you want to eat.

Fruit sauces, such as an orange or cherry sauce on duck, are, by the way, chancy menu items, since a true fruit sauce is difficult to make and a passable shortcut is easy. The cook simply burns white sugar, mixes it with stock, brandy, frozen orange juice concentrate and orange rind, or canned cherries and cherry syrup.

A word of caution: Forgoing a sauce won't make a bit of difference if you choose to embellish a food with extra toppings. A baked potato, for example, has almost no fat and about 150 calories. When the same baked potato has 2 teaspoons of butter, 2 tablespoons of sour cream, plus bacon bits, the saturated-fat level climbs and the calories more than double to about 350. (And there are nitrites, salt, sugar, and preservatives in the bacon bits.)

Natural and health food restaurants deserve special attention here, because you can eat all your meals in such restaurants and be miserably nourished. That's because commercial health foods, in and of themselves, are no guarantee of good food. In general, restaurants that play down the health food aspect and simply concentrate on fresh whole foods are your best bet. Avoid fast-food health food restaurants that offer sweetened foods: frozen yogurt, honey-saturated muffins, carob chip cookies, and so on. In reputable natural food restaurants, watch out for foods that are comparatively high in fat. Avocados, olives, nuts, granola, eggs, and cheese are all good examples. Avocados are 17% fat; 30% to 40% of the calories in granola come from the vegetable oil it's roasted in; ounce for ounce, hard cheese contains more saturated fat than beef; natural ice creams have more fat than regular ice creams because they're made with a higher percentage of butterfat. Some examples of high-calorie/high-fat items on natural-food-restaurant menus are quiche made with cheese, heavy cream, and eggs; lasagna, enchiladas, or vegetarian casseroles made with cheese, sour cream, and/or lots of butter; fruit-flavored frozen yogurt topped with raisins, coconut, and granola; sandwiches and salads made with egg, cheese, avocado, and nuts, then spread or dressed with tahini or peanut butter.

Of all natural food restaurants, macrobiotic restaurants seem to use the fewest sweeteners, offer a minimum of dairy foods (if any at all), and offer no meat. As a result, sugar and fat are not problems—unless you specifically order a fried dish. Do be careful of salt in macrobiotic restaurants, however. Sea salt may be used, but sea salt has the same effect on blood pressure that regular table salt has. Tamari and shoyu (naturally fermented soy sauces) may also be used—liberally. One tablespoon of tamari contains three grams of salt, which is the daily limit suggested by many nutritionists.

Finally, remember that in a restaurant you're paying for the right to eat exactly what you want and to eat well. Chefs and waiters say that the people who politely ask for what they want eat much better than the people who sit back without a preference.

But there's another reason why asking for what you want is important: When enough people asked for saccharine, restaurants began putting those pink packets on every table. The same was true of Sanka. A 1979 menu-census report shows that as a result of customer demand, 40% of restaurants, schools, colleges, and employee cafeterias now have salad bars. Also, the number of restaurants offering fresh vegetables and egg dishes has increased significantly, while an average 15% of the restaurants surveyed have taken high-priced beef items, roast beef sandwiches, and hamburgers *off* the menu. According to the Hospitality Industry Foundation, people are now beginning to ask for unsalted butter, skim milk, and whole wheat bread. In a few years, they say, these foods have a good chance of becoming standard restaurant items.

General Index

Recipe Index

About the Author

KAREN MACNEIL was born in 1954. She received her B.A.from Pace College. She regularly writes about food, wine, restaurants, and travel for *Travel and Leisure, Food & Wine, Cook's Magazine, Gentleman's Quarterly, Wine, Self, Town & Country, Bon Appetit,* and several European magazines. She lives in New York City.